Treasury Department
January 18. 1792

There are various arrangements
between the Government and
d States, which will better
sonal conference than
request therefore that such
hear proper to the Director,

The Founding Fathers

Engraving by John F. E. Prud'homme after a miniature, circa 1790, by Archibald Robertson

The Founding Fathers

ALEXANDER HAMILTON

A Biography in His Own Words

Edited by
MARY–JO KLINE

With an Introduction by
HAROLD C. SYRETT
Editor, *The Papers of Alexander Hamilton*

JOAN PATERSON KERR
Picture Editor

Published by NEWSWEEK, New York
Distributed by HARPER & ROW, PUBLISHERS, INC.

We dedicate this series of books to the memory of
Frederick S. Beebe
friend, mentor, and "Founding Father" of Newsweek Books

Alexander Hamilton, A Biography in His Own Words,
has been produced by the Newsweek Book Division:

Joseph L. Gardner, Editor

Janet Czarnetzki, Art Director

Thomas Froncek, Assistant Editor

Susan Storer, Picture Researcher

S. Arthur Dembner, Publisher

This book is based on Volumes 1-19 of *The Papers of Alexander Hamilton,*
edited by Harold C. Syrett and published by Columbia University Press.
The texts of documents to be published in forthcoming volumes of this edition
have been supplied by Mr. Syrett, and permission to reproduce excerpts
from these documents has been obtained from their owners.

For information address Harper & Row, Publishers, Inc.,
10 East 53rd Street, New York, N.Y. 10022.
Published simultaneously in Canada by Fitzhenry & Whiteside Limited, Toronto.

Contents

Introduction

by Harold C. Syrett
Editor, The Papers of Alexander Hamilton

Despite differences in party, background, and ideology, many recent American political leaders have shared an almost pathological interest in how posterity will judge their accomplishments. Some of them have meticulously tried to preserve all that they have written and all that has been written to them, and on more than one occasion they have rushed into print in an apparent effort to set the record straight before historians have had an opportunity to examine that record. Every President of the United States since Franklin D. Roosevelt has arranged for the establishment of a special library to house his papers as well as those of many of his associates. Some Presidents have written their own versions of the events in which they were the principal participants, while more than one Chief Executive has appointed to his staff an academician whose responsibilities have presumably included that of court historian. Lesser figures in each administration, along with state and city officials, have published books and articles drawing on information that they had acquired in office. For those too inept or too lazy to write their memoirs, there has been no shortage of ghost writers and tape recorders. Most such efforts constitute in varying degrees a contribution to history, but all of them also represent a species of special pleading.

The Founding Fathers were also interested, if not obsessed, with the verdict of history. Although they seldom published their memoirs, many of them were careful to preserve their own records of the momentous times in which they lived. In this respect the first three Presidents of the United States are representative. George Washington had clerks or secretaries make letter book or letterpress copies of his letters, saved the letters that he received, and kept a diary that unfortunately contains little more than the names of visitors to Mount Vernon and reports on crops and the weather. John Adams was merely the first in his family to keep a diary and letter book and to preserve a vast amount of the avalanche of letters that descended on him during a long and eventful life. Like Washington and Adams, Thomas Jefferson retained the letters of his correspondents, but he also itemized in a ledger all his outgoing and incoming mail, and for part of his life he entered in the *Anas* his versions of each day's events and gossip. All three men left a legacy to mankind that in each case included a large corpus of papers telling what they and their contemporaries had done and thought during the formative years of the Republic.

As an immigrant, a parvenu, and an outspoken champion of aristocratic values,

6

Alexander Hamilton has always seemed the least typical of the Founding Fathers. In addition, he was often openly contemptuous of the opinions of his contemporaries, and there is little or no evidence that he was interested in telling future generations how they should view his record as a soldier, public servant, and political leader. He made no systematic effort to save the letters he received, and he did not copy in a letter book those that he sent. Nor did he record for his own amusement or for the edification of posterity accounts of his participation in the American Revolution, Continental Congress, New York legislature, Annapolis Convention, Constitutional Convention, New York ratifying convention, and Washington Administration.

It is difficult to avoid the conclusion that Hamilton was so concerned with the present that he gave little thought to what Americans would think of him in the future. Instead of diaries, he kept journals and ledgers that he considered either essential to his program of self-education or necessary for the day-to-day practice of his profession as a lawyer. During the American Revolution he filled his company's paybook with quotations and snippets of miscellaneous information from standard sources, and while studying for admission to the bar he wrote for his own use "Practical Proceedings in the Supreme Court of the State of New York." While practicing as a lawyer he kept cash books, which contain little beyond his legal and household accounts, and a register of cases, which lists some of the suits in which he served as an attorney from 1795 until his death. It is, perhaps, significant that the so-called Reynolds Pamphlet, his most famous—if not his only—example of special pleading, was designed to convince his contemporaries rather than their descendants that his lapses of private morality offered convincing proof of his public rectitude.

When Hamilton died on July 12, 1804, he left his widow an estate encumbered with debts and a collection of public and private papers that, according to his friend Gouverneur Morris, were "in wretched Disorder." In the remaining fifty years of her life Elizabeth Hamilton devoted her formidable energies to the care and feeding of her seven children and to an unrelenting campaign to perpetuate and enhance her husband's reputation through the exploitation of his writings. In her efforts to win for Hamilton the popular acclaim that she thought he deserved, she not unexpectedly met repeated rebuffs and discouragement, for she initiated her campaign during the ascendancy of the Virginia Dynasty and carried it on into and beyond the age of Jackson. But she was not easily discouraged; and before she died in 1854, she had not only acquired numerous copies and originals of Hamilton manuscripts to add to the collection that she had inherited, but she had also helped to persuade the United States Government to purchase and publish her husband's papers.

To Elizabeth Hamilton it seemed obvious that the most effective way to make Americans aware of her husband's achievements would be a biography based on his extant papers. At various times she commissioned—cajoled might be more accurate—James M. Mason, Joseph Hopkinson, Timothy Pickering, Francis Baylies, and Francis Hawks to write a biography. She was, however, uniformly unfortunate in her selection of authors. Some of them abandoned the project because of her interference; others backed out when it proved impossible to find a publisher; Pickering died before he could begin, let alone complete, the project; and Hawks used the papers entrusted to him to publish not a biography, but the first and only volume of a projected multivolumed edition of Hamilton's works. Understandably upset and disgusted with the outside talent that she had recruited, she turned to her own family and selected John C. Hamilton as his father's biographer.

In 1834 he published Volume I of *The Life of Alexander Hamilton*. Six years later he published two volumes under the same title, but "these...were nearly all burned while in the process of binding." Both editions covered only the early life of their subject, and it was not until 1857–60 that John C. Hamilton brought out his seven-volume edition of the *History of the Republic of the United States of America, as Traced in the Writings of Alexander Hamilton and of his Contemporaries*. Despite its obvious bias and leisurely pace, the *History of the Republic* remained the most authoritative biography of Hamilton until a century later when it was supplanted by Broadus Mitchell's *Alexander Hamilton*.

Although Elizabeth Hamilton did not live to see a complete and major biography of her husband, she made easier the task of his future biographers by searching for and finding manuscripts that were not part of the collection she had inherited. In these endeavors she enlisted the assistance of her sons, and James A. Hamilton and John C. Hamilton proved particularly helpful. All three wrote to Hamilton's contemporaries for materials, took frequent trips to talk with the owners of Hamilton manuscripts, and did not hesitate to use flattery or threats to attain their objectives. On one occasion Mrs. Hamilton resorted to the courts in her efforts to secure manuscripts she thought were rightfully hers. On another, James A. Hamilton wrote to Chief Justice John Marshall, the biographer of Washington, asking for papers in the Washington manuscripts "of which Genl Hamilton was the author." Not surprisingly, Marshall replied that the manuscripts in question were part of Washington's estate and that he had no authority to lend or give them away.

As she grew older, Elizabeth Hamilton became increasingly convinced that the most efficacious way of insuring her husband's fame was to have the Federal Government purchase and publish his papers. In June, 1848, when she was ninety-one, she wrote: "I have been for a very long time engaged in an application to Congress which in the probable course of human events will be the last, as it is the most interesting, business of my protracted life." She did not have long to wait, for on August 12, 1848, Congress provided in a routine appropriations bill twenty thousand dollars for the purchase "of the papers and manuscripts of the late Alexander Hamilton" and six thousand dollars for their "printing and publishing." Mrs. Hamilton did not record whether she found it ironical — or even distasteful — that this section of the bill was directly preceded by a similar provision appropriating the same amounts for the purchase and publication of the papers and manuscripts of Thomas Jefferson.

In 1849 Elizabeth Hamilton delivered her husband's manuscripts to the State Department, which subsequently transferred them to the Library of Congress. In 1850–51 John C. Hamilton published his seven-volume edition of *The Works of Alexander Hamilton*. The title page of these volumes announced that they were "published from the original manuscripts deposited in the Department of State, by order of the Joint Library Committee of Congress." Henry Cabot Lodge's edition of *The Works of Alexander Hamilton* in 1885 supplemented rather than supplanted John C. Hamilton's volumes, for although Lodge's edition contains some material not found in the earlier work, it also omits several letters and documents printed in the 1850–51 edition. Because John C. Hamilton's edition of his father's works includes most, but not all, of the items in the collection that his mother sold to the Government, it provides a rough guide to the range and nature of the papers that she had inherited and accumulated. During the past century the Hamilton papers in the Library of Congress have been augmented by several notable gifts and purchases. Perhaps the most important addition to the original collection were the manuscripts provided by Allan McLane Hamilton, Alexander Hamilton's grandson and a pioneering student of mental illness. These manuscripts, which deal mainly with Hamilton's family life and law practice, provided most of the material for Allan McLane Hamilton's *The Intimate Life of Alexander Hamilton,* which was published in 1910.

The collection of papers that Elizabeth Hamilton turned over to the Government in 1849 has more than justified the time and effort she expended on her husband's memory, for it has remained to this day an indispensable source for every serious student of Alexander Hamilton and the era that he helped to shape. It contains, however, less than a third of Hamilton's extant papers. Many of his most significant letters are in the papers of his contemporaries — most notably in those of George Washington — in the Library of Congress. Much, but not all, of his official correspondence and reports as Secretary of the Treasury are located in the National Archives. There are, moreover, large numbers of letters to and from Hamilton in the manuscript collections of such repositories as the New York Public Library, New York Historical Society, Columbia University, Connecticut Historical Society, Massachusetts Historical Society, Historical Society of Pennsylvania, and the Henry E. Huntington Library. Many Hamilton manuscripts can also be found in the public and private archives of Canada, Great Britain (including four letters in Windsor Castle), Denmark, the Netherlands, and France. Finally, a relatively large number of Hamilton manuscripts, like those of most other famous men, are owned by individuals who have either inherited them or have purchased them for essentially the same reasons that motivate stamp collectors.

It is impossible, of course, even to estimate how many Hamilton manuscripts have been destroyed either by acts of nature or by misguided defenders of his and their own reputations. Some of his official correspondence as Secretary of the Treasury is known to have been burned in fires in buildings occupied by his successors during the first two decades of the new government. Moreover, one can only wonder what happened to those Hamilton manuscripts that Gouverneur Morris in 1807 "promised to examine and select" so that they would "not . . . fall into the hands of those who might publish them." The evidence also seems clear that Elizabeth Hamilton systematically searched out and destroyed all the letters that she had written to her husband. If she did not, the result was much the same, for not a single letter of hers to Alexander Hamilton has survived, while the collections in the Library of Congress and in other repositories contain countless letters that she wrote to others.

Several Hamilton documents have survived only in printed versions. For example, none of the manuscripts of Hamilton's contributions to *The Federalist* is known to exist, and the same applies to the many other articles he wrote for newspapers. Because most such articles by Hamilton and his contemporaries were signed by pseudonyms, it is difficult, if not impossible, to determine the name of the author in any given instance. The contents of such articles provide an unreliable guide to their authorship, for many of Hamilton's fellow Federalists not only shared his views but also contributed pseudonymous essays to the press. Nor does style provide an adequate clue to the identity of these writers. Among eighteenth-century polemicists the method of presentation was almost as standardized as that used in classical tragedies. It is true that statisticians with the aid of a computer have recently been able to determine the authorship of some of the issues of *The Federalist,* but to date no one has had either the money or the fortitude to apply the same techniques to the thousands of articles that filled the newspapers in the first years of the new nation.

Although scholars interested in the formative years of the American Republic have long realized that the bulk of Hamilton manuscripts in the Library of Congress represented only a fraction of what he had written and what had been written to him, it is only recently that a systematic attempt has been made to assemble and publish a comprehensive, annotated edition of Hamilton's papers. The idea for such an undertaking originated with President Nicholas Murray Butler of Columbia University, who during the last two decades of his life repeatedly called for a definitive edition of the papers of his institution's most famous alumnus. But first the Depression—for modern editorial projects are expensive—and then World War II and its aftermath intervened. Following Butler's death in 1947, John A. Krout, who served successively as professor of history, graduate dean, and provost at Columbia, worked tirelessly to turn Butler's proposal into a reality, and he more than any other individual deserves the major credit for the establishment at Columbia in 1955 of an editorial project known as the Papers of Alexander Hamilton. Initial financing was provided by the Rockefeller Foundation, with subsequent grants being furnished by Time Inc. and the Ford Foundation. A few weeks after the grant from the Rockefeller Foundation, an editorial staff began the task of gathering and editing Hamilton's papers.

In the years since 1955 the staff of the Papers of Alexander Hamilton has collected photocopies of approximately 19,000 documents, some of which contain no more than a single sentence, while others run for hundreds of pages. Although this may appear to be a sizable body of historical materials for the study of one man's life, it is in reality quite small when compared to the 63,000 items that have been accumulated by Julian P. Boyd as Editor of *The Papers of Thomas Jefferson*. The disparity in the two collections explains why Hamilton's writings will be published in approximately twenty-five volumes, while considerably more than twice that number will be needed for Jefferson's writings. No one—certainly not the editorial staff—can estimate what the relative lengths of the two editions might have been had Aaron Burr proved to be the less efficient duelist.

Each document—or more accurately each copy of a document—arriving at the office of the Papers of Alexander Hamilton must be catalogued and typed, and then the typescript has to be checked and double checked for accuracy. Until quite recently accurate transcription more often than not represented the final step in the editorial process. For example, almost all the multivolumed editions of *Works* or *Letters* that were published in the nineteenth century contain nothing more than the texts of documents. Even John C. Fitzpatrick's thirty-nine-volume edition of the *Writings of George Washington*, published between 1931 and 1944, provides the reader with little or no annotation for what are some of the most important sources of eighteenth-century American history. Present-day editors of historical documents are, however, neither lazy nor reticent, and there are some instances in which the editor's footnotes take up more space than the materials that they are designed to explain or illuminate. In the volumes of *The Papers of Alexander Hamilton* that have been published to date an attempt has been made to find some middle ground between scarcity and abundance.

The Papers of Alexander Hamilton present only a partial view of their subject's life, for they treat only in the most cursory fashion his career as an attorney—a career in which he spent approximately the same number of years as he did as a soldier and officeholder and in which his contributions were in many respects as notable as those he made as a public official and political leader. With these facts in mind Columbia University in 1960 established the Legal Papers of Alexander Hamilton to collect, edit, and publish a "documentary reconstruction of Hamilton's professional life" in a "period when the law was in rapid process of change and when the outcome of any juristic controversy depended as well upon a lawyer's mastery of pleading as upon his powers of mastery." Under the editorship of Julius Goebel, Jr., and the sponsorship of the William Nelson Cromwell Foundation, this project has published two volumes of a projected three-volume edition of *The Law Practice of Alexander Hamilton*. Based in large part on manuscripts in Hamilton's papers in the Library of Congress and on the surviving judicial records of city, state, and Federal courts, *The Law Practice of Alexander Hamilton*—to quote from its scholarly critics—"blazes a new trail in the field of biographical research and exposition," "imparts a totally new set of dimensions to the image of Alexander Hamilton," and "takes its place...as an adornment to scholarship and a lasting memorial to the patience and good sense of its editor."

In preparing the present biography of Alexander Hamilton, Mary-Jo Kline has for the most part used the materials printed in *The Papers of Alexander Hamilton* and *The Law Practice of Alexander Hamilton* and the papers that will appear in the subsequent volumes in these two editions of Hamilton's writings. Whenever possible she has permitted Hamilton and his contemporaries to speak for themselves. The result is a felicitous and penetrating account of Hamilton and his times that will enable the reader to draw his own conclusions concerning one of the most significant and controversial figures in the entire history of the United States.

EDITORIAL NOTE

Most of the Hamilton writings reprinted in this biography have been excerpted from the longer original documents being published in their entirety by Columbia University Press. Omissions at the beginning or ending of a document are indicated by ellipses only if the extract begins or ends in the middle of a sentence; omissions within a quoted passage are also indicated by ellipses. The original spellings have been retained; editorial insertions are set within square brackets

Chronology of Hamilton and His Times

Alexander Hamilton born in Danish West Indies	1755?
	1765 British Stamp Act brings first major Colonial protests
Begins working for Nicholas Cruger in St. Croix	1768
Sails for North America, fall or winter, 1772–73	1772 Samuel Adams organizes new committees of correspondence
Enters King's College (now Columbia University), New York City; publishes first pamphlet, "A Full Vindication of the Measures of the Congress..."	1774 Parliament passes Coercive Acts; First Continental Congress meets
Publishes "The Farmer Refuted"	1775 Battles of Lexington and Concord
Named Captain of New York Provincial Artillery	1776 Declaration of Independence signed; British capture Long Island and New York City
Becomes Washington's aide and lieutenant colonel in Continental Army; present during American defeats at Brandywine Creek and Germantown; winters with Army at Valley Forge	1777 Howe takes Philadelphia; Burgoyne surrenders to the Americans at Saratoga; Articles of Confederation adopted
Sees action at Battle of Monmouth Court House	1778 American alliance with France
Serves with Washington in New Jersey; combats rumors that he had been fomenting an Army rebellion against Congress	1779 Spain declares war on England; Iroquois Confederacy subdued by American expedition; naval victory of John Paul Jones
Becomes involved in movement for governmental reforms; is denied request for field duty; marries Elizabeth Schuyler, December 14	1780 Charleston falls to British; French force under Rochambeau reaches Newport; Battle of Camden; Arnold's treason revealed
Breaks with Washington, resigns from Army; publishes *Continentalist* essays; rejoins Army and leads assault on British redoubt at Yorktown	1781 Articles of Confederation ratified; executive departments created; Cornwallis surrenders at Yorktown
Birth of first son, Philip; resigns from Army; serves as New York receiver of Continental taxes; admitted to bar; represents New York in Congress	1782 Carleton succeeds Howe as British commander; preliminary articles of peace signed at Paris
Leads congressional fight for impost and half pay; moves family to New York City; opens first law office	1783 Newburgh Addresses circulated; threat of Army mutiny forces Congress to flee Philadelphia; definitive peace treaty signed at Paris; Britain recognizes American independence
Publishes *Letters from Phocion*; helps organize Bank of New York; serves as counsel in *Rutgers* v. *Waddington*, case testing supremacy of United States law over laws of states	1784 Congress makes New York temporary capital; diplomatic corps reorganized; John Jay becomes Secretary for Foreign Affairs
Elected to New York Assembly; serves as New York delegate to Annapolis Convention	1786 Annapolis Convention; Shays' Rebellion
Attends Constitutional Convention at Philadelphia; begins publishing *The Federalist* essays	1787 Constitution ratified by first three states

Leads Federalists at New York's ratifying convention at Poughkeepsie; elected to Continental Congress	1788	Constitution adopted, having been ratified by eleven states; first Federal elections held
Named Secretary of the Treasury	1789	New Federal Government organized; Washington inaugurated as President, Adams as Vice President; beginning of French Revolution
Moves with wife and four children to Philadelphia; submits reports on public credit and a national bank; leads battle for Federal assumption of state debts	1790	Jefferson takes office as Secretary of State; Congress assumes state debts and agrees to locate the national capital in the South
Defends constitutionality of a national bank; begins affair with Maria Reynolds; submits report on manufactures	1791	Legislative Assembly governs France; Congress enacts whiskey excise; growth of Republican opposition in Congress
Defends policies in the press; accused privately of misdirecting public funds, denies charges, confessing to affair with Mrs. Reynolds and use of own funds to pay blackmail	1792	New York financial panic; war of the First Coalition of European powers against France; National Convention replaces Legislative Assembly in France, monarchy abolished
Opponents' attempts at censure defeated in Congress; informs President of intention to resign; works to undermine support for France during Citizen Genêt affair; stricken, with wife, during yellow fever epidemic	1793	Louis XVI executed; Reign of Terror; France declares war on Britain, Holland, and Spain; United States proclaims neutrality; Randolph becomes Secretary of State
Treasury Department investigated by House committee; Hamilton leads call for military expedition to suppress Whisky Rebellion; takes the field against the rebels	1794	Growing friction between the United States and Britain; Jay named special envoy to England; Jay's treaty concluded; led by Kosciusko, Poles revolt against Russia
Submits last report on public credit; resigns from Cabinet; leads fight for Jay's treaty; publishes first *Camillus* essay	1795	French Directory succeeds National Convention; Jay's treaty ratified; signing of Pinckney's treaty with Spain
Argues case for "carriage" tax; drafts Washington's Farewell Address	1796	Adams elected President, Jefferson elected Vice President
Works for support of peace commission; publishes pamphlet on the Reynolds affair	1797	Adams names peace commission to France; XYZ affair revealed
Named Major General and Inspector General of the Army	1798	Beginning of America's Quasi War with France; Alien and Sedition Acts adopted
Urges military expedition to suppress Fries' Rebellion; influence over Cabinet members brings clash with Adams; proposals for reorganization of Army accepted by Congress	1799	War of the Second Coalition against France; death of Washington; Directory replaced by Consulate of Napoleon Bonaparte
Disbands troops, resigns Army command; circulates letter opposing Adams; supports Jefferson after electoral tie with Burr	1800	Treaty of Mortefontaine ends Quasi War with France; Federalists Adams and Pinckney opposed by Jefferson and Burr in presidential election; capital moved to District of Columbia
Son Philip dies in duel; publishes *The Examination*	1801	House chooses Jefferson to be President, Burr to be Vice President; beginning of Tripolitan War
Proposes reform of Federalist party; moves family to the Grange in upper Manhattan	1802	
Defends freedom of the press in *People* v. *Crosswell*; begins campaign against Aaron Burr; wounded in duel with Burr, Alexander Hamilton dies, July 12; buried in Trinity churchyard in lower Manhattan	1804	Aaron Burr defeated for Governor of New York; Napoleon begins rule as Emperor of France, 1804–14

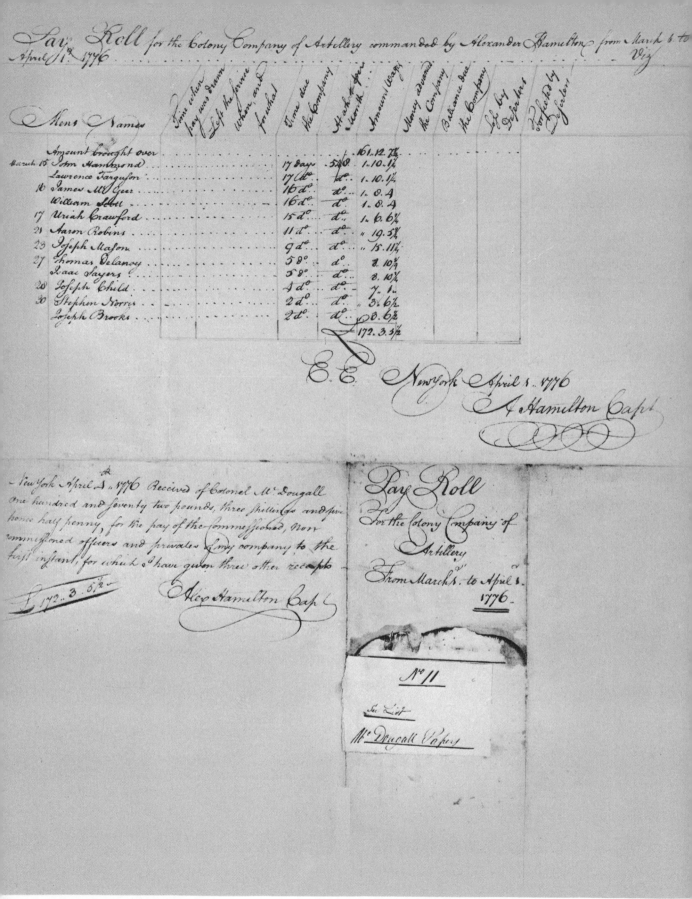

Pay Roll for the Colony Company of Artillery commanded by Alexander Hamilton from March 6 to April 1st 1776 ...... Viz

Mens Names	Time when pay was drawn	Left the service when and furnished	Time due the company	Rate of pay Month	Amount Wages	Money advanc'd the Company	Ballance due the Company	Lost by Deserters	Forfeited by Deserters
Amount brought over					161.12.7½				
March 15 John Hammond			17 days	54/.	1.10.1½				
Lawrence Farguson			17 d°.	d°.	1.10.1½				
16 James McGeer			16 d°.	d°.	1. 8. 4				
William Scott			16 d°.	d°.	1. 8. 4				
17 Uriah Crawford			15 d°.	d°.	1. 6. 6½				
21 Aaron Robins			11 d°.	d°.	„ 19. 5½				
23 Joseph Mason			9 d°.	d°.	„ 15. 11½				
27 Thomas Delanoy			5 d°.	d°.	8. 10½				
Isaac Sayers			5 d°.	d°.	8. 10½				
28 Joseph Child			4 d°.	d°.	7. 1.				
30 Stephen Norris			2 d°.	d°.	„ 3. 6½				
Joseph Brooks			2 d°.	d°.	„ 3. 6½				
					172. 3. 5½				

E. E.   New York April 8. 1776

A Hamilton Capt.

New York April 8 1776 Received of Colonel McDougall One hundred and seventy two pounds, three shillings and five pence half penny, for the pay of the Commessioned, Non commessioned officers and privates of my company to the first instant, for which I have given three other receipts

£ 172. 3. 5½

Alex Hamilton Capt

Pay Roll
For the Colony Company of
Artillery
From March 6. to April 8.
1776.

N° 11

See List
McDougall Papers

Captain Alexander Hamilton's payroll record of March, 1776, for his New York artillery company in the Revolution

Chapter 1

Up from Obscurity

I n the first twenty-one years of his life, Alexander Hamilton struggled for a chance to prove himself and gain recognition of his abilities. By chance, this struggle brought him to the North American Colonies at the moment when loyal British subjects had begun to explore the idea of creating a new nation. Of all the Founding Fathers, Hamilton was especially suited to fight for a new society where men could live together free of ancient customs and outworn prejudices. An illegitimate child, Hamilton had neither family, fortune, nor tradition to call his own. Indeed, historians are not even sure of the time or place of his birth.

To the best of our knowledge, the future American statesman was born on one of the British Virgin Islands, in the Leeward group of the West Indies, probably in January, 1755. Several years before, his mother, Rachel Fawcett Lavien, had left her husband to become the common-law wife of James Hamilton, a Scottish merchant. For a time, young Alexander and his older brother, James, had an apparently normal family life. But in 1765 their father decided to go his own way, leaving Rachel Lavien and her two illegitimate sons to fend for themselves. Rachel quickly proved, however, that she had a better head for business than her bankrupt "husband." For three years she operated a prosperous store on the Danish island of St. Croix, but her efforts to provide for her boys were short-lived. She died in February, 1768, and the courts awarded all her property to the son she had borne by her estranged husband, John Lavien. In effect, Alexander and his brother were orphaned at the ages of thirteen and fifteen. Still, although their charming but irresponsible father did nothing to help them, the boys found that their mother had given them a particularly valuable legacy—the example of her pride and hard work. In short order, young James found work as an apprentice to a carpenter, and Alexander became a clerk in the office of Nicholas Cruger, a New York merchant who operated a trading firm in St. Croix.

The circumstances of Hamilton's boyhood years make it difficult to present a balanced picture of his early life in his own words. For a man's youthful writings to survive there must be people willing to save such documents—proud parents to treasure his school exercise books, close friends to preserve his first letters. It is almost equally important that a future statesman remain in one place during his early years of obscurity, so that historians will know where to look for records of his boyhood and young manhood. Obviously, Hamilton's youth did not lend itself to the preservation of his manuscripts. Most of the letters that have survived from this period are business correspondence copied in his employer's letter books. A number of poems and articles published in various Colonial newspapers have also been preserved. But the only personal letter that has survived from the time when Hamilton lived in St. Croix is one that he sent to Edward Stevens, a young friend who had been sent to school in New York. Though in general we can only guess at the thoughts of this lonely, brilliant boy, his letter to "Ned" gave a vivid picture of the hopes and dreams that the fourteen-year-old Hamilton concealed as he worked over Nicholas Cruger's account books.

Young Hamilton's letter to his friend, Edward (Ned) Stevens

St Croix Novemr. 11th 1769

This just serves to acknowledge receipt of yours per Cap Lowndes which was delivered me Yesterday.... As to what you say respecting your having soon the happiness of seeing us all, I wish, for an accomplishment of your hopes provided they are Concomitant with your welfare, otherwise not, tho doubt whether I shall be Present or not for to confess my weakness, Ned, my Ambition is prevalent that I contemn the grov'ling and condition of a Clerk or the like, to which my Fortune &c. condemns me and would willingly risk my life tho' not my Character to exalt my Station. Im confident, Ned that my Youth excludes me from any hopes of immediate Preferment nor do I desire it, but I mean to prepare the way for futurity. Im no Philosopher you see and may be jusly said to Build Castles in the Air. My Folly makes me ashamd and beg youll Conceal it, yet Neddy we have seen such Schemes successfull when the Projector is Constant I shall Conclude saying I wish there was a War.

I am D[ea]r Edward Yours

ALEX HAMILTON

By early 1771, Hamilton had begun to experiment with a means to "prepare the way for futurity." On April 6, the printer of the *Royal Danish American Gazette,* St. Croix's English-language newspaper, published the following contribution from Nicholas Cruger's young clerk.

[April, 1771]

I am a youth about seventeen, and consequently such an attempt as this must be presumptuous; but if, upon perusal, you think the following piece worthy of a place in your paper, by inserting it you'll much oblige

Your obedient servant,

A.H.

Just Imported from Quebeck, in the Brigt. Harriot, and to be fold by the fubfcriber, at Mr. Barry's Tavern, very reafonable for cafh or crop pay,

A CARGO OF EXCELLENT DRAUGHT AND SADDLE HORSES, fingle and in pairs.—Alfo, Englifh Peafe, Brown Bread, Pickled and Smoaked Salmon.

BENEDICT ARNOLD.

Chriftianftæd, December 11, 1773.

In 1773 a St. Croix newspaper ran this advertisement from a West Indies horse trader with a name later famous, Benedict Arnold.

In yonder mead my love I found
Beside a murm'ring brook reclin'd:
Her pretty lambkins dancing round
Secure in harmless bliss.
I bad the waters gently glide,
And vainly hush'd the heedless wind,
Then softly kneeling by her side,
I stole a silent kiss—

She wak'd, and rising sweetly blush'd
By far more artless than the dove:
With eager haste I onward rush'd,
And clasp'd her in my arms;
Encircled thus in fond embrace
Our panting hearts beat mutual love—
A rosy-red o'er spread her face
And brighten'd all her charms.

Silent she stood, and sigh'd consent
To every tender kiss I gave;
I closely urg'd—to church we went,
And hymen join'd our hands.
Ye swains behold my bliss complete;
No longer then your own delay;
Believe me love is doubly sweet
In wedlocks holy bands.—

As the year 1771 wore on, Hamilton had little time for poetry, but he found an opportunity to prove his abilities in another area. On October 15, Nicholas Cruger sailed to New York "by reason of a very ill state of health," and his sixteen-year-old clerk was left in charge of business in St. Croix. Since Cruger's father and brothers owned trading firms in New York, England, and various West Indian ports, the office in St. Croix was part of a family network of international scope. During Cruger's absence, young Alexander Hamilton was responsible for making the daily decisions that such a business entailed. For five months, he handled the firm's correspondence and carried out his employer's orders. This letter to Nicholas Cruger gave a hint of the problems that Hamilton faced.

St Croix Novem. 12 1771

Markets are just the same excepting in the price of Butter which is now reducd.... Your Philadelphia flour is realy very bad, being of a most swarthy complexion & withal very untractable; the Bakers complain that they cannot by any means get it to rise. Wherefore & in consideration of the quantity of flour at Market and the little demand for it I have some thought not to refuse 8½ [pieces of eight] from any good person that will give it.... Upon opening several barrels I have observ'd a kind of Worm very common in flour about the surface, which is an indication of Age. It could not have been very new when twas shipd and for all these reasons I conceive it highly necessary to lessen the price or probably I may be oblig'd in the end to sell it at a much greater disadvantage....

No appearance of the Thunderbolt nor no News from Curracoa.

Heads and tails of a piece of eight, a Spanish silver dollar

The *Thunderbolt* mentioned above was a sloop owned by Cruger and his partners and commanded by Captain William Newton. When the ship reached St. Croix in mid-November, Hamilton handled the details of her voyage to the Dutch island of Curaçao and gave the captain his orders in the following letter.

St Croix Nov. 16 1771

Here with I give you all your dispatches & desire youll proceed immediately to Curracoa. You are to deliver your Cargo there to Teleman Cruger Esqr. agreeable to your Bill Lading, whose conditions you must follow in every respect concerning the disposal of your Vessell after your arrival. You know it is intended that you shall go from thence to the Main for a load of Mules & I must beg if you do, you'll be very choice in Quality of your Mules and bring as many as your Vessell can conveniently contain. By all means take in a large supply of provendor. Remember you are to make three trips this Season & unless you are very diligent, you will be too late as our Crops will be early in.

Take care to avoid the Gaurda Costos [Spanish customs officials]. I place an intire reliance upon the prudence of your Conduct.

A map decoration, circa 1770, advertises the West Indies trade.

For ten weeks, Hamilton anxiously awaited Newton's return from Curaçao with his cargo of mules from the Spanish Main. On January 29, 1772, the sloop reached St. Croix, and Hamilton faced more problems, as he reported to Tileman Cruger, his employer's brother in Curaçao.

St Croix Febru 1, 1772

Two days ago Capt Newton deliverd me your favour without date & 41 Mules in such order that I have been oblig'd to send all of them to pasture, and of which I expect at least a third will die. The highest offer made me for 20 of the best was 70 ps. [pieces of eight], whereas if they had been in good order I could readily have obtain'd £40 round, which I all along entertaind the most sanguine hopes of. Thus you see how unfortunate the Thunderbolts first Voyage has been. But we must try a second time. Accordingly I have put on Board her some Codfish, Rum & Bread as per Inclosd Bill Lading & wish them to a good Market.

Capt Newton is to supply himself with Grass on his way down & I must beg the favour of you by all means to buy or hire him a few Guns which is agreeable to Mr. Crugers directions to me. I should do it here if it were possible but there are none to be had upon any terms whatever & it would be undoubtedly a great pity that such a Vessell should be lost for the want of them....

It is thought by Judges that the Sloop Thunderbolt ought to carry 60 Mules. If you think so, please to desire the Capt to do it. I have mentioned it to him, but he insists that 48 are as many as she can conveniently hold. The more she brings the better. But I do not pretend to be a Judge of the matter & therefore leave it to you. But Without the utmost dispatch her second Voyage may miscarry like the first. Please to send by the Sloops return a full state of accounts between you & Mr. Cruger that I may enter all things properly.

A busy, palm-lined road on St. Croix

Despite the failure of Newton's first voyage, Hamilton immediately sent the captain back on another expedition. Three weeks after the *Thunderbolt* set sail for the second time, Hamilton dispatched this account of the sloop's misadventures to Nicholas Cruger in New York.

St Croix February 24 1772

Your Sloop Thunderbolt arrivd here the 29th of the preceding Month with 41 More Skeletons. A worse parcel of Mules never was seen; she took in at first 48 & lost 7

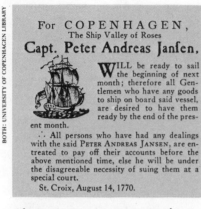

For COPENHAGEN,
The Ship Valley of Roses
Capt. Peter Andreas Janſen,

WILL be ready to sail the beginning of next month; therefore all Gentlemen who have any goods to ship on board said vessel, are desired to have them ready by the end of the present month.

∴ All persons who have had any dealings with the said PETER ANDREAS JANSEN, are entreated to pay off their accounts before the above mentioned time, else he will be under the disagreeable necessity of suing them at a special court.

St. Croix, August 14, 1770.

Above: A captain announces the departure of his merchant ship from St. Croix; opposite: Hamilton's letter describing the hurricane that struck the island in 1772

on the passage. I sent all that were able to walk to pasture, in Number 33. The other 8 could hardly stand for 2 Minutes together & in spite of the greatest care 4 of them are now in Limbo. The Surviving 4 I think are out of Danger, and shall likewise be shortly sent to pasture. I refusd two great offers made me upon their first landing to Wit 70 ps. a head for the Choice of 20, and 15 ps. a Head for the abovementioned Invalids, which may give you a proper idea of the condition they were in. Taking this along with it—that if they had been such as we had reason to hope they would be—I could with pleasure have had £40 round, so unfortunate has the Voyage been. However by sending them to pasture I expect to get £100 round for those now alive. 17 are already gone at that price and as they recruit fast the rest I hope will soon go at the same.... The Sloop was 27 days on her passage from the Main—not for want of swiftness, for tis now known she Sails well, but from continual Calms & the little wind she had was quite against her. Capt Newton seemd to be much concernd at his Ill luck tho I believe he had done all in his power to make the voyage Successful. But no Man can command the Winds. The Mules were pretty well chosen & had been once a good parcel. I receivd only a few lines from your Brother; no Sales nor anything else; he excusd himself being Sick. I desird him as directed to furnish the Sloop with a few Guns but she went intirely defenceless to the Main; notwithstanding several Vessells had been obligd to put back to get out of the way of the Launches with which the Coast swarms. When Capt Newton urgd him to hire a few Guns for the Sloop He replied to this effect—that I only had mentiond the matter to him but that you had never said a word about it. This last time I mentiond it again & begd the Captain to hire 4 Guns himself if your Brother did not which he has promisd to do. The Expence will not be above 15. or 20 ps., and one escape may not be followd by a second, neither do I see any reason to run the risque of it.

Although Hamilton had made a favorable impression on the Crugers and their business associates during the winter of 1771–72, he returned to "the grov'ling and condition of a Clerk" when Nicholas Cruger came back to St. Croix in March. But while he dutifully copied

Cruger's letters during the spring and summer, the boy still kept his eyes open for his own "futurity." It was a natural disaster, however, not a war (as he had predicted to Edward Stevens in 1769) that gave Hamilton his chance to escape ledgers and account books. On August 31, 1772, a hurricane swept St. Croix, and a few days later Hamilton wrote an account of the storm in a letter to his father. A copy of the letter reached Hugh Knox, a Presbyterian minister and journalist on the island, and Knox arranged to have the letter published in the *Royal Danish American Gazette* of October 3, 1772. It was this letter that won the boy local fame and an opportunity to leave Nicholas Cruger's countinghouse.

St. Croix, Sept. 6, 1772

I take up my pen just to give you an imperfect account of one of the most dreadful Hurricanes that memory or any records whatever can trace, which happened here on the 31st ultimo at night.

It began about dusk, at North, and raged very violently till ten o'clock. Then ensued a sudden and unexpected interval, which lasted about an hour. Meanwhile the wind was shifting round to the South West point, from whence it returned with redoubled fury and continued so 'till near three o'clock in the morning. Good God! what horror and destruction. Its impossible for me to describe or you to form any idea of it. It seemed as if a total dissolution of nature was taking place. The roaring of the sea and wind, fiery meteors flying about it in the air, the prodigious glare of almost perpetual lightning, the crash of the falling houses, and the ear-piercing shrieks of the distressed, were sufficient to strike astonishment into Angels. A great part of the buildings throughout the Island are levelled to the ground, almost all the rest very much shattered; several persons killed and numbers utterly ruined; whole families running about the streets, unknowing where to find a place of shelter; the sick exposed to the keeness of water and air without a bed to lie upon, or a dry covering to their bodies; and our harbours entirely bare. In a word, misery, in all its most hideous shapes, spread over the whole face of the country. A strong smell of gunpowder added somewhat to the terrors of the night; and it was observed that the rain was surprizingly salt. Indeed the water is so brackish and full of sulphur that there is hardly any drinking it. . . .

[After this factual account of the storm, Hamilton turned to his own "reflections and feelings on this frightful and melancholy occasion."]

*The logo of St. Croix's
English-language newspaper*

*A nineteenth-century woodcut
shows a hurricane striking the
harbor of the island of St. Thomas.*

Where now, oh! vile worm, is all thy boasted fortitude and resolution? What is become of thine arrogance and self sufficiency? Why dost thou tremble and stand aghast? How humble, how helpless, how contemptible you now appear....

Death comes rushing on in triumph veiled in a mantle of tenfold darkness. His unrelenting scythe, pointed, and ready for the stroke. On his right hand sits destruction, hurling the winds and belching forth flames: Calamity on his left threatening famine disease and distress of all kinds. And Oh! thou wretch, look still a little further; see the gulph of eternal misery open. There mayest thou shortly plunge—the just reward of thy vileness. Alas! whither canst thou fly? Where hide thyself? Thou canst not call upon thy God; thy life has been a continual warfare with him....

Thus did I reflect, and thus at every gust of the wind, did I conclude, 'till it pleased the Almighty to allay it. Nor did my emotions proceed either from the suggestions of too much natural fear, or a conscience over-burthened with crimes of an uncommon cast. I thank God, this was not the case. The scenes of horror exhibited around us, naturally awakened such ideas in every thinking breast, and aggravated the deformity of every failing of our lives.

[Although this letter was supposedly only a private message for his father, Alexander Hamilton closed his account of the hurricane with an appeal for public charity and high praise for the Governor General.]

But see, the Lord relents. He hears our prayer. The Lightning ceases. The winds are appeased. The warring elements are reconciled and all things promise peace. The darkness is dispell'd and drooping nature revives at the approaching dawn. Look back Oh! my soul, look back and tremble. Rejoice at thy deliverance, and humble thyself in the presence of thy deliverer.

Yet hold, Oh vain mortal! Check thy ill timed joy. Art thou so selfish to exult because thy lot is happy in a season of universal woe? Hast thou no feelings for the miseries of thy fellow-creatures? And art thou incapable of the soft pangs of sympathetic sorrow? Look around thee and shudder at the view. See desolation and ruin where'er thou turnest thine eye! See thy fellow-creatures pale and lifeless; their bodies mangled, their souls snatched into eternity, unexpecting. Alas! perhaps unprepared! Hark the bitter groans of distress. See sickness and infirmities exposed to the inclemencies of wind and water! See tender infancy pinched with hunger and hanging on the mothers knee for food! See the unhappy mothers anxiety. Her poverty denies relief, her breast heaves with pangs of maternal pity, her heart is bursting, the tears gush down her cheeks. Oh sights of woe! Oh distress unspeakable! My heart bleeds, but I have no power to solace! O ye, who revel in affluence, see the afflictions of humanity and bestow your superfluity to ease them. Say not, we have suffered also, and thence withold your compassion. What are your sufferings compared to those? Ye have still more than enough left. Act wisely. Succour the miserable and lay up a treasure in Heaven.

I am afraid, Sir, you will think this description more the effort of imagination than a true picture of realities. But I can affirm with the greatest truth, that there is not a single circumstance touched upon, which I have not absolutely been an eye witness to.

Our General [Ulrich Wilhelm Roepstorff, Governor General of St. Croix] has issued several very salutary and humane regulations, and both in his publick and private measures, has shewn himself *the Man.*

Juft Publifhed
And to be fold by the Printer hereof
A SERMON,
By the Rev. HUGH KNOX, on occafion of the late Storm—*Price 6 Old Bitts.*
Alfo Ditto's Difcourfes in two Volumes, neatly bound—*Ps. 2. 4. Reals.*
Alfo Ditto's Printed Letter, to the Rev. Mr. Green—*Price Rx. 1.*
Alfo other fingle Sermons by ditto—*Price 6 Old Bitts.*

The Reverend Hugh Knox published his own thoughts on the hurricane.

Impressed by Hamilton's obvious intelligence and talents, several wealthy residents of St. Croix subscribed to a fund for the young man's education. Soon after his account of the hurricane was published, Hamilton sailed for North America, where friends of Nicholas Cruger and his family could look out for his welfare and arrange for his schooling. First, Hamilton spent a year in New Jersey, where he received private tutoring that prepared him for admission to college. During this period, he lived in the homes of men like Elias Boudinot, a kindly lawyer who remained Hamilton's lifelong friend. For Hamilton, who had had no home or family of his own since his mother's death, the year in New Jersey was a heart-warming experience. In 1774, after he entered King's College (now Columbia University) in New York, Hamilton expressed some of his feelings for the Boudinots in a poem written to commemorate the death of their daughter Maria.

[New York, September 4, 1774]

For the sweet babe, my doating heart
Did all a Mother's fondness feel;
Carefull to act each tender part
and guard from every threatening ill.

But alass! availd my care?
The unrelenting hand of death,
Regardless of a parent's prayr
Has stoped my lovely Infant's breath—

With rapture number Oer thy Charms,
While on thy harmless sports intent,
Or pratling in my happy arms—

No more thy self Important tale
Some embryo meaning shall convey,
Which should th' imperfect accents fail,
Thy speaking looks would still display—

Thou'st gone, forever gone—yet where,
Ah! pleasing thought; to endless bliss.
Then, why Indulge the rising tear?
Canst thou, fond heart, lament for this?

Let reason silence nature's strife,
And weep Maria's fate no more;
She's safe from all the storms of life,
And Wafted to a peacefull Shore.

Elias Boudinot

In the winter of 1774, there were many distractions for undergraduates at King's College. New York politics had always been characterized by battles in the columns of local newspapers and skirmishes with handbills and pamphlets, and a new war of words was erupting over the growing anti-imperial movement. In September, the First Continental Congress had assembled in Philadelphia to consider the effects of the "Intolerable Acts," by which the British Parliament hoped to stifle Colonial protests. To implement their opposition to British policies, the congressmen adopted measures for economic retaliation—creating a "Continental Association," which decreed nonimportation and nonconsumption of British goods.

Loyalist opposition to the Congress and its Association found a spokesman in the New York press when "A Westchester Farmer" began his attacks on Congress in local newspapers in November, 1774. A month later, readers were introduced to a new political analyst, "A Friend to America," who published "A Full Vindication of the Measures of the Congress" in reply to the Farmer's criticisms. In reality, the "Friend to America" was Hamilton, and his article of December 15, 1774, showed how quickly he had mastered the issues in the Colonial dispute and how well he had learned the arguments that would further the Whig cause.

New-York [December 15] 1774

And first, let me ask these restless spirits, whence arises that violent antipathy they seem to entertain, not only to the natural rights of mankind; but to common sense and common modesty. That they are enemies to the natural rights of mankind is manifest, because they wish to see one part of their species enslaved by another. That they have an invincible aversion to common sense is apparent in many respects: They endeavour to persuade us, that the absolute sovereignty of parliament does not imply our absolute slavery; that it is a Christian duty to submit to be plundered of all we have, merely because some of our fellow-subjects are wicked enough to require it of us, that slavery, so far from being a great evil, is a great blessing; and even, that our contest with Britain is founded entirely upon the petty duty of 3 pence per pound on East India tea; whereas the whole world knows, it is built upon this interesting question, whether the inhabitants of Great-Britain have a right to dispose of the lives and properties of the inhabitants of America, or not? And lastly, that these men have discarded all pretension to common modesty, is clear from hence, first, because they, in the plainest terms, call an august body of men, famed for their patriotism and abilities, fools or knaves, and of course the people whom they represented cannot be exempt from the same opprobrious appellations; and secondly, because they set themselves up as standards of wisdom and probity, by contradicting and censuring the public voice in favour of those men....

[Hamilton's "Vindication" then went on to prove that enslavement of the American Colonies was inevitable unless British policies were reversed.]

The only distinction between freedom and slavery consists in this: In the former state, a man is governed by the laws to which he has given his consent, either in person, or by his representative: In the latter, he is governed by the will of another. In the one case his life

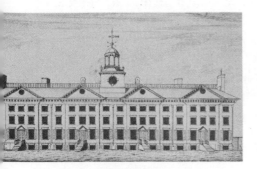

A view of Columbia College, 1790

The Reverend Samuel Seabury, author of the Loyalist essays signed by "A Westchester Farmer"

and property are his own, in the other, they depend upon the pleasure of a master. It is easy to discern which of these two states is preferable. No man in his senses can hesitate in choosing to be free, rather than a slave.

That Americans are intitled to freedom, is incontestible upon every rational principle. All men have one common original: they participate in one common nature, and consequently have one common right. No reason can be assigned why one man should exercise any power, or pre-eminence over his fellow creatures more than another; unless they have voluntarily vested him with it. Since then, Americans have not by any act of their's impowered the British Parliament to make laws for them, it follows they can have no just authority to do it.

Besides the clear voice of natural justice in this respect, the fundamental principles of the English constitution are in our favour. It has been repeatedly demonstrated, that the idea of legislation, or taxation, when the subject is not represented, is inconsistent with *that*. Nor is this all, our charters, the express conditions on which our progenitors relinquished their native countries, and came to settle in this, preclude every claim of ruling and taxing us without our assent....

What then is the subject of our controversy with the mother country? It is this, whether we shall preserve that security to our lives and properties, which the law of nature, the genius of the British constitution, and our charters afford us; or whether we shall resign them into the hands of the British House of Commons, which is no more privileged to dispose of them than the Grand Mogul? What can actuate those men, who labour to delude any of us into an opinion, that the object of contention between the parent state and the colonies is only three pence duty upon tea? or that the commotions in America originate in a plan, formed by some turbulent men to erect it into a republican government?...

[The Farmer had argued that Americans should confine themselves to petitioning the Crown, not electing congresses or threatening Britain with economic retaliation, but Hamilton contended that only these stronger measures could impress King and Parliament.]

The only scheme of opposition, suggested by those, who

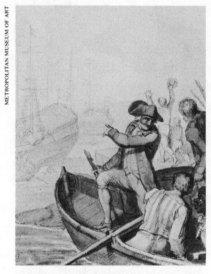

A contemporary wash drawing of the Boston Tea Party

have been, are averse from a non-importation and non-exportation agreement is, by REMONSTRANCE and PETITION. The authors and abettors of this scheme, have never been able to *invent* a single argument to prove the likelihood of its succeeding. On the other hand, there are many standing facts, and valid considerations against it.

In the infancy of the present dispute, we had recourse to this method only. We addressed the throne in the most loyal and respectful manner...but...our address was treated with contempt and neglect. The first American congress did the same, and met with similar treatment....

There is less reason now than ever to expect deliverance, in this way, from the hand of oppression. The system of slavery, fabricated against America, cannot at this time be considered as the effect of inconsideration and rashness. It is the offspring of mature deliberation. It has been fostered by time, and strengthened by every artifice human subtilty is capable of....

This being the case, we can have no resource but in a restriction of our trade, or in a resistance *vi* & *armis*. It is impossible to conceive any other alternative. Our congress, therefore, have imposed what restraint they thought necessary. Those, who condemn or clamour against it, do nothing more, nor less, than advise us to be slaves....

[Even more important, Hamilton had to prove to Americans that nonimportation would work—that the "inconveniencies" of doing without British goods for a few months would be balanced by swift changes in British policies.]

No person, that has enjoyed the sweets of liberty, can be insensible of its infinite value, or can reflect on its reverse, without horror and detestation. No person, that is not lost to every generous feeling of humanity, or that is not stupidly blind to his own interest, could bear to offer himself and posterity as victims at the shrine of despotism, in preference to enduring the short lived inconveniencies that may result from an abridgment, or even entire suspension of commerce....

The evils which may flow from the execution of our measures, if we consider them with respect to their extent and duration, are comparatively nothing. In all human probability they will scarcely be felt. Reason and experience teach us, that the consequences would be too fatal to Great Britain to admit of delay. There is an immense trade between her and the colonies.... The experiment we have made heretofore, shews us of how much importance our commercial connexion is to her; and gives us the highest assurance of obtaining immediate redress by suspending it.

From these considerations it is evident, she must do something decisive. She must either listen to our complaints, and restore us to a peaceful enjoyment of our violated rights; or she must exert herself to enforce her despotic claims by fire and sword. To imagine she would prefer the latter, implies a charge of the grossest infatuation of madness itself....

[While his "Vindication" met the general arguments against Congress's Association, Hamilton realized that he must speak directly to one specific group, the farmers of New York, whom Loyalists hoped to win over by declaring that nonimportation was merely a scheme to enrich merchants and townspeople. In a postscript to his "Vindication," Hamilton skillfully played on local pride, making a special "Address" to the Colony's shrewd, independent rural citizens.]

The reason I address myself to you, in particular, is, [not] because I am one of your number, or connected with you in interest more than with any other branch of the community. I love to speak the truth, and would scorn to prejudice you in favour of what I have to say, by taking upon me a fictitious character as other people have done. I can venture to assure you, the true writer of the piece signed by A. W. FARMER, is not in reality a Farmer. He is some ministerial emissary, that has assumed the name to deceive you, and make you swallow the intoxicating potion he has prepared for you. But I have a better opinion of you than to think he will be able to succeed. I am persuaded you love yourselves and children better than to let any designing men cheat you out of your liberty and property, to serve their own purposes. You would be a disgrace to your ancestors, and the bitterst enemies to yourselves and to your posterity, if you did not act like men, in protecting and defending those rights you have hitherto enjoyed....

*An English cartoon of 1773
contrasts Britain's prosperity under
George II and George III.*

[Having described the economic consequences of non-importation for New Yorkers, Hamilton appealed to the farmers' pride and dislike of authority.]

Are you willing then to be slaves without a single struggle? Will you give up your freedom, or, which is the same thing, will you resign all security for your life and property, rather than endure some small present inconveniencies? Will you not take a little trouble to transmit the advantages you now possess to those, who are to come after you? I cannot doubt it. I would not suspect you of so much baseness and stupidity, as to suppose the contrary.

Pray who can tell me why a farmer in America is not as honest and good a man, as a farmer in England? or why has not the one as good a right to what he has earned by his labour, as the other? I can't, for my life, see any distinction between them. And yet it seems the English farmers are to be governed and taxed by their own Assembly, or Parliament; and the American farmers are not.... The latter are to be loaded with taxes by men three thousand miles off; by men, who have no interest, or connexions among them; but whose interest it will be to burden them as much as possible; and over whom they cannot have the least restraint. How do you like this doctrine my friends? Are you ready to own the English farmers for your masters? Are you willing to acknowledge their right to take your property from you, [how] and when they please? I know you scorn the thought....

The Farmer cries, "tell me not of delegates, congresses committees, mobs, riots, insurrections, associations; a plague on them all. Give me the steady, uniform, unbiassed influence of the courts of justice. I have been happy under their protection, and I trust in God, I shall be so again."

I say, tell me not of the British Commons, Lords, ministry, ministerial tools, placemen, pensioners, parasites. I scorn to let my life and property depend upon the pleasure of any of them. Give me the steady, uniform, unshaken security of constitutional freedom; give me the right to be tried by a jury of my own neighbours, and to be taxed by my own representatives only....

[In summarizing his "Address" to the farmers of the

province, Hamilton deftly pictured the Westchester Farmer as a British agent who secretly despised the very people to whom he had appealed.]

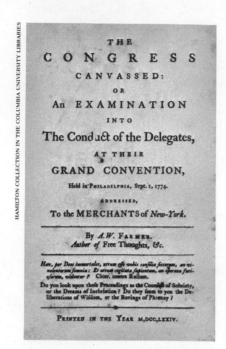

THE
CONGRESS
CANVASSED:
OR
An EXAMINATION
INTO
The Conduct of the Delegates,
AT THEIR
GRAND CONVENTION,
Held in Philadelphia, Sept. 1, 1774.

ADDRESSED,
To the MERCHANTS of New-York.

By *A.W.* FARMER.
Author of Free Thoughts, *&c.*

Hæc, per Deos immortales, utrum esse vobis consilia siccorum, an vigilantorum somnia: Et utrum cogitata sapientum, an optata furiosorum, videntur? Cicer. contra Rullum.

Do you look upon these Proceedings as the Counsels of Sobriety, or the Dreams of Inebriation? Do they seem to you the Deliberations of Wisdom, or the Ravings of Phrenzy?

PRINTED IN THE YEAR M,DCC,LXXIV.

Title page, 1774, of the attack on Congress by "A Westchester Farmer"

Will you then, my friends, allow yourselves, to be duped by this artful enemy? will you follow his advices, disregard the authority of your congress, and bring ruin on yourselves and posterity? will you act in such a manner as to deserve the hatred and resentment of all the rest of America? I am sure you will not. I should be sorry to think, any of my countrymen would be so mean, so blind to their own interest, so lost to every generous and manly feeling.

The sort of men I am opposing give you fair words, to persuade you to serve their own turns; but they think and speak of you in common in a very disrespectful manner. I have heard some of their party talk of you, as the most ignorant and mean-spirited set of people in the world. They say, that you have no sense of honour or generosity . . . and that you are so ignorant, as not to be able to look beyond the present; so that if you can once be persuaded to believe the measures of your congress will involve you in some little present perplexities, you will be glad to do anything to avoid them; without considering the much greater miseries that await you at a little distance off. . . . I flatter myself you will convince them of their error, by shewing the world, you are capable of judging what is right and [best], and have resolution to pursue it.

All I ask is, that you will judge for yourselves. I don't desire you to take my opinion or any man's opinion, as the guide of your actions. I have stated a number of plain arguments; I have supported them with several well-known facts: It is your business to draw a conclusion and act accordingly.

I caution you, again and again, to beware of the men who advise you to forsake the plain path, marked out for you by the congress. They only mean to deceive and betray you. . . . If you join with the rest of America in the same common measure, you will be sure to preserve your liberties inviolate; but if you separate from them, and seek for redress alone, and unseconded, you will certainly fall a prey to your enemies, and repent your folly as long as you live.

(Text continued on page 42)

A Picture Portfolio

An Ambitious Young Man

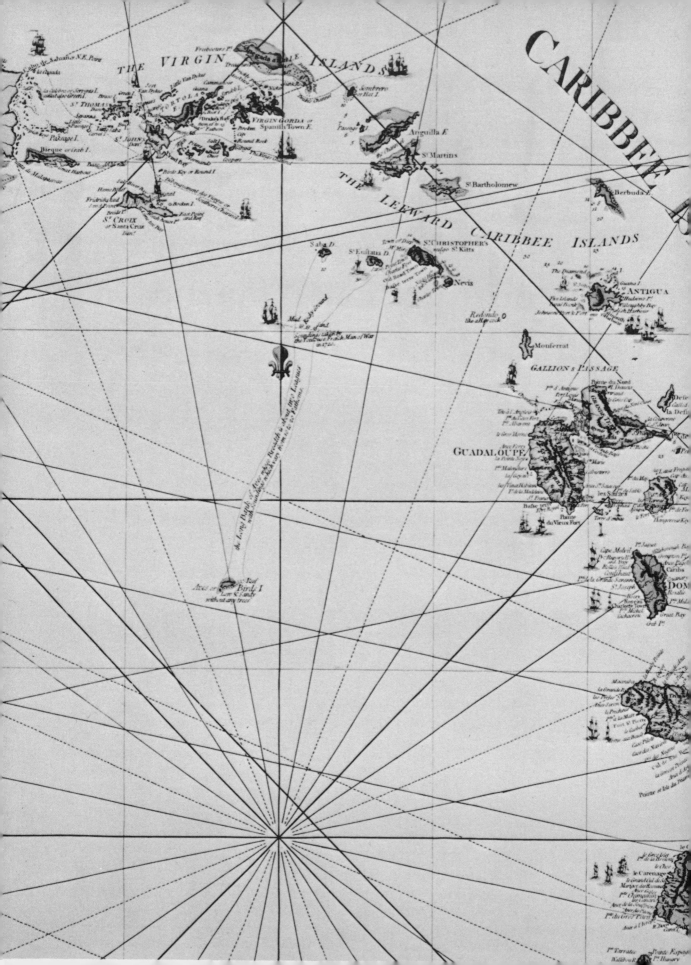

CARIBBEAN BOYHOOD

For many, life on a Caribbean island in the eighteenth century could be extremely pleasant. Residing in great houses and surrounded by outbuildings for their managers and slaves, the owners of a typical plantation such as Prosperity (above) on St. Croix made a comfortable living off the main crop of sugar cane. Their mills (one can be seen in the center of the water color) processed the cane into sugar and rum, both commodities much in demand by the world far from their sunny shores. For young Alexander Hamilton, however, life was a series of hurdles to be overcome. The "bastard brat of a Scotch pedlar," as John Adams was later to call him, Hamilton is thought to have been born in January, 1755, on the tiny British island of Nevis (under the word "Leeward" on the map at left). Illegitimacy, abandonment, poverty, and tragic loss marked the early years of the highly intelligent boy and undoubtedly did much to supply the urgent drive that characterized his later career.

33

MERCHANT'S APPRENTICE

Christiansted, the main port of St. Croix, was a beehive of trading activity in Hamilton's day. It is pictured below as it appeared from the harbor at that time, and at right in a view looking from the town out to the bay. Young Alexander was apprenticed to Nicholas Cruger (below, far right), whose place of business was located on the lower end of King Street (the colonnaded buildings leading directly to the wharves in the water color at right). Cruger dealt in a variety of merchandise, as his advertisements in the local paper (below, right) indicate. Hamilton kept Cruger's books and wrote many of his letters, and when his employer went to America in 1771, sixteen-year-old Alexander was left in charge. A measure of his application to the job can be seen in a progress report to Cruger: "Believe me Sir I dun as hard as is proper."

Just Imported, and to be sold

By Nicholas Cruger,

SUPERfine and Common Philadelphia Flour,
  Do. Do. New-York Do.
Rye Do.
Shipbread in tierces and barrels,
Kegs Water Bread,
Corn in hhds.
Dry Codfish in bbls.
Pickled Fish in bbls.
Burlington Pork,
Hams,
New Irish Butter,
Oats in hhds. and by the bushel,
Tobacco in hhds.
Bohea and Congo Tea in chests and cannisters,
Madeira Wine in pipes,
White Pine Albany plank,
Georgia Pitch Pine Joist,
Scantling and Shingles,
White Oak Staves and Heading,
Red Oak do.
Lime in hhds.
Sailduck,
White Lead and Yellow Oaker ground in oil,
Nails and Brads of different sorts,
HL Hinges, Hooks, Fenders & Stags for Spouts,
A parcel of seasoned Main & Porto-Rico Mules.
Do. of Draught Cattle.
    St. Croix, December 4, 1773.

Just imported from the Windward Coast of A-
FRICA, and to be sold on Monday next, by
Messrs. Kortright & Cruger,
At said CRUGER's Yard,
Three Hundred Prime
S L A V E S.
❖ The terms will be made known at the
place of sale.
  Jan. 23, 1771.

BLOWN INTO HISTORY

The otherwise idyllic Caribbean islands are subject to frequent hurricanes. In 1772, a disastrous storm
sweeping over St. Croix made such a
vivid impression on Hamilton that he
wrote a long letter to his father, then
living on St. Vincent Island, describing its horrors. Although the aquatint
at left depicts the devastation of
another of the Virgin Islands after a
hurricane, the effect on St. Croix was
much the same—five hundred buildings, including Cruger's store, were
damaged or destroyed. A minister
named Hugh Knox saw the youth's
letter and had it published in the
Royal Danish-American Gazette (logo,
above), where it received considerable acclaim. Through Knox's efforts,
combined with Cruger's New York
contacts, it was arranged for Hamilton
to go north to college. The ambitious
young man was on his way, thanks to
a hurricane that has been aptly
described as having "blown Alexander Hamilton into history."

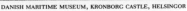

DANISH MARITIME MUSEUM, KRONBORG CASTLE, HELSINGOR

CONFIDENT SCHOLAR

Armed with letters of credit through the generosity of Cruger, young Hamilton headed in 1773 for Elizabethtown, New Jersey, where Hugh Knox had arranged for him to prepare for college. Because Hamilton in characteristic fashion wanted to follow a course of independent study, Princeton turned him down. King's College in New York, now known as Columbia University (seen above as it looked when Hamilton first saw it), agreed to take him on his own terms. The matricula of 1774 (right) has Alexander Hamilton's name second from the bottom, though it is possible he was admitted a year earlier. His responsibilities during his formative years with Cruger's firm stood him in good stead; he arrived on the mainland with a businessman's knowledge of American commerce. Not yet twenty but confident and ambitious, he met New York head on and soon began to make himself known in the northern metropolis.

Admissions Anno 1774.

David Clarkson.
Schuyler Lupton.
Jacob Shaw.
John Gaine.
John Whitaker. *Left College 2d Year*
Samuel Deall.
Horatio Smith.
Paul Kendall.
John Brickell.
Daniel Moore.
Edward Cornwallis Venericke. *Left College 2d Year*
James Stiles. *Left the College in the 2d Year*
James Depeyster.
Tristim Lowther
Thomas Attwood.
Alexander Hamilton.

Nicholas Romeyn S.M.

39

IMPASSIONED PAMPHLETEER

At college Hamilton joined a student literary society and closely followed the pamphlet war that was raging in the Thirteen Colonies. Even at the tender age of ten, he had been made aware of the controversial Stamp Act when boatloads of men from the neighboring island of St. Kitts had come to Nevis to help destroy the stamped papers. Most of the men he first met in America were patriots, Colonial residents with strong grievances against the mother country, and Hamilton soon joined their ranks as a pamphleteer of considerable talents. His first effort (right) was in answer to a Loyalist pamphlet that had appeared in November of 1774, just three weeks after the Continental Congress had adjourned. Hamilton, however, was apparently opposed to violence, and when a group of angry New Yorkers threatened to attack the home of Myles Cooper, the Loyalist president of King's College (below), it was Hamilton—according to a popular but unsubstantiated legend—who stood in the doorway and talked eloquently to the mob long enough to allow Cooper to escape out the back door.

A
FULL VINDICATION
OF THE
Meafures of the Congrefs,
FROM
The CALUMNIES of their ENEMIES;
In ANSWER to
A LETTER,
Under the Signature of
A. W. FARMER,
WHEREBY
His *Sophiftry* is expofed, his *Cavils* confuted, his *Artifices* detected, and his *Wit* ridiculed ;

IN
A GENERAL ADDRESS
To the Inhabitants of America,
AND
A Particular Addrefs
To the FARMERS *of the Province of New-York.*

by Alexander Hamilton.

Veritas magna eft & prævalebit.
Truth is powerful, and will prevail.

N E W - Y O R K :
Printed by JAMES RIVINGTON. 1774.

(Text continued from page 30)

May God give you wisdom to see what is your true interest, and inspire you with becoming zeal for the cause of virtue and mankind.

A FRIEND TO AMERICA.

Within a few weeks of the publication of Hamilton's "Vindication" of the Continental Association, the Westchester Farmer made a counterattack in his "View of the Controversy Between Great-Britain and her Colonies." Using his pseudonym of "A Friend to America," Hamilton renewed his fight and replied with a lengthy pamphlet dated February 23, 1775. This piece, "The Farmer Refuted: or A more impartial and comprehensive View of the Dispute...," summarized Hamilton's position on the tragic controversy that threatened the Empire.

New-York [February 23, 1775]

Whatever opinion may be entertained of my sentiments and intentions, I attest that being, whose all-seeing eye penetrates the inmost recesses of the heart, that I am not influenced (in the part I take) by any unworthy motive—that, if I am in an error, it is my judgment, not my heart, that errs. That I earnestly lament the unnatural quarrel, between the parent state and the colonies; and most ardently wish for a speedy reconciliation, a perpetual and *mutually* beneficial union, that I am a warm advocate for limitted monarchy and an unfeigned well-wisher to the present Royal Family.

But on the other hand, I am inviolably attached to the essential rights of mankind, and the true interests of society. I consider civil liberty, in a genuine unadulterated sense, as the greatest of terrestrial blessings. I am convinced, that the whole human race is intitled to it; and, that it can be wrested from no part of them, without the blackest and most aggravated guilt.

I verily believe also, that the best way to secure a permanent and happy union, between Great-Britain and the colonies, is to permit the latter to be as free, as they desire. To abridge their liberties, or to exercise any power over them, which they are unwilling to submit to, would be a perpetual source of discontent and animosity. A continual jealousy would exist on both sides. This would lead to tyranny, on the one hand, and to sedition and rebellion, on the other. Impositions, not really grievous in themselves, would be thought so; and the murmurs

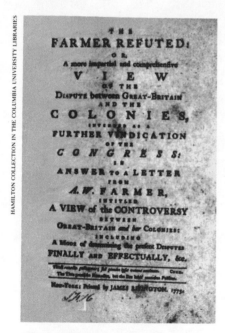

The title page of Hamilton's 1775 pamphlet "The Farmer Refuted"

arising from thence, would be considered as the effect of a turbulent ungovernable spirit. These jarring principles would, at length, throw all things into disorder; and be productive of an irreparable breach, and a total disunion.

That harmony and mutual confidence may speedily be restored, between all the parts of the British empire, is the favourite wish of one, who feels the warmest sentiments of good will to mankind, who bears no enmity to you, and who is,

A SINCERE FRIEND TO AMERICA.

Within a few months the nature of the controversy disputed by Hamilton and the Westchester Farmer had changed drastically. In December, 1774, Hamilton had declared that it would be "the grossest infatuation of madness itself" for Britain to "enforce her despotic claims by fire and sword," but the skirmishes at Lexington and Concord in April, 1775, showed that such "madness" was now a reality. Accordingly, Hamilton took a much harder line in his next publication, "Remarks on the Quebec Bill." The bill, passed by the British Government in 1774, provided for the protection of the Catholic Church and for the administration of French law and judicial practice in the French-Canadian provinces that Britain had won in the French and Indian War a decade earlier. But Protestants in neighboring Colonies saw these provisions as a threat to their own religious freedom.

[New York, June 15, 1775]

Therefore it is apparent, that a system of French laws has been re-established, in the province of Quebec, and an indefinite power vested in the King, to vary and alter those laws, as also to constitute such courts of criminal civil and ecclesiastical jurisdiction, and to introduce such a form of criminal law, as he shall judge necessary; I say since all this is deducible, from the express letter of the act; or in other words, since the whole legislative, executive, and judiciary powers are ultimately and effectually, though not immediately, lodged in the King, there can be no room to doubt, that an arbitrary government has been really instituted throughout the extensive region now comprised in the province of Quebec.

In Part Two of his "Remarks," Hamilton discussed Britain's new toleration of Catholicism in Canada and warned Americans to take care lest their own freedom be destroyed by this British "plot."

[New York, June 22, 1775]

Had there been really provision made, to be applied at the discretion of his Majesty, I should still consider this act as an atrocious infraction on the rights of Englishmen, in a point of the most delicate and momentous concern. No protestant Englishman would consent to let the free exercise of his religion depend upon the mere pleasure of any man, however great or exalted. The privilege of worshipping the deity in the manner his conscience dictates, which is one of the dearest he enjoys, must in that case be rendered insecure and precarious. Yet this is the unhappy situation, to which the protestant inhabitants of Canada are now reduced. The will of the King must give law to their consciences. It is in his power to keep them for ever dispossessed of all religious immunities; and there is too much reason to apprehend, that the same motives which instigated the act, would induce him to give them as little future encouragement as possible....

This act develops the dark designs of the ministry more fully than any thing they have done; and shews, that they have formed a systematic project of absolute power. The present policy of it is evidently this. By giving a legal sanction to the accustomed dues of the priests, it was intended to interest them in behalf of administration; and by means of the dominion they possess over the minds of the laity, together with the appearance of good will towards their religion, to prevent any dissatisfaction, which might arise from the loss of their civil rights, and to propitiate them to the great purposes in contemplation; first the subjugation of the colonies and afterwards that of Britain itself....

What can speak in plainer language, the corruption of the British Parliament, than its act; which invests the King with absolute power over a little world...and makes such ample provision for the popish religion, and leaves the protestant, in such dependent disadvantageous situation that he is like to have no other subjects, in this part of his domain, than Roman catholics; who, by reason of their implicit devotion to their priests, and the superlative reverence they bear to those, who countenance and favour their religion, will be the voluntary instruments of ambition; and will be ready, at all times, to second the oppressive designs of administration against

In this English comment on the Quebec Act, a bishop is prevented from landing in America.

the other parts of the empire.

Hence...it behoves us to be upon our guard against the deceitful wiles of those, who would persuade us, that we have nothing to fear from the operation of the Quebec act. We should consider it as being replete with danger, to ourselves, and as threatening ruin to our posterity. Let us not therefore suffer ourselves to be terrified at the prospect of an imaginary and fictitious Sylla, and, by that means, be led blindfold into a real and destructive Charybdis.

In the months that followed the publication of his "Remarks on the Quebec Bill," Hamilton was an unhappy observer of the methods used by some men to defend America's liberties. He himself had already faced mob violence in May, 1775, when he protected Myles Cooper, the Tory president of King's College, from a group of angry New Yorkers. Such vigilante action increased in the city and on November 20, a leader of the Sons of Liberty named Isaac Sears took a band of followers across the border from Connecticut into Westchester County and Manhattan to seize New York Loyalists. On November 23, they destroyed the printing presses of James Rivington, the leading Tory newspaperman in New York City, and carried some of his equipment back to Connecticut. Alarmed by these acts, Hamilton wrote to John Jay, one of New York's delegates to the Continental Congress, to report on the situation and to suggest legislation that would discourage such raids in the future.

New York Novem 26. 1775

Though I am fully sensible how dangerous and pernicious Rivington's press has been, and how detestable the character of the man is in every respect, yet I cannot help disapproving and condemning this step.

In times of such commotion as the present, while the passions of men are worked up to an uncommon pitch there is great danger of fatal extremes. The same state of the passions which fits the multitude, who have not a sufficient stock of reason and knowlege to guide them, for opposition to tyranny and oppression, very naturally leads them to a contempt and disregard of all authority. The due medium is hardly to be found among the more intelligent, it is almost impossible among the unthinking populace. When the minds of these are loosened from their attachment to ancient establishments and courses, they seem to grow giddy and are apt more or less to run into anarchy. These principles, too true in them-

45

selves, and confirmed to me both by reading and my own experience, deserve extremely the attention of those, who have the direction of public affairs. In such tempestuous times, it requires the greatest skill in the political pilots to keep men steady and within proper bounds, on which account I am always more or less alarmed at every thing which is done of mere will and pleasure, without any proper authority. Irregularities I know are to be expected, but they are nevertheless dangerous and ought to be checked, by every prudent and moderate mean. From these general maxims, I disapprove of the irruption in question, as serving to cherish a spirit of disorder at a season when men are too prone to it of themselves....

[Quite aside from general principles of justice and law and order, Hamilton pointed out, there were several very practical reasons for putting an end to such highhanded actions by New England radicals.]

Antipathies and prejudices have long subsisted between this province and New England. To this may be attributed a principal part of the disaffection now prevalent among us. Measures of the present nature, however they may serve to intimidate, will secretly revive and increase those ancient animosities, which though smothered for a while will break out when there is a favorable opportunity.

Besides this, men coming from a neighbouring province to chastise the notorious friends of the ministry here, will hold up an idea to our ennemies not very advantageous to our affairs. They will imagine that the New Yorkers are totally, or a majority of them, disaffected to the American cause, which makes the interposal of their neighbours necessary: or that such violences will breed differences and effect that which they have been so eagerly wishing, a division and quarrelling among ourselves. Every thing of such an aspect must encourage their hopes.

Upon the whole the measure is condemned, by all the cautious and prudent among the whigs, and will evidently be productive of secret jealousy and ill blood if a stop is not put to things of the kind for the future.

All the good purposes that could be expected from such

James Rivington

a step will be answered; and many ill consequences will be prevented if your body gently interposes a check for the future.... Believe me sir it is a matter of consequence and deserves serious attention.

The tories it is objected by some are growing insolent and clamorous: It is necessary to repress and overawe them. There is truth in this; but the present remedy is a bad one. Let your body station in different parts of the province most tainted, with the ministerial infection, a few regiments of troops, raised in Philadelphia the Jerseys or any other province except New England. These will suffice to strengthen and support the Whigs who are still I flatter myself a large majority and to suppress the efforts of the tories. The pretence for this would be plausible. There is no knowing how soon the Ministry may make an attempt upon New York. There is reason to believe they will not be long before they turn their attention to it. In this there will be some order & regularity, and no grounds of alarm to our friends.

I am sir with very great Esteem—Your most hum servant

A. HAMILTON

Encouraged by Jay's response to his letter, Hamilton continued the correspondence. Although he was not yet old enough to vote or hold office, Hamilton was quite ready to give political advice to an older man like Jay, who was a distinguished lawyer ten years his senior. This he did when he learned that local Loyalists had persuaded Governor William Tryon to call for elections for a new provincial assembly in New York. The Tories hoped that a new assembly, recognized by the Crown and dedicated to "constitutional" government, would distract attention from the "illegal" congresses and committees of the disaffected colonists. Hamilton, seeing a way of turning the elections to Whig advantage, outlined his ideas in another letter to Jay.

N York Decemr. 31st. 1775

The tories will be no doubt very artful and intriguing, and it behoves us to be very vigilant and cautious. I have thrown out a hand bill or two to give the necessary alarm, and shall second them by others.

It appears to me that as the best way to keep the attention of the people united and fixed to the same point it would be expedient that four of our Continental delegates should be candidates for this city and county.

...The minds of all our friends will naturally tend to these, and the opposition will of course be weak and contemptible, for the whigs I doubt not constitute a large majority of the people. If you approve the hint, I should wish for your presence here. Absence you know is not very favorable to the influence of any person however great.

I shall give you farther notice, as I see the scheme advance to execution.

Governor Tryon called for new assembly elections on January 2, 1776. Two days later, Hamilton wrote to Jay in Philadelphia, urging him to return from the Continental Congress and lead the fight in New York.

A view from Long Island of New York and its harbor in 1776

[New York, January 4, 1776] You will find by the papers, that a proclamation has been issued for dissolving the old Assembly; writs are making out for the election of a new.

The tories seem to give out that there will be no opposition, but I suspect this as an artifice to throw the people off their guard. I doubt not however the whig Interest will prevail.

I should be glad to see you here with all convenient dispatch; though perhaps your presence may not be absolutely necessary, yet I like not to hazard any thing, or to neglect any step which may have the least tendency to insure success.

Hamilton's political judgment was accurate. But though the Whig slate of delegates to the assembly was elected without opposition in New York City on February 1, 1776, the victory had only symbolic importance. The assembly met briefly on February 14 and adjourned at once, never to convene again. Royal government collapsed, and Governor Tryon retreated to the safety of His Majesty's Ship *Duchess of Gordon*, anchored in New York Harbor. As the spring of 1776 approached, Hamilton, like all New York Whigs, forgot royal assemblies and "constitutional" government and turned his attention to the provincial and continental congresses and the military organizations needed for their defense. New Yorkers knew that they could expect a British invasion of their province as soon as the winter storms ended. Hamilton's youthful wish seemed fulfilled. Although he had come to North America for an education, he had, instead, found a war to insure his fame and "futurity."

Chapter 2

A Soldier's Progress

For a young man with a taste for military glory, there seemed no better place to be than New York in 1776, for in the summer and fall of that year the approach of the British fleet made the city the center of military operations. When the New York congress ordered the recruitment of an artillery company in January, 1776, Alexander Hamilton did not hesitate to volunteer. In March, on the recommendation of an officer and friend, Alexander McDougall, Hamilton was named Captain of the Provincial Company of Artillery.

Hamilton's abilities as a conscientious and businesslike leader were evident from his earliest days of military service. He not only had to recruit and train his own men; he also had to see that they were fed, clothed, and paid. While many young New Yorkers may have fought the enemy as bravely as Hamilton did, few battled the local authorities so stubbornly to provide for their troops. Toward the end of May, 1776, when he learned that his soldiers were not receiving the benefits of a new pay scale, Hamilton sent this indignant letter to the provincial congress.

[New York, May 26, 1776]

I am not personally interested in having an augmentation agreeable to the above rates, because my own pay will remain the same that it now is; but I make this application on behalf of the company, as I am fully convinced such a disadvantageous distinction will have a very pernicious effect on the minds and behaviour of the men. They do the same duty with the other companies and think themselves entitled to the same pay. They have been already comparing accounts and many marks of discontent have lately appeared on this score. As to the circumstance of our being confined to the defence of the Colony, it will have little or no weight, for there are but few in the company who would not as willingly leave the Colony on any necessary expedition as stay in it; and they will not therefore think it reasonable to have their pay curtailed on such a consideration.

At the Battle of Long Island in the last week of August, 1776, the British defeated the American forces and won possession of New York City. It was either during this campaign or in the retreat of Continental troops across New Jersey in the autumn that Washington was struck by Hamilton's abilities and asked him to become his aide-de-camp with the rank of lieutenant colonel in the Continental Army. Although Hamilton had declined a similar appointment to another general's staff, he accepted Washington's offer. He received his new commission on March 1, 1777, and in the weeks that followed he had a brisk introduction to his duties.

But if Hamilton hoped that his new position would bring him military advancement and fame, he soon had reason for doubt. The theater of operations now shifted from New Jersey to Pennsylvania, and although Hamilton was close to the scene of action, he was seldom exposed to fire. More and more Washington began relying on his skills—both as a writer who could draft endless official letters and as a trustworthy officer who could accept responsibility for the uninspiring but necessary tasks of administration. This was not the war of which Hamilton had dreamed in St. Croix, but it was precisely the kind of war to which he was best suited—a war of paperwork and politics, of diplomacy and detail. Writing to his friend Brigadier General Alexander McDougall, Hamilton explained that the general's inquiries about fortifications in New York had gone unanswered because of Washington's illness.

> Head Qrs. Morris Town [New Jersey]
> March 10th. 1777
> [His Excellency] has been very much indisposed for three or four days past, insomuch that his attention to business is pronounced by the Doctor to be very improper; and we have made a point of keeping all from him which was not indispensibly necessary. I detained your express a day in hopes of a convenient opportunity to communicate your letter to him; but though he has grown considerably better than he was, I find he is so much pestered with matters, which cannot be avoided, that I am obliged to refrain from troubling him on the occasion; especially as I conceive the only answer he would give, may be given by myself.
>
> It is greatly to be lamented that the present state of things does not admit of having the requisite number of

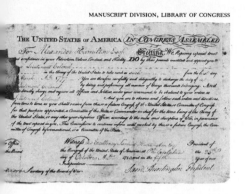

Hamilton's commission as lieutenant colonel in the Continental Army

troops at every post: on the contrary the most important, are deficient.... 'Till matters get into a better train, it is impossible but those posts must suffer which, from their situation ought only to be the objects of a secondary attention. We have, I think, the most decisive evidence that the enemy's operations will be directed on this quarter; to this end they are drawing all their forces into the Jerseys, and as soon as the weather will permit 'tis expected they will move towards Philadelphia. Not being very numerous 'tis unlikely they should attempt such an object, without collecting their whole force; and for that reason 'tis not much to be apprehended they should make any stroke of the kind you mention.

Although Hamilton's first loyalties were now to his Commander and to the Continental Army, he did not forget New York or ignore any opportunities to maintain his ties to political leaders in that state. When the Committee of Correspondence of the New York Convention suggested that he furnish them with military news of special interest to their state, Hamilton responded promptly.

[Morristown, New Jersey, March 20, 1777] With chearfulness, I embrace the proposal of corresponding with your convention, through you; and shall from time to time as far as my leisure will permit, and my duty warrant, communicate such [transactions] as shall happen, such pieces of intelligence as shall be received and such comments upon them as shall appear necessary, to convey a true idea of what is going on in the military line. Let me caution you however, that whatever opinions I shall give, in the course of our correspondence, are to be considered merely as my private sentiments; and are never to be interpreted as an echo of those of the *General*; since they will not be really so, and a construction of the kind may lead into errors and be productive of inconveniences.

The house in Kingston, where the New York Convention met in 1777 to approve the state constitution

Throughout March, Hamilton assured the New York Committee that the enemy would make "no grand movement" before May, but he soon had to temper his optimism. When the Committee inquired about rumors that the British might advance up the Hudson River, Hamilton admitted that the enemy had moved earlier than expected. But he still contended that Albany was not the primary target.

Head Quarters, Morristown [New Jersey]
April 5th. 1777

The opinion I advanced respecting the Enemy's not moving before the beginning of May seems to be Shaken. ...We have received information that they are embarking about three thousand men on board of transports....

As to your apprehensions of an attempt up the North River I immagine you may discard any uneasiness on that score, though it will be at all times adviseable to be on the watch....Philadelphia is an object calculated to strike and attract their attention. It has all along been the main source of supplies towards the war and the getting it into their possession would deprive us of a wheel we could very badly spare in the great political and military machine.

Although military affairs grew more serious in May, Hamilton could still devote himself to drafting a lengthy reply to his friend Gouverneur Morris's comments on the new New York constitution. Morris, a member of the state constitutional convention, described the plan as "deficient for the Want of Vigor in the executive unstable from the very Nature of popular elective Governments and dilatory from the Complexity of the Legislature." In mid-May, Hamilton explained his own views of the "frame of government."

Head Quarters Morris Town [New Jersey]
May 19th. 1777

That there is a want of vigor in the executive, I believe will be found true. To determine the qualifications proper for the chief executive Magistrate requires the deliberate wisdom of a select assembly, and cannot be safely lodged with the people at large. That instability is inherent in the nature of popular governments, I think very disputable; unstable democracy, is an epithet frequently in the mouths of politicians; but I believe that from a strict examination of the matter, from the records of history, it will be found that the fluctuation of governments in which the popular principle has borne a considerable sway, has proceeded from its being compounded with other principles and from its being made to operate in an improper channel. Compound governments, though they may be harmonious in the beginning, will introduce distinct interests; and these interests will clash, throw the state into convulsions & produce a change

This elegant Morristown mansion served as Washington's headquarters during the winter of 1779–80.

Revolution, LOSSING

or dissolution. When the deliberative or judicial powers are vested wholly or partly in the collective body of the people, you must expect error, confusion and instability. But a representative democracy, where the right of election is well secured and regulated & the exercise of the legislative, executive and judiciary authorities, is vested in select persons, chosen *really* and not *nominally* by the people, will in my opinion be most likely to be happy, regular and durable. That the complexity of your legislature will occasion delay and dilatoriness is evident and I fear may be attended with much greater evil; as expedition is not very material *in making* laws, especially when the government is well digested and matured by time. The evil I mean is, that in time, your senate, from the very name and from the mere circumstance of its being a separate member of the legislature, will be liable to degenerate into a body purely aristocratical. And I think the danger of an abuse of power from a simple legislative would not be very great, in a government where the equality and fulness of popular representation is so wisely provided for as in yours. On the whole, though I think there are the defects intimated, I think your Government far the best that we have yet seen, and capable of giving long and substantial happiness to the people. Objections to it should be suggested with great caution and reserve.

Pay book of Hamilton's artillery company for August, 1776

While Britain's General William Howe concealed his intentions in the spring of 1777, a young officer in Washington's "family" even had moments for flirtation. During his stay in New Jersey before the Revolution, Alexander Hamilton had become acquainted with the family of William Livingston, the first governor of the state after independence. When Livingston's daughter Catharine asked Hamilton to send her news of the military and political situation, he was only too glad to oblige. He teased Catharine with a lighthearted warning that he would not confine himself to public affairs.

> Morris Town [New Jersey] April 11th. 1777
> I challenge you to meet me in whatever path you dare; and if you have no objection, for variety and amusement, we will even sometimes make excursions in the flowery walks, and roseate bowers of Cupid. You know, I am renowned for gallantry, and shall always be able to entertain you with a choice collection of the prettiest things

imaginable. I fancy my knowledge of you affords me a tolerably just idea of your taste, but lest I should be mistaken I shall take it kind, if you will give me such intimations of it, as will remove all doubt, and save me the trouble of finding it out with certainty myself....

After knowing exactly your taste, and whether you are of a romantic, or discreet temper, as to love affairs, I will endeavour to regulate myself by it. If you would choose to be a goddess, and to be worshipped as such, I will torture my imagination for the best arguments, the nature of the case will admit, to prove you so. You shall be one of the graces, or Diana, or Venus, or something surpassing them all. And after your deification, I will cull out of every poet of my acquaintance, the choicest delicacies, they possess, as offerings at your Goddesships' shrine. But if, conformable to your usual discernment, you are content with being a mere mortal, and require no other incense, than is justly due to you, I will talk to you like one [in] his sober senses; and, though it may be straining the point a little, I will even stipulate to pay you all the rational tribute properly applicable to a fine girl.

But amidst my amorous transports, let me not forget, that I am also to perform the part of a politician and intelligencer....

Of this, I am pretty confident, that the ensuing campaign will effectually put to death all their hopes; and establish the success of our cause beyond a doubt. You and I, as well as our neighbours, are deeply interested to pray for victory, and its necessary attendant peace; as, among other good effects, they would remove those obstacles, which now lie in the way of that most delectable thing, called matrimony;—a state, which, with a kind of magnetic force, attracts every breast to it, in which sensibility has a place, in spite of the resistance it encounters in the dull admonitions of prudence, which is so prudish and perverse a dame, as to be at perpetual variance with it.

Governor William Livingston

Alexander Hamilton's courtship of "Kitty" Livingston should not be taken too seriously. Five years his senior, Catharine enjoyed flirting and flattery, but cautiously avoided marriage to any of her suitors until 1786. For his part, Hamilton soon had little time for romance, for it was becoming clear that General Howe had an objective in mind. The problem for Washington's headquarters was to sort out the reports of spies, deserters, and prisoners of war to determine what that objective was. By early May, Hamilton had to qualify his confident predictions that the British would turn south, as he warned the New York Committee of Correspondence.

Head Quarters Morris Town [New Jersey]
May 7th. 1777

We have reason to suspect the enemy will soon evacuate Brunswick and push for Amboy; whence they will no doubt embark for some expedition by water...either... to Philadelphia or up the North River....The testimony of every person, that comes from them, confirms this fact, that their horses are in such miserable condition as to render them incapable of any material operations by land. If therefore proper care be taken...to prevent their collecting supplies of good horses among ourselves, I know not how it will be possible for them to penetrate any distance into the Country. As far as it may depend upon them, I hope the Convention will attend to this circumstance & will take effectual measures to put it out of their power to gain such supplies in any part of your state, towards which they may direct their movements.

General William Howe

On May 28, Washington moved his headquarters to Middle Brook, New Jersey, only seven miles from the British post at Brunswick. Middle Brook could be defended easily and was a better point from which to observe Howe's troop movements and to try to figure out his course. For weeks, Howe and Washington played a cat-and-mouse game in New Jersey as the British general tried to draw the Americans away from Middle Brook and the Continental Commander wisely stood his ground. When Howe evacuated Brunswick in the third week of June and withdrew his forces to Amboy, Washington finally ordered his troops into the field. On June 26, Howe moved to cut off the Americans and block their return to the safety of Middle Brook. Although the Continental Army escaped the British trap, Hamilton realized that his Commander would be criticized for choosing to make a timely retreat rather than risk his soldiers in open battle. To prevent such attacks on Washington, Hamilton wrote in confidence to Robert R. Livingston in New York.

Head Quarters Camp at Middle Brook [New Jersey]
June 28 1777

I know the comments that some people will make on our Fabian conduct. It will be imputed either to cowardice or to weakness: But the more discerning, I trust, will not

Fort Ticonderoga map by Trumbull

find it difficult to conceive that it proceeds from the truest policy, and is an argument neither of the one nor the other. The liberties of America are an infinite stake. We should not play a desperate game for it or put it upon the issue of a single cast of the die. The loss of one general engagement may effectually ruin us, and it would certainly be folly to hazard it, unless our resources for keeping up an army were at an end, and some decisive blow was absolutely necessary; or unless our strength was so great as to give certainty of success. Neither is the case. America can in all probability maintain its army for years, and our numbers though such as would give a reasonable hope of success are not such as should make us intirely sanguine.... England herself, from the nature of her polity can furnish few soldiers and even these few can ill be spared to come to America in the present hostile appearance of affairs in Europe....

Their affairs will be growing worse—our's better;—so that delay will ruin them. It will serve to perplex and fret them, and precipitate them into measures, that we can turn to good account. Our business then is to avoid a General engagement and waste the enemy away...in a desultory teazing way.

After the engagement of June 26, Howe discarded his plan to lure Washington into open battle in New Jersey and withdrew to Staten Island. In July, headquarters learned that Britain's General John Burgoyne had captured the American post at Fort Ticonderoga in northern New York. Once again, the American command was baffled by British strategy. Believing that Howe might turn north up the Hudson River and join forces with Burgoyne, Washington moved his headquarters to Smiths Clove in Orange County, New York. From there, Hamilton wrote to Gouverneur Morris, vainly trying to understand the curious British movements.

[Smiths Clove, New York, July 22, 1777]
I am doubtful whether Burgoigne will attempt to penetrate far, and whether he will not content himself with harassing our back settlements by parties assisted by the savages.... This doubt arises from some appearances that indicate a Southern movement of General Howes army, which, if it should really happen, will certainly be a barrier against any further impressions of Burgoigne; for it cannot be supposed he would be rash enough to plunge into the bosom of the Country, without an expec-

tation of being met by General Howe.... I confess however that the appearances I allude to do not carry a full evidence in my mind; because ... I cannot conceive upon what principle of common sense or military propriety Howe can be running away from Burgoigne to the Southward.

Luckily, Hamilton's grasp of British military objectives was better than that of Sir William Howe. An administrative comedy of errors destroyed the Crown's carefully laid plans to seize New York and divide the United States. According to a program drawn up in London in March, 1777, General Burgoyne was to march south from Canada to be met at Albany by Howe's forces from southern New York. Howe knew nothing of this plan. Instead, on July 23, he and his army sailed from Staten Island for an attack on Philadelphia. Washington turned his men south to check this move. Not until August 16 did Howe receive orders to capture Philadelphia in time to aid in a "junction" with Burgoyne. Had Howe seen these instructions earlier, or had they been stated more clearly, he could have adjusted his timetable and attempted to move up the Hudson. As it was, reports from the north indicated that Burgoyne was advancing easily through the New York wilderness and was in no need of aid. Indeed, as Hamilton pointed out to Robert R. Livingston, the conduct of New Yorkers indicated that the state might well be frightened into submission.

> Head Quarters Camp
> near German Town [Pennsylvania]
> 7 Augt 1777

> I am with you exceeding anxious for the Safety of your State ... ; the panic in the army (I am afraid pretty high up) and the want of zeal in the Eastern States are the only alarming Considerations, for tho Burgoine should be weak in numbers as I suppose him, if the army Tumble at his name, & those who Command it ready to fly from the most defencible Ground at the Terror of small Scouting Parties of Indians, and, if to Crown the Whole the Eastern States go to Sleep & leave New York dismembered & Exhausted, as it is, to play the whole Game against a Skilfull & Enterprising Antagonist; I say if that is to be the Case, we can look for nothing but Misfortune upon Misfortune, & Conquest without a blow.

On August 22, Howe's fleet was sighted in Chesapeake Bay, and Washington knew, at last, that Philadelphia was the British objective. Marching from Germantown, American forces camped at Wilmington, Delaware. While the British slowly fanned out from their landing point near modern Elkton, Maryland, Hamilton gave Gouverneur Morris yet another report on the puzzling movements of the British commander.

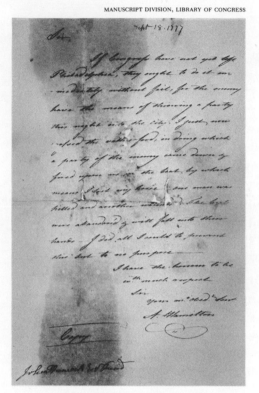

Hamilton's letter to John Hancock, September 18, 1777, advising Congress to leave Philadelphia

Head Quarters Wilmington [Delaware]
September 1st 1777

He still lies there [Greys Hill, Pennsylvania] in a state of inactivity; in a great measure I believe from the want of horses, to transport his baggage and stores. It seems he sailed with only about three weeks provendor and was six at sea. This has occasioned the death of a great number of his horses, and has made skeletons of the rest. He will be obliged to collect a supply from the neighbouring country before he can move....

This Country does not abound in good posts. It is intersected by such an infinity of roads, and is so little mountainous that it is impossible to find a spot not liable to capital defects. The one we now have is all things considered the best we could find, but there is no great depindence to be put upon it. The enemy will have Philadelphia, if they dare make a bold push for it, unless we fight them a pretty general action. I opine we ought to do it, and that we shall beat them soundly if we do. The Militia seem pretty generally stirring. Our army is in high health & spirits. We shall I hope have twice the enemy's numbers. I would not only fight them, but I would attack them; for I hold it an established maxim, that there is three to one in favour of the party attacking.

Ten days later, "pretty general action" at Brandywine Creek brought defeat for the Americans. Luckily, Howe did not press his victory, and Washington was able to withdraw in good order. On September 18, Hamilton led a party to destroy flour at Daversers Ferry on the Schuylkill River before Howe's troops could seize these supplies. Early in the day, Hamilton wrote a hurried note to John Hancock, the president of Congress, warning him to leave Philadelphia. Fearing that Hancock might not receive his first message, Hamilton sat down that evening to give him a fuller report on enemy activities.

[Warwick Furnace, Pennsylvania],
Sepr. 18th 1777 9OClock at night

The enemy are on the road to Sweedes ford [the site of modern Norristown, Pennsylvania], the main body about

The British took refuge from the patriots in the Chew House during the Battle of Germantown.

four miles from it. They sent a party this evening to Davesers ferry, which fired upon me and some others in crossing it, killed one man, wounded another, and disabled my horse. They came on so suddenly that one boat was left adrift on the other side, which will of course fall into their hands and by the help of that they will get possession of another, which was abandonned by those who had the direction of it and left afloat, in spite of every thing that I could do to the contrary. These two boats will convey 50 men across at a time so that in a few hours they may throw over a large party, perhaps sufficient to overmatch the militia who may be between them and the city. This renders the situation of Congress extremely precarious if they are not on their guard; my apprehensions for them are great, though it is not improbable they may not be realized.

Not Washington but Horatio Gates, the commander of the Northern Army, emerged as the hero of the American campaign of 1777. Unable to prevent the British occupation of Philadelphia on September 26, Washington was also defeated at Germantown on October 4. By contrast, Burgoyne surrendered his entire army to Gates at Saratoga on October 17. Although many historians argue that Benedict Arnold deserved the credit for the American success in New York, it was Gates, a man jealous of Washington's power and popularity, who was acclaimed the victor. A few days later Washington and his advisers reached a decision that would bring the rivalry with Gates into the open. Gates was to be asked to send troops from the Northern Army to bolster the American position around Philadelphia. Hamilton was given the thankless assignment of riding to Albany to persuade Gates to part with a "very considerable part of the army at present under his command." On his arrival in Albany on November 5, Hamilton received Gates's promise to release one of the three brigades still at that post. Later in the day, Hamilton complained to Gates that he had been tricked.

Albany [New York], Novemr. 5th. 1777
By inquiry, I have learned that General Patterson's brigade, which is the one you propose to send is, by far, the weakest of the three now here, and does not consist of more than about 600 rank and file fit for duty. It is true there is a militia regiment with it of about 200, but the term of service . . . is so near expiring, that it would be past by the time the men could arrive at the place of their destination, and to send them would be to fatigue

Washington's troops waited on the banks of the Brandywine to meet Howe en route to Philadelphia.

the men to no purpose. Under these circumstances, I cannot consider it either as compatible with the good of the service or my instructions from His Excellency General Washington, to consent, that that brigade be selected from the three, to go to him; but I am under the necessity of requiring, by virtue of my orders from him, that one of the others be substituted instead of this. . . .

Knowing that General Washington wished me to pay great deference to your judgment, I ventured so far to deviate, from the instructions he gave me as to consent, in compliance with your opinion that two brigades should remain here instead of one. . . . When I preferred your opinion to other considerations, I did not imagine you would pitch upon a brigade little more than half as large as the others; and finding this to be the case I indispensibly owe it to my duty, to desire in His Excellency's name, that another brigade may go instead of the one intended.

The next day, Hamilton reported the touchy situation at Albany to his Commander in Chief.

Albany [New York], November [6] 1777

I felt the importance of strengthening you as much as possible, but on the other hand, I found insuperable inconviences in acting diametrically opposite to the opinion of a Gentleman, whose successes have raised him into the highest importance. General Gates has won the intire confidence of the Eastern States; if disposed to do it by addressing himself to the prejudices of the people he would find no difficulty to render a measure odious; which it might be said, with plausibility enough to be believed, was calculated to expose them to unnecessary danger, not withstanding their exertions during the campaign had given them the fullest title to repose and security. General Gates has influence and interest elsewhere; he might use it, if he pleased, to discredit the measure there also. On the whole it appeared to me dangerous to insist on sending more troops from hence while General Gates appeared so warmly opposed to it. Should any accident or inconvenience happen in consequence of it, there would be too fair a pretext for censure, and many people are too-well-disposed to lay hold of it. At any rate it might be considered as using him ill to

Hamilton's certification that a man in his artillery company had lost his arm in battle and so was entitled to disability pay

take a step so contrary to his judgment in a case of this nature. These considerations...determined me not to insist upon sending either of the other brigades remaining here. I am afraid what I have done may not meet with your approbation as not being perhaps fully warranted by your instructions; but I ventured to do what I thought right, hoping that at least the goodness of my intention will excuse the error of my judgment.

After Hamilton rejoined the main Army at its new winter headquarters at Valley Forge at the end of December, 1777, he became increasingly concerned over the failure of the Continental Congress to provide for the Army's welfare. While some soldiers struggled to throw up huts in the snow and others froze and starved, Congress seemed more interested in political infighting than in aiding the Army. Moreover, Washington's rivalry with Gates had become a political issue in Congress, and every suggestion of military reform was scrutinized carefully—and slowly. Despairing of prompt action from Congress, Hamilton decided to enlist the aid of George Clinton, New York's newly elected governor, who had proved an invaluable ally in dealing with Gates. Accordingly, he wrote to the governor on "a matter...which requires the attention of every person of sense and influence [: the] degeneracy of representation in the great council of America."

Head Quarters [Valley Forge Pennsylvania]
Feb'y 13. 1778.

It is a melancholy truth Sir, and the effects of which we dayly see and feel, that there is not so much wisdom in a certain body, as there ought to be, and as the success of our affairs absolutely demands. Many members of it are no doubt men in every respect, fit for the trust, but this cannot be said of it as a body. Folly, caprice a want of foresight, comprehension and dignity, characterise the general tenor of their actions. Of this I dare say, you are sensible, though you have not perhaps so many opportunities of knowing it as I have. Their conduct with respect to the army especially is feeble indecisive and improvident—insomuch, that we are reduced to a more terrible situation than you can conceive....

Each State in order to promote its own internal government and prosperity, has selected its best members to fill the offices within itself, and conduct its own affairs. Men have been fonder of the emoluments and conveniences, of being employed at home, and local attachment, falsely operating, has made them more provi-

General Horatio Gates

61

The War of Independence BY BENSON J. LOSSING, 1850

A nineteenth-century engraving of Washington's camp at Valley Forge during the winter of 1777–78

dent for the particular interests of the states to which they belonged, than for the common interests of the confederacy.... You should not beggar the councils of the United States to enrich the administration of the several members. Realize to yourself the consequences of having a Congress despised at home and abroad. How can the common force be exerted, if the power of collecting it be put in weak foolish and unsteady hands? How can we hope for success in our European negociations, if the nations of Europe have no confidence in the wisdom and vigor, of the great Continental Government?

Late in March, the problem of exchanging prisoners of war with the British became Hamilton's personal concern. Although Howe and Washington had agreed to such an exchange in 1776, arguments over the interpretation of their agreement, and congressional interference, had seriously impeded any exchange. On March 28, 1778, Hamilton and three others were named to a commission to meet with Howe's representatives at Germantown. Their first attempt at negotiation failed, but Hamilton and his colleagues agreed to a second round of talks. That "national character" that Hamilton treasured was threatened again, as the commissioners reported to Washington after their return to Valley Forge.

[Valley Forge, Pennsylvania, April 15, 1778]
[April 7]... The Commissioners... opened [the meeting] by informing us, that [General Howe] meant the Treaty to be of a personal nature, founded on the mutual confidence and honor of the contracting Generals; and had no intention, either of binding the nation, or extending the cartel beyond the limits and duration of his own command....

In answer, we assigned them our reasons at large, for thinking there was a material defect, in their powers, which must render any Treaty, we could form, nugatory and unequal; nugatory, because the private faith of an individual could not in the nature of things be a competent, or proper security for a treaty of public import; and unequal, because, on the one hand, from the express terms of our powers, the public faith would be plighted for our engagements, and on the other, General Howe alone would be bound for the performance of theirs.

The Commissioners from General Howe... intimated an impropriety in treating with us, on a national ground, in a contest of such a nature as the present, which might

Trumbull sketched these starving American prisoners aboard the British prison ship Jersey, *which was anchored in New York Harbor.*

imply an acknowlegement inconsistent with their claims. We observed to them, that if there was any inconsistency at all, it would operate equally against the forming a cartel, on any principle whatever, and against the whole business of exchange;...to remove, as far as was in our power, every impediment to the execution of our commission we proposed, that a clause should be admitted into the cartel, declaring, that no expressions contained in it, should be construed to affect the political claims of either country, in any thing, not directly necessary to the due and faithful observance of the Treaty....

[The British general, however, refused to alter the wording of his commission, and after a brisk exchange of notes and memoranda, the talks ended fruitlessly, as Hamilton and his fellow officers regretfully reported to Washington.]

We are sorry the views of General Sir William Howe were so far different from yours as to render them impracticable. Your powers to us were the standard, by which we were to judge of the sufficiency of his. The former are founded on the broad basis of national faith; the latter, on the narrow one of private faith. A dissimilarity, in so material a point, appeared to us a solid, and on our part, an insuperable objection. We considered the formation of a Treaty, by which such momentous concerns would be affected, with no other sanction, than the personal honor and interest of an individual—not only as incompatible with our commission; but as repugnant to reason, to the nature of the business, and to common usage, in similar cases. A Treaty so formed would, in our conception, be merely nominal, or at best of temporary operation, certainly ceasing with personal command—liable, at any time, to be violated by public authority, without the imputation of public dishonor, and highly derogatory to the dignity of these United States.

After his frustrating negotiations with the British, the summer of 1778 seemed to offer Hamilton his long-awaited chance for military glory. With the news of a Franco-American alliance, General Sir Henry Clinton, Howe's successor as British commander, was ordered to

Hamilton's oath of allegiance as aide-de-camp to General Washington

evacuate Philadelphia. Fearful of the arrival of a French fleet, Clinton withdrew his troops overland to New York. On June 19, Washington, with Hamilton at his side, left Valley Forge to pursue the British across New Jersey. Although his advisers urged him to merely harass the British instead of meeting them in open battle, Washington decided on more decisive action. The Marquis de Lafayette and General Anthony Wayne were sent forward, and the Marquis was to engage the enemy as he wished. Assigned to assist Lafayette, Hamilton rode ahead to scout British positions. From a tavern near Allentown, New Jersey, he sent Washington his first bulletin.

> Robins Tavern
> 8 Miles from Allen Town [New Jersey]
> 12 OClock [June 26, 1778]

The Marquis de Lafayette

Our reason for halting is the extreme distress of the troops for want of provisions. General Wayne's detachment is almost starving and seem both unwilling and unable to march further 'till they are supplied. If we do not receive an immediate supply, the whole purpose of our detachment must be frustrated. This morning we missed doing any thing from a deficiency of intelligence. On my arrival at Cranbury yesterday evening, I proceeded...to take measures for cooperating with the different parts of the detachment and to find what was doing to procure intelligence. I found every precaution was neglected—no horse was near the enemy, or could be heard of 'till late in the morning; so that before we could send out parties and get the necessary information, they were in full march and as they have marched pretty expeditiously we should not be able to come up with them during the march of this day; if we did not suffer the impediment we do on the score of provisions. We are intirely at a loss where the army is, which is no inconsiderable check to our enterprise; if the army is wholly out of supporting distance, we risk the total loss of the detachment in making an attack. If the army will countenance us we may do something clever. We feel our personal honor as well as the honor of the army and the good of the service interested and are heartily desirous to attempt whatever the disposition of our men will second and prudence authorise. It is evident the enemy wish to avoid not to engage us.

Two days later, on the plain near Monmouth Court House, the enemy had no choice but "to engage us." Even then the battle was almost lost because of the indecision of General Charles Lee, Washington's second-in-command. A week after the battle, Hamilton reported on the event to his old friend Elias Boudinot, now a member of Congress. His account began with a denunciation of Lee and the officers who had advised a cautious campaign of harassment.

[New Brunswick, New Jersey
July 5, 1778]

I can hardly persuade myself to be in good humour with success so far inferior to what we, in all probability should have had, had not the finest opportunity America ever possessed been fooled away by a man, in whom she has placed a large share of the most ill judged confidence. You will have heard enough to know, that I mean General Lee. This man is either a driveler in the business of soldiership or something much worse. To let you fully into the silly and pitiful game he has been playing, I will take the tale up from the beginning....

When we came to Hopewell Township, The General unluckily called a council of war, the result of which would have done honor to the most honorab[le] society of midwives, and to them only. The purport was, that we should keep at a comfortable distance from the enemy, and keep up a vain parade of annoying them by detachment. In persuance of this idea, a detachment of 1500 men was sent off under General [Charles] Scot to join the other troops near the enemy's lines. General Lee was *primum mobile* of this sage plan; and was even opposed to sending so considerable a force....

General Charles Lee, by Trumbull

[As Hamilton recalled, Lee's behavior became even more erratic when the "advanced corps" under Lafayette was ordered forward on June 25, and became totally incomprehensible when that corps met the enemy on the morning of June 28.]

General Lee's conduct with respect to the command of this corps was truly childish. According to the incorrect notions of our army his seniority would have intitled him to the command of the advanced corps; but he in the first instance declined it, in favour of the Marquis [de Lafayette]. Some of his friends having blamed him for doing it, and Lord Stirling [Major General William Alexander] having shown a disposition to interpose his claim, General Lee very inconsistently reasserted his

pretensions. The matter was a second time accommo-
dated; General Lee and Lord Stirling agreed to let the
Marquis command. General Lee a little time after, re-
canted again and became very importunate. The General
[Washington], who had all along observed the greatest
candor in the matter, grew tired of such fickle behaviour
and ordered the Marquis to proceed....

The advanced corps came up with the enemys rear a
mile or two beyond the court House; I saw the enemy
drawn up, and am persuaded there were not a thousand
men; their front from different accounts was then ten
miles off. However favourable this situation may seem
for an attack it was not made; but after changing their
position two or three times by retrograde movements
our advanced corps got into a general confused retreat
and even route would hardly be too strong an expression.
Not a word of all this was officially communicated to the
General; as we approached the supposed place of action
we heard some flying rumours of what had happened in
consequence of which the General rode forward and
found the troops retiring in the greatest disorder and the
enemy pressing upon their rear. I never saw the general
to so much advantage. His coolness and firmness were
admirable. He instantly took measures for checking the
enemy's advance, and giving time for the army, which
was very near, to form and make a proper disposition.
He then rode back and had the troops formed on a very
advantageous piece of ground; in which and in other
transactions of the day General Greene & Lord Stirling
rendered very essential service, and did themselves great
honor. The sequel is, we beat the enemy and killed and
wounded at least a thousand of their best troops. America owes a great deal to General Washington for this day's
work; a general route dismay and disgrace would have
attended the whole army in any other hands but his. By
his own good sense and fortitude he turned the fate of
the day.

*A nineteenth-century engraving of
the battleground at Monmouth*

The American victory at Monmouth did much to silence
Washington's critics in Congress, but another problem rose to plague the
Commander's military family. The massive naval aid sent from France
proved to be of questionable value. A joint attack on British forces in Rhode
Island in August failed when the Count D'Estaing, the French admiral,

sailed to Boston to repair his ships rather than remain near Newport to aid Continental troops under generals John Sullivan and Nathanael Greene. After extricating his stranded men, Sullivan was understandably indignant, and openly expressed his doubts as to the value of America's ally in the war against Britain. Early in September, Hamilton explained the situation to Elias Boudinot, pointing out the delicate path that Boudinot and his fellow congressmen would have to take in the matter.

Head Quarters [White Plains, New York]
Sepr 8th. 78.

The military action in Rhode Island, August, 1778

The Frenchmen expect the state will reprobate the conduct of their General, and by that means, make atonement for the stain he has attempted to bring upon French honor. Something of this kind seems necessary and will in all likelihood be expected by the Court of France; but the manner of doing it suggests a question of great delicacy and difficulty, which I find myself unable to solve.

The temper with which General Sullivan was actuated was too analogous to that which appeared in the generality of those concerned with him in the expedition, and to the sentiments prevailing among the people. Though men of discression will feel the impropriety of his conduct; yet there are too many who will be ready to make a common cause with him against any attempt of the public authority to convince him of his presumption, unless the business is managed with great address and circumspection. The credit universally given him for a happy and well conducted retreat, will strengthen the sentiments in his favour, and give an air of cruelty to any species of disgrace, which might be thrown upon a man, who will be thought rather to deserve the esteem and applause of his country. To know how to strike the proper string will require more skill, than I am master of; but I would offer this general hint, that there should be a proper mixture of the *sweet* and *bitter* in the potion which may be administered.

As the campaign of 1778 drew to a close, Hamilton, like the rest of Washington's staff, began to speculate on the enemy's plans for the coming year. It is significant that in discussing this problem in a letter to his friend Alexander McDougall, who was now a major general, Hamilton considered America's economic distress to be as important a factor as military considerations were in determining British policy.

Miniature, by John Ramage, of Major General Alexander McDougall

[Fredericksburg, New York, November 8, 1778]
It is a question very undecided in my mind whether the enemy will evacuate or not. Reasoning *a priori* the arguments seem to be strongest for it, from the exhausted state of the British resources, the naked condition of their dominions every where, and the possibility of a Spanish War. But on the other hand naval superiority must do a great deal in the business. This, I think, considering all things appears clearly enough to be on the side of Britain.... The preserving posts in these States will greatly distress our trade and give security to the British West India trade. They will also cover the West Indies, and restrain any operations of ours against the British dominions on the Continent. These considerations and the depreciated state of our currency, will be strong inducements to keep New York and Rhode Island, if not with a view to conquest with a view to temopary advantages, and making better terms in a future negotiation....

The depreciation of our Currency really casts a gloom on our prospects; but my sentiments on this subject are rather peculiar. I think bad as it is, it will continue to draw out the resources of the country a good while longer; and especially if the enemy make such detachments, of which there is hardly a doubt, as will oblige them to act on the defensive. This will make our public expenditures infinitely less and will allow the states leisure to attend to the arrangement of their finances as well as the country tranquillity to cultivate its resources.

While Hamilton kept in touch with old friends like McDougall, he had also begun to make new friends among Washington's family of junior officers. The closest of these was John Laurens of South Carolina, the son of Henry Laurens, a powerful planter and political figure. A charming, fearless soldier who had served as a volunteer aide to the Commander since 1777, John Laurens had been wounded at Monmouth and had little patience with Charles Lee's attempts to exonerate his own conduct at Washington's expense. Finally, in December, 1778, young Laurens challenged Lee to a duel, and Hamilton, as his friend's second, accompanied him to the edge of a woods near Philadelphia at 3:30 P.M., on December 23. Laurens and Lee chose pistols as weapons and agreed that each was to advance toward the other and fire at will; then the affair of honor began. The next day, Hamilton and Evan Edwards, Lee's second, drew up an official account of the afternoon's events.

[Philadelphia, December 24, 1778]

They approached each other within about five or six paces and exchanged a shot almost at the same moment. As Col Laurens was preparing for a second discharge, General Lee declared himself wounded. Col Laurens, as if apprehending the wound to be more serious than it proved advanced towards the general to offer his support. The same was done by Col Hamilton and Major Edwards under a similar apprehension. General Lee then said the wound was inconsiderable, less than he had imagined at the first stroke of the Ball, and proposed to fire a second time. This was warmly opposed both by Col Hamilton and Major Edwards, who declared it to be their opinion, that the affair should terminate as it then stood. But General Lee repeated his desire, that there should be a second discharge and Col Laurens agreed to the proposal. Col Hamilton observed, that unless the General was influenced by motives of personal enmity, he did not think the affair ought to be persued any further; but as General Lee seemed to persist in desiring it, he was too tender of his friend's honor to persist in opposing it. The combat was then going to be renewed; but Major Edwards again declaring his opinion, that the affair ought to end where it was, General Lee then expressed his confidence in the honor of the Gentlemen concerned as seconds, and said he should be willing to comply with whatever they should cooly and deliberately determine. Col. Laurens consented to the same....

[Stepping to one side, Hamilton and Edwards agreed that the duel should end. At the same time, Lee and Laurens discussed their differences more fully—and came to the same conclusion.]

On Col Hamilton's intimating the idea of personal enmity, as beforementioned, General Lee declared he had none, and had only met Col. Laurens to defend his own honor—that Mr. Laurens best knew whether there was any on his part. Col Laurens replied, that General Lee was acquainted with the motives, that had brought him there, which were that he had been informed from what he thought good authority, that General Lee had spoken of General Washington in the grossest and most opprobri-

Above: A South Carolina note for two shillings and six pence; below: a Continental note for four dollars

ous terms of personal abuse, which He Col Laurens thought himself bound to resent, as well on account of the relation he bore to General Washington as from motives of personal friendship, and respect for his character. General Lee acknowleged that he had given his opinion against General Washingtons military character to his particular friends and might perhaps do it again. He said every man had a right to give his sentiments freely of military characters, and that he did not think himself personally accountable to Col Laurens for what he had done in that respect. But said he never had spoken of General Washington in the terms mentioned, which he could not have done; as well because he had always esteemed General Washington as a man, as because such abuse would be incompatible with the character, he would ever wish to sustain as a Gentleman.

Upon the whole we think it a piece of justice to the two Gentlemen to declare, that after they met their conduct was strongly marked with all the politeness generosity coolness and firmness, that ought to characterise a transaction of this nature.

A few months later, Hamilton and his friend were separated when Laurens returned home to advocate a radical scheme for South Carolina's defense. Laurens hoped to raise battalions of slaves to supplement the militia; the black soldiers would be promised their freedom in return for their military service. When Laurens rode to Philadelphia to seek congressional endorsement of his plan, he carried the following letter of introduction from Hamilton to John Jay, then the president of Congress. Jay, a long-time opponent of slavery, could prove to be a valuable ally to Laurens.

[Middlebrook, New Jersey, March 14, 1779]
It appears to me, that an expedient of this kind, in the present state of Southern affairs, is the most rational, that can be adopted, and promises very important advantages. Indeed, I hardly see how a sufficient force can be collected in that quarter without it; and the enemy's operations there are growing infinitely serious and formidable. I have not the least doubt, that the negroes will make very excellent soldiers, with proper management.... It is a maxim with some great military judges, that with sensible officers soldiers can hardly be too stupid.... I mention this, because I frequently hear

it objected to the scheme of embodying negroes that they are too stupid to make soldiers. This is so far from appearing to me a valid objection that I think their want of cultivation (for their natural faculties are probably as good as ours) joined to that habit of subordination which they acquire from a life of servitude, will make them sooner became soldiers than our White inhabitants. Let officers be men of sense and sentiment, and the nearer the soldiers approach to machines perhaps the better.

I foresee that this project will have to combat much opposition from prejudice and self-interest. The contempt we have been taught to entertain for the blacks, makes us fancy many things that are founded neither in reason nor experience; and an unwillingness to part with property of so valuable a kind will furnish a thousand arguments to show the impracticability or pernicious tendency of a scheme which requires such a sacrifice. But it should be considered, that if we do not make use of them in this way, the enemy probably will; and that the best way to counteract the temptations they will hold out will be to offer them ourselves. An essential part of the plan is to give them their freedom with their muskets. This will secure their fidelity, animate their courage, and I believe will have a good influence upon those who remain, by opening a door to their emancipation. This circumstance, I confess, has no small weight in inducing me to wish the success of the project; for the dictates of humanity and true policy equally interest me in favour of this unfortunate class of men.

John Laurens

John Laurens's departure for South Carolina forced Hamilton to make a difficult and painful confession: he had allowed himself to grow fond of another human being. In a letter to Laurens, Hamilton did his best to explain his feelings and the reasons why he had tried, throughout most of his life, to avoid forming close friendships or "particular attachments."

[Middlebrook, New Jersey, April, 1779]
Cold in my professions, warm in my friendships, I wish, my Dear Laurens, it might be in my power, by action rather than words, to convince you that I love you. I shall only tell you that 'till you bade us Adieu, I hardly knew the value you had taught my heart to set upon you. Indeed, my friend, it was not well done. You know the

opinion I entertain of mankind, and how much it is my desire to preserve myself free from particular attachments, and to keep my happiness independent on the caprice of others. You should not have taken advantage of my sensibility to steal into my affections without my consent. But as you have done it and as we are generally indulgent to those we love, I shall not scruple to pardon the fraud you have committed, on condition that for my sake, if not for your own, you will always continue to merit the partiality, which you have so artfully instilled into me....

[Having confided in Laurens this far, Hamilton let his thoughts turn to deeper attachments and, only half-jokingly, listed the qualifications he would wish to find in a wife.]

And Now my Dear as we are upon the subject of wife, I empower and command you to get me one in Carolina. Such a wife as I want will, I know, be difficult to be found, but if you succeed, it will be the stronger proof of your zeal and dexterity. Take her description—She must be young, handsome (I lay most stress upon a good shape) sensible (a little learning will do), well bred (but she must have an aversion to the word *ton*) chaste and tender (I am an enthusiast in my notions of fidelity and fondness) of some good nature, a great deal of generosity (she must neither love money nor scolding, for I dislike equally a termagent and an œconomist). In politics, I am indifferent what side she may be of; I think I have arguments that will easily convert her to mine. As to religion a moderate stock will satisfy me. She must believe in god and hate a saint. But as to fortune, the larger stock of that the better. You know my temper and circumstances and will therefore pay special attention to this article in the treaty. Though I run no risk of going to Purgatory for my avarice; yet as money is an essential ingredient to happiness in this world—as I have not much of my own and as I am very little calculated to get more either by my address or industry; it must needs be, that my wife, if I get one, bring at least a sufficiency to administer to her own extravagancies. NB You will be pleased to recollect in your negotiations that I have no invincible antipathy to the *maidenly beauties* & that I am willing to take the *trouble* of them upon myself.

If you should not readily meet with a lady that you think answers my description you can only advertise in the public papers and doubtless you will hear of many competitors for most of the qualifications required, who will be glad to become candidates for such a prize as I am. To excite their emulation, it will be necessary for you to give an account of the lover—his *size*, make, quality of mind and *body*, achievements, expectations, fortune, &c. In drawing my picture, you will no doubt be civil to your friend; mind you do justice to the length of my nose.

Hamilton diverted himself from the dull routine at camp that summer by composing a letter of introduction for Mrs. Judah Fitzgerald to present to Governor George Clinton of New York. Clinton, concerned for the outcome of an American expedition against the Iroquois in the western part of his state, was in sore need of the comic relief offered by Hamilton's letter.

[West Point, New York] Aug 24th. 79

The bearer of this is an *old woman* and of course the most troublesome animal in the world. She wants to go into New York. It was in vain we told her no inhabitant could be permitted by us to go within the enemy's lines without permission from the civil power. Old and decrepid as she is, she made the tour of the family and tried her blandishments upon each. I assured her Governor Clinton could have no possible motive for detaining her within his territories and would readily give his consent to her emigration. But nothing would satisfy her except a line from General Washington to the Governor. As she showed a disposition to remain with us 'till she carried her point, with true female perseverance—as we are rather straitened in our quarters, and not one of the Gentlemen of the family would agree to share his bed with her—And as you must at all events have the favour of a visit from her—I at last promised her a letter to you, the direct and sole end of which is to get rid of her. I dare say, your Excellency will think you make a very good bargain for the state, by getting rid of her also in the manner she wishes. She seems too to be in distress and have a claim upon our compassion.

Governor George Clinton

In the first week of September, Hamilton's good humor vanished. William Gordon, an eccentric Massachusetts clergyman, was spreading a story that Hamilton had declared that "it was high time for the people to rise, join General Washington, and turn Congress out of doors." Hamilton demanded that Gordon disclose the source of this tale, but the cleric tried to placate him with assurances that the words in question must have been spoken "unguardedly"; worse still, he refused to name the supposed witness to the incident until Hamilton promised not to challenge this mysterious informant to a duel. Furious, Hamilton sent this indignant reply to Gordon.

[West Point, New York, September 5, 1779] An opinion of my *inexperience* seems to have betrayed you into mistakes: Whatever you may imagine, Sir, I have read the *world* sufficiently to know that, though it may often be *convenient* to the propagator of a calumny to conceal the inventor, he will stand in need of no small address, to escape the suspicions & even the indignation of the honest & of the disinterested. Nor can I but persist in believing, that ... the delicacy of your sentiments will be alarmed at the possibility of incurring this danger, & will prevent your exposing yourself to it, by refusing or delaying any longer, to comply with so reasonable a demand.

... The good sense of the present times has happily found out, that to prove your own innocence, or the malice of an accuser, the worst method, you can take, is to run him through the body, or shoot him through the head. And permit me to add, that while you felt an aversion to duelling, on the principles of religion, you ought, in charity, to have supposed others possessed of the same scruples,—of whose impiety you had no proofs.... The crime alleged to me is of such enormity, that, if I am guilty, it ought not to go unpunished; &, if I am innocent I should have an opportunity of indicating my innocence. The truth in either case should appear; & it is incumbent upon you, Sir, to afford the means, either by accusing me to my civil, or military superiors, or by disclosing the author of the information.

William Gordon

A few days later, renewing his correspondence with John Laurens, Hamilton reassessed America's position in view of Spain's recent declaration of war against England and predicted that the northern states no longer had much to fear from British arms.

The French Admiral Count D'Estaing

[West Point, New York, September 11, 1779] Negotiation not conquest will then be [Britain's] object; the acquisition of two or three of the Southern states would be the counterballance to the loss of her Islands, give credit in Europe, facilitate honorable pacification or procure it. The plan of operations, I suppose in that case would be this—to evacuate Rhode Island, leave a garrison of eight thousand men for the defence of New York and its dependencies, detach five thousand to the West Indies to assist in garrisoning their remaining Islands, and then they will have five thousand to send to the Southward....

The plan here suggested, you will perhaps think with me is not the worst the enemy could adopt in their present circumstances. Its goodness is perhaps the strongest reason against its being undertaken; but they may blunder upon the right way for once, and we ought to be upon our guard.

In September, the Army's strategy was determined by naval considerations. The English fleet, under Admiral Arbuthnot, had reached New York, while the French Admiral Count D'Estaing had sailed to Georgia to aid in an assault on British-held Savannah. After conferring with the Chevalier de la Luzerne, France's minister to the United States, Washington made tentative plans for joint operations in the North. It was expected that D'Estaing would return soon from his Georgia expedition, and it was hoped that he would cooperate in some limited operation such as an attack upon New York City before sailing to the West Indies for the winter campaign. In order to communicate with the French admiral as quickly as possible, Hamilton and Brigadier General Louis Du Portail were sent to Philadelphia, where D'Estaing's fleet was to appear. After a few days, Hamilton and Du Portail pressed on to the New Jersey coast in hopes of sighting the elusive fleet, as they reported to Washington.

Great Egg Harbor Landing [New Jersey]
Octr. 26: 1779

We propose to remain till the arrival of the Count, till intelligence from him decides the inutility of a longer stay or 'till we receive your Excellency's orders of recall. We have now a better relation to the different points in which we are interested and have taken the necessary precautions to gain the earliest notice of whatever happens....

By recent information...we find that so late as the

fourth of this month the Count was yet to open his batteries against the enemy at Savannah. The time that will probably intervene between this and their final reduction... and his arrival on this coast may we fear exhaust the season too much to permit the cooperation to which our mission relates. We do not however despair; for if the Count has been fully successful to the Southward, and should shortly arrive which may be the case, the enterprise may possibly still go on.

Unwittingly, Washington had sent Hamilton on a wild goose chase. A week before Hamilton and Du Portail established their lonely outpost at Great Egg Harbor, D'Estaing had sailed for the West Indies, ignoring General Benjamin Lincoln's pleas that he continue the siege of Savannah; he thus had failed the American cause in Georgia as fully as he had a year before off Rhode Island. When Hamilton returned to headquarters at Morristown, there was yet another letter from William Gordon, in which the clergyman again refused to name his mysterious "informant." Thoroughly disgusted and having "no hope of bringing this affair to a more satisfactory conclusion," Hamilton put an end to the correspondence.

His fruitless search for D'Estaing and his message from William Gordon must have seemed to Hamilton an appropriate climax to a particularly frustrating period of his military career. He had seen no action since the Battle of Monmouth eighteen months earlier. His hopes for a part in a Franco-American expedition against New York were crushed. Furthermore, he had already begun to resent his work as Washington's aide. To a restless young man with dreams of glory, it must have seemed in December, 1779, that he had traded the hated "condition of a Clerk" in St. Croix for the same position in the Continental service. On the other hand, his experience on Washington's staff had given Hamilton a superb education in America's economic and political problems, and the warmth of that "family" enabled him to form close friendships. During the next two years that experience would serve him well in his efforts to find a more satisfying place in American life and the Continental Army.

Chapter 3

Triumphs in Love and War

To Americans of the second half of the twentieth century, Alexander Hamilton's obsession with military glory might seem rather puzzling, but for a young man who found himself, in 1780, with "no property here, no connexions," a reputation could be won most easily on the battlefield. For an ambitious man like Hamilton, military heroism had more than symbolic significance. Eventually, as a command in the field began to seem more and more elusive, Hamilton turned to other areas where "connexions" or "property" might be acquired. But at the beginning of 1780 he could see little future for himself in America. When he learned that his friend John Laurens had attempted to win a diplomatic assignment for him from Congress, Hamilton viewed the occasion as simply another proof of the futility of his life. In a letter to Laurens, Hamilton thanked his friend for his kindness, but made it clear that more than this would be needed to end his depression.

> [Morristown, New Jersey] Jany 8t. [1780] Believe me my Dr Laurens I am not insensible of the first mark of your affection in recommending me to your friends for a certain commission. However your partiality may have led you to overrate my qualifications that very partiality must endear you to me; and all the world will allow that your struggles and scruples upon the occasion deserve the envy of men of vertue....
>
> ...Not one of the four in nomination but would stand a better chance than myself; and yet my vanity tells me they do not all merit a preference. But I am a stranger in this country. I have no property here, no connexions. If I have talents and integrity, (as you say I have) these are justly deemed very spurious titles in these enlightened days, when unsupported by others more solid....

I have strongly sollicited leave to go to the Southward. It could not be refused; but arguments have been used to dissuade me from it, which however little weight they may have had in my judgment gave law to my feelings. I am chagrined and unhappy but I submit. In short Laurens I am disgusted with every thing in this world but yourself and *very* few more honest fellows and I have no other wish than as soon as possible to make a brilliant exit. 'Tis a weakness; but I feel I am not fit for this terrestreal Country.

Fortunately, the dull camp routine at Morristown during the winter of 1779–80 left Washington's family of young officers ample time for other diversions. A "dancing assembly" was formed, and the daughters of good patriots were only too delighted to participate. Among the ladies who visited headquarters was Elizabeth Schuyler, daughter of Major General Philip Schuyler. While the guest of her aunt and uncle in Morristown, "Betsey" caught Hamilton's eye and their romance progressed rapidly. In February, the young officer wrote to Elizabeth's sister Margarita, who had remained in Philadelphia where their father served in Congress. Although Hamilton had not met Margarita, he confessed to her that her older sister "by some odd contrivance" had "found out the secret of interesting me in every thing that concerns her."

[Morristown, New Jersey, February, 1780]
I have already confessed the influence your sister has gained over me; yet notwithstanding this, I have some things of a very serious and heinous nature to lay to her charge. She is most unmercifully handsome and so perverse that she has none of those pretty affectations which are the prerogatives of beauty. Her good sense is destitute of that happy mixture of vanity and ostentation which would make it conspicuous to the whole tribe of fools and foplings as well as to men of understanding so that as the matter now stands it is very little known beyond the circle of these. She has good nature affability and vivacity unembellished with that charming frivolousness which is justly deemed one of the principal accomplishments of a *belle*. In short she is so strange a creature that she possesses all the beauties virtues and graces of her sex without any of those amiable defects, which from their general prevalence are esteemed by connoisseurs necessary shades in the character of a fine woman. The most determined adversaries of Hymen can

Philip Schuyler, by Trumbull

General Schuyler's headquarters at Morristown, where Hamilton and Elizabeth Schuyler first met

find in her no pretext for their hostility, and there are several of my friends, philosophers who railed at love as a weakness, men of the world who laughed at it as a phantasie, whom she has presumptuously and daringly compelled to acknowlege its power and surrender at discretion. I can the better assert the truth of this, as I am myself of the number. She has had the address to overset all the wise resolutions I had been framing for more than four years past, and from a rational sort of being and a professed contemner of Cupid has in a trice metamorphosed me into the veriest inamorato you perhaps ever saw.

In the second week of March, Hamilton's courtship was interrupted by the recurring problem of prisoners of war. On the ninth, Hamilton and two other officers set out for Perth Amboy, New Jersey, for negotiations with the British. As this tender letter to Elizabeth Schuyler clearly illustrates, Hamilton had declared his feelings before he left Morristown.

[Perth Amboy, New Jersey] Thursday Forenoon
[March 17, 1780]

My dearest girl

...Every moment of my stay here becomes more and more irksome; but I hope two or three days will put an end to it. Col Webb tells me you have sent for a carriage to go to Philadelphia. If you should set out before I return have the goodness to leave a line informing me how long you expect to be there. I beg too you will not suffer any considerations respecting me to prevent your going; for though it will be a tax upon my love to part with you so long, I wish you to see that city before you return.... Only let me entreat you to endeavour not to stay there longer than the amusements of the place interest you, in complaisance to friends; for you must always remember your best friend is where I am....

If I were not afraid of making you vain, I would tell you that Mrs. Carter, Peggy [Elizabeth Schuyler's sisters], and yourself are the dayly toasts of our table; and for this *honor* you are chiefly indebted to the British Gentlemen....

Our interview is attended with a great deal of sociability and good humour; but I begin notwithstanding to be tired of our British friends. They do their best to

Elizabeth Schuyler Hamilton

be agreeable and are particularly civil to me; but after all they are a compound of grimace and jargon; and out of a certain fashionable routine are as dull and empty as any Gentlemen need to be. One of their principal excellencies consists in swallowing a large quantity of wine every day, and in this I am so unfortunate that I shall make no sort of figure with them.

Returning to Morristown with his colleagues after two and a half weeks of fruitless negotiations with the British, Hamilton continued his courtship of Elizabeth Schuyler, who, he had now discovered, matched perfectly the requirements for a wife that he had sent to John Laurens in his half-joking letter of a year before. Not only would her father's influence as one of the wealthiest and most powerful men in New York more than compensate for Hamilton's own lack of connections; her good humor and even temper would make her an excellent wife for the sensitive, often moody, young officer. Philip Schuyler and his wife, journeying from Philadelphia to meet their daughter's suitor and consider his proposal, agreed to the match on April 8, and plans were made for a wedding in the late fall. But the prospect of a brilliant marriage did not distract Hamilton from other aspects of his "futurity." He still dreamed of military glory, and for a few days in June there seemed a chance of action. British forces under the Hessian General Knyphausen had landed near Elizabethtown, New Jersey, and Hamilton was sent forward to investigate the situation. From a vantage point near Springfield, New Jersey, he sent his report to Washington.

[Near Springfield, New Jersey, June 8, 1780]
I have seen the enemy; those in view I calculate at about three thousand; there may be and probably enough are others out of sight. They have sent all their horse to the other side except about fifty or sixty. Their baggage it is agreed on all hands has also been sent across and their wounded. It is not ascertained that any of their infantry have passed to the other side....

Different conjectures may be made. The present movement may be calculated to draw us down and betray us into an action. They may have desisted from their intention of passing till night for fear of our falling upon their rear. I believe this is the case; for as they have but few boats it would certainly be a delicate manœuvre to cross in our face. We are taking measures to watch their motions to night as closely as possible. An incessant but *very light* skirmishing.

The Jersey militia managed to halt the British raiders, and Hamilton returned to his duties as an aide. But, as he wrote to his friend John Laurens at the end of June, he was infuriated by the militia's poor showing and by the inability of the states to take joint action at this critical time.

[Ramapo, New Jersey, June 30, 1780]
My Dear Laurens, our countrymen have all the folly of the ass and all the passiveness of the sheep in their compositions. They are determined not to be free and they can neither be frightened, discouraged nor persuaded to change their resolution. If we are saved France and Spain must save us. I have the most pigmy-feelings at the idea, and I almost wish to hide my disgrace in universal ruin. Don't think I rave; for the conduct of the states is enough most pitiful that can be imagined. Would you believe it—a German baron at the head of five thousand men, in the month of June insulted and defied the main American army with the Commander in Chief at their head with impunity, and made them tremble for the security of their magazines forty miles in the country.

The Schuyler home near Albany (above) and Schuyler's mills (below) were destroyed by the British in 1777 and rebuilt after the war.

BOTH: *Revolution,* LOSSING

The military situation was not as bleak as Hamilton believed it to be. Lafayette had recently returned from France with news of substantial aid—an expeditionary force under the capable Comte de Rochambeau. Hamilton's mood may have been affected by Elizabeth's departure for Albany. Lonely and miserable, he wrote to her early in July.

[Preakness, New Jersey, July 2–4, 1780]
I love you more and more every hour. The sweet softness and delicacy of your mind and manners, the elevation of your sentiments, the real goodness of your heart, its tenderness to me, the beauties of your face and person, your unpretending good sense and that innocent simplicity and frankness which pervade your actions; all these appear to me with increasing amiableness and place you in my estimation above all the rest of your sex.

I entreat you my Charmer, not to neglect the charges I gave you particularly that of taking care of your self, and that of employing all your leisure in reading. Nature has been very kind to you; do not neglect to cultivate her gifts and to enable yourself to make the distinguished figure in all respects to which you are intitled to aspire. You excel most of your sex in all the amiable qualities; endeavour to excel them equally in the splendid ones.

You can do it if you please and I shall take pride in it. It will be a fund too, to diversify our enjoyments and amusements and fill all our moments to advantage....

Yrs. my Angel with inviolable Affection

ALEX HAMILTON

•

While watching impatiently with the rest of Washington's staff for the appearance of Rochambeau's fleet, Hamilton complained to Betsey Schuyler that his affection for her prevented him from enjoying anything else.

Col. Dey's house Bergen County [New Jersey]
July 6th. [1780]

Here we are my love in a house of great hospitality— in a country of plenty—a buxom girl under the same roof—pleasing expectations of a successful campaign— and every thing to make a soldier happy, who is not in love and absent from his mistress. As this is my case I cannot be happy; but it is a maxim of my life to enjoy the present good with the highest relish & to soften the present evil by a hope of future good. I alleviate the pain of absence by looking forward to that delightful period which gives us to each other forever; and my imagination serves up such a feast of pleasure as almost makes me forget the deprivation I now experience. But alas my Dear girl this does not always do. The illusion will not always soothe; my heart every now and then cries: You are separated from the lovely partner of your life; four long months must elapse before this separation ends; your sweet girl with nothing to engage or divert her attention is perhaps suffering the keenest anxiety for the situation of her lover not only absent from her but exposed to a thousand imaginary dangers.

But my dearest quiet your apprehensions (for I know your tender fond mind is of too apprehensive a cast) and let your thoughts run only upon those delights which our reunion will afford.

Adieu my angel, be happy and love me as well as I love you

A HAMILTON

Comte de Rochambeau, by Peale

Rochambeau reached Newport four days later and Lafayette was sent north to "fix our plan of operations" with the French commander. Both Lafayette and Hamilton were hoping that allied strategy would involve an attack on New York City, where both could win military fame, and in mid-July, Hamilton wrote of their scheme to François de Barbé-Marbois, the young secretary to the French diplomatic mission in Philadelphia.

François de Barbé-Marbois

[Preakness, New Jersey, July 20, 1780]
New York in all probability will be our object; if we can have a naval superiority, I shall not doubt our success; if we have not the event will be very precarious; and in success the advantages infinitely less. The enemy will save a great part of their army; stores & their shipping of course will be safe, and the whole may fall upon some other part where we may be vulnerable.

I shall take occasion to assure you that it appears clear to a demonstration that with a superiority by land and sea you can infallibly possess the port of New York, and by seige or blockade, reduce the whole fleet and army. What will be done or can be done to secure an object of such magnitude, I cannot judge; only of this I am confident that your court will do every thing possible. The proofs she has already given would make it ingratitude to doubt her future intentions.

Hope for an early campaign against New York faded when a British fleet under Admiral Thomas Graves threatened French forces at Newport. Washington marched north to divert British attention and naval power from Rhode Island, and by August not even Hamilton could pretend that a New York campaign was likely. His dreams of an early military expedition died hard, and the unpleasant turn of events even affected his attitude toward his marriage. Writing to Elizabeth Schuyler late in August, Hamilton began in a lighthearted fashion but soon adopted a more serious tone.

[Teaneck, New Jersey, August, 1780]
Though I am not sanguine in expecting it, I am not without hopes this Winter will produce a peace and then you must submit to the mortification of enjoying more domestic happiness and less fame. This I know you will not like, but we cannot always have things as we wish.

The affairs of England are in so bad a plight that if no fortunate events attend her this campaign, it would seem impossible for her to proceed in the war. But she is an obstinate old dame, and seems determined to ruin her whole family, rather than to let Miss America go on

Rochambeau's forces step ashore at Newport, Rhode Island, July, 1780.

flirting it with her new lovers, with whom, as giddy young girls often do, she eloped in contempt of her mothers authority. I know you will be ready to justify her conduct and tell me the ill treatment she received was enough to make any girl of spirit act in the same manner. But I will one day cure you of these refractory notions about the right of resistance, (of which I foresee you will be apt to make a very dangerous application), and teach you the great advantage and absolute necessity of implicit obedience.

But now we are talking of times to come, tell me my pretty damsel have you made up your mind upon the subject of housekeeping? Do you soberly relish the pleasure of being a poor mans wife? Have you learned to think a home spun preferable to a brocade and the rumbling of a waggon wheel to the musical rattling of a coach and six? . . . If you cannot my Dear we are playing a comedy of all in the wrong, and you should correct the mistake before we begin to act the tragedy of the unhappy couple.

Hamilton had meantime found an engrossing pastime to distract him from his loneliness. Long critical of American government, he now began formulating remedies for the nation's ills. In a letter to James Duane, New York's powerful congressman, he outlined his developing political theories and discussed the need for a strong central government that could provide "method and energy" in administering America's affairs. As a spokesman for administrative reform in Congress, Duane could be counted on to listen carefully to Hamilton's "ideas on the defects of our present system, and the changes necessary to save us from ruin."

[Liberty Pole, New Jersey, September 3, 1780] The fundamental defect is a want of power in Congress. It is hardly worth while to show in what this consists, as it seems to be universally acknowleged, or to point out how it has happened, as the only question is how to remedy it. It may however be said that it has originated from three causes—an excess of the spirit of liberty which has made the particular states show a jealousy of all power not in their own hands; and this jealousy has led them to exercise a right of judging in the last resort of the measures recommended by Congress, and of acting according to their own opinions of their propriety or necessity, a diffidence in Congress of their own powers, by which they have been timid and indecisive in their resolutions, constantly making concessions to the states, till they have scarcely left themselves the shadow of power; a want of sufficient means at their disposal to answer the public exigencies and of vigor to draw forth those means; which have occasioned them to depend on the states individually to fulfill their engagements with the army, and the consequence of which has been to ruin their influence and credit with the army, to establish its dependence on each state separately rather than *on them*, that is rather than on the whole collectively....

Another defect in our system is want of method and energy in the administration. This has partly resulted from the other defect, but in a great degree from prejudice and the want of a proper executive. Congress have kept the power too much into their own hands and have meddled too much with details of every sort. Congress is properly a deliberative corps and it forgets itself when it attempts to play the executive. It is impossible such a body, numerous as it is, constantly fluctuating, can ever act with sufficient decision, or with system. Two thirds of the members, one half the time, cannot know what has gone before them or what connection the subject in hand has to what has been transacted on former occasions. The members, who have been more permanent, will only give information, that promotes the side they espouse, in the present case, and will as often mislead as enlighten....

The first step must be to give Congress powers competent to the public exigencies. This may happen in two ways, one by resuming and exercising the discretionary powers I suppose to have been originally vested in them for the safety of the states...the other by calling immediately a convention of all the states with full authority to conclude finally upon a general confederation, stating to them beforehand explicitly the evils arising from a want of power in Congress, and the impossibility of supporting the contest on its present footing, that the delegates may come possessed of proper sentiments as well as proper authority to give to the meeting....

...The Convention should assemble the 1st of November next, the sooner, the better; our disorders are too violent to admit of a common or lingering remedy.... A convention may agree upon a confederation; the states individually hardly ever will. We must have one at all

In this British cartoon of 1779, the horse "America" is shown throwing his master, George III.

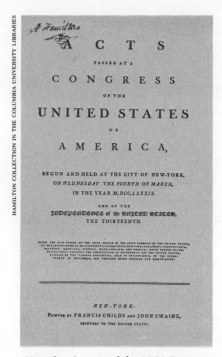

Hamilton's copy of the 1780 "Acts of Congress" bears his signature.

The Continental Congress, 1780, as shown in an English engraving

events, and a vigorous one if we mean to succeed in the contest and be happy hereafter.... Congress ought to confess... plainly and unanimously the impracticability of supporting our affairs on the present footing and without a solid coercive union....

The second step I would recommend is that Congress should instantly appoint the following great officers of state—A secretary for foreign affairs—a President of war—A President of Marine—a Financier—A President of trade....

Congress should choose for these offices, men of the first abilities, property and character in the continent—and such as have had the best opportunities of being acquainted with the several branches....

These offices should have nearly the same powers and functions as those in France analogous to them, and each should be chief in his department, with subordinate boards composed of assistant clerks &c. to execute his orders....

[Next, Congress must reform the American Army. Under Hamilton's plan, terms of enlistment were to be standardized, and officers were to be rewarded with a pension of "half pay"—a yearly payment equal to half their annual salaries in the Army.]

The advantages of securing the attachment of the army to Congress, and binding them to the service by substantial ties are immense. We should then have discipline, an army in reality, as well as in name. Congress would then have a solid basis of authority and consequence, for to me it is an axiom that in our constitution an army is essential to the American union.

The providing of supplies is the pivot of every thing else.... There are four ways all which must be united—a foreign loan, heavy pecuniary taxes, a tax in kind, a bank founded on public and private credit.

As to a foreign loan I dare say, Congress are doing every thing in their power to obtain it. The most effectual way will be to tell France that without it, we must make terms with great Britain....

Concerning the necessity of heavy pecuniary taxes I need say nothing, as it is a point in which everybody is agreed....

As to a tax in kind, the necessity of it results from this principle—that the money in circulation is not a sufficient representative of the productions of the country....

How far it may be practicable to erect a bank on the joint credit of the public and of individuals can only be certainly determined by the experiment; but it is of so much importance that the experiment ought to be fully tried....

If a Convention is called the minds of all the states and the people ought to be prepared to receive its determinations by sensible and popular writings, which should conform to the views of Congress. There are epochs in human affairs, when *novelty* even is useful. If a general opinion prevails that the old way is bad, whether true or false, and this obstructs or relaxes the operation of the public service, a change is necessary if it be but for the sake of change. This is exactly the case now. 'Tis an universal sentiment that our present system is a bad one, and that things do not go right on this account. The measure of a Convention would revive the hopes of the people and give a new direction to their passions, which may be improved in carrying points of substantial utility....

And, in future, My Dear Sir, two things let me recommend, as fundamental rules for the conduct of Congress—to attach the army to them by every motive, to maintain an air of authority (not domineering) in all their measures with the states. The manner in which a thing is done has more influence than is commonly imagined. Men are governed by opinion; this opinion is as much influenced by appearances as by realities; if a Government appears to be confident of its own powers, it is the surest way to inspire the same confidence in others; if it is diffident, it may be certain, there will be a still greater diffidence in others, and that its authority will not only be distrusted, controverted, but contemned.

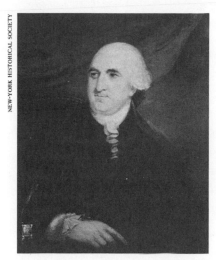

James Duane helped draft the Articles of Confederation and later became the mayor of New York.

Before he could dispatch his letter to Duane, Hamilton heard of Horatio Gates's defeat at Camden, South Carolina, on August 16—a battle that has been described as "the most disastrous defeat ever inflicted on an American army." Gates compounded his disgrace by retreating at record speed, putting almost two hundred miles between himself and the remnants of the Southern Army in three and a half days. Writing again to Duane,

Hamilton did not miss this chance to bolster his arguments for Army reform and to attack his old enemy, Gates.

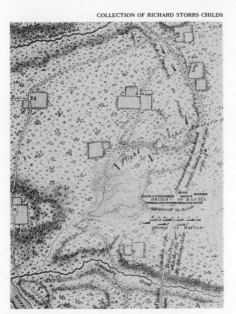

A British map of the Battle of Camden, South Carolina—a disaster for America's Southern Army

[Bergen County, New Jersey] Sept 6. 1780
I have heard since of Gates defeat, a very good comment on the necessity of changing our system.... What think you of the conduct of this great man? I am his enemy personally, for unjust and unprovoked attacks upon my character, therefore what I say of him ought to be received as from an enemy.... But did ever any one hear of such a disposition or such a flight? His best troops placed on the side strongest by nature, his worst, on that weakest by nature, and his attack made with these. 'Tis impossible to give a more complete picture of military absurdity. It is equally against the maxims of war, and common sense....

But was there ever an instance of a General running away as Gates has done from his whole army? and was there ever so precipitous a flight? One hundred and eighty miles in three days and a half. It does admirable credit to the activity of a man at his time of life. But it disgraces the General and the Soldiers.

Meanwhile, Hamilton's fight for reform was winning him enemies on all sides in Congress and in the Army. As he explained in a letter to John Laurens, his position was becoming increasingly difficult.

[New Bridge, New Jersey, September 12, 1780]
You told me, my remedies were good, but you were afraid would not go down at this time. I tell you necessity must force them down; and that if they are not speedily taken the patient will die. She is in a gallopping consumption, and her case will soon become desperate. Indeed, my Dear friend, to drop allegory, you can hardly conceive in how dreadful a situation we are. The army, in the course of the present month, has received only four or five days rations of meal, and we really know not of any adequate relief in future.... The officers are out of humour.... 'Tis in vain you attempt to appease; you are almost detested as an accomplice with the administration. I am losing character my friend, because I am not over complaisant to the spirit of clamour, so that I am in a fair way to be out with every body. With one set, I am considered as a friend to military pretensions however exorbitant, with another as a man, who secured by my

situation from sharing the distress of the army, am inclined to treat it lightly. The truth is I am an unlucky, honest man, that speak my sentiments to all and with emphasis. I say this to you because you know it and will not charge me with vanity. I hate Congress—I hate the army—I hate the world—I hate myself. The whole is a mass of fools and knaves; I could almost except you and [Richard Kidder] Meade.

In the last week of September, Hamilton accompanied Washington to Hartford, Connecticut, for conferences with the French. On their return journey, they witnessed an incident that temporarily overshadowed any disappointments over French aid or congressional inefficiency. For sixteen months, Benedict Arnold, the American commander at West Point, had been secretly negotiating with the British, and by the end of August, 1780, he had agreed to surrender the plans of fortifications at West Point. Sir Henry Clinton's aide, John André, was sent north to meet Arnold's agent, Joshua Hett Smith, but at 9 A.M. on September 25, Arnold learned that Smith and André had been captured. Washington and his party were to arrive at West Point later in the day, and Arnold lost no time in departing for safety to New York City. By the time Washington and Hamilton reached West Point, Arnold had vanished, and, as Hamilton reported to Elizabeth Schuyler, Washington's aides had to deal with the traitor's hysterical wife.

[Robinson's House, Highlands, New York]
Sepr 25 [1780]

The fortifications at West Point, as seen at the close of the war

In the midst of my letter, I was interrupted by a scene that shocked me more than any thing I have met with—the discovery of a treason of the deepest dye. The object was to sacrifice West Point. General Arnold had sold himself to André for this purpose. The latter came but in disguise and in returning to New York was detected. Arnold hearing of it immediately fled to the enemy. I went in persuit of him but was much too late, and I could hardly regret the disappointment, when on my return, I saw an amiable woman frantic with distress for the loss of a husband she tenderly loved—a traitor to his country and to his fame, a disgrace to his connections. It was the most affecting scene I ever was witness to. She for a considerable time intirely lost her senses. The General went up to see her and she upbraided him with being in a plot to murder her child; one moment she raved; another she melted into tears; sometimes she

Margaret Shippen Arnold, as sketched by Major André in 1778

pressed her infant to her bosom and lamented its fate occasioned by the imprudence of its father in a manner that would have pierced insensibility itself.... We have every reason to believe she was intirely unacquainted with the plan, and that her first knowlege of it was when Arnold went to tell her he must banish himself from his Country and from her forever. She instantly fell into a convulsion and he left her in that situation.

This morning she is more composed. I paid her a visit and endeavoured to sooth her by every method in my power, though you may imagine she is not easily to be consoled. Added to her other distresses, She is very apprehensive the resentment of her country will fall upon her ... for the guilt of her husband.... She received us in bed, with every circumstance that could interest our sympathy. Her sufferings were so eloquent that I wished myself her brother, to have a right to become her defender. As it is, I have entreated her to enable me to give her proofs of my friendship.

Could I forgive Arnold for sacrificing his honor reputation and duty I could not forgive him for acting a part that must have forfieted the esteem of so fine a woman. At present she almost forgets his crime in his misfortune, and her horror at the guilt of the traitor is lost in her love of the man. But a virtuous mind cannot long esteem a base one, and time will make her despise, if it cannot make her hate.

Margaret Shippen Arnold, who was well aware of her husband's plans, did not deserve Hamilton's chivalrous concern, although she certainly should have won his applause for her acting ability. Another party in the scheme, Major John André, was a more sympathetic figure. The young British officer charmed his captors, and when André was judged a spy and sentenced to hang, Hamilton did his best to give the Englishman what help he could. On the day of André's death, Hamilton explained his conduct to Elizabeth Schuyler.

[Tappan, New York, October 2, 1780]

To justify myself to your sentiments, I must inform you that I urged a compliance with Andre's request to be shot and I do not think it would have had an ill effect; but some people are only sensible to motives of policy, and sometimes from a narrow disposition mistake it. When André's tale comes to be told, and present resentment is over, the refusing him the privilege of choosing the manner of death will be branded with too much obduracy.

It was proposed to me to suggest to him the idea of an exchange for Arnold; but I knew I should have forfieted his esteem by doing it, and therefore declined it. As a man of honor he could not but reject it and I would not for the world have proposed to him a thing, which must have placed me in the unamiable light of supposing him capable of a meanness, or of not feeling myself the impropriety of the measure. I confess to you I had the weakness to value the esteem of a *dying* man; because I reverenced his merit.

Nine days after André's execution (by hanging), Hamilton sent a lengthy account of the English officer's story to John Laurens. "Never," he told Laurens, "did any man suffer death with more justice, or deserve it less."

André made these sketches the day before his execution: a self-portrait and a view of his crossing of the Hudson for his meeting with Arnold.

[Preakness, New Jersey, October 11, 1780] There was something singularly interesting in the character and fortunes of André. To an excellent understanding well improved by education and travel, he united a peculiar elegance of mind and manners, and the advantage of a pleasing person. . . . By his merit he had acquired the unlimited confidence of his general and was making a rapid progress in military rank and reputation. But in the height of his career, flushed with new hope from the execution of a project the most beneficial to his party . . . he was at once precipitated from the summit . . . and saw all the expectations of his ambition blasted and himself ruined. . . .

. . . In going to the place of execution, he bowed familiarly as he went along to all those with whom he had been acquainted in his confinement. A smile of complacency expressed the serene fortitude of his mind. Arrived at the fatal spot, he asked with some emotion, *must* I then die in this manner? He was told it had been unavoidable. "I am reconciled to my fate (said he) but not to the mode." Soon however recollecting himself, he added, "it will be but a momentary pang," and springing upon the cart performed the last offices to himself with a composure that excited the admiration and melted the hearts of the beholders. Upon being told the final moment was at hand, and asked if he had any thing to say, he answered:

"nothing, but to request you will witness to the world, that I die like a brave man."

By the end of October, Hamilton was thinking of little besides his plans for marriage. He confessed to Betsey that she occupied his sleeping as well as his waking hours, and as proof he wrote his "Dear girl" an account of a dream he had had.

[Preakness, New Jersey, October 27, 1780]
I had a charming dream two or three night ago. I thought I had just arrived at Albany and found you asleep on a green near the house, and beside you in an inclined posture stood a Gentleman whom I did not know. He had one of your hands in his, and seemed fixed in silent admiration. As you may imagine, I reproached him with his presumption and asserted my claim. He insisited on a prior right; and the dispute grew heated. This I fancied awoke you, when yielding to a sudden impulse of joy, you flew into my arms and decided the contention with a kiss. I was so delighted that I immediately waked, and lay the rest of the night exulting in my good fortune. Tell me pray you who is this rival of mine. Dreams you know are the messengers of Jove.

Hamilton's wedding plans were delayed when two of Washington's other aides were called home to Virginia. While he waited for these officers to return and relieve him, Hamilton used his time to work out another plan for a New York expedition with Lafayette. Although Washington had refused to consider his earlier requests for a command in the field, Hamilton wrote again to his commander in hopes of persuading him that he could serve in this projected campaign.

[Passaic Falls, New Jersey, November 22, 1780]
Sometime last fall when I spoke to your Excellency about going to the Southward, I explained to you candidly my feelings with respect to military reputation, and how much it was my object to act a conspicuous part in some enterprise that might perhaps raise my character as a soldier above mediocrity. You were so good as to say you would be glad to furnish me with an occasion. When the expedition to Staten Island was on foot a favourable one seemed to offer. . . . I made an application for it through the Marquis, who informed me of your refusal on two principles—one that giving me a

whole batalion might be a subject of dissatisfaction, the other that if an accident should happen to me, in the present state of your family, you would be embarrassed for the necessary assistance.

The project you now have in contemplation affords another opportunity. I have a variety of reasons that press me to desire ardently to have it in my power to improve it....

I take this method of making the request to avoid the embarrassment of a personal explanation; I shall only add that however much I have the matter at heart, I wish your Excellency intirely to consult your own inclination; and not from a disposition to oblige me, to do any thing, that may be disagreeable to you. It will, nevertheless, make me singularly happy if your wishes correspond with mine.

Hamilton's request for a military command was again turned down. But if there was to be no military glory for him in 1780, the young officer could console himself with the prospect of a happy marriage. At the end of November, he rode to Albany, where he and Elizabeth Schuyler were married on December 14. Married life agreed with him perfectly, as he confessed to his sister-in-law Margarita Schuyler soon after his return to headquarters.

A reception given by General and Mrs. Washington (right), to honor Hamilton and his bride, who are seen at left, beneath the chandelier

[New Windsor, New York, January 21, 1781] Because your sister has the talent of growing more amiable every day, or because I am a fanatic in love, or both—or if you prefer another interpretation, because I have address enough to be a good dissembler, she fancies herself the happiest woman in the world, and would need persuade all her friends to embark with her in the matrimonial voyage. But I pray you do not let her advice have so much influence as to make you matrimony-mad. 'Tis a very good thing when their stars unite two people who are fit for each other, who have souls capable of relishing the sweets of friendship, and sensibilities.... But its a dog of life when two dissonant tempers meet, and 'tis ten to one but this is the case. When therefore I join her in advising you to marry, I add be cautious in the choice. Get a man of sense, not ugly enough to be pointed at—with some good-nature—a few grains of feeling—a little taste—a little imagination—and above all a good deal of decision to keep you in order; for that I foresee will be no easy task. If you can find one with all these qualities, willing to marry you, marry him as soon as you please.

I must tell you in confidence that I think I have been very fortunate.

By early 1781, prospects for military and civilian reform had improved considerably. Mutiny among Continental troops in New Jersey and Pennsylvania had persuaded Congress to consider the plan for executive "departments" that James Duane had prepared six months before; and after three years, Maryland at last seemed ready to ratify the Articles of Confederation. Still, as Hamilton confided to Barbé-Marbois, it was too early to rejoice.

[New Windsor, New York, February 7, 1781] The first step to reformation as well in an administration as in an individual is to be sensible of our faults. This begins to be our case; and there are several symptoms that please me at this juncture. But we are so accustomed to doing right by halves, and spoiling a good intention in the execution, that I always wait to see the end of our public arrangements before I venture to expect good or ill from them. The plan of executive ministers is undoubtedly a good one, and by some men has been fruitlessly insisted upon for three or four years back; but whether it will work a present good or evil must depend on the choice of the persons. This is a bad omen. I am not at all informed of the persons in nomination.

The accession of Maryland to the confederacy will be a happy event if it does not make people believe that the Confederacy gives Congress power enough and prevent their acquiring more; if it has this effect it will be an evil, for it is unequal to the exigencies of the war or to the preservation of the union hereafter.

Nine days later, Hamilton's place in the Continental military establishment was threatened. His frustrations as an aide, his failure to gain a command, had finally taken their toll on the headstrong young officer. In mid-February, Hamilton wrote to his father-in-law of an "unexpected change" in his situation.

Head Quarters New Windsor [New York] Feby 18, 81 I am no longer a member of the General's family. This information will surprise you and the manner of the change will surprise you more. Two day ago The General

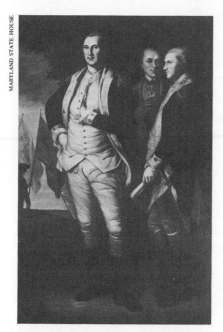

Washington, Tilghman, and Lafayette at Yorktown, by C. W. Peale, 1784

and I passed each other on the stairs. He told me he wanted to speak to me. I answered that I would wait upon him immediately. I went below and delivered Mr. Tilghman [Lieutenant Colonel Tench Tilghman] a letter to be sent to The Commissary containing an order of a pressing and interesting nature. Returning to The General I was stopped in the way by the Marquis De la Fayette and we conversed together about a minute on a matter of business. He can testify how impatient I was to get back, and that I left him in a manner which but for our intimacy would have been more than abrupt. Instead of finding the General as usual in his room, I met him at the head of the stairs, where accosting me in a very angry tone, "Col Hamilton (said he), you have kept me waiting at the head of the stairs these ten minutes. I must tell you Sir you treat me with disrespect." I replied without petulancy, but with decision "I am not conscious of it Sir, but since you have thought it necessary to tell me so we part" "Very well Sir (said he) if it be your choice" or something to this effect and we separated.

I sincerely believe my absence which gave so much umbrage did not last two minutes.

In less than an hour after, Tilghman came to me in the Generals name assuring me of his great confidence in my abilities, integrity usefulness &c and of his desire in a candid conversation to heal a difference which could not have happened but in a moment of passion. I requested Mr. Tilghman to tell him, 1. that I had taken my resolution in a manner not to be revoked: 2. that as a conversation could serve no other purpose than to produce explanations mutually disagreeable, though I certainly would not refuse an interview if he desired it yet I should be happy he would permit me to decline it—3. that though determined to leave the family the same principles which had kept me so long in it would continue to direct my conduct towards him when out of it. 4. that however I did not wish to distress him or the public business, by quitting him before he could derive other assistance by the return of some of the Gentlemen who were absent: 5. And that in the mean time it depended on him to let our behaviour to each other be the same as if nothing had happened.

He consented to decline the conversation and thanked me for my offer of continuing my aid, in the manner I had mentioned.

Thus we stand....

I always disliked the office of an Aide de Camp as having in it a kind of personal dependance. I refused to serve in this capacity with two Major General's at an early period of the war. Infected however with the enthusiasm of the times, an idea of the Generals character which experience soon taught me to be unfounded overcame my scruples and induced me to *accept his invitation* to enter into his family. I believe you know the place I held in The Generals confidence and councils of which will make it the more extraordinary to you to learn that for three years past I have felt no friendship for him and have professed none. The truth is our own dispositions are the opposites of each other & the pride of my temper would not suffer me to profess what I did not feel. Indeed when advances of this kind have been made to me on his part they were received in a manner that showed at least I had no inclination to court them, and that I wished to stand rather upon a footing of military confidence than of private attachment. You are too good a judge of human nature not to be sensible how this conduct in me must have operated on a man to whom all the world is offering incense. With this key you will easily unlock the present mystery. At the end of the war I may say many things to you concerning which I shall impose upon myself 'till then an inviolable silence.

The General is a very honest man. His competitors have slender abilities and less integrity. His popularity has often been essential to the safety of America, and is still of great importance to it. These considerations have influenced my past conduct respecting him, and will influence my future. I think it is necessary he should be supported.

His estimation in your mind, whatever may be its amounts, I am persuaded has been formed on principles which a circumstance like this cannot materially affect; but if I thought it could diminish your friendship for him, I should almost forego the motives that urge me to justify myself to you. I wish what I have said to make no other impression than to satisfy you I have not been in the wrong. It is also said in confidence, for as a public knowledge of the breach would in many ways have an ill effect. it will probably be the policy of both sides to conceal it and cover the separation with some plausible pretext. I am importuned by such friends as are privy to the affair, to listen to a reconciliation: but my resolution is unalterable.

With his departure from headquarters not far off, Hamilton began sounding out friends on other opportunities in the Continental service. He cautiously wrote on the subject to Nathanael Greene, Gates's successor as commander of the Southern Army.

> Hd. Qrs. New Windsor [New York] April 19. 81 [Robert Hanson] Harrison has left the General to be a Chief Justice of Maryland. I am about leaving him to be anything that fortune may cast up. I mean in the military line. This, my dear General, is not an affair of calculation but of feeling. You may divine the rest, and I am sure you will keep your divinations to yourself.
>
> The enemy have gotten so much in the way of intercepting our mails that I am afraid of seeing whatever I write spring up the Week after in Rivingtons Gazette. This obliges me to be cautious. Adieu, My Dear General. Let me beg you will believe that whatever change there may be in my situation there never will be any in my respect, esteem, and affection for you.
>
> A HAMILTON
>
> PS. Let me know if I could find any thing worth my while to do in the Southern army. You know I shall hate to be nominally a soldier.

A view of Albany, 1789

Late in April, Hamilton made one more appeal to Washington for a command in the field. When his request was refused, the disheartened young officer, together with his wife, Elizabeth, left for an extended visit with the Schuyler family in Albany. Historians can only guess at Hamilton's reasons for suddenly interrupting this vacation at the beginning of July to hurry to Washington's new camp at Dobbs Ferry, New York. Perhaps he was shrewd enough to see that this would be the year in which the French alliance would secure Britain's defeat, and that the fall campaign would be his last opportunity to serve. Perhaps he simply became bored with the quiet town of Albany. In any case, shortly after his arrival at Dobbs Ferry on July 8, Hamilton was writing triumphantly to his wife.

> [Camp near Dobbs Ferry, New York, July 10, 1781]
>
> Finding when I came here that nothing was said on the

subject of a command, I wrote the General a letter and enclosed him my commission. This morning Tilghman came to me in his name, pressed me to retain my commission, with an assurance that he would endeavor by all means to give me a command nearly such as I could have desired in the present circumstances of the army. Though I know my Betsy would be happy to hear I had rejected this proposal, it is a pleasure my reputation would not permit me to afford her. I consented to retain my commission and accept my command.

I hope my beloved Betsy will dismiss all apprehensions for my safety; unhappily for public affairs, there seems to be little prospect of activity, and if there should be Heaven will certainly be propitious to any attachment so tender, so genuine as ours. . . .

My good, my tender, my fond, my excellent Betsy, Adieu. You know not how much it must ever cost me to pronounce this word. God bless and preserve you.

Troops at Dobbs Ferry saw little action that month as Washington and Rochambeau debated whether to attack Sir Henry Clinton's forces in New York City or to strike at the army of Charles, Lord Cornwallis, in Virginia. While the American and French commanders weighed the reports of their scouts, Hamilton wrote to his young wife.

[Dobbs Ferry, New York, July 13, 1781] I remonstrate with my heart on the impropriety of suffering itself to be engrossed by an individual of the human race when so many millions ought to participate in its affections and in its cares. But it constantly presents you under such amiable forms as seem too well to justify its meditated desertion of the cause of country humanity, and of glory I would say, if there were not something in the sound insipid and ridiculous. . . .

Indeed Betsey, I am intirely changed—changed for the worse I confess—lost to all the public and splendid passions and absorbed in you. Amiable woman! nature has given you a right to be esteemed to be cherished, to be beloved; but she has given you no right to monopolize a man, whom, to you I may say, she has endowed with qualities to be extensively useful to society. . . . Assist me in this; reproach me for an unmanly surrender . . . to love and teach me that your esteem will be the price of my acting well my part as a member of society.

On August 14, Washington learned that the French fleet of the Comte de Grasse had sailed for Chesapeake Bay. Plans for an attack on New York were discarded and the Yorktown campaign was born. On the evening of August 20, the French army and half of the Continental forces at Dobbs Ferry began their historic march south to Virginia. In a letter written at Haverstraw, New York, Hamilton gently broke the news to his wife.

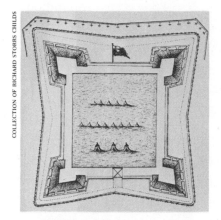

Plan of a typical British redoubt of the Revolutionary period

Haverstraw [New York] Aug 22d. 81

A part of the army My Dear girl is going to Virginia, and I must of necessity be separated at a much greater distance from my beloved wife....I am unhappy beyond expression, I am unhappy because I am to be so remote from you, because I am to hear from you less frequently than I have been accustomed to do....I am wretched at the idea of flying so far from you without a single hour's interview to tell you all my pains and all my love. But I cannot ask permission to visit you. It might be thought improper to leave my corps at such a time and upon such an occasion. I cannot persuade myself to ask a favour at Head Quarters. I must go without seeing you. I must go without embracing you. Alas I must go.

Expecting relief from the British navy, Cornwallis confidently withdrew his forces to the towns of Yorktown and Gloucester Point, on opposite banks of the York River. But the French navy, which had disappointed Americans so often in the past, now proved its worth by blocking the British fleet. As Hamilton waited on the Virginia peninsula for the siege of Yorktown to begin, he received word from Elizabeth that she was pregnant and that their first child would be born in January. Hamilton immediately wrote to his "darling Wife," his "beloved Angel."

[Camp before Yorktown, Virginia, October 12, 1781]

You shall engage shortly to present me with *a boy.* You will ask me if a girl will not answer the purpose. By no means. I fear, with all the mothers charms, she may inherit the caprices of her father and then she will enslave, tantalize and plague one half the sex, out of pure regard to which I protest against a daughter....

In an instant my feelings are changed. My heart disposed to gayety is at once melted into tenderness. The idea of a smiling infant in my Betseys arms calls up all the father in it. In imagination I embrace the mother and embrace the child a thousand times. I can scarce refrain from shedding tears of joy. But I must not indulge these sensations; they are unfit for the boisterous scenes of war and whenever they intrude themselves make me but half a soldier.

Two days later, Hamilton found the military glory he had been seeking for so long. To strengthen their position, the Allies had to capture the British "redoubts" numbered 9 and 10 near the York River. These redoubts were temporary posts surrounded by earthworks, ditches, and other barriers. Lafayette was given command of the assault on number 10, and after considerable wrangling over the rights of rank, his friend Hamilton was given the honor of leading the four hundred men who actually attacked the post. At nightfall on October 14, six cannon fired their signal, and Hamilton led his men against number 10 while a French column moved on number 9. The French prudently waited for their axemen to clear away brush, and for their caution they lost precious time and valuable men. Hamilton led his men quickly through ditches, bushes, and fallen trees. Suffering light casualties, they seized their objective and were evacuating British prisoners while the French were still struggling to secure redoubt number 9. Although Hamilton's exploits at Yorktown may not have been the most important military actions in the Revolution, he had at least proved to his adopted country, and to himself, that he was a capable soldier. The next day, Lieutenant Colonel Hamilton proudly sent this report of the engagement to Lafayette.

[Camp before Yorktown, Virginia, October 15, 1781]

Agreeable to your orders we advanced in two columns with unloaded arms, the right composed of Lt. Col [Jean-Joseph Sourbader de] Gimat's batalion and my own commanded by Major [Nicholas] Fish, the left of a detachment commanded by Lt Col [John] Laurens, destined to take the enemy in reverse, and intercept their retreat. The column on the right was preceded by a van guard of twenty men [led] by Lt. [John] Mansfield, and a detachment of sappers and miners, commanded by Capt [James] Gilliland for the purpose of removing obstructions.

The redoubt was commanded by Major [Patrick] Campbell, with a detachment of British and German troops, and was completely in a state of defence.

The rapidity and immediate success of the assault are the best comment on the behaviour of the troops. Lt Col Laurens distinguished himself by an exact and vigor-

The American attack on Yorktown

Illumination.

COLONEL TILGHMAN, Aid de Camp to his Excellency General WASHINGTON, having brought official acounts of the SURRENDER of Lord Cornwallis, and the Garrisons of York and Gloucester, those Citizens who chuse to ILLUMINATE on the GLORIOUS OCCASION, will do it this evening at Six, and extinguish their lights at Nine o'clock.

Decorum and harmony are earnestly recommended to every Citizen, and a general discountenance to the least appearance of riot.

October 24, 1781.

A broadside of 1781 announces an "illumination" to celebrate the American victory at Yorktown

ous execution of his part of the plan, by entering the enemy's work with his corps among the foremost, and making prisoner the commanding officer of the redoubt. Lt Col Gimat's batalion which formed the van of the right attack and which fell under my immediate observation, encouraged by the decisive and animated example of their leader, advanced with an ardor and resolution superior to every obstacle. They were well seconded by Major Fish with the batalion under his command, who when the front of the column reached the abatis, unlocking his corps to the left, as he had been directed, advanced with such celerity, as to arrive in time to participate in the assault....

I do but justice to the several corps when I have the pleasure to assure you, there was not an officer nor soldier whose behaviour, if it could be particularized, would not have a claim to the warmest approbation. As it would have been attended with delay and loss to wait for the removal of the abatis and palisades the ardor of the troops was indulged in passing over them.

There was a happy coincidence of movements. The redoubt was in the same moment invelopped and carried on every part. The enemy are intitled to the acknowlegement of an honorable defence....

Our killed and wounded you will perceive by the inclosed return. I sensibly felt at a critical period the loss of the assistance of Lt. Col Gimat, who received a musket ball in his foot, which obliged him to retire from the field....

Inclosed is a return of the prisoners. The killed and wounded of the enemy did not exceed eight. Incapable of imitating examples of barbarity, and forgetting recent provocations, the soldiery spared every man, who ceased to resist.

On October 19, Cornwallis surrendered his army of eight thousand men to the Americans. The Revolution was not yet over and many more American soldiers and French sailors would die in skirmishes and naval engagements before peace treaties were concluded. But the war had ended for Alexander Hamilton. He could now leave the Army with honor and join Betsey in Albany before the birth of their son, Philip, on January 22, 1782. At the end of February, Hamilton rode to Philadelphia to make his civilian status official. The Secretary of War, Benjamin Lincoln, had meantime requested that Hamilton be retained in the service because of "his superior abilities & knowledge." Hamilton, wishing to make his position clear, wrote to Washington offering a conditional resignation from active military duty.

[Philadelphia, March 1, 1782]

As I have many reasons to consider my being employed hereafter in a precarious light, the bare possibility of rendering an equivalent will not justify to my scruples the receiving any future emoluments from my commission. I therefore renounce from this time all claim to the compensations attached to my military station during the war or after it. But I have motives which will not permit me to resolve on a total resignation. I sincerely hope a prosperous train of affairs may continue to make it no inconvenience to decline the services of persons, whose zeal, in worse times, was found not altogether useless; but as the most promising appearances are often reversed by unforeseen disasters, and as unfortunate events may again make the same zeal of some value, I am unwilling to put it out of my power to renew my exertions in the common cause, in the line, in which I have hitherto acted. I shall accordingly retain my rank while I am permitted to do it, and take this opportunity to declare, that I shall be at all times ready to obey the call of the public, in any capacity civil, or military (consistent with what I owe to myself) in which there may be a prospect of my contributing to the final attainment of the object for which I embarked in the service.

Cornwallis surrenders to Washington and Rochambeau at Yorktown in this 1790 English engraving.

After Yorktown, America would most frequently call on Hamilton in his "civil" rather than his military capacity. Although Hamilton himself probably considered his service at Yorktown the most significant aspect of his life during 1780 and 1781, historians would quarrel with him. By accident or design, he had, in these two years, laid the foundation for his civilian career. By his marriage to Elizabeth Schuyler he had provided himself with a powerful political base in the state of New York. By his support of Army and congressional reform he had marked himself as a promising administrator and economic theorist. In the years of peace, few men would remember redoubt 10, but many would recall the perceptive comments of the young lieutenant colonel who had seen the flaws of the Confederation, and many would listen carefully when he repeated his arguments for political reform.

A Picture Portfolio

In Search of Military Glory

"I WISH THERE WAS A WAR"

In November, 1769, Alexander Hamilton wrote wistfully from St. Croix to his boyhood friend Ned Stevens in New York, saying, "I wish there was a war." The lad was not so much expressing a bellicose mood as he was dreaming of military glory—the only way a young man without an influential family or his own means could escape an unpromising future. Hamilton, of course, could not have known that the gathering storms of revolution would not only come to involve him but would also catapult him into the very center of the military action—and later would lead him into the political affairs of a new nation. While still at King's College in New York, Hamilton joined a volunteer company and "became exceedingly expert in the manual exercise." He then asked for the command of an artillery company, which the provincial congress authorized early in 1776, and he was duly appointed a captain at the age of twenty-one. Pictured at right in uniform, he was described by an older soldier as "a mere stripling, small slender, almost delicate in frame... with a cocked hat pulled down over his eyes...." In the actions that took place in New York and New Jersey during that desperate year, Hamilton came to the attention of General Washington, and on March 1, 1777, he was appointed to the Commander in Chief's staff (below) and commissioned a lieutenant colonel, a position he held for most of the next four years.

HEAD-QUARTERS, Morristown, March 1, 1777.

ALEXANDER HAMILTON ESQUIRE is appointed AID DE-CAMP to the Commander in Chief; and is to be respected and obeyed as such.

EXTRACT of General Orders.

Alexd Scammell
Adjt Genl

106

HAMILTON TAKES A BRIDE

The brightest event of Hamilton's wartime service took place in the winter of 1779 when Betsey Schuyler (left) came to headquarters at Morristown, New Jersey, to visit her aunt. Daughter of the wealthy and influential Major General Philip Schuyler and his wife, Catherine Van Renssalaer Schuyler (left, above), the charming Betsey was eagerly courted by Hamilton. When they were married the following year, at her parents' home in Albany, he is thought to have presented her with the miniature by Charles Willson Peale above; the 1780 likeness is set in a highly decorative embroidered frame.

ARENAS OF COMBAT

Hamilton's two periods of significant combat in the Revolution came at the war's beginning and toward its end and in actual time amounted to slightly more than a year. As the Continental Army retreated through New Jersey in 1777, he was involved in the battles at Trenton and Princeton (below), and later at Monmouth. Major General Charles Lee, whom Washington had sent ahead at Monmouth, disobeyed orders; and when the Commander in Chief (at right on the black horse) came charging up to confront him, Hamilton and Lafayette (hatless) were right behind him. In Lee's subsequent court-martial Hamilton testified against him; while his closest friend, Lieutenant Colonel John Laurens (left), another aide who worshiped Washington, sought satisfaction with Lee in a duel in which Hamilton acted as his second. Neither man was wounded; but when Laurens was killed in combat five years later, Hamilton lost a valued confidant.

OVERLEAF:

At the war's climax, Hamilton again returned to military combat, successfully leading his troops in an attack on a British redoubt at Yorktown—a scene recorded in a panoramic painting by Eugene Lami.

A GLORIOUS FINALE

On October 19, 1781, the British surrendered at Yorktown and Alexander Hamilton's four years of military service at Washington's side ended. The day before, Cornwallis had sent a message to Washington proposing a cessation of hostilities for twenty-four hours and a meeting "at Mr. Moore's house [below], to settle terms for the surrender of the posts at York and Gloucester." Pleading illness, Cornwallis did not attend the surrender ceremony, and Washington appointed General Benjamin Lincoln to receive the surrender from Cornwallis's second-in-command. In the detail of John Trumbull's painting at left, Washington is astride the black horse, flanked by a number of his officers. Hamilton, in a position of honor he richly deserved, stands erect to the right of the gray horse, with his friend John Laurens beside him. Congress recognized Hamilton's contributions by adopting in January, 1782, a report citing his "superior abilities and knowledge of his profession" and including him among those officers to be retained in service. And Washington recognized Hamilton's worth by recalling him to his side several years later, naming him to his first Cabinet as Secretary of the Treasury. Hamilton's boyhood wish for a war had reaped a rich harvest.

Chapter 4

The War of Finance

In 1782, Alexander Hamilton found that for those men who shared his dreams for America the Revolution was only beginning. As an Army officer, he had grown dissatisfied with a government that let its troops go unfed, unclothed, and unpaid. As a civilian, he found himself in a circle of men dedicated to providing the United States with a peacetime government that would be more "respectable" and "energetic" than was the creaking, inefficient administrative machine that had hitherto directed America's affairs. This group of "nationalists" that fought to reform American government in 1782 and 1783 centered on the personality and policies of Robert Morris of Philadelphia. Appointed by Congress to head the Office of Finance, Morris chose as his assistant Gouverneur Morris, Hamilton's friend from New York days. Although the two Morrises were not related by blood, they were brothers in their determination to use the Office of Finance as a base for broader reform. While Hamilton was proving his military valor in the fall campaign of 1781, the Morrises were proving their worth as financial administrators by keeping the Army in the field. After Yorktown, they were ready to use their prestige to begin a wider program of financial policies that would strengthen the power and prestige of the national government.

In this "War of Finance," Alexander Hamilton was an obvious recruit for the Morrises' civilian "army" of men who believed that the American union could survive only if it was strong and efficient. Working first as an agent of the Office of Finance in New York and later as a member of Congress, Hamilton proved a courageous and daring warrior. The "impost," the "permanent fund," "half pay," "uniting the interest of the public creditors" —these were the battle cries of his campaign, and although they may sound strange today, they were part of a strategy as carefully thought out as any military expedition. Hamilton and the Morrises were determined to establish Continental revenues so that the national government would no longer have to make annual, often ignored, "requisitions" of funds from the states. By establishing an impost, a duty on imported goods, they hoped to set up a "permanent fund" for the payment of the public debt. By manipulating the Army's demands for "half-pay" pensions, they tried to unite the restless troops with the owners of government securities in hopes that this formidable body of public creditors might force the states to grant the impost and other "Continental" taxes. Eventually, however, Hamilton and his friends would go too far in their attempt to make the government work as they felt it must to preserve its independence. Hamilton's daring and dedication would turn to a recklessness and near fanaticism that was to damage the nationalist cause for years to come.

Originally, however, when he returned to his home in the spring of 1782, Hamilton had no plans other than to raise a family and to launch a private career that would enable him to support his wife and child. Shortly after his eldest son, Philip, was born in January, 1782, he wrote to his friend Richard Kidder Meade to disclaim interest in anything but the joys of family life—and the possibility of arranging a match between his infant son and Meade's newborn daughter.

> Philadelphia March 1782
> You cannot imagine how entirely domestic I am growing. I lose all taste for the pursuits of ambition, I sigh for nothing but the company of my wife and my baby. The ties of duty alone or imagined duty keep me from renouncing public life altogether. It is however probable I may not be any longer actively engaged in it....
>
> Betsy is so fond of your family that she proposes to form a match between her Boy & your girl provided you will engage to make the latter as amiable as her mother.
>
> Truly My Dear Meade, I often regret that fortune has cast our residence at such a distance from each other. It would be a serious addition to my happiness if we lived where I could see you every day but fate has determined it otherwise.

Domestic as he was, Hamilton could not resist a chance to express his views on public affairs. In the summer of 1781, four of his essays as "The Continentalist" had appeared in a Fishkill, New York, newspaper. In April, 1782, the fifth essay was published with this warning for Americans who resisted the policies of Congress and the Office of Finance.

> [Fishkill, New York, April 18, 1782]
> It is too much characteristic of our national temper to be ingenious in finding out and magnifying the minutest disadvantages, and to reject measures of evident utility even of necessity to avoid trivial and sometimes imaginary

evils. We seem not to reflect, that in human society, there is scarcely any plan, however salutary to the whole and to every part, by the share, each has in the common prosperity, but in one way, or another, and under particular circumstances, will operate more to the benefit of some parts, than of others. Unless we can overcome this narrow disposition and learn to estimate measures, by their general tendency, we shall never be a great or a happy people, if we remain a people at all.

Robert Morris needed men who would argue for his program, and "The Continentalist" only confirmed what he already knew of Alexander Hamilton's talents. In 1781, after he accepted his appointment from Congress as Superintendent of Finance, Morris had received a long letter of congratulations from the young colonel making it clear that they thought alike on financial and political matters. Accordingly, when Morris learned that Hamilton had left active military duty, he promptly offered him a post as "Receiver" of taxes, with responsibility for collecting New York's share of the eight million dollars requested from the states by Congress. Hamilton at first declined on the grounds that the salary for the office— 25 per cent of taxes received—was not enough to allow him to take time from his legal studies in Albany. But when Morris assured him that his salary would be based on New York's full quota of taxes, whether or not that amount was actually collected, Hamilton wrote back accepting the appointment.

[Albany, June 17, 1782]

Hamilton's appointment as New York receiver of Continental taxes, signed and sealed by Robert Morris, 1782

In accepting it I have only one scruple, arising from a doubt whether the service I can render in the present state of things will be an equivalent for the compensation.... As the matter now stands there seems to be little for a Continental Receiver to do.... There is only one way in which I can imagine a prospect of being materially useful that is in seconding your applications to the State. In popular assemblies much may sometimes be brought about by personal discussions, by entering into details and combating objections as they rise. If it should at any time be thought adviseable by you to empower me to act in this capacity, I shall be happy to do every thing that depends on me to effectuate your views.

Robert Morris was only too happy to have Hamilton act as his lobbyist with the New York legislature, since that was precisely one of the roles he planned for his receivers. The young New Yorker shared

Morris's conviction that in the War of Finance, no chance should be lost for a useful skirmish with state assemblies. When the New York legislature was called into special session in July, 1782, to consider the problems of national finance, Hamilton set out to meet the lawmakers. But although the legislature was supposed to devote itself to "the Necessity of providing competent Means for a vigorous Prosecution of the War," after six days of conferences with a legislative committee, Hamilton had no encouraging news for Morris on revenue matters. However, he did see promise in a resolution passed by the legislature calling for a "general Convention" to amend the Confederation.

The high bluffs and rolling hills of the Poughkeepsie area, with Henry Livingston's estate and the Hudson River in the foreground

Poughkepsie [New York] July 22d. 1782

I think this a very eligible step though I doubt of the concurrence of the other states; but I am certain without it, they never will be brought to cooperate in any reasonable or effectual plan. Urge reforms or exertions and the answer constantly is what avails it for one state to make them without the concert of the others? It is in vain to expose the futility of this reasoning; it is founded on all those passions which have the strongest influence on the human mind.

The Legislature have also appointed at my instance a Committee to devise in the recess a more effectual system of taxation and to communicate with me on this subject. A good deal will depend on the success of this attempt. Convinced of the absurdity of multiplying taxes in the present mode, where in effect the payment is voluntary, and the money received exhausted in the collection, I have laboured chiefly to instil the necessity of a change in the plan, and though not so rapidly as the exigency of public affairs requires, truth seems to be making some progress.

Before the legislature adjourned, Hamilton was elected a New York delegate to the Continental Congress, his term to begin in November. This honor did nothing to help the young receiver collect taxes —or even to collect the statistics on state finances that Robert Morris demanded. As he waited, none too hopefully, for these "returns," Hamilton had time to prepare for Morris a "full view of the situation and temper" of New York. The scanty information that had come to the receiver's office convinced Hamilton that New York's finances were marked by an unfavorable balance of trade, which had caused "an *extreme* and *universal* scarcity of money." Local politics, he explained to the superintendent in his report, were no more encouraging.

117

The first session of America's Continental Congress is depicted in this French engraving, circa 1783.

Albany Augt. 13th. 1782

Here we find the general disease which infects all our constitutions, an excess of popularity. There is no *order* that has a will of its own. The inquiry constantly is what will *please* not what will *benefit* the people. In such a government there can be nothing but temporary expedient, fickleness and folly.

But the point of view in which this subject will be interesting to you is that which relates to our finances. I gave you in a former letter a sketch of our plan of taxation; but I will now be more particular.

The general principle of it is an assessment, according to *circumstances and abilities collectively considered.*

The ostensible reason for adopting this vague basis was a desire of equality: It was pretended, that this could not be obtained so well by any fixed tariff of taxable property, as by leaving it to the discretion of persons chosen by the people themselves, to determine the ability of each citizen. But perhaps the true reason was a desire to discriminate between the *whigs* and *tories*. This chimerical attempt at perfect equality has resulted in total inequality....

The Legislature first *asseses,* or quotas the several counties. Here the evil begins. The members cabal and intrigue to throw the burthen off their respective constituents. Address and influence, more than considerations of real ability prevail. A great deal of time is lost and a great deal of expence incurred before the juggle is ended and the necessary compromises made.

The Supervisors ... in each county, meet ... and assign their proportions to the sub-divisions of the county; and in the distribution play over the same game, which was played in the Legislature.

The Assessors ... according to their fancies, determine the proportion of each individual; a list of which [is] made out and ... is a warrant to the collectors....

It now remains for the collectors to collect the tax, and it is the duty of the supervisors to see that they do it. Both these offices ... are elective; and of course there is little disposition to risk the displeasure of those who elect....

You will perceive Sir, I have neither flattered the state nor encouraged high expectations. I thought it my duty to exhibit things as they are not as they ought to be. I shall be sorry, if it give an ill-opinion of the state for want of equal candor in the representations of others; for however disagreeable the reflection, I have too much reason to believe that the true picture of other states would be in proportion to their circumstances equally unpromising. All my inquiries and all that appears induces this opinion. I intend this letter *in confidence to yourself* and therefore I indorse it *private.*

In the last week of August, Hamilton received urgent appeals for cash from Philadelphia but continued to get only evasions and excuses from New York authorities. Two months as a Continental receiver had only confirmed his cynicism about his fellow citizens. Writing to Richard Kidder Meade from Albany, Hamilton shared his thoughts on mankind, his seven-month-old son, and his plans for the future.

Albany Augt 27th. 1782

Experience is a continued comment on the worthlessness of the human race and the few exceptions we find have the greater right to be valued in proportion as they are rare. I know few men estimable, fewer amiable & when I meet with one of the last description it is not in my power to withhold my affection.

You reproach me with not having said enough about our little stranger. When I wrote last I was not sufficiently acquainted with him to give you his character. I may now assure you that your daughter when she sees him will not consult you about the choice or will only do it in respect to the rules of decorum. He is truly a very fine young gentleman, the most agreable in his conversation and manners of any I ever knew — nor less remarkable for his intelligence and sweetness of temper. You are not to imagine by my beginning with his mental qualifications that he is defective in personal. It is agreed on all hands, that he is handsome, his features are good, his eye is not only sprightly and expressive but it is full of benignity. His attitude in sitting is by connoisseurs esteemed graceful and he has a method of waving his hand that announces the future orator. He stands however rather awkwardly and his legs have not all the delicate slimness of his fathers. It is feared He may never excel as much in dancing which is probably the only accomplishment in which he will not be a model. If he has any fault in manners, he laughs too much. He has now passed his Seventh

*A five-hundred-dollar bond issued
by the Continental treasury in 1781*

Month. . . .

As to myself I shall sit down in New York when it opens
& the period we are told approaches. No man looks forward to a Peace with more pleasure than I do, though
no man would sacrifice less to it than myself, If I were
not convinced the people sigh for peace. I have been
studying the Law for some months and have lately been
licenced as an attorney. I wish to prepare myself by October for Examination as a Counsellor but some public
avocations may possibly prevent me.

I had almost forgotten to tell you, that I have been . . .
elected . . . a member of Congress. . . . I do not hope to
reform the State although I shall endeavour to do all the
good I can.

The New York legislature had named a special committee on taxation, which was to meet on September 15, 1782. The committee's sessions offered Hamilton a last chance to make a contribution as
a receiver, since he would have to resign this post to take his seat in Congress
in November. But, as he reported to Robert Morris on October 5, the committee did little.

[Albany, October 5, 1782]
In spite of my efforts, they have parted without doing
any thing decisive. They have indeed agreed upon several
matters and those of importance but they have not reduced them to the form of a report, which in fact leave
every thing afloat to be governed by the impressions of
the moment when the legislature meet.

The points agreed upon are these—that there shall be
an actual valuation of land and a tax of so much in the
pound. . . . That there shall be also a tariff of all personal
property to be also taxed at so much in the pound—that
there shall be a specific tax on carriages clocks watches
& other similar articles of luxury—that money at usury
shall be taxed at a fixed rate in the pound excluding that
which is loand to the public—that houses in all towns
shall be taxed at a certain proportion of the annual rent
—that there shall be a poll tax on all single men from
fifteen upwards and that the Collection of the taxes
should be advertised to the lowest bidder at a fixed rate
P[er] Cent bearing all subordinate expences.

Among other things which were rejected I pressed
hard for an excise on distilled liquors; but all that could

be carried on these articles was a license on taverns.

The Committee were pretty generally of opinion that the system of funding for payment of old debts & for procuring further credit was wise & indispensable but a majority thought it would be unwise in one state to contribute in this way alone.

Nothing was decided on the quantum of taxes which the state was able to pay; those who went furthest would not exceed 70000 £ of which fifty for the use of the United states.

When Hamilton was elected to Congress in the summer of 1782, he showed some guarded enthusiasm for the idea of carrying on the War of Finance in Philadelphia. Further encouraged by news of peace negotiations in Europe, he tried to recruit his friend John Laurens for the finance campaign.

[Albany, August 15, 1782]

Your wishes in one respect are gratified; this state has pretty unanimously delegated me to Congress. My time of service commences in November.... We have great reason to flatter ourselves peace on our own terms is upon the carpet....

I fear there may be obstacles but I hope they may be surmounted.

Peace made, My Dear friend, a new scene opens. The object then will be to make our independence a blessing. To do this we must secure our *union* on solid foundations; an herculean task and to effect which mountains of prejudice must be levelled!

It requires all the virtue and all the abilities of the Country. Quit your sword my friend, put on the *toga,* come to Congress. We know each others sentiments, our views are the same: we have fought side by side to make America free, let us hand in hand struggle to make her happy.

Hamilton (left) and his friend John Laurens appear in this detail from Trumbull's painting of the British surrender at Yorktown.

Laurens probably never read his friend's letter. On August 27, he was killed in a skirmish with British troops at Combahee Ferry, South Carolina. Hamilton was stunned by the news. He had always been reluctant to give his trust or friendship to any man, and Laurens had gained his confidence and affection completely. In mid-October, Hamilton tried to explain his feelings to Nathanael Greene.

[Albany, October 12, 1782]

I feel the deepest affliction at the news we have just received of the loss of our dear and inestimable friend Laurens. His career of virtue is at an end. How strangely are human affairs conducted, that so many excellent qualities could not ensure a more happy fate? The world will feel the loss of a man who has left few like him behind, and America of a citizen whose heart realized that patriotism of which others only talk. I feel the loss of a friend I truly and most tenderly loved, and one of a very small number.

As Hamilton prepared for his trip to Philadelphia, he found that he had lost much of his zest for Continental service. With his closest friend dead, he was forced to leave his wife and child at a time when he needed the security of his family most. It is not surprising that he insisted to Lafayette that he was "already tired" of public life.

CULVER PICTURES, INC.

Gouverneur Morris

[Albany, November 3, 1782]

I have been employed for the last ten months in rocking the cradle and studying the art of fleecing my neighbours. I am now a Grave Counsellor at law, and shall soon be a grand member of Congress.... I am going to throw away a few months more in public life and then I retire a simple citizen and good paterfamilias. I set out for Philadelphia in a few days. You see the disposition I am in. You are condemned to run the race of ambition all your life. I am already tired of the career and dare to leave it.

But you would not give a pin for my letter unless politics or war made a part of it. You tell me they are employed in building *a peace;* And other accounts say it is nearly finished; I hope the work may meet with no interruptions: it is necessary for America; especially if your army is taken from us as we are told will soon be the case.... These states are in no humour for continuing exertions; if the war lasts, it must be carried on by external succours. I make no apology for the inertness of this country. I detest it; but since it exists I am sorry to see other resources diminish.

Once Hamilton had taken his seat in Congress, his interest in public affairs revived quickly. There he found other men, including Robert and Gouverneur Morris and James Madison, a young congressman from Virginia, who were as eager as he was to press for reform. The most urgent problem facing them in the winter of 1782–83 was the fate of the Continental duty on imports. Under the Articles of Confederation, the impost could not go into effect without the consent of all thirteen states. By November, 1782, only Rhode Island still withheld its approval. Shortly before Hamilton took his seat on November 25, Congress received unofficial word that Rhode Island had flatly rejected the impost. At Hamilton's suggestion, Congress voted to send a delegation to Rhode Island to plead for the import duty. On December 11, Hamilton presented a draft letter for the delegation to deliver to Governor William Greene in Providence.

Robert Morris, by Peale

Philadelphia [December 11, 1782]

Congress are equally affected and alarmed by the information they have received that the Legislature of your state at their last meeting have refused their concurrence in the establishment of a duty on imports. They consider this measure as so indispensable to the prosecution of the war, that a sense of duty and regard to the common safety compel them to renew their efforts to engage a compliance with it; and in this view they have determined to send a deputation of three of their members to your state.... The Gentlemen they have appointed will be able to lay before you a full and just representation of the public affairs....

They will only briefly observe that the increasing discontents of the army, the loud clamours of the public creditors, and the extreme disproportion between the current supplies and the demands of the public service are so many invincible arguments for the fund recommended by Congress. They feel themselves unable to devise any other, that will be more efficacious, less exceptionable or more generally agreeable; and if this is rejected they anticipate calamities of a most menacing nature, with this consolation however, that they have faithfully discharged their trust, and that the mischiefs which may follow cannot be attributed to them.

Before the delegation could depart for Rhode Island with Hamilton's carefully drafted message, Congress received a harsh letter from William Bradford, speaker of the state's assembly. Confirming the legislature's veto of the impost, Bradford remarked that Rhode Island would cease to "suspect the virtue of the present Congress" only when Congress's resolutions were "founded on the great principles of liberty, and a general interest." Hamilton, Madison, and Thomas FitzSimons of Pennsylvania were named to prepare a reply to the speaker's letter. Their report, almost wholly Hamilton's work, closed with a stinging rebuttal.

[Philadelphia] December 16, 1782

It is certainly pernicious to leave any government in a situation of responsibility, disproportioned to its power.

The conduct of the war is intrusted to Congress and the public expectation turned upon them without any competent means at their command to satisfy the important trust. After the most full and solemn deliberation under a collective view of all the public difficulties, they recommend a measure, which appears to them the corner stone of the public safety: They see this measure suspended for near two years—partially complied with by some of the states, rejected by one of them and in danger on that account to be frustrated; the public embarrassments every day increasing, the dissatisfaction of the army growing more serious, the other creditors of the public clamouring for justice, both irritated by the delay of measures for their present relief or future security, the hopes of our enemies encouraged to protract the war, the zeal of our friends depressed by an appearance of remissness and want of exertion, on our part, Congress harrassed, the national character suffering and the national safety at the mercy of events.

William Bradford

By December, 1782, one group of public creditors had become especially anxious for settlement of its claims. As the conclusion of a peace treaty now seemed imminent, Army officers and enlisted men were beginning to wonder whether they would be reimbursed for back pay and other expenses. On December 31, the same day that Congress learned that Virginia had withdrawn its approval of the impost, a delegation from the Army at West Point arrived in Philadelphia to petition Congress for the back pay and half-pay pensions that had been promised to officers. This coincidence gave a new turn to nationalist strategy, as Hamilton hinted in a letter to Governor George Clinton.

Philda. [January 12] 1783

We have now here a deputation from the army, and feel a mortification of a total disability to comply with their just expectations. If, however, the matter is taken up in a proper manner, I think their application may be turned to a good account. Every day proves more & more the insufficiency of the confederation. The proselytes to this opinion are increasing fast....

Hamilton and Madison, named to consider the Army petition, clearly demonstrated the "turn" to which military claims could be put. They argued that the half-pay pensions might be paid in government securities, which would be supported, of course, by a permanent fund provided by the impost. The Army delegates, headed by Hamilton's old friend General Alexander McDougall, gave added weight to the nationalists' argument by testifying that the Army might react violently if its claims were ignored. To back up the general's testimony another of Hamilton's friends, Colonel John Brooks, returned to camp in mid-February to report to his fellow officers on the mood of Congress, and apparently to encourage some sort of concrete demonstration of military unrest. In the meantime, Hamilton sent Washington the following outline of the role he expected the Commander to play in the finance campaign. A similar proposal was sent by Gouverneur Morris and Alexander McDougall to General Henry Knox.

[Philadelphia, February 13, 1783]

If the war continues it would seem that the army must in June subsist itself *to defend the* country; if peace should take place it *will* subsist itself to *procure justice to itself.* It appears to be a prevailing opinion in the army that the disposition to recompence their services will cease with the necessity for them, and that if they once lay down their arms, they will part with the means of obtaining justice. It is to be lamented that appearances afford too much ground for their distrust.

It becomes a serious inquiry what will be the true line of policy. The claims of the army urged with moderation, but with firmness, may operate on those weak minds which are influenced by their apprehensions more than their judgments; so as to produce a concurrence in the measures which the exigencies of affairs demand. They may add weight to the applications of Congress to the several states. So far an useful turn may be given to them. But the difficulty will be to keep a *complaining* and *suffering army* within the bounds of moderation....

[Hamilton had come to the point. Washington was to control the Army's protests and advance the cause of Continental financial policies.]

This Your Excellency's influence must effect. In order to [do] it, it will be adviseable not to discountenance their endeavours to procure redress, but rather by the intervention of confidential and prudent persons, *to take the direction of them.* This however must not appear: it is

No. *92,325* — State of *So Carolina 8 March* 1785

N the final Settlement of an Account between the United ates and *Edward Floyd* there appeared be due to *him* the Sum of *Thirty three* 30/90 Dollars: I do therefore cer- y, that the said Sum is payable with Interest at six per Cent. m the *Twenty third* Day of *March* 1783 to e said *Edward Floyd* or Bearer.

Soldiers in the Continental Army were reimbursed for back pay with *"final Settlement"* certificates signed by Paymaster John Pierce.

Washington's headquarters at Newburgh, New York

of moment to the public tranquillity that Your Excellency should preserve the confidence of the army without losing that of the people. This will enable you in case of extremity to guide the torrent, and bring order perhaps even good, out of confusion. 'Tis a part that requires address; but 'tis one which your own situation as well as the welfare of the community points out.

I will not conceal from Your Excellency a truth which it is necessary you should know. An idea is propagated in the army that delicacy carried to an extreme prevents your espousing its interests with sufficient warmth. The falsehood of this opinion no one can be better acquainted with than myself; but it is not the less mischievous for being false. Its tendency is to impair that influence, which you may exert with advantage, should any commotions unhappily ensue, to moderate the pretensions of the army and make their conduct correspond with their duty.

The great *desideratum* at present is the establishment of general funds, which alone can do justice to the Creditors of the United States (of whom the army forms the most meritorious class), restore public credit and supply the future wants of government. This is the object of all men of sense; in this the influence of the army, properly directed, may cooperate.

A week after Colonel Brooks's departure for West Point there was still no word of Army unrest and still no answer from Washington or Henry Knox. Nevertheless, the nationalists continued their campaign in Philadelphia, pressing their fight for the impost and insisting that the Army was near mutiny. On the evening of February 20, at a private conference, Hamilton and Richard Peters, Secretary of the Board of War, gave their version of the "temper, transactions & views of the army." James Madison, who took notes during the meeting, left a record of their remarks.

[Philadelphia, February 20, 1783]
Mr. Hamilton & Mr. Peters . . . informed the company that the army had secretly determined not to lay down their arms until due provision & a satisfactory prospect should be afforded on the subject of their pay; that there was reason to expect that a public declaration to this effect would soon be made; that plans had been agitated if not formed for subsisting themselves after such declaration; that as a proof of their earnestness on this subject the Commander was already become extremely unpopular

Colonel Walter Stewart

among almost all ranks from his known dislike to every unlawful proceeding, that this unpopularity was daily increasing & industriously promoted by many leading characters.... Mr. Hamilton said that he knew Genl. Washington intimately and perfectly, that his extreme reserve, mixed sometimes with a degree of asperity of temper both of which were said to have increased of late, had contributed to the decline of his popularity; but that his virtue his patriotism & his firmness would it might be depended upon never yield to any dishonorable or disloyal plans into which he might be called; that he would sooner suffer himself to be cut into pieces; that he, (Mr. Hamilton) knowing this to be his true character wished him to be the conductor of the army in their plans for redress, in order that they might be moderated & directed to proper objects, & exclude some other leader who might foment and misguide their councils; that with this view he had taken the liberty to write to the Genl. on this subject and to recommend such a policy to him.

By the beginning of March it was clear that John Brooks's mission had failed and that neither Knox nor Washington would become involved in a plan to use the Army for political purposes. Time was running out for the nationalists. There were now unofficial reports that a provisional peace treaty had been signed, and it was obvious that the states would be reluctant to establish permanent funds once hostilities were ended. From New York, however, came encouraging news. At Army headquarters in Newburgh, a group of officers led by Colonel Walter Stewart, who had just arrived from Philadelphia to assume his duties as an Inspector of the Army, had begun circulating the "Newburgh Addresses," which attacked Congress and the Commander in Chief and warned that the Army would not lay down its arms until its claims were met. There is no evidence that Hamilton or the Morrises had any connection with Stewart, although their opponents believed otherwise. When Washington wrote to Hamilton demanding to know what part the nationalists had played in the budding revolt, Hamilton sent him this reply.

Philadelphia, March 17. 1783

Your Excellency mentions that it has been surmised the plan in agitation was formed in Philadelphia; that combinations have been talked of between the public creditors and the army; and that members of Congress had incouraged the idea. This is partly true. I have myself urged in Congress the propriety of uniting the influence of the public creditors, & the army as a part of them, to prevail upon the states to enter into their views. I have expressed the same sentiments out of doors. Several other members of Congress have done the same. The meaning however of all this was simply that Congress should adopt such a plan as would embrace the relief of all the public creditors including the army; in order that the personal influence of some, the connections of others, and a sense of justice to the army as well as the apprehension of ill consequences might form a mass of influence in each state in favour of the measures of Congress. In this view, as I mentioned to Your Excellency in a former letter, I thought the discontents of the army might be turned to a good account. I am still of opinion that their earnest, but respectful applications for redress will have a good effect.

As to any combination of *Force* it would only be productive of the horrors of a civil war, might end in the ruin of the Country & would certainly end in the ruin of the army.

For a time it seemed as if the nationalist gamble might pay off. While quelling the mutiny, Washington was able to turn the occasion into a stirring reaffirmation of the Army's sense of honor and duty, and on March 21, Hamilton reintroduced a plan for half pay to Congress. But events were moving too fast for Hamilton and his friends. Prospects for a settlement with the Army or the creation of a permanent fund grew dimmer when, on March 24, the preliminary treaty of peace between Britain and the Allies was read in Congress. A few days later Washington received Hamilton's candid appraisal of the Army's chances of receiving justice either from Congress or the states.

Phila. Mar 25th 1783

Here I write as a citizen zealous for the true happiness of this country, as a soldier who feels what is due to an army which has suffered everything and done much for the safety of America.

I sincerly wish *ingratitude* was not so natural to the human heart as it is. I sincerely wish there were no seeds of it in those who direct the councils of the United States. But while I urge the army to moderation, and advise Your Excellency to take the direction of their discontents, and endeavour to confine them within the bounds of duty, I cannot as an honest man conceal from you, that I am afraid their distrusts have too much foundation. Republican jealousy has in it a principle of hostility to an army whatever be their merits, whatever be their claims to the gratitude of the community. It acknowleges their services with unwillingness and rewards them with reluctance. I see this temper, though smothered with great care, involuntarily breaking out upon too many occasions. I often feel a mortification, which it would be impolitic to express, that sets my passions at variance with my reason. Too many I perceive, if they could do it with safety or colour, would be glad to elude the just pretensions of the army. I hope that this is not the prevailing disposition.

But supposing the Country ungrateful what can the army do? It must submit to its hard fate. To seek redress by its arms would end in its ruin. The army would moulder by its own weight and for want of the means of keeping together. The soldiery would abandon their officers. There would be no chance of success without having recourse to means that would reverse our revolution. I make these observations not that I imagine Your Excellency can want motives to continue your influence in the path of moderation; but merely to show why I cannot myself enter into the views of coertion which some Gentlemen entertain, for I confess could force avail I should almost wish to see it employed. I have an indifferent opinion of the honesty of this country, and ill-forebodings as to its future system.

Your Excellency will perceive I have written with sensations of chagrin and will make allowance for colouring; but the general picture is too true.

God send us all more wisdom.

An English engraving of the signing of the preliminary peace treaty between Britain and the Allies

When Washington replied, Hamilton felt even more "chagrin," for it was apparent that the Commander had not accepted his version of the history of the Newburgh "Conspiracy." Many officers, Washington wrote Hamilton, had become convinced that "some members" of Congress had intended to use the Army "as mere Puppits to establish Continental funds" and would "make a sacrafice of the Army and all its interests" to win these revenues. Hamilton replied promptly—if not too honestly.

[Philadelphia, April 8, 1783]
I do not wonder at the suspicions that have been infused, nor should I be surprised to hear that I have been pointed

out as one of the persons concerned in playing the game described. But facts must speak for themselves. The Gentlemen who were here from the army; General Mc. Dougall who is still here will be able to give a true account of those who have supported the just claims of the army, and of those who have endeavoured to elude them.

There are two classes of men Sir in Congress of very Different views—one attached to state, the other to Continental politics. The last have been strenuous advocates for funding the public debt upon solid securities, the former have given every opposition in their power and have only been dragged into the measures which are now near being adopted by the clamours of the army and other public creditors. The advocates for Continental funds have blended the interests of the army with other Creditors from a conviction, that no funds for partial purposes will go through those states to whose citizens the United States are largely indebted—or if they should be carried through from impressions of the moment would have the necessary stability; for the influence of those unprovided for would always militate against a provision for others, in exclusion of them. It is in vain to tell men who have parted with a large part of their property on the public faith that the services of the army are intitled to a preference. They would reason from their interest and their feelings. These would tell them that they had as great a title as any other class of the community to public justice, and that while this was denied to them, it would be unreasonable to make them bear their part of a burthen for the benefit of others. This is the way they would reason & as their influence in some of the states was considerable they would have been able to prevent any partial provision. . . .

[Hamilton then described the tactics of the opposing groups in Congress with regard to commutation and pensions.]

The opinions on this head have been two. One party was for referring the several lines to their states to make such commutation as they should think proper—the other for making the commutation by Congress and funding it on continental security. I was of this last opinion and so were all those who will be represented as having made

The Commander in Chief, General Washington, in a 1782 engraving

use of the army as puppets. Our principal reasons were 1st by referring the lines to their respective states, those which were opposed to the half pay would have taken advantage of the officers necessities, to make the commutation far short of an equivalent. 2dly. The inequality which would have arisen in the different states when the officers came to compare...would have been a new source of discontent. 3dly. such a reference was a continuance of the old wretched state system, by which the ties between Congress and the army have been nearly dissolved—by which the resources of the states have been diverted from the common treasury & wasted; a system which Your Excellency has often justly reprobated.

...I assure you upon my honor Sir I have given you a candid state of facts to the best of my judgment. The men against whom the suspicions you mention must be directed are in general the most sensible the most liberal, the most independent and the most respectable characters in our body as well as the most unequivocal friends to the army. In a word they are the men who think continentally.

Hamilton had been half right in predicting that the outcome of the "storm" at Newburgh would "add new lustre" to the Army's "character" and "strengthen the hands of Congress." Congress reaffirmed the Government's commitment to half pay, but refused to listen to Hamilton's pleas for strong, nationalist tax measures. On April 18, a new impost was recommended to the states, but this time the provision for the import duty was so watered down that Hamilton could not bring himself to vote for the revenue measure—even though it was earmarked for the payment of the public debt. A month later, Hamilton outlined his reasons for opposing the new impost to Governor Clinton.

Philadelphia May 14 1783

1st That it does not designate the funds (except the impost) on which the whole interest is to arise; and by which ...the collection would have been easy, the fund productive and necessarily increasing with the increase of the Country.

2dly. That the duration of the fund is not coextensive with the debt but limited to twenty five years, though there is a moral certainty that in that period, the principal will not by the present provision be fairly extinguished.

3dly That the nomination and appointment of the collectors of the revenue are to reside in each state . . . the consequence of which will be, that those states which have little interest in the fund by having a small share of the public debt due to their own citizens will take care to appoint such persons as are least likely to collect the revenue.

The evils resulting from these defects will be that in many instances the objects of the revenues will be improperly chosen and will . . . on experiment prove insufficient—that for want of a vigorous collection in each state, the revenue will be unproductive in many and will fall chiefly upon those states which are governed by most liberal principles; that for want of an adequate security, the evidences of the public debt will not be transferrable for anything like their value—that this . . . will deprive the public of the benefit of an increased circulation, and of course will disable the people from paying the taxes for want of a sufficient medium. . . .

[Although Hamilton declared he would be "happy" if his gloomy predictions were proved false, he made it clear that he did not expect that he would have to admit any error in judgment.]

I hope our state will consent to the plan proposed; because it is her interest at all events to promote the payment of the public debt on Continental funds (independent of the general considerations of Union & propriety). I am much mistaken if the debts due from the United States to the citizens of the state of New York do not considerably exceed its proportion of the necessary funds, of course it has an immediate interest that there should be a Continental provision for them. But there are superior motives that ought to operate in every state, the obligations of national faith honor and reputation.

Individuals have been already too long sacrificed to public convenience. It will be shocking and indeed an eternal reproach to this country, if we begin the peaceable enjoyment of our independence by a violation of all the principles of honesty & true policy. . . .

P. S.   It is particularly interesting that the state should have a representation here. Not only many matters are depending which require a full representation in Congress and there is now a thin one; but those matters are

A view of the Philadelphia State House, as it appeared in 1778

of a nature so particularly interesting to our state, that we ought not to be without a voice in them. I wish two other Gentlemen of the delegation may appear as soon as possible for it would be very injurious to me to remain much longer here. Having no future view in public life, I owe it to myself without delay to enter upon the care of my private concerns in earnest.

As the last lines of this letter suggest, Hamilton was now more than ready to end his career in the wartime Congress. He outlined his plans and his complaints in a letter to Nathanael Greene.

[Philadelphia, June 10, 1783]

I expect to leave this shortly for that place [Albany] and to remain there 'till New York is evacuated [by the British]; on which event I shall set down there seriously on the business of making my fortune....

There is so little disposition either in or out of Congress to give solidity to our national system that there is no motive to a man to lose his time in the public service; who has no other view than to promote its welfare. Experience must convince us that our present establishments are Utopian before we shall be ready to part with them for better.

Soon, however, the discontents of the Army forced Hamilton to change his plans for returning to New York. Soldiers from the regiment stationed at Lancaster, Pennsylvania, had begun a march on Philadelphia to demand a settlement of their accounts, and Hamilton was named to a congressional committee that was to confer with the Executive Council of the State of Pennsylvania on measures for dealing with the mutinous troops. On the afternoon of June 21, several hundred angry, unpaid members of the Continental Army surrounded the State House to demand a hearing from Congress. Hamilton reported to Congress on his committee's meetings with state authorities on June 22 and June 23.

[Philadelphia] June 24, 1783

The Committee ... beg leave to report:

That the Council had a high respect for the representative sovereignty of the United States and were disposed to do every thing in their power to support its dignity. That they regretted the insult which had happened.... That they had consulted a number of well-informed officers of the militia, and found that nothing in the present state of things was to be expected from that quarter. That the Militia of the city in general were not only ill provided for service, but disinclined to act upon the present occasion. That the Council did not believe any exertions were to be looked for from them, except in case of further outrage and actual violence to person and property. That in such a case a respectable body of citizens would arm for the security of their property and of the public peace; but it was to be doubted what measure of outrage would produce this effect; and in particular it was not to be expected merely from a repetition of the insult which had happened....

[When the council declared that a "policy of coertion" against the rebellious troops was unnecessary, Hamilton's committee replied indignantly.]

That the excesses of the mutineers had passed those bounds within which a spirit of compromise might consist with the dignity and even the safety of government. That impunity for what had happened might encourage to more flagrant proceedings, invite others to follow the example and extend the mischief.... That these considerations had determined Congress to adopt decisive measures. That ... they had not neglected other means of ultimately executing their purpose but had directed the Commander in Chief to march a detachment of troops towards the city. That whatever moderation it might be prudent to exercise towards the mutineers, when they were once in the power of government it was necessary in the first instance to place them in that situation. That Congress would probably continue to persue this object unless it should be superseded by unequivocal demonstrations of submission on the part of the mutineers. That they had hitherto given no satisfactory evidence of this disposition, having lately presented the officers they had chosen to represent their grievances with a formal commission in writing, enjoining them if necessary to use compulsory means for redress, and menacing them with death in case of their failing to execute their views....

The Committee finding that there was no satisfactory ground to expect prompt and adequate exertions on the part of the Executive of this state ... were bound by the resolution under which they acted to advice the president to summon Congress to assemble at Princeton or Trenton on Thursday.

Congress beat an undignified and hasty retreat to Princeton, New Jersey, leaving the mutineers to the authorities in Philadelphia. By this time, Hamilton was growing more and more anxious to end his term in Congress—a legislature that could neither provide for the Army that had won American independence, nor raise funds to pay the nation's debts, nor even insure the safety of the building in which it assembled. Still, Hamilton had enough faith in the body to prepare a lengthy resolution enumerating the defects of the Articles of Confederation and calling for a convention to amend the articles. He began by listing "essential points" in which the confederation was "defective."

Hamilton's letter informing Governor Clinton that Congress had removed to Princeton to avoid mutineers from the Army barracks in Philadelphia

[Princeton, New Jersey, July, 1783]

First and generally in confining the power of the fœderal government within too narrow limits, withholding from it that efficacious authority and influence in all matters of general concern which are indispensable to the harmony and welfare of the whole—embarrassing general provisions by unnecessary details and inconvenient exceptions incompatible with their nature tending only to create jealousies and disputes respecting the proper bounds of the authority of the United States and of that of the particular states, and a mutual interference of the one with the other.

Secondly. In confounding legislative and executive powers in a single body . . . contrary to the most approved and well founded maxims of free government which require that the legislative executive and judicial authorities should be deposited in distinct and separate hands.

Thirdly. In the want of a Fœderal Judicature having cognizance of all matters of general concern in the last resort, especially those in which foreign nations, and their subjects are interested; from which defect, by the interference of the local regulations of particular states militating directly or indirectly against the powers vested in the Union, the national treaties will be liable to be infringed, the national faith to be violated and the public tranquillity to be disturbed. . . .

[After listing seven more specific ways in which the Articles of Confederation failed to provide for America's interests in finance, trade, and national security, Hamilton turned to broader defects in the system.]

11thly. In requiring the assent of *nine* states to matters of principal importance and of seven to all others...a rule destructive of vigour, consistency or expedition in the administration of affairs, tending to subject the *sense* of the majority to *that* of the minority...the evils of which...must always make the spirit of government, a spirit of compromise and expedient, rather than of system and energy.

12thly. In vesting in the Fœderal government the sole direction of the interests of the United States in their intercourse with foreign nations, without empowering it to pass all general laws in aid and support of the laws of nations; for the want of which authority, the faith of the United States may be broken, their reputation sullied, and their peace interrupted by the negligence or misconception of any particular state.

[Having completed his analysis of the faults of the present Government, Hamilton closed his "Resolution" with his proposals for a remedy.]

And Whereas it is essential to the happiness and security of these states, that their union, should be established on the most solid foundations, and it is manifest that this desireable object cannot be effected but by a government capable both in peace and war of making every member of the Union contribute in just proportion to the common necessities, and of combining and directing the forces and wills of the several parts to a general end; to which purposes in the opinion of Congress the present confederation is altogether inadequate.

And Whereas on the spirit which may direct the councils and measures of these states at the present juncture may depend their future safety and welfare; Congress conceive it to be their duty freely to state to their constituents the defects which by experience have been discovered in the present plan of the Fœderal Union and solemnly to call their attention to a revisal and amendment of the same:

Therefore Resolved that it be earnestly recommended to the several states to appoint a convention to meet...

Adams, Morris, Hamilton, and Jefferson are shown conferring at the Continental Congress.

with full powers to revise the confederation and to adopt and propose such alterations as to them shall appear necessary to be finally approved or rejected by the states respectively—and that a Committee...be appointed to prepare an address upon the subject.

Congress never heard this draft resolution for a convention; the manuscript carries Hamilton's terse notation: "abandoned for want of support." Finally, at the end of July, 1783, Hamilton left Congress. His mood at the time was best expressed in a letter he sent to his old friend John Jay, one of the commissioners who had negotiated America's treaty of peace with Britain.

[Philadelphia, July 25, 1783]

We have now happily concluded the great work of independence, but much remains to be done to reach the fruits of it. Our prospects are not flattering. Every day proves the inefficacy of the present confederation, yet the common danger being removed, we are receding instead of advancing in a disposition to amend its defects. The road to popularity in each state is to inspire jealousies of the power of Congress, though nothing can be more apparent than that they have no power; and that for the want of it, the resources of the country during the war could not be drawn out, and we at this moment experience all the mischiefs of a bankrupt and ruined credit. It is to be hoped that when prejudice and folly have run themselves out of breath we may return to reason and correct our errors.

Hamilton returned gladly to the joys of raising a family and the challenge of building a law practice in New York. It was a fortunate decision both for him and for the nation he had tried to serve. By July, 1783, the American public and Hamilton needed a rest from the strain of eight years of war and revolution. Since 1775, Hamilton's fellow citizens had undergone political upheaval, economic hardship, and military danger; there was little national energy left for the "exertions" Hamilton and other nationalists had demanded. For his part, Hamilton, in his desire to introduce reforms, had lost his sense of perspective about the role of a public servant in a republic. If he was to serve America, he first had to learn more about that nation. A few quiet years as a New York lawyer would permit him to observe his neighbors more closely. When he returned to public life, he would not repeat his mistakes of 1783.

137

Chapter 5

Devil's Advocate

When Alexander Hamilton returned to New York in August, 1783, he might have sincerely believed that he could pursue his private career without troubling himself with public affairs. But he soon learned that a conscientious nationalist could not even earn a living without confronting flaws of government and threats to the nation's "character." One of the most bothersome issues involved New York's reaction to the provisions of the Treaty of Paris, under which Britain and the United States had agreed that neither nation would permit the persecution of any persons for the part they had taken in the war. New Yorkers showed no inclination to end such actions. Beginning in 1779 with the Confiscation Act, under which "attainted" Loyalists forfeited their property, the state legislature had enacted a series of harsh laws against British sympathizers. Under the Trespass Act of 1783, New Yorkers who had fled from their homes could bring action against those who had remained behind British lines and occupied their property.

This list of laws brought Hamilton a harvest of legal fees. In all, he handled at least forty-five cases under the Trespass Act and twenty more under other anti-Loyalist laws. But although Hamilton's success in many of these trials won him a reputation as an able and resourceful attorney, he was too concerned with the nation's "character" to view the treaty violations with anything but disgust. He knew that the continued enforcement of these laws might endanger America's national prestige. In June, 1783, when he was still serving New York in the Continental Congress, Hamilton had written to Governor George Clinton expressing his concern about his home state's refusal to comply with the treaty's provisions. Hamilton pointed out that since the preliminary articles of peace had not yet been ratified, New York's violations of the treaty might give Britain an excuse to postpone complying with other provisions of the agreement.

Philadelphia June 1st 1783

...with a treaty which has exceeded the hopes of the

most sanguine . . . I think it the height of imprudence to run any risk. Great Britain without recommencing hostilities may evade parts of the treaty. She may keep possession of the frontier posts, she may obstruct the free enjoyment of the fisheries, she may be indisposed to such extensive concessions in matters of commerce as it is our interest to aim at; in all this she would find no opposition from any foreign power; and we are not in a condition to oblige her to any thing. If we imagine that France, obviously embarrassed herself in her Finances would renew the war to oblige Great Britain to the restoration of our frontier posts, or to a compliance with the stipulations respecting the fisheries . . . we speculate much at random. . . . Are we prepared, for the mere gratification of our resentments to put those great national objects to the hazard — to leave our western frontier in a state of insecurity — to relinquish the fur trade and to abridge our pretensions to the fisheries? Do we think national character so light a thing as to be willing to sacrifice the public faith to individual animosity? . . .

[Britain had less to lose than America if the provisions of the treaty were not observed. Under the peace terms, Britain had recognized American independence, granted fishing rights, and agreed to surrender the western posts; America had given little in return.]

What equivalent do we give for this? Congress are to recommend the restoration of property to those who have adhered to her, and expressly engage that no future injury shall be done them on person liberty or property. This is the sole condition on our part where there is not an immediate reciprocity . . . and stands as the single equivalent for all the restitutions and concessions to be made by Great Britain. Will it be honest in us to violate this condition or will it be prudent to put it in competition with all the important matters to be performed on the other side? Will foreign nations be willing to undertake any thing with us or for us, when they find that the nature of our governments will allow no dependence to be placed upon our engagements?

I have omitted saying any thing of the impolicy of inducing by our severity a great number of useful citizens, whose situations do not make them a proper

In this English cartoon the peace treaty of 1783 is attacked for supposedly leaving Loyalists at the mercy of the vengeful Americans.

Robert R. Livingston, circa 1804

object of resentment to abandon the country to form settlements that will hereafter become our rivals animated with a hatred to us which will descend to their posterity. Nothing however can be more unwise than to contribute as we are doing to people the shores and wilderness of Nova-scotia, a colony which by its position will become a competitor with us among other things in that branch of commerce in which our navigation and navy will essentially depend. I mean the fisheries in which I have no doubt the state of New York will hereafter have a considerable share. . . .

Those who consult only their passions might choose to construe what I say as too favourable to a set of men who have been the enemies of the public liberty; but those for whose esteem I am most concerned will acquit me of any personal considerations and will perceive that I only urge the cause of national honor, safety and advantage. We have assumed an independent station; we ought to feel and to act in a manner consistent with the dignity of that station.

I anxiously wish to see every prudent measure taken to prevent those combinations which will certainly disgrace us, if they do not involve us in other calamities. Whatever distinctions are judged necessary to be made in the case of those persons who have been in opposition to the common cause, let them be made by legal authority on a fair construction of the treaty, consistent with national faith and national honor.

After having returned to New York, Hamilton realized that persecution of the Tories could have far-reaching economic consequences for the state. Having passed through New York City on his way to Albany, he afterward sent this report to Robert R. Livingston, chancellor of New York State.

[Albany, August 13, 1783]
The spirit of emigration has greatly increased of late. Some violent papers sent into the city have determined many to depart, who hitherto have intended to remain. Many merchants of second class, characters of no political consequence, each of whom may carry away eight or ten thousand guineas have I am told lately applied for shipping to convey them away. Our state will feel for twenty years at least, the effects of the popular phrenzy.

While he waited for British troops to evacuate Manhattan, Hamilton shared his thoughts on America's political "peace establishment" with Washington and congratulated his former chief on the General's farewell address to the Army and the nation.

[Albany, September 30, 1783]

In a letter which I wrote to you several months ago I intimated that it might be in your power to contribute to the establishment of our Fœderal union upon a more solid basis. I have never since explained myself. At the time I was in hopes Congress might have been induced to take a decisive ground—to inform their constituents of the imperfections of the present system and of the impossibility of conducting the public affairs with honor to themselves and advantage to the community with powers so disproportioned to their responsibility; and having done this in a full and forcible manner, to adjourn the moment the definitive treaty was ratified. In retiring at the same juncture I wished you in a solemn manner to declare to the people your intended retreat from public concerns, your opinion of the present government and of the absolute necessity of a change.

Before I left Congress I dispaired of the first and your circular letter to the states had anticipated the last. I trust it will not be without effect though I am persuaded it would have had more combined with what I have mentioned. At all events, without compliment Sir, It will do you honor with the sensible and well meaning; and ultimately it is to be hoped with the people at large—when the present epidemic phrenzy has subsided.

A late-eighteenth-century view of Broadway and St. Paul's Chapel

While the "epidemic phrenzy" ran its course, Hamilton took the oaths required of a lawyer who wished to practice in New York courts and found a home for his family at 57 Wall Street in Manhattan. As soon as British forces left the city at the end of November, those Tories who had chosen to remain found themselves in need of legal advice. Hamilton's own disgust with public affairs and the demands of his growing practice led him to place this notice in the *New-York Packet.*

[New York, December 27, 1783]

I observe in Mr. Holt's paper [*The Independent New-York Gazette*] of this day, a nomination [for the state assembly] for the ensuing election, in which my name is included. I thank the authors of it for the honour they intended me; but being determined to decline public

141

office, I think it proper to declare my determination, to avoid . . . distracting the votes of my fellow citizens.

Yet the interests of his clients did not allow Hamilton to ignore politics or public opinion. In January, 1784, he published his first *Letter from Phocion to the Considerate Citizens of New-York On the Politics of the Day*, which was concerned primarily with an "alien bill" passed in the state legislature in 1783. The bill, which would have threatened the civil rights of any man who had remained behind British lines during the Revolution, had been vetoed by the State Council of Revision but was about to be reconsidered by the legislature. Hamilton opened his pamphlet with an indictment of politicians who would "practise upon the passions of the people."

[New York, January 1–27, 1784]

It is . . . a common observation, that men, bent upon mischief, are more active in the pursuit of their object, than those who aim at doing good. Hence it is in the present moment, we see the most industrious efforts to violate, the constitution of this state, to trample upon the rights of the subject, and to chicane or infringe the most solemn obligations of treaty; while dispassionate and upright men almost totally neglect the means of counteracting these dangerous attempts. A sense of duty alone calls forth the observations which will be submitted to the good sense of the people in this paper, from one who has more inclination than leisure to serve them; and who has had too deep a share in the common exertions in this revolution, to be willing to see its fruits blasted by the violence of rash or unprincipled men, without at least protesting against their designs.

The persons alluded to, pretend to appeal to the spirit of Whiggism, while they endeavour to put in motion all the furious and dark passions of the human mind. The spirit of Whiggism, is generous, humane, beneficent and just. These men inculcate revenge, cruelty, persecutions, and perfidy. The spirit of Whiggism cherishes legal liberty, holds the rights of every individual sacred, condemns or punishes no man without regular trial and conviction of some crime declared by antecedent laws, reprobates equally the punishment of the citizen by arbitrary acts of legislature, as by the lawless combinations of unauthorised individuals: While these men are advocates for expelling a large number of their fellow-citizens unheard, untried; or if they

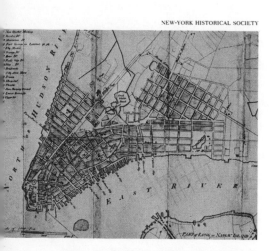

New York City in 1789 was confined to the lower tip of Manhattan and was bordered on the north by farms.

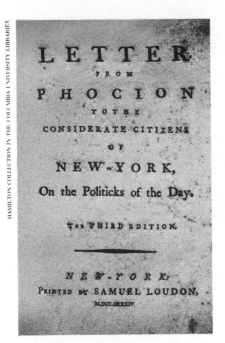

Title page from Hamilton's first Letter from Phocion, *dated 1784*

cannot effect this, are for disfranchising them, in the face of the constitution, without the judgment of their peers, and contrary to the law of the land....

[New Yorkers would endanger not only their own rights as citizens but also their economic future by expelling wealthy merchants with badly needed capital. There was, Hamilton insisted, nothing to fear from leaving former British sympathizers in peace.]

Viewing the subject in every possible light, there is not a single interest of the community but dictates moderation rather than violence. That honesty is still the best policy; that justice and moderation are the surest supports of every government, are maxims, which however they may be called trite, at all times true, though too seldom regarded, but rarely neglected with impunity. Were the people of America, with one voice, to ask, What shall we do to perpetuate our liberties and secure our happiness? The answer would be, "govern well" and you have nothing to fear either from internal disaffection or external hostility. Abuse not the power you possess, and you need never apprehend its diminution or loss. But if you make a wanton use of it, if you furnish another example, that despotism may debase the government of the many as well as the few, you like all others that have acted the same part, will experience that licentiousness is the fore-runner to slavery....

These sentiments are delivered to you in the frankness of conscious integrity, by one who *feels* that solicitude for the good of the community which the zealots, whose opinions he encounters profess, by one who pursues not as they do, the honour or emoluments of his country, by one who, though he has had, in the course of the Revolution, a very *confidential* share in the public councils, civil and military, and has as often, at least, met danger in the common cause as any of those who now assume to be the guardians of the public liberty, asks no other reward of his countrymen, than to be heard without prejudice for their own interest.

A month after this letter appeared, Hamilton gave his friend Gouverneur Morris a picture of New York politics and legal practice.

New York Feby. 21. 1784

Legislative folly has afforded so plentiful a harvest to us lawyers that we have scarcely a moment to spare from the substantial business of reaping. Today being sunday I have resolved to give an hour to friendship and to you....

I ought...to give you an account of what we are doing here; but I will in the lump tell you that we are doing those things which we ought not to do, and leaving undone those things which we ought to do. Instead of wholesome regulations for the improvement of our polity and commerce; we are labouring to contrive methods to mortify and punish tories and to explain away treaties.

Let us both erect a temple to time; only regretting that we shall not command a longer portion of it to see what will be the event of the American drama.

Hamilton's first *Letter from Phocion* did not go unchallenged. A reply from "Mentor" appeared in short order, and a second *Letter from Phocion* was necessary to answer "Mentor's" charges and to prepare public opinion for the stand Hamilton would take in the New York courts as the defense attorney for Joshua Waddington, a New Yorker who was being sued under the state's Trespass Act. Hamilton pointed out that more than the fate of a few Tories, more than the honor of the state or even of the nation, were involved.

[New York, April, 1784]

Those, who are at present entrusted with power, in all these infant republics, hold the most sacred deposit that ever was confided to human hands. 'Tis with governments as with individuals, first impressions and early habits give a lasting bias to the temper and character. Our governments hitherto have no habits. How important to the happiness not of America alone, but of mankind, that they should acquire good ones....

The world has its eye upon America. The noble struggle we have made in the cause of liberty, has occasioned a kind of revolution in human sentiment. The influence of our example has penetrated the gloomy regions of despotism, and has pointed the way to inquiries, which may shake it to its deepest foundations. Men begin to ask every where, who is this tyrant, that dares to build his greatness on our misery and degradation? What commission has he to sacrifice millions to the wanton appetites of himself and the few minions that surround his throne? . . .

If the consequences prove, that we really have asserted the cause of human happiness, what may not be expected from so illustrious an example? In a greater or less degree, the world will bless and imitate!

But if experience, in this instance, verifies the lesson long taught by the enemies of liberty; that the bulk of mankind are not fit to govern themselves, that they must have a master, and were only made for the rein and the spur: We shall then see the final triumph of despotism over liberty. . . . With the greatest advantages for promoting it, that ever a people had, we shall have betrayed the cause of human nature.

Let those in whose hands it is placed, pause for a moment, and contemplate with an eye of reverence, the vast trust committed to them. Let them retire into their own bosoms and examine the motives which there prevail. Let them ask themselves this solemn question —Is the sacrifice of a few mistaken, or criminal individuals, an object worthy of the shifts to which we are reduced to evade the constitution and the national engagements? Then let them review the arguments that have been offered . . . and if they even doubt the propriety of the measures, they may be about to adopt, let them remember, that in a doubtful case, the constitution ought never to be hazarded, without extreme necessity.

New York Attorney General Egbert Benson, a Hamilton opponent in the case of Rutgers v. Waddington

Before the *Second Letter from Phocion* appeared, Hamilton had been retained by Joshua Waddington, the defendant in a suit brought by Mrs. Elizabeth Rutgers under the Trespass Act. Mrs. Rutgers, the operator of a brewery, had fled New York City in 1776. During the occupation, British civil authorities, and later the military, had given permission to two English merchants to operate the brewery, and Mrs. Rutgers was now seeking back rent and damages of eight thousand pounds from Waddington, who was an agent for the merchants. In his plea on Waddington's behalf, Hamilton argued that the Trespass Act violated the "law of nations" by not allowing citizens to plead military orders as a defense for actions that might otherwise have been illegal. Using traditional legal phrases, he also implied that the act was void because it violated the Treaty of Paris.

[April 21, 1784]

Joshua Waddington further saith, that the... action... against him ought not to have and maintain; because he saith that after the passing the act of the Legislature of this state... a certain definitive treaty of peace between the King of Great Britain and... the United States of America... was entered into made and concluded...; which said definitive treaty of peace hath been since ... by the said United States of America in Congress... approved ratified and confirmed, and was afterwards... announced published and notified to all the good Citizens of the said United States... the said proclamation requiring and enjoining all bodies of Magistracy, Legislative executive and judiciary, all persons bearing office civil and military of whatever rank... and all... the good Citizens of the said States of every vocation and condition, that reverencing those stipulations entered into on their behalf under the authority of that foederal bond by which their existence as an independent people is bound up together and is known and acknowleged by the nations of the world and with that good faith which is every mans surest guide— ... they should carry into effect the said definitive Articles and every clause and sentence thereof strictly and completely... in virtue of which said definitive treaty, all right claim pretension and demand whatsoever which either of the said contracting parties and the Subjects and Citizens of either of the said contracting parties might otherwise have had to any compensation, recompence, retribution or indemnity whatsoever; for or by reason of any injury or damage... which either of the said contracting parties might have done or caused to be done to the other:... and the Subjects and Citizens of the other... in consequence of or in any wise relating to the war... virtually and effectually relinquished renounced and released to each other to all intents constructions and purposes whatsoever.

A check, signed by Aaron Burr, drawn on the Bank of New York

R*utgers* v. *Waddington* was at best a qualified success for Hamilton. The New York Mayor's Court, while avoiding ruling on the legality of the Trespass Act, held that the legislature had not intended to overrule the "law of nations," since nothing to that effect was specifically stated in the act. The court also ruled that Mrs. Rutgers was entitled to collect rent only for the period when the merchants held her property under the orders of a civilian and not for the years when they were licensed by British military authorities.

The Trespass and Confiscation acts were not Hamilton's only concerns in 1784. In the preceding summer, his wife's brother-in-law, John Barker Church, had sailed for Europe, leaving Hamilton in charge of his interests in New York. Church and his partner, Jeremiah Wadsworth, hoped to found a commercial bank in Manhattan, but Robert R. Livingston, the state chancellor, sponsored a rival scheme for a bank whose capital would be largely in pledges of land. Hamilton set about mobilizing support for a "money bank," and the Bank of New York was organized on March 15. Three weeks later, Hamilton, who had originally favored competition in banking, conveyed his modified views on the subject in a letter to Gouverneur Morris.

[New York, April 7, 1784]

Page from New York Mayor's Court docket, 1784, signed by Hamilton

...you will believe me when I tell you, that on more deliberate consideration, I was led to view the competition in a different light from that in which it at first struck me. I had no doubt that it was against the interests of the proprietors; but on a superficial view I perceived benefits to the community which on a more close inspection I found were not real.

You well call our proceedings here *strange doings;* if some folks were paid to counteract the prosperity of the state, they could not take more effectual measures than they do. But it is in vain to attempt to kick against the Pricks.

Discrimination bills—Partial taxes—schemes to engross public property in the hands of those who have present power—to banish the real wealth of the state and substitute paper bubbles are the only dishes that suit the public palate at this time.

For the remainder of the year, Hamilton was engrossed in the details of establishing the Bank of New York and handling his growing law practice. Meanwhile, the pleasures of life in New York were increased when John Jay and his family returned from Europe in the summer. Jay, who became Secretary for Foreign Affairs, joined Hamilton in leading a reform movement that both had been advocating for several years—the end of slavery. Early in February, 1785, they met with other antislavery New Yorkers to form the Society for Promoting the Manumission of Slaves. The minutes of that meeting provide a record of some of Hamilton's activities.

[New York, February 4, 1785]

Ordered—That Colonel Hamilton, Colonel [Robert] Troup and Mr. [White] Matlack be a Committee to Report

"What the unhappy Children of Africa endure"—an illustration from an emancipation broadside of 1807

a Line of Conduct to be recommended to the Members of the Society in relation to any Slaves possessed by them; and also to prepare a Recommendation to all such Persons as have manumitted or shall Manumit Slaves to transmit their names and the names and Ages of the Slaves manumitted; in Order that the same may be Registered and the Society be the better Enabled to detect Attempts to deprive such Manumitted Persons of their Liberty.

Hamilton's family responsibilities, meantime, were increasing. A baby girl, Angelica, had been added to the family, and Betsey Schuyler Hamilton looked after her children while her husband traveled the "circuit" of New York courts. A letter written in mid-March shows that Hamilton found his "Angel" to be a competent businesswoman as well as a loving wife.

> [West Chester, New York, March 17, 1785]
> I have just written to you My beloved by the person who will probably be the bearer of this. Col Burr just tells me, that the house we live in is offered for sale at £2100. I am to request you to agree for the purchase for me, if at that price. If you cannot do better, you may engage that the whole shall be paid in three months; but I could wish to pay half in a short time and the other half in a year. Adieu my Angel
>
> A HAMILTON

In the spring of 1785, Hamilton again found his name being put forward for public office. Again he refused to run, but when the state legislature defeated a petition for a charter of incorporation for the Bank of New York, he set out to persuade other "men of respectability" to enter politics. Toward the end of April he broached the subject to Robert Livingston, the lord of the Manor of Livingston.

> [April 25, 1785]
> ...the situation of the state at this time is so critical that it is become a serious object of attention to those who are concerned for the *security of property* or the prosperity of government, to endeavour to put men in the Legislature whose principles are not of the *levelling kind*. The spirit of the present Legislature is truly alarming, and appears evidently directed to the confusion of all property and principle. The truth is that the state

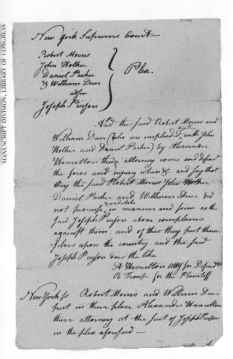

*One of Hamilton's pleas before the
New York Supreme Court, July, 1785*

is now governed by a couple of New England adventurers.... A number of attempts have been made by this junto to subvert the constitution and destroy the rights of private property.... All men of respectability, in the city, of whatever party, who have been witnesses of the despotism and iniquity of the Legislature, are convinced, that the principal people in the community must for their own defence, unite to overset the party I have alluded to. I wish you to be persuaded Sir, that I would not take the liberty to trouble you with these remarks with a view to serving any particular turn; but, from a thorough conviction, that the safety of all those who have any thing to lose calls upon them to take care that the power of government is intrusted to proper hands. Much depends on the ensuing election. You Sir have much in your power; and I have no doubt you will have heared from other quarters and from your immediate connections, a like account of public affairs to that which I have now given.

In the summer and early fall of 1785, Hamilton devoted much of his time to research on a commission that was to settle a boundary dispute between New York and Massachusetts. Among his business letters, receipts, and legal documents from this period, there is one poignant reminder of Hamilton's boyhood, of the life he had left behind in the West Indies. In June, Hamilton received a letter from his older brother James, a carpenter. James's letter has been lost, but Alexander's reply gives a good idea of James's circumstances and of Alexander's wish to help his brother and reunite his family.

New York, June 22, 1785.
The situation you describe yourself to be in gives me much pain, and nothing will make me happier than, as far as may be in my power, to contribute to your relief. I will cheerfully pay your draft upon me for fifty pounds sterling, whenever it shall appear. I wish it was in my power to desire you to enlarge the sum; but though my future prospects are of the most flattering kind my present engagements would render it inconvenient to me to advance you a larger sum. My affection for you, however, will not permit me to be inattentive to your welfare, and I hope time will prove to you that I feel all the sentiment of a brother. Let me only request of you to exert your industry for a year or two more where

Angelica Schuyler Church

Cornelia Schuyler

you are, and at the end of that time I promise myself to be able to invite you to a more comfortable settlement in this Country. Allow me only to give you one caution, which is to avoid if possible getting in debt. Are you *married* or *single*? If the *latter*, it is my wish for many reasons it may be agreeable to you to continue in that state.

But what has become of our dear father? It is an age since I have heared from him or of him, though I have written him several letters. Perhaps, alas! he is no more, and I shall not have the pleasing opportunity of contributing to render the close of his life more happy than the progress of it. My heart bleeds at the recollection of his misfortunes and embarrassments. Sometimes I flatter myself his brothers have extended their support to him, and that he now enjoys tranquillity and ease. At other times I fear he is suffering in indigence. I entreat you, if you can, to relieve me from my doubts, and let me know how or where he is, if alive, if dead, how and where he died. Should he be alive inform him of my inquiries, beg him to write to me, and tell him how ready I shall be to devote myself and all I have to his accommodation and happiness.

I do not advise your coming to this country at present, for the war has also put things out of order here, and people in your business find a subsistence difficult enough. My object will be, by-and-by, to get you settled on a farm.

Believe me always your affectionate friend and brother,

ALEX. HAMILTON.

Alexander Hamilton never saw his brother again, for James Hamilton died the following year. Fortunately, Hamilton had found a family that he adopted as completely as any man could—the Schuylers. His wife's parents, brothers, and sisters had accepted him as one of their own, and Hamilton repaid their affection in full. When he learned that his sister-in-law, Angelica Schuyler Church, and her husband might remain in Europe, Hamilton pleaded with his "Dear Sister" to reconsider.

[New York, August 3, 1785]

You have I fear taken a final leave of America and of those that love you here. I saw you depart from Philadelphia with peculiar uneasiness, as if foreboding you were not to return. My apprehensions are confirmed and unless I see you in Europe I expect not to see you again.

This is the impression we all have; judge the bitterness it gives to those who love you with the *love of nature* and to me who feel an attachment for you not less lively.

I confess for my own part I see one great source of happiness snatched away. My affection for Church and yourself made me anticipate much enjoyment in your friendship and neighbourhood. But an ocean is now to separate us.

Let me entreat you both not precipitately to wed yourselves to a soil less propitious to you than will be that of America: You will not indeed want friends wherever you are on two accounts: One is You will have no need of them: another is that You have both too many qualities to engage friend ship. But go where you will you will find no *such* friends as those you have left behind.

In the fall of 1785, local "prejudices" and party politics again began to interrupt Hamilton's private pursuits. On September 13, the Pennsylvania legislature, dominated by the "Constitutionalist" party, repealed the charter of the Bank of North America. The bank still held a charter from Congress—but not from the state in which it was located. Since Hamilton's wife's brother-in-law John Barker Church and Church's associate Jeremiah Wadsworth were large stockholders in this bank, the battles between Pennsylvania's Constitutionalists and Republicans became a pressing concern for Hamilton. Toward the end of October he wrote urgently to Wadsworth in Hartford, Connecticut.

[New York, October 29, 1785]

What do you intend to do or what would you advise to be done for Mr Church? To sell unless at a great disadvantage is not practicable. To leave *so considerable a sum* in a Company of this kind not incorporated is too dangerous. To force it out of their hands is an uphill business. In this choice of difficulties I will submit to you what occurs to me.

It is believed the Republican party has prevailed at the last election, not in so decisive a manner however as to insure a decisive influence; but sufficiently in all probability to effect a revival of the act of Incorporation.

COLLECTION OF MRS. JOSEPH CARSON

One of the earliest existing checks drawn on the Bank of North America

151

Should this happen, It will in some degree restore the credit of stock and make it easier to part with it, without any considerable loss.

I should think therefore it would be prudent to wait the result of the next meeting of their Legislature; if the Charter is not then revived, I should be of opinion to insist that measures may be taken to decide the Question whether the bank still remains an incorporated body by virtue of the original act of Congress or not.... The mode of deciding it will be easy. It will be to get some person to refuse to pay a note to the bank, and to have an action instituted against him in behalf of the bank in their corporate capacity. If the Courts allow this action to be maintained it must be on the principle that the Bank still subsists a corporation in Pensylvania.

If the decision is in favour of the corporate existence of the bank, the proprietors will then know in what situation they are and may either continue such with greater safety or part with their interest with less disadvantage. If it is decided that the bank does not continue a corporation, you can then insist on your money being returned to you and may compel its being done. It seems to me essential you should ascertain upon what footing you stand.

Jeremiah Wadsworth

Wadsworth replied immediately, reporting that he had already had doubts about the Bank of North America and had made an unsuccessful attempt to force the bank to return the funds he had invested. Hamilton accordingly prepared a letter of instructions to Wadsworth, who was to act as the agent for John Church and four other stockholders in the bank. At a meeting of the shareholders on January 9, 1786, Wadsworth presented the letter as a summary of his position.

[New York, January 3, 1786]

Those who subscribed to the Bank of North America on the faith of the Pensylvania Charter might with great reason urge that so material a change in its situation is, at all events, with respect to them, a dissolution of the contract upon which their subscriptions were made; and that they have a right to reclaim their property. But not being disposed to agitate any questions injurious to the Institution, we are content to wave this right, so long as there remains any prospect of the bank being continued with safety and advantage. This prospect

This set of scales for weighing coins was used by a Connecticut town clerk during the late eighteeenth century.

however we deem inseparable from its existence as a corporation; and if this cannot be maintained all hopes of security or utility in our apprehension fail.

Nothing will give us greater pleasure than to find that the Bank of North America has a solid foundation in the Charter of the United States; and that it will on experiment be considered in this light by the laws of that state in which from its position its operations would be carried on; but it appears to us essential that the experiment should be made without delay, in order that it may be ascertained in what light it will be considered by those laws. If these should pronounce that it is no corporation, no prudent alternative is left but to remove it to another state, where it will be protected by the laws, or to leave all those who wish to do it at liberty to withdraw their shares.

While on the one hand public as well as private considerations concur to restrain us from advising any measures incompatible with the Interest of the bank; on the other hand we cannot help feeling great anxiety to know what our *true situation* is; and to extricate ourselves from *one* (if such *it* is) in which we might hazard much more than we intended.

Slowly but surely, Hamilton's interest in public affairs was being revived. In early 1786, an old cause—the impost—called Hamilton to action. The import duty recommended by Congress in April, 1783, had been approved by every state but Georgia and New York. Georgia was on the verge of granting its approval, but New York, which enjoyed a sizable revenue from state taxes on imports, was reluctant to share this source of wealth with the Federal treasury. Hamilton drafted a petition to the state legislature advocating acceptance of the tax in the spring session.

[New York, January–March, 1786]

The Petition of the Subscribers Inhabitants of the City of New York respectfully sheweth...

That the anxiety which Your Petitioners have all along felt from motives of a more general nature is at the present junction increased by this particular consideration that the State of New York now stands almost alone, in a non compliance with a measure in which the sentiments and wishes of the Union at large appear to unite and by a further delay may render itself responsible for consequences too serious not to affect every considerate man.

That in the opinion of Your Memorialists all the considerations important to a state—all the motives of public honor faith reputation interest and safety conspire to urge a compliance with these resolutions.

That Government without revenue cannot subsist. That the mode provided in the Confederation for supplying the treasury of the United States has in experiment been found inadequate.

That the system proposed will in all probability prove much more efficacious, and is in other respects as unexceptionable as the various circumstances and interests of these states will permit.

That any objection to it as a measure not warranted by the confederation is refuted by the thirteenth article which provides that alterations may be made if agreed to by Congress and confirmed by the Legislatures of each State....

That as to danger in vesting the United States with these funds, Your Memorialists consider their interests and liberties as not less safe in the hands of their fellow citizens delegated to represent them for one year in Congress than in the hands of their fellow citizens delegated to represent them for one year or four years in the Senate and Assembly of this state.

That Government implies trust; and every government must be trusted so far as is necessary to enable it to attain the ends for which it is instituted; without which insult and oppression from abroad confusion and convulsion at home.

To the south, meanwhile, there were promising signs for nationalists. James Madison and George Washington had successfully sponsored arbitration that ended a dispute between Virginia and Maryland over navigation rights on the Potomac River. This in turn led to a call from the Virginia assembly for a convention to "take into consideration the trade of the states" and "seek a uniform system in their commercial regulations." By now Hamilton was ready once again to play an active role in the nationalist cause, as was evident in a letter he sent to Nathaniel Hazard. Hazard, a New York ironmonger, had asked Hamilton's help in supporting a petition addressed to the legislature on behalf of New Yorkers who were indebted to British merchants. Hamilton's reply was "politic" in more than one respect.

The State House at Annapolis, site of the Annapolis Convention, 1786

[New York, April 24, 1786]
I would not be understood to declare any opinion concerning the principles of the Bill, with which I am not sufficiently acquainted to form a decided opinion. I have merely made your letter the occasion of Introducing the subject to General Schuyler; whose sentiments are as favorable to your wishes as you could desire.

I make this observation from that spirit of candour which I hope will always direct my conduct. I am aware that I have been represented as an enemy to the wishes of what you call your corps. If by this has been meant that I do not feel as much as any man, not immediately interested, for the distresses of those merchants who have been in a great measure the victims of the revolution, the supposition does not do Justice either to my head or my heart. But if it means that I have always viewed the mode of relieving them as a matter of peculiar delicacy and difficulty it is well founded.

I should have thought it unnecessary to enter into this explanation, were it not that I am held up as a candidate at the ensuing Election; and I would not wish that the step I have taken in respect to your letter should be considered as implying more than it does: For I woud never wish to conciliate at the expence of candour. On the other hand, I confide in your liberality not to infer more than I intend from the explanation I have given.

Six days later, Hamilton was elected to the assembly from New York County. In May, when the legislature agreed to send commissioners to the convention, which was to be held in September at Annapolis, Maryland, Hamilton was among those elected to the delegation. At about this same time he also had the satisfaction of celebrating the birth of his third child, Alexander, Jr. Leaving his growing family at the end of the summer, Hamilton traveled to Annapolis, and shortly after reaching his destination he wrote to his wife to assure her of his safe arrival.

[Annapolis, September 8, 1786]
I was not very well on the first part of the journey; but my health has been improved by travelling and is now as good as I could wish. Happy, however I cannot be, absent from you and my darling little ones. I feel that nothing can ever compensate for the loss of the enjoyments I leave at home, or can ever put my heart at tolerable ease. In the bosom of my family alone must

my happiness be sought, and in that of my Betsey is every thing that is charming to me. Would to heaven I were there! Does not your heart re-echo the wish?

In reality my attachments to home disqualify me for either business or pleasure abroad; and the prospect of a detention here for Eight or ten days perhaps a fortnight fills me with an anxiety which will best be conceived by my Betseys own impatience.

I am straitened for time & must conclude. . . . Kiss my little ones a thousand times for me. . . . Think of me with as much tenderness as I do of you and we cannot fail to be always happy[.]

Events proved that Hamilton was by no means so "disqualified" for public service by his "attachments to home" as he expected to be. On the surface, the Annapolis Convention seemed a poor starting place for reform of the American Government. Only five states were represented, and the delegates met for only four days. But the fact that this convention could do nothing constructive in the area of commercial regulation made it possible for some of the commissioners to suggest another convention where there would be a fuller representation of the states and where a broader range of topics might be discussed. The delegates from New Jersey had been instructed to discuss "other important matters" as well as trade, and Hamilton seized on this idea in drafting the address issued by the convention at the close of its sessions.

[Annapolis, September 14, 1786]
Your Commissioners cannot forbear to indulge an expression of their earnest and unanimous wish, that speedy measures may be taken, to effect a general meeting, of the States, in a future Convention, for the same and such other purposes, as the situation of public affairs, may be found to require. . . .

In this persuasion your Commissioners submit an opinion, that the Idea of extending the powers of their Deputies, to other objects, than those of Commerce, . . . will deserve to be incorporated into that of a future Convention. . . .

That there are important defects in the system of the Fœderal Government is acknowledged by the Acts of all those States, which have concurred in the present Meeting; That the defects, upon a closer examination, may be found greater and more numerous, than even these acts imply, is at least so far probable . . . as may

The insignia of the Society of the Cincinnati, as it appeared on an invitation to a Society banquet

The minutes of the meeting of the Annapolis Convention of September 11, 1786, showing those present to include Hamilton and James Madison

reasonably be supposed to merit a deliberate and candid discussion, in some mode, which will unite the Sentiments and Councils of all the States. In the choice of the mode your Commissioners are of opinion, that a Convention of Deputies from the different States, for the special and sole purpose of entering into this investigation, and digesting a plan for supplying such defects as may be discovered to exist, will be entitled to a preference....

Your Commissioners, with the most respectful deference, beg leave to suggest their unanimous conviction, that it may essentially tend to advance the interests of the union, if the States, by whom they have been respectively delegated, would themselves concur, and use their endeavours to procure the concurrence of the other States, in the appointment of Commissioners, to meet at Philadelphia on the second Monday in May next, to take into consideration the situation of the United States, to devise such further provisions as shall appear to them necessary to render the constitution of the Foederal Government adequate to the exigencies of the Union; and to report such an Act for that purpose to the United States in Congress Assembled, as when agreed to, by them, and afterwards confirmed by the Legislatures of every State will effectually provide for the same.

Though your Commissioners could not with propriety address these observations and sentiments to any but the States they have the honor to Represent, they have nevertheless concluded from motives of respect, to transmit Copies of this report to the United States in Congress assembled, and to the executives of the other States.

After Hamilton returned to New York to await the reconvening of the state legislature in January, 1787, an opportunity arose for him to advance the nationalist cause. The Society of the Cincinnati, a fraternal organization of Revolutionary officers, had been attacked for its supposedly aristocratic pretensions, and the national society had suggested reforms in the bylaws. As a member of the committee named by the New York chapter to correspond with other state societies, Hamilton drafted comments on some of the proposed alterations in the national charter. One such proposal called for the deletion of a clause that stated that one of the group's fundamental principles was "to promote and cherish between the respective States that Union and national honor so essentially necessary, to their Happiness and the future dignity of the American empire." Hamilton argued vigorously that the passage should be retained.

[New York, November, 1786]

We flatter ourselves, we speak the sense of the Society of which we are members, as well as our own, in declaring, that we reverence the sentiment contained in that clause, too much to be willing to see it expunged. Nor can we believe that its continuance will on reflection, give umbrage to any whose views are not unfriendly to those principles which form the Basis of the Union and the only sure foundation of the tranquility and happiness of this Country. To such men it can never appear criminal, that a class of citizens who have had so conspicuous an Agency in the American Revolution as those who compose the Society of the Cincinnati should pledge themselves to each other, in a voluntary association, to support, by all means consistent with the laws, That noble Fabric of United Independence, which at so much hazard, and with so many sacrifices they have contributed to erect; a Fabric on the Solidity and duration of which the value of all they have done must depend! And America can never have cause to condemn, an Institution, calculated to give energy and extent to a sentiment, favorable to the preservation of that Union, by which she established her liberties, and to which she must owe her future peace, respectability and prosperity. Experience, we doubt not, will teach her, that the members of the Cincinnati, always actuated by the same virtuous and generous motives, which have hitherto directed their conduct, will pride themselves in being, thro every vicissitude of her future fate, the steady and faithful supporters of her Liberty, her Laws and her Government.

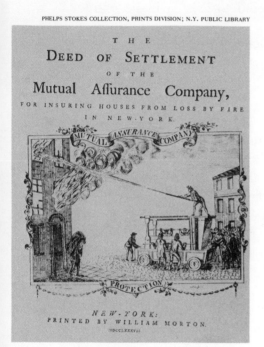

A 1787 deed of settlement of the Mutual Assurance Company, of which Hamilton was an early director

Hamilton had had almost three and a half years of retirement from public life in which to study state and national problems. Now, with the New York Assembly about to reconvene, he faced a test of his ability to adapt to the realities of American politics. If he proved himself in that legislature, he could go on to serve America, "her Liberty, her Laws and her Government," at the coming Constitutional Convention in Philadelphia, where he would need all his skills as a forceful courtroom lawyer to win his case for a strong national government.

Chapter 6

Prelude to Nationhood

When Alexander Hamilton took his seat in the New York Assembly in January, 1787, he was well aware that Governor George Clinton, the leader of the forces that had fought Continental measures after the war, would oppose any future attempt to surrender state power to a national government. A capable and conscientious man, Clinton had been a popular and effective governor since 1777. First and always a state leader rather than a national politician, he cited constitutional reasons for his opposition to a national impost; but clearly, a more important factor was his reluctance to see nationwide taxes deprive the state of its own highly profitable levies.

Conflict between Hamilton and Clinton was inevitable, for the points Hamilton was determined to win in the legislature were diametrically opposed to the views held by the governor. Hamilton hoped, first of all, that the legislature would reconsider the list of qualifications it had attached to its approval of the impost in the spring of 1786—qualifications that could not be accepted by other states. He also intended to do all he could to modify the laws concerning Loyalists. Most important, Hamilton intended to use every opportunity to convince the legislature that the crisis in national affairs demanded that New York participate in the Philadelphia Convention. To achieve his objectives, he shrewdly pictured Clinton as a man who had enjoyed power so long that he was no longer willing to share it, as a man who might even be willing to infringe on the rights of the citizens of his state. In contrast, Hamilton represented himself as the defender of the state constitution, the champion of popular rights. Although his oratory did not persuade the legislature to vote with him in every case, he did win the respect of the legislators and was named a delegate to the convention.

The legislative session opened on January 13, 1787, with the governor's annual message, in which Clinton summarized his reasons for having ignored a congressional request that the legislature be called into special session to reconsider its position on the impost. Hamilton, a member of the committee

159

that was to prepare the assembly's reply, submitted a draft that contained no reference to the governor's action. Clinton's supporters demanded that the assembly express its approval of Clinton's decision. The battle was on. In his first speech in this debate, Hamilton dwelled on the governor's contention that a special session would have impaired "the right of free deliberation on matters not stipulated by the [Articles of] Confederation."

[New York, January 19, 1787]

In particular I think it must strike us all, that there is something singularly forced in intimating, that an application of Congress to the governor of the state to convene a new legislature to consider a very important national subject, has any thing in it dangerous to the freedom of our deliberations. I flatter myself we should all have felt ourselves, as much at liberty to have pursued our sentiments, if we had met upon an extraordinary call, as we now do when met according to our own appointment.

There yet remains an important light, in which the subject merits consideration, I mean as it respects the executive authority of the state itself. By deciding that the application of Congress upon which the debate turns was not such an extraordinary occasion as left the governor at liberty to call the legislature, we may form a precedent of a very dangerous tendency; we may impose a sense on the constitution very different from the true meaning of it—and may fetter the present, or a future executive with very inconvenient restraints. A few more such precedents may tie up the hands of a governor in such a manner, as would either oblige him to act at an extreme peril or to omit acting when public exigencies required it. The mere sense of one governor would be no precedent for his successor, but that sense approved by both houses of the legislature would become a rule of conduct....

[Hamilton then turned to the argument that there was a "danger" in implying that Congress could "compel" state legislatures to convene.]

Admitting in the fullest extent that it would be dangerous to allow to Congress the power of requiring the legislature to be convened at pleasure, yet no injury nor inconvenience can result from supposing the call of the United States on a matter by them deemed of importance to be an occasion sufficiently extraordinary to *authorise*,

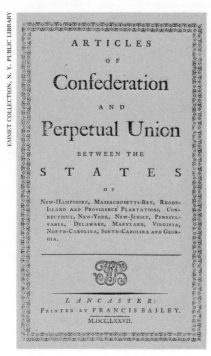

ARTICLES

OF

Confederation

AND

Perpetual Union

BETWEEN THE

STATES

OF

NEW-HAMPSHIRE, MASSACHUSETTS-BAY, RHODE-ISLAND AND PROVIDENCE PLANTATIONS, CONNECTICUT, NEW-YORK, NEW-JERSEY, PENNSYLVANIA, DELAWARE, MARYLAND, VIRGINIA, NORTH-CAROLINA, SOUTH-CAROLINA AND GEORGIA.

LANCASTER:
PRINTED BY FRANCIS BAILEY.
M,DCC,LXXVII.

Title page of the Articles of Confederation, published in 1777

not to *oblige* the governor to comply with it.

I cannot forbear remarking, that it is a common artifice to endeavour to insinuate a resemblance between the king under the former government, and Congress; though no two things can be more unlike each other. Nothing can be more dissimilar than a monarch, permanent, hereditary, the source of honor and emolument; and a republican body composed of a number of individuals appointed annu[a]lly, liable to be recalled within the year, and subject to a continual rotation, which with few exceptions, is the fountain neither of honor nor emolument. If we will exercise our judgments we shall plainly see that no such resemblance exists, and that all inferences deducted from the comparison must be false.

Upon every occasion, however foreign such observations may be, we hear a loud cry raised about the danger of intrusting power to Congress, we are told it is dangerous to trust power any where; that *power* is liable to *abuse* with a variety of trite maxims of the same kind.... To these we might oppose other propositions equally true and equally indefinite. It might be said that too little power is as dangerous as too much, that it leads to anarchy, and from anarchy to despotism. But the question still recurs, what is this *too much or too little?* where is the measure or standard to ascertain the happy mean?

Powers must be granted, or civil Society cannot exist; the possibility of abuse is no argument against the *thing*; this possibility is incident to every species of power however placed or modified.

Governor George Clinton

Samuel Jones of Queens County led the forces demanding praise for Clinton's stand. In his reply to Hamilton's speech, Jones argued that there would be no constitutional issue in the assembly's expressing its approval, and he elaborated on the perils of letting Congress interfere in local government. When Jones concluded, Hamilton rose to make his second speech of the day. After answering the points Jones had raised, Hamilton introduced a new issue—a particularly significant one in view of the call for a national convention.

[New York, January 19, 1787]

Sir, are we not to respect federal decisions; are we on the contrary to take every opportunity of holding up their resolutions and requests in a contemptible and insignificant light, and tell the world, their calls, their requests are nothing to us, that we are bound by none of their measures; do not let us add to their embarrassment, for it is but a slender tie that at present holds us, you see alas what contempt we are falling into since the peace; you see to what our commerce is exposed to on every side. You see us the laughing stock, the sport of foreign nations, and what may this lead to? I dread Sir, to think. Little will it avail then to say, we could not attend to your wise and earnest requests without inconvenience; little will it avail to say it would have hurt individual interest to have left our farms. These things are trifling when compared to bringing the Councils and powers of the Union into universal contempt, by saying their call was unimportant. . . . See, gentlemen, before you feel what may be your situation hereafter. There is more involved in this measure than what presents itself to your view.

The first round of legislative battle went to Clinton when the assembly voted to include a brief commendation in its reply to the governor's message. Hamilton had more success in debates on a bill regulating state elections. A provision was introduced barring any "person receiving a pension from, or holding any office or place under" the national government from holding a seat in the state legislature. In a speech, reported in the *Daily Advertiser*, Hamilton shrewdly presented himself as a defender of the state constitution.

[New York, January 27, 1787]
It is impossible to suppose that the Convention who framed the constitution were inattentive to this point. It is a matter of too much importance not to have been well considered, they have fixed the qualification of electors with precision; they have defined those of Senator and Governor; but they have been silent as to the qualifications of Members of Assembly. It may be said that, being silent, they have left the matter to the discretion of the legislature. But is not the language of the framers of the constitution rather this?—we will fix the qualifications of electors—we will take care that persons absolutely indigent shall be excluded—we will provide that the right of voting shall be on a broad and secure basis—and we will trust to the discretion of the electors themselves the choice of those who are to represent them in assembly. Every qualification implies a disqualification: The persons who do not possess the

qualification required become ineligible. Is not this to restrain the freedom of choice allowed by the constitution to the body of electors?...

By the constitution every citizen is eligible to a seat in the Assembly. If we say certain descriptions of persons shall not be so eligible, what is this but to deprive all those who fall within that description of an essential right allowed them by the constitution?...

[If the legislature of 1787 broke faith with the constitution, Hamilton charged, future legislatures could carry the principle further. Then he turned to specific problems that the bill could cause.]

I have hitherto confined my self to the general principle of the clause. There are however particular objections, one just occurs to me—there are officers who have been wounded in the service, and who now have pensions under the United States as the price of their blood; would it be just, would it not be cruel on this account to exclude men from a share in the administration of that government which they have at every hazard contributed to establish?...

If the committee however should resolve to adopt it; for the sake of consistency, they must carry it one step further—they must say that no member of Congress shall hold a seat. For surely if it be dangerous that the servants of Congress should have a seat in this house, it is more dangerous that the members themselves should be allowed this privilege.

But I would not be understood to advocate this extention of the clause. I am against the whole business. I am for adhering strictly to the present provisions of the constitution, I repeat it if we once break the ground of innovation, we may open a door to mischiefs what we neither know nor think of.

The façade and floor plans of New York's old City Hall on Wall Street, where the state assembly met in 1787

Hamilton carried his point; the clause on Continental pensioners and officeholders was deleted. A day later, he condemned another article in the elections bill, which would have required inspectors to "take aside" illiterate voters "and examine them" concerning their choices on the ballot. This time, Hamilton managed to emerge as the champion of the rights of the uneducated masses.

[New York, January 30, 1787]

It was very justly remarked . . . that the unlettered person from his want of knowing personally the candidates will not when taken aside recollect the names even of them, or at least but a few; in this case the inspector not only may, but must suggest the names to him otherwise how can he vote? What then is the consequence? Certainly if he is a man connected with party, he will vote for his friend, for notwithstanding the inspector may be an honest man, and bound by an oath on this occasion, yet, we know how easy it is for people to interpret such oaths to accommodate themselves, especially when they think they are rendering service to their country, they find a thousand ingenious contrivances, a thousand subterfuges to reconcile it to their preferences.

But . . . it not only is dangerous but it is totally contrary to the very genius and intention of balloting; which means that a man's vote should be secret and known but to himself—yet you not only permit him but even oblige him to discover his vote. . . . this clause is a violation of the right we wish to give ourselves of voting concealed, and it deprives the unlettered person of what his fellow citizen who has it in his power to read, has secured to him. I would wish these persons might be left to themselves, for there would be then less danger than when the influence was regular.

On February 9, an impost bill was reintroduced in the assembly. Fighting for the bill's unconditional acceptance, Hamilton repeated the arguments he had perfected over four years to show that the impost would not infringe on state rights or state constitutions. In the end, he turned to an aspect of the situation that was closest to his heart.

[New York, February 15, 1787]

Let us ask ourselves what will be the consequence of rejecting the bill; what will be the situation of our national affairs if they are left much longer to float in the chaos in which they are now involved.

Can our national character be preserved without paying our debts. Can the union subsist without revenue. Have we realized the consequences which would attend its dissolution.

If these states are not united under a federal government, they will infalliably have wars with each other;

and their divisions will subject them to all the mischiefs of foreign influence and intrigue. The human passions will never want objects of hospitality. The western territory is an obvious and fruitful source of contest. Let us also cast our eye upon the mass of this state, intersected from one extremity to the other by a large navigable river. In the event of a rupture with them, what is to hinder our metropolis from becoming a prey to our neighbours? Is it even supposeable that they would suffer it to remain the nursery of wealth to a distinct community?

These subjects are delicate, but it is necessary to contemplate them to teach us to form a true estimate of our situation.

Wars with each other would beget standing armies — a source of more real danger to our liberties than all the power that could be conferred upon the representatives of the union. And wars with each other would lead to opposite alliances with foreign powers, and plunge us into all the labyrinths of European politics....

The application is easy; if there are any foreign enemies, if there are any domestic foes to this country, all their arts and artifices will be employed to effect a dissolution of the union. This cannot be better done than by sowing jealousies of the federal head and cultivating in each state an undue attachment to its own power.

The New York legislature agreed to grant the impost revenue to Congress, but ruled that while the collectors should be accountable to the Continental government they should be appointed by the state. Hamilton had better luck in fighting for the rights of former Tories, many of whom had since pledged their allegiance to the state and some of whom were now members of the assembly itself. As chairman of a committee named to revise the Trespass Act, Hamilton recommended repeal of the article that prevented a defendant from claiming that he had occupied property under military orders. Hamilton's successful argument of his case was reported in the *Daily Advertiser.*

[New York, March 21, 1787]

[Hamilton said:] The courts of justice were at present in a delicate dilemma, obliged either to explain away a positive law of the state or openly violate the national faith by counteracting the very words and spirit of the treaties now in existance. Because the treaty declares a general amnesty, and this state, by this law, declares that no person shall plead any military order for a trespass committed during the war. He said no state was so much interested in the due observance of the treaty, as the state of New-York; the British having possession of its western frontiers. And which they hold under the sanction of our not having complied with our national engagements. He hoped the house would have too much wisdom, not to do away with this exception; and indeed he expected the bill would be readily agreed to.

Hamilton was as impatient with "local interests" of his own state as he was with those of other states. In March, he attempted to dispose of one of New York's pet projects—the state's claims to the "Hampshire Grants," or what is now the state of Vermont. Although settlers in this region had effectively asserted their independence in the first years of the Revolution, New Yorkers still dreamed of reasserting authority over the area. Hamilton introduced a bill to recognize Vermont's independence and argued for a more realistic policy.

[New York, March 14, 1787]
I believe there is not a member of this house but considers the independence of the district [or] territory in question as a matter fixed and inevitable, all our efforts to a different point have hitherto proved fruitless, and it is long since we seem to have entirely given up the controversy. Vermont is in fact *independent,* but she is not *confederated.* And I am constrained to add that the means which they employ to secure that independence, are objects of the utmost alarm to the safety of this state, and to the confederation at large. Are they not wisely inviting and encouraging settlers by an exemption from taxes, and availing themselves of the discontents of a neighbouring state, by turning it to the aggrandizement of their own power.

Is it not natural to suppose, that a powerful people both by numbers and situation; unconnected as they now stand, and without any relative importance in the union. Irritated by neglect, or stimulated by revenge, I say, is it not probable under such circumstances they will provide for their own safety, by seeking connections elsewhere? And who that hears me doubts, but that these connections have *already* been formed with the British in Canada.... Whatever may be the present temper of that people, it is easy to foresee what it will become under

John Lansing

the influence of their leaders. Confederated with a foreign nation, we can be at no loss to anticipate the consequences of such a connection, nor the dangers to this country. . . . In their present situation they bear no part of our public burdens; if they were a part of the confederacy they must of course participate in them. They are useless to us now, and if they continue as they are, they will be formidable to us hereafter.

Congress had followed the advice of the Annapolis Convention and called on the states to select delegates to meet in Philadelphia in May. Hamilton persuaded the assembly to send a five-man delegation to the convention, but the senate, which had voted down his Vermont bill, refused to send more than three delegates to Philadelphia. A larger delegation could have included some of New York's distinguished nationalists; as it was, the legislature sent Hamilton, John Lansing, and Robert Yates—the last two, good Clintonians. In the last week of the session, Hamilton made a final stand for another factor in the national character when the assembly considered Congress's request that the states pass blanket repeals of all acts "repugnant to the treaty of peace." As in other instances, the assembly followed Hamilton's lead, but the senate ignored the ideas he presented. Hamilton's speech was reported in the *Daily Advertiser.*

[New York, April 17, 1787]

He urged the committee to consent to the passing of the bill, from the consideration, that the state of New-York was the only state to gain any thing by a strict adherence to the treaty. There was no other state in the union that had so much to expect from it. . . . With respect to the bill as it was drafted in conformity to the recommendation of Congress; he viewed it as a wise, and a salutary measure; one calculated to meet the approbation of the different states, and most likely to answer the end proposed. Were it possible to examine an intricate maze of laws, and to determine which of them, or what parts of laws were opposed to the treaty, it still might not have the intended effect, as different parties would have the judging of this matter. What one should say was a law not inconsistent with the peace, another might say was so, and there would be no end, no decision of the business. Even some of the states might view laws in a different manner. The only way to comply with the treaty, was to make a general and unexceptionable repeal. . . . He thought it must be obvious to every member of the com-

*A view of Philadelphia in 1777, as
seen from across the Delaware River*

mittee, that as there was no law in direct opposition to the treaty, no difficulty could arise from passing the bill. . . . He declared that the full operation of the bill, would be no more than merely to declare the treaty the law of the land. And that the judges viewing it as such, shall do away [with] all laws that may appear in direct contravention of it. Treaties were known constitutionally, to be the law of the land, and why be afraid to leave the interpretation of those laws, to the judges; the constitution knows them as the interpreters of the law. He asked if there was any member of the committee that would be willing to see the first treaty of peace ever made by this country violated. This he did not believe, he could not think that any member on that floor harboured such sentiments.

When the legislature voted to hold its next session in Poughkeepsie, Hamilton announced that he would not be a candidate for reelection. If he was reluctant to ride up the Hudson to serve New York, he was quite ready to travel to Philadelphia to serve America. On May 18, he and Yates took their seats at the convention; two weeks later they were joined by John Lansing. In the Philadelphia State House, Hamilton renewed acquaintance with old friends and fellow warriors in the nationalist cause—George Washington, James Madison, Robert and Gouverneur Morris. After Washington was named presiding officer, the convention considered the "Virginia Plan" of government—a plan that provided for a national legislature with representation based on population and an executive and judiciary chosen by the legislators. New Jersey, speaking for the smaller states, presented a series of amendments to the Confederation that would have remedied specific flaws in the old Articles, but would not change the basis of equal representation for all states in the Congress.

Hamilton, who did not agree with either plan, gave the convention his own views in a marathon five-hour speech. Although Hamilton's arguments and the "Plan of Government" that he introduced were not especially influential or persuasive, the speech is historically significant in that it gives the most "correct view" of the form of government that Hamilton felt would be best for America. James Madison recorded Hamilton's oration and afterward, realizing its historical importance, asked Hamilton to check the notes he had taken, to insure their accuracy. As recorded by Madison, Hamilton began by outlining with almost brutal frankness his views of the Confederation in America and of loose confederations in general.

[June 18, 1787]

He was particularly opposed to that [plan] from N. Jersey,

In the engraving above, Washington presides over the Constitutional Convention; below, a plan of the meeting hall, credited to Trumbull.

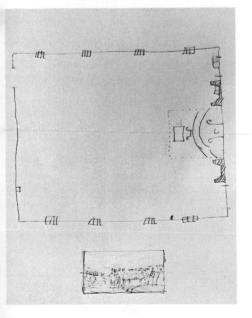

being fully convinced, that no amendment of the Confederation, leaving the States in possession of their Sovereignty could possibly answer the purpose. On the other hand he confessed he was much discouraged by the amazing extent of Country in expecting the desired blessings from any general sovereignty that could be substituted. As to the powers of the Convention, he thought the doubts started on that subject had arisen from distinctions & reasonings too subtle. A *federal* Gov[ernmen]t. he conceived to mean an association of independent Communities into one. Different Confederacies have different powers, and exercise them in different ways. In some instances the powers are exercised over collective bodies; in others over individuals.... Great latitude therefore must be given to the signification of the term.... He agreed moreover ... that we owed it to our Country, to do on this emergency whatever we should deem essential to its happiness. The States sent us here to provide for the exigences of the Union. To rely on & propose any plan not adequate to these exigences, merely because it was not clearly within our powers, would be to sacrifice the means to the end. It may be said that the *States* can not *ratify* a plan not within the purview of the article of Confederation providing for alterations & amendments. But may not the States themselves in which no constitutional authority equal to this purpose exists in the Legislatures, have had in view a reference to the people at large....

[Hamilton asserted that the "great question" for the convention was, "What provision shall we make for the happiness of our Country?" Both the Virginia and New Jersey plans, he declared, had serious flaws and did not meet the basic needs of the nation.]

The great & essential principles necessary for the support of Government are 1. an active & constant interest in supporting it. This principle does not exist in the States in favor of the federal Govt.... They constantly pursue internal interests adverse to those of the whole.... All these when opposed to; invariably prevail over the requisitions & plans of Congress. 2. The love of power. Men love power. The same remarks are applicable to this principle. The States have constantly shewn a disposition rather to regain the powers delegated by them than to part with more, or to give effect to what they had parted with. The ambition of their demagogues is known to hate the controul of the Genl. Government....3. An habitual attachment of the people. The whole force of this tie is on the side of the State Govt. Its sovereignty is immediately before the eyes of the people; its protection is immediately enjoyed by them. From its hand... all those acts which familiarize & endear Govt. to a people, are dispensed to them. 4. *Force* by which may be understood a *coertion of laws* or *coertion of arms.* Cong[res]s. have not the former except in few cases. In particular States, this coercion is nearly sufficient; tho'...in most cases, not entirely so. A certain portion of military force is absolutely necessary in large communities....But how can this force be exerted on the States collectively. It is impossible. It amounts to a war between the parties. Foreign powers also will not be idle spectators....5. *influence.* he did not mean corruption, but a dispensation of those regular honors & emoluments, which produce an attachment to the Govt. Almost all the weight of these is on the side of the States; and must continue so as long as the States continue to exist. All the passions then we see, of avarice, ambition, interest, which govern most individuals, and all public bodies, fall into the current of the States, and do not flow in the stream of the Genl. Govt. The former therefore will generally be an overmatch for the Genl. Govt. and render any confederacy, in its very nature precarious.

Continuing his oration, Hamilton presented historical examples of the failure of confederacies, closely analyzed the British system of government, and discoursed on the nature of executive power. He then offered his colleagues his plan for an American government. His draft of that plan has survived and is printed here in full. Hamilton's ideal, however, was far removed from the practical compromises that the convention worked into the Constitution of 1787.

[Philadelphia, June 18, 1787]

I   The Supreme Legislative Power of the United States of America to be vested in two distinct bodies of men— the one to be called the *Assembly* the other the *senate*; who together shall form the Legislature of the United States, with power to pass all *laws whatsoever,* subject

Hamilton's notes for his speech
proposing a plan of government

to the *negative* hereafter mentioned.

II   The Assembly to consist of persons elected *by the People* to serve for three years.

III   The Senate to consist of persons elected to serve during *good behaviour*. Their election to be made by *Electors* chosen for that purpose by the People. In order to this The States to be divided into election districts. On the death removal or resignation of any senator his place to be filled out of the district from which he came.

IV   The Supreme Executive authority of the United States to be vested in a *governor* to be elected to serve *during good behaviour*. His election to be made by *Electors* chosen by *electors* chosen by the people in the election districts aforesaid or by electors chosen for that purpose by the respective legislatures—provided that [if] an election be not made within a limited time the President of the Senate shall...be the Governor. The Governor to have *a negative* upon all laws about to be passed and to have the execution of all laws passed—to be the Commander in Chief of the land and naval forces and of the Militia of the United States—to have the direction of war, when authorised or began—to have with the *advice* and *approbation* of the Senate the power of making all treaties—to have the appointment of the *heads or chief* officers of the departments of finance war and foreign affairs—to have the *nomination* of all other officers (ambassadors to foreign nations included) subject to the approbation or rejection of the Senate—to have the power of pardoning all offences but *treason*, which he shall not pardon without the approbation of the Senate.

V   On the death resignation or removal of the Governor his authorities to be exercised by the President of the Senate.

VI   The Senate to have the sole power of *declaring war*—the power of advising and approving all treaties—the power of approving or rejecting all appointments of officers except the heads or chiefs of the departments of finance war and foreign affairs.

VII   The Supreme Judicial authority of the United States to be vested in twelve Judges, to hold their offices during good behaviour with adequate and permanent salaries. This Court to have original jurisdiction in all causes of capture and an appellative jurisdiction (from the Courts of the several states) in all causes in which the revenues of the general government or the citizens of foreign nations are concerned.

VIII The Legislature of the United States to have power to institute Courts in each state for the determination of all causes of capture and of all matters relating to their revenues, or in which the citizens of foreign nations are concerned.

IX The Governor Senators and all Officers of the United States to be liable to impeachment for mal and corrupt conduct, and upon conviction to be removed from office and disqualified for holding any place of trust or profit. All impeachments to be tried by a Court to consist of the judges of the Supreme Court chief or Senior Judge of the superior Court of law of each state — provided that such judge hold his place during good behaviour and have a permanent salary.

X All laws of the particular states contrary to the constitution or laws of the United States to be utterly void. And the better to prevent such laws being passed the Governor or President of each state shall *be appointed by the general government* and shall have a *negative* upon the laws about to be passed in the state of which he is governor or President.

XI No state to have any forces land or naval — and the *Militia* of all the states to be under the sole and *exclusive direction* of the United States *the officers* of which to be appointed and commissioned by them.

William Paterson, who proposed the "New Jersey Plan" of government on behalf of the smaller states

After reading his Plan of Government to the delegates, Hamilton concluded with these remarks, which were jotted down by his colleague Robert Yates.

[Philadelphia, June 18, 1787]

I confess that this plan and that from Virginia are very remote from the idea of the people. Perhaps the Jersey plan is nearest their expectation. But the people are gradually ripening in their opinions of government — they begin to be tired of an excess of democracy — and

*what even is the Virginia plan, but pork still, with a
little change of the sauce.*

Although the delegates chose to use the Virginia Plan
rather than Hamilton's as the basis for their debates, they did not forget
what he had proposed on June 18. "Small-state" men were especially
alarmed by his remarks. As the members of the convention discussed the
proposition that "a National Government ought to be established," Madison
recorded Hamilton's attempts to placate these representatives.

[Philadelphia, June 19, 1787]

[Hamilton] took this occasion of observing for the
purpose of appeasing the fears of the small States, that
two circumstances would render them secure under a
National Govt. in which they might lose the equality
of rank they now held: one was the local situation of the
3 largest States Virga. Masts. & Pa. They were separated
from each other by distance of place, and equally so, by
all the peculiarities which distinguish the interests of
one State from those of another. No combination therefore could be dreaded. In the second place, as there was
a gradation in the States from Va. the largest down to
Delaware the smallest, it would always happen that ambitious combinations among a few States might &
w[oul]d. be counteracted by defensive combinations of
greater extent among the rest. No combination has been
seen among large Counties merely as such, ag[ain]st.
lesser Counties. The more close the Union of the States,
and the more compleat the authority of the whole: the
less opportunity will be allowed the stronger States to
injure the weaker.

*Edmund Randolph, who put forward
the "Virginia Plan" of government*

As the convention began to consider the upper house
of the new Congress, Hamilton realized that his proposal for a Senate with
life terms would not be accepted, but he joined James Madison in arguing
for as long a term for Senators as possible. Again, the notes on the debate
are Madison's.

[Philadelphia, June 26, 1787]

He [Hamilton] concurred with Mr. Madison in thinking
we were now to decide for ever the fate of Republican
Government; and that if we did not give to that form
due stability and wisdom, it would be disgraced & lost
among ourselves, disgraced & lost to mankind for ever.

He acknowledged himself not to think favorably of Republican Government; but addressed his remarks to those who did think favorably of it, in order to prevail on them to tone their Government as high as possible. He professed himself to be as zealous an advocate for liberty as any man whatever, and trusted he should be as willing a martyr to it though he differed as to the form in which it was most eligible.

The hardest problem to be solved, however, was not the length of the Senators' terms, but the basis on which Senate seats would be distributed. The Virginia Plan proposed that seats in both houses be assigned in proportion to population; smaller states demanded protection for state interests in at least one part of the national legislature. Hamilton spoke on behalf of a Senate with a "popular" base, not equal representation for all states. Madison recorded his remarks.

[Philadelphia, June 29, 1787]

...as States are a collection of individual men which ought we to respect most, the rights of the people composing them, or of the artificial beings resulting from the composition. Nothing could be more preposterous or absurd than to sacrifice the former to the latter. It has been s[ai]d. that if the smaller States renounce their *equality*, they renounce at the same time their *liberty*. The truth is it is a contest for power, not for liberty. Will the men composing the small States be less free than those composing the larger. The State of Delaware having 40,000 souls will *lose power*, if she has 1/10 only of the votes allowed to Pa. having 400,000: but will the people of Del: *be less free*, if each citizen has an equal vote with each citizen of Pa....

[Hamilton warned that this was a "critical moment" that demanded all the wisdom the delegates possessed.]

It had been said that respectability in the eyes of foreign Nations was not the object at which we aimed; that the proper object of republican Government was domestic tranquility & happiness. This was an ideal distinction. No Governmt. could give us tranquility & happiness at home, which did not possess sufficient stability and strength to make us respectable abroad. This was the critical moment for forming such a Government. We

A view of Philadelphia's New Market

should run every risk in trusting to future amendments. As yet we retain the habits of union. We are weak & sensible of our weakness. Henceforward the motives will become feebler, and the difficulties greater. It is a miracle that we were now here exercising our tranquil & free deliberations on the subject. It would be madness to trust to future miracles. A thousand causes must obstruct a reproduction of them.

Later that day, Hamilton left the convention to return to his business affairs in New York. Although his own ideas on government had met a cool reception, he had not lost interest in the proceedings in Philadelphia, as he made clear in a letter to George Washington.

[New York, July 3, 1787]

In my passage through the Jerseys and since my arrival here I have taken particular pains to discover the public sentiment and I am more and more convinced that this is the critical opportunity for establishing the prosperity of this country on a solid foundation. I have conversed with men of information not only of this City but from different parts of the state; and they agree that there has been an astonishing revolution for the better in the minds of the people. The prevailing apprehension among thinking men is that the Convention, from a fear of shocking the popular opinion, will not go far enough. They seem to be convinced that a strong well mounted government will better suit the popular palate than one of a different complexion. Men in office are indeed taking all possible pains to give an unfavourable impression of the Convention; but the current seems to be running strongly the other way.

A plain but sensible man, in a conversation I had with him yesterday, expressed himself nearly in this manner. The people begin to be convinced that their "excellent form of government" as they have been used to call it, will not answer their purpose; and that they must substitute something not very remote from that which they have lately quitted.

These appearances though they will not warrant a conclusion that the people are yet ripe for such a plan as I advocate, yet serve to prove that there is no reason to despair of their adopting one equally energetic, if the Convention should think proper to propose it. They serve to prove that we ought not to allow too much weight to objections drawn from the supposed repugnancy of the people to an efficient constitution. . . .

Not having compared ideas with you, Sir, I cannot judge how far our sentiments agree; but . . . my anxiety for the event of the deliberations of the Convention induces me to make this communication of what appears to be the tendency of the public mind. I own to you Sir that I am seriously and deeply distressed at the aspect of the Councils which prevailed when I left Philadelphia. I fear that we shall let slip the golden opportunity of rescuing the American empire from disunion anarchy and misery. No motley or feeble measure can answer the end or will finally receive the public support. Decision is true wisdom and will be not less reputable to the Convention than salutary to the community.

Having spent the summer looking after his law practice, Hamilton returned to Philadelphia in the first week of September to find that most of the questions concerning the new plan of government had been settled. One major problem remained—the election of the President. The Committee of Detail, appointed in July, had suggested a Chief Executive chosen by the national legislature for a seven-year term. Another committee, appointed September 4, proposed that he be named instead by electors chosen in each state. Hamilton's presentation of his own view was recorded by Madison.

[Philadelphia, September 6, 1787]
Mr. HAMILTON said that he had been restrained from entering into the discussions by his dislike of the Scheme of Govt. in General; but as he meant to support the plan to be recommended, as better than nothing, he wished in this place to offer a few remarks. He liked the new modification, on the whole, better than that in the printed Report [made by the Committee of Detail]. In this the President was a Monster elected for seven years, and ineligible afterwards; having great powers, in appointments to office, & continually tempted by this constitutional disqualification to abuse them in order to subvert the Government. Although he should be made re-eligible, still if appointed by the Legislature, he would be tempted to make use of corrupt influence to be continued in office. It seemed peculiarly desireable therefore that some other mode of election should be devised. Con-

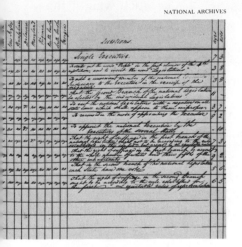

*A voting record kept during
the Constitutional Convention*

sidering the different views of different States, & the different districts Northern Middle & Southern, he concurred with those who thought that the votes would not be concentered, and that the appointment would consequently in the present mode devolve on the Senate. The nomination to offices will give great weight to the President. Here then is a mutual connection & influence, that will perpetuate the President, and aggrandize both him & the Senate. What is to be the remedy? He saw none better than to let the highest number of ballots, whether a majority or not, appoint the President. What was the objection to this? Merely that too small a number might appoint. But as the plan stands, the Senate may take the candidate having the smallest number of votes, and make him President.

The convention agreed with Hamilton that this modification—the basis of the Electoral College—was preferable. On September 10, Elbridge Gerry of Massachusetts suggested a change in the article concerning future amendments to the Constitution. As it stood, amendments could come only when two thirds of the states applied to Congress, and Gerry feared that a majority of the states might make alterations "that may subvert the State-Constitutions altogether." Hamilton seconded Gerry's motion, but explained that he did so for quite different reasons.

[Philadelphia, September 10, 1787]

It had been wished by many and was much to have been desired that an easier mode for introducing amendments had been provided by the articles of Confederation It was equally desireable now that an easy mode should be established for supplying defects which will probably appear in the New System The mode proposed was not adequate. The State Legislatures will not apply for alterations but with a view to increase their own powers. The National Legislature will be the first to perceive and will be the most sensible to the necessity of amendments, and ought also to be empowered, whenever two thirds of each branch should concur to call a Convention. There could be no danger in giving this power, as the people would finally decide in the case.

After the delegates agreed to the articles of the new Constitution, problems of protocol still remained. There was, of course,

177

the delicate question of the manner in which the Constitution should be ratified. When Elbridge Gerry demanded that Congress be given the opportunity to pass on the Constitution, Hamilton supported him. For the second time on September 10, Hamilton spoke on behalf of one of Gerry's motions, but again for very different reasons from those that had motivated the Massachusetts delegate.

Elbridge Gerry of Massachusetts

[Philadelphia, September 10, 1787]

Mr. HAMILTON concurred with Mr. Gerry as to the indecorum of not requiring the approbation of Congress. He considered this as a necessary ingredient in the transaction. He thought it wrong also to allow nine States . . . to institute a new Government on the ruins of the existing one. He wd. propose as a better modification . . . that the plan should be sent to Congress in order that the same if approved by them, may be communicated to the State Legislatures, to the end that they may refer it to State Conventions; each Legislature declaring that if the Convention of the State should think the plan ought to take effect among nine ratifying States, the same shd. take effect accordingly.

By September 17, the last day of the convention, many of the delegates had already left Philadelphia. Some who had remained were so bitterly opposed to the Constitution that had been approved that they refused to add their signatures to the document. Hamilton presented his arguments in favor of signing.

[Philadelphia, September 17, 1787]

Mr. HAMILTON expressed his anxiety that every member should sign. A few characters of consequence, by opposing or even refusing to sign the Constitution, might do infinite mischief by kindling the latent sparks which lurk under an enthusiasm in favor of the Convention which may soon subside. No man's ideas were more remote from the plan than his were known to be; but is it possible to deliberate between anarchy and Convulsion on one side, and the chance of good to be expected from the plan on the other.

In the two weeks following the convention's adjournment, Hamilton jotted down some "Conjectures about the New Constitution," in which he weighed the chances for ratification of the document by the various states.

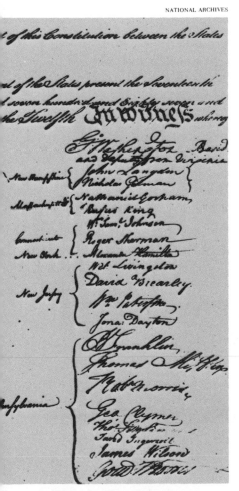

Hamilton was the only New York delegate to sign the Constitution.

[September 17–30, 1787]

The new constitution has in favour of its success these circumstances—a very great weight of influence of the persons who framed it, particularly in the universal popularity of General Washington—the good will of the commercial interest throughout the states which will give all its efforts to the establishment of a government capable of regulating protecting and extending the commerce of the Union—the good will of most men of property in the several states who wish a government of the union able to protect them against domestic violence and the depredations which the democratic spirit is apt to make on property; and who are besides anxious for the respectability of the nation—the hopes of the Creditors of the United States that a general government possessing the means of doing it will pay the debt of the Union—a strong belief in the people at large of the insufficiency of the present confederation to preserve the existence of the Union and of the necessity of the union to their safety and prosperity; of course a strong desire of a change and a predisposition to receive well the propositions of the Convention....

But the causes operating against its adoption are powerful and there will be nothing astonishing in the Contrary.

If it do not finally obtain, it is probable the discussion of the question will beget such struggles animosities and heats in the community that this circumstance conspiring with the *real necessity* of an essential change in our present situation will produce civil war. Should this happen, whatever parties prevail it is probable governments very different from the present in their principles will be established. A dismemberment of the Union and monarchies in different portions of it may be expected. It may however happen that no civil war will take place; but several republican confederacies be established between different combinations of the particular states....

If the government be adopted, it is probable general Washington will be the President of the United States. This will insure a wise choice of men to administer the government and a good administration. A good administration will conciliate the confidence and affection of the people and perhaps enable the government to acquire more consistency than the proposed constitution seems to promise for so great a Country. It may then triumph altogether over the state governments and reduce them to an intire subordination, dividing the larger states into smaller districts....

If this should not be the case, in the course of a few years, it is probable that the contests about the boundaries of power between the particular governments and the general government and the *momentum* of the larger states in such contests will produce a dissolution of the Union. This after all seems to be the most likely result.

But it is almost arrogance in so complicated a subject, depending so intirely on the incalculable fluctuations of the human passions, to attempt even a conjecture about the event.

There was one element in the battle for ratification that was not subject to "conjecture"—the bitter opposition of Governor George Clinton of New York. In July, after having left Philadelphia, Hamilton learned that Clinton had "in public company" criticized the convening of the Constitutional Convention and declared that "the result of their deliberations, whatever it might be, would only serve to throw the community into confusion." In an anonymous letter published in the *Daily Advertiser*, Hamilton offered the governor "the following reflections."

[New York, July 21, 1787]

First. That from the almost universal concurrence of the states in the measure of appointing a Convention, and from the powers given to their Deputies... it appears clearly to be the general sense of America, that the present confederation *is not* "equal to the purposes of the union," but requires material alterations.

Secondly. That the concurrence of the legislatures of twelve out of the thirteen states... in a measure of so extraordinary a complexion, the direct object of which is the abridgement of their own power, in favor of a general government, is of itself a strong presumptive proof that there exist real evils; and that these evils are of so extensive and cogent a nature, as to have been capable of giving an impulse from one extremity of the United States to the other....

[Hamilton then went on to itemize these "evils," which had crippled the American economy and degraded "our national character and consequence" to such an extent that "the very existence of the union is in imminent danger." He closed with a personal attack on Clinton.]

The residence of Governor Clinton on Pearl Street in lower Manhattan

Eighthly. That however justifiable it might be in the governor to oppose the appointment of a convention, if the measure were still under deliberation; and if he sincerely believed it to be a pernicious one, yet the general voice of America having decided in its favor, it is *unwarrantable* and *culpable in any man*, in so serious a posture of our national affairs, to endeavour to prepossess the public mind against the hitherto undetermined and unknown measures of a body to whose councils America has, in a great measure, entrusted its future fate, and to whom the people in general look up, under the blessing of heaven, for their political salvation.

Ninthly. That such conduct in a man high in office, argues greater attachment to his *own power* than to the *public good*, and furnishes strong reason to suspect a dangerous predetermination to oppose whatever may tend to diminish the *former*, however it may promote the *latter*.

If there be any man among us, who acts so unworthy a part, it becomes a free and enlightened people to observe him with a jealous eye, and when he sounds the alarm of danger from another quarter, to examine whether they have not more to apprehend from *himself*.

After Hamilton returned to his duties in Philadelphia, "A Republican" replied to his charges against Clinton. The *Daily Advertiser* carried Hamilton's rebuttal, in which he disputed the claim that printing Clinton's remarks was "calculated to produce the evil pretended to be guarded against."

[New York, September 15, 1787]

If his Excellency was predetermined to oppose the measures of the Convention, as his conduct indicates, he would take care himself to propagate his sentiments, in the manner in which it could be done with the most effect. This appears to have been his practice. It was therefore proper that the antidote should go along with the poison; and that the community should be apprised, that he was capable of forming such a predetermination, before, it can be presumed, he had any knowlege of the measures themselves, on which to found his judgment.

181

A cry is attempted to be raised against the publication . . . as if it were an invasion of the right of the first Magistrate of the State to deliver his sentiments on a matter of public concern. The fallacy of this artifice will easily be detected. The Governor has an undoubted right to give his sentiments freely on every public measure. . . . But every *right* may be abused by a *wrong exercise* of it. . . . The only question then is, whether he has in the present instance used his right properly, or improperly—whether it became him, by *anticipation*, to endeavour to prejudice the community against the "unknown and undetermined" measures of a body, to which the general voice of the union had delegated the important trust of concerting and proposing a plan for reforming the national constitution? Let every man answer this question to himself.

The apologists for the Governor, in the intemperate ardor of their zeal for his character, seem to forget another *right*, very precious to the citizens of a free country, *that* of examing the conduct of their rulers. . . .

But, observations of either kind might mutually have been spared. There is no danger that the rights of a man, at the head of the Government (possessing all the influence to be derived from long continuance in office, the disposition of lucrative places, and *consummate talents* for popularity) can be injured by the voice of a private individual. There is as little danger, that the spirit of the people of this State will ever tolerate attempts to seduce, to awe, or to clamor them out of the privilege of bringing the conduct of men in power to the bar of public examination.

Hamilton's public career in the first nine months of 1787 ended, as it had begun, with an attack upon George Clinton. By September of that year Hamilton had already begun concentrating his energies on winning the ratification of the Federal Constitution—an issue that would cause statewide differences, that would lead to the creation of rival political organizations, and that would influence the course of state and national history for years to come. The time had come for Hamilton the Continentalist to become Hamilton the Federalist.

Chapter 7

The Federalist

O f all the compromises involved in the creation of the Constitution, few were as remarkable as Alexander Hamilton's bargain with his own principles. Although "no man's ideas were more remote from the plan" than his, no man worked harder to see that the plan succeeded. Since the Constitution would not take effect until two thirds of the states had ratified it, Hamilton and his allies had to fight for the Federalist cause on several fronts.

Their first victory came in appropriating the name Federalist. Originally, the term had been applied to defenders of the Articles of Confederation, but it was now being used by those who sought to replace the "federal" form of government with the "national" regime promised under the new Constitution. Supporters of the federal plan, who opposed the Constitution, complained that they were unfairly labeled Antifederalists. They could do nothing but grumble, however, for Hamilton had laid his party's claim to the Federalist title in the public press. *The Federalist* papers, a series of more than eighty essays produced between October 27, 1787, and May 28, 1788, presented the definitive defense of the new Constitution and the political theories of its supporters. Signed "Publius," the essays were written in collaboration first with John Jay and later with James Madison, but since Hamilton himself produced two thirds of these articles, as well as arranging for their publication and distribution, he had time for little else in the eight months following the Philadelphia Convention.

During these first months after the Constitution was submitted to the states, Hamilton's words were primarily written for or spoken to the public. Few of the documents that appear in this chapter are reprinted from manuscripts in Hamilton's own hand. His drafts of *The Federalist* essays have vanished, and only rough outlines of his speeches have survived. Historians must rely on printed versions of the "Publius" articles and on newspaper reports and other records of his orations. What little private correspondence

Hamilton engaged in at this time also deals primarily with the increasingly bitter dispute over ratification. Particularly troublesome was the whispered campaign launched against him by the Clintonians. By October, 1787, the attack had become so harsh that Hamilton turned to Washington for aid.

[New York, October 11–15, 1787]

Among many contemptible artifices practiced by them, they have had recourse to an insinuation that I *palmed* myself upon you and that you *dismissed* me from your family. This I confess hurts my feelings, and if it obtains credit, will require a contradiction.

You... know how destitute of foundation such insinuations are. My confidence in your justice will not permit me to doubt your readiness to put the matter in its true light in your answer to this letter....

The New Constitution is as popular in this City as it is possible for any thing to be—and the prospect thus far is favourable to it throughout the state. But there is no saying what turn things may take when the flood of official influence is let loose against it. This is to be expected, for though the Governor has not publicly declared himself his particular connections and confidential friends are loud against it.

Washington replied promptly, asserting that both charges were "entirely unfounded," but he also expressed his "unfeigned concern" over the bitter division between Hamilton and Clinton. When Hamilton answered Washington, he did not raise the point again.

[New York, October 30, 1787]

I am much obliged to Your Excellency for the explicit manner in which you contradict the insinuations mentioned in my last letter. The only use I shall make of your answer will be to put it into the hands of a few friends.

The constitution proposed has in this state warm friends and warm enemies. The first impressions every where are in its favour; but the artillery of its opponents makes some impression. The event cannot yet be foreseen. The inclosed is the first number of a series of papers to be written in its defence.

The paper sent to Washington was the first of *The Federalist* essays. On Saturday, October 27, readers of New York's *Inde-*

pendent Journal: or, the General Advertiser were introduced to "Publius," whose object was to persuade voters to elect Federalist (that is, pro-Constitution) delegates to the state's ratifying convention.

[New York, October 27, 1787]

To the People of the State of New York.

AFTER an unequivocal experience of the inefficacy of the subsisting Fœderal Government, you are called upon to deliberate on a new Constitution for the United States of America. The subject speaks its own importance; comprehending in its consequences, nothing less than the existence of the UNION, the safety and welfare of the parts of which it is composed, the fate of an empire, in many respects, the most interesting the world. It has been frequently remarked, that it seems to have been reserved to the people of this country, by their conduct and example, to decide the important question, whether societies of men are really capable or not, of establishing good government from ref[l]ection and choice, or whether they are forever destined to depend, for their political constitutions, on accident and force. If there be any truth in the remark, the crisis, at which we are arrived, may with propriety be regarded as the æra in which that decision is to be made; and a wrong election of the part we shall act, may, in this view, deserve to be considered as the general misfortune of mankind....

...My Countrymen, I own to you, that, after having given it an attentive consideration, I am clearly of opinion, it is your interest to adopt [the new Constitution]. I am convinced, that this is the safest course for your liberty, your dignity, and your happiness....I will not amuse you with an appearance of deliberation, when I have decided. I frankly acknowledge to you my convictions, and I will freely lay before you the reasons on which they are founded....

I propose in a series of papers to discuss the following interesting particulars—*The utility of the* UNION *to your political prosperity*—*The insufficiency of the present Confederation to preserve that Union*—*The necessity of a government at least equally energetic with the one proposed to the attainment of this object*—*The conformity of the proposed constitution to the true principles of republican government*—*Its analogy to your own state constitution*—*and lastly, The additional security, which*

The Independent Journal *was one of the New York papers in which* The Federalist *essays first appeared.*

its adoption will afford to the preservation of that species of government, to liberty and to property.

The extent of Hamilton's contributions to *The Federalist* makes it impossible to include even a representative sampling of these essays. A substantial portion of *No. 13*, however, the shortest of Hamilton's pieces, is reprinted here to give an idea of their content and style. In this article, Publius was still concerned with "the utility of the UNION," this time in matters of "œconomy."

[New York, November 28, 1787]

If the States are united under one government, there will be but one national civil list to support; if they are divided into several confederacies, there will be as many different national civil lists to be provided for.... The entire separation of the States into thirteen unconnected sovereignties is a project too extravagant and too replete with danger to have many advocates. The ideas of men who speculate upon the dismemberment of the empire, seem generally turned towards three confederacies; one consisting of the four northern, another of the four middle, and a third of the five southern States. There is little probability that there would be a greater number. According to this distribution each confederacy would comprise an extent of territory larger than that of the kingdom of Great-Britain. No well informed man will suppose that the affairs of such a confederacy can be properly regulated by a government, less comprehensive in its organs or institutions, than that, which has been proposed by the Convention. When the dimensions of a State attain to a certain magnitude, it requires the same energy of government and the same terms of administration; which are requisite in one of much greater extent. This idea admits not of precise demonstration, because there is no rule by which we can measure the momentum of civil power, necessary to the government of any given number of individuals; but when we consider that the island of Britain, nearly commensurate with each of the supposed confederacies, contains about eight millions of people, and when we reflect upon the degree of authority required to direct the passions of so large a society to the public good, we shall see no reason to doubt that the like portion of power would be sufficient to perform the same task in

Hamilton's bookplate

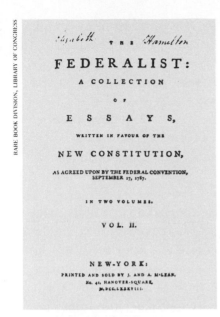

Elizabeth THE *Hamilton*

FEDERALIST:

A COLLECTION

OF

E S S A Y S,

WRITTEN IN FAVOUR OF THE

NEW CONSTITUTION,

AS AGREED UPON BY THE FEDERAL CONVENTION,
SEPTEMBER 17, 1787.

IN TWO VOLUMES.

VOL. II.

NEW-YORK:

PRINTED AND SOLD BY J. AND A. M·LEAN,
No. 41, HANOVER-SQUARE,
M,DCC,LXXXVIII.

*The title page of Volume II
of* The Federalist *papers, bearing
the name of Elizabeth Hamilton*

a society far more numerous. Civil power properly organised and exerted is capable of diffusing its force to a very great extent; and can in a manner reproduce itself in every part of a great empire by a judicious arrangement of subordinate institutions. . . .

If in addition to the consideration of a plurality of civil lists, we take into view the number of persons who must necessarily be employed to guard the inland communication, between the different confederacies, against illicit trade, and who in time will infallibly spring up out of the necessities of revenue; and if we also take into view the military establishments, which it has been shewn would unavoidably result from the jealousies and conflicts of the several nations, into which the States would be divided, we shall clearly discover, that a separation would be not less injurious to the œconomy than to the tranquillity, commerce, revenue and liberty of every part.

PUBLIUS

By April, 1788, six states had ratified the Constitution. James Madison had departed from New York in March to prepare for his work in the Virginia Convention, leaving Hamilton to supervise the publication of the remaining *Federalist* essays. There were some difficulties in literary collaboration by mail, as this letter to Madison shows.

[New York, April 3, 1788]

I think . . . the principles we have talked of, in respect to the legislative authorities, are not only just but will apply to the other departments. Nor will the consequences appear so disagreeable, as they may seem at first sight, when we attend to the true import of the rule established. The states *retain* all the authorities they were *before* possessed of, not alienated in the three modes pointed out; but this does not include cases which are the *creatures* of the New Constitution. For instance, the crime of treason against the United States *immediately*, is a crime known only to the New Constitution. There of course *was* no power in the state constitutions to pardon that crime. There will therefore be none under the new &c. This or something like it seems to me to afford the best solution of the difficulty.

I send you the Fœderalist from the beginning to the conclusion of the commentary on the Executive branch. If

187

our suspicions of the author be right, he must be too much engaged to make a rapid progress in what remains. . . .

We are told that your election has succeeded; with which we all felicitate ourselves. I will thank you for an account of the result generally.

In this state our prospects are much as you left them — a moot point which side will prevail. Our friends to the Northward are active.

Between April 2 and May 28, 1788, Publius was silent. Involved with his legal work and with the outcome of elections in other states, Hamilton was also worried about the election of delegates in New York, where the Antifederalists had built a strong statewide organization of county committees. Votes were cast on the last Tuesday in April, and the results showed that *The Federalist* papers had had little effect on "the People of the State of New York," to whom they were addressed. As one New Yorker remarked, Publius was not "intelligible to the common people." Hamilton, Jay, and Robert R. Livingston were easy winners in Manhattan. But, as Hamilton wrote to Madison in mid-May, it was clear that Clinton's forces had triumphed upstate.

TO THE
INDEPENDENT ELECTORS
OF THE
CITY of NEW-YORK.

THERE was a time when a majority of the citizens of New-York were so opposed to lawyers as members of the legislature, that a *single* gentleman of that profession, though confessedly a man of abilities, *and in other respects*, of unimpeachable character, could not obtain a majority of suffrages, principally owing to the circumstance of his being of that profession.

But the times are changed, and we are changed with them. We now find a list of candidates proposed for convention, SEVEN of whom are either lawyers or law characters, and no less than THREE are named as members of the legislature.

No prejudice ought to be entertained against the profession of the law, confined to its proper sphere; but there are cogent reasons to be offered against admitting too large a number in the legislature. Every man will be inclined to promote his own trade. The more dubious and obscure the laws are, the more will the business of the profession be increased. It will therefore be for the interest of the lawyers to frame the laws in such a manner as to be equivocal and hard to be understood.

There are also good reasons against electing many lawyers in the convention.—We are for adopting the constitution; but still we wish that they, who compose the convention, may propose amendments, after the manner of Massachusetts.—In this opinion, so far as we are able to collect it, are a large majority of our fellow citizens. If the new constitution needs amendment, it wants in no part more than in that which relates to the judicial department—the courts of law, as they are to be formed under the constitution, will prove oppressive and expensive, and will introduce very great confusion by their interference with the state judiciaries; and it is wished that the convention may recommend alterations in this and some other articles after its adoption. But the lawyers will be under a strong bias to oppose the necessary amendments to this part of the plan. The increase of lawsuits, and of the expences of carrying them on, though it will be oppressive to the people in general, will be to the advantage of the profession of the law—It will therefore be more for the public good, to chuse a less number of lawyers—give them a full share in the representation, and elect two. There are other gentlemen who are not lawyers—characters firmly attached to the adoption of the system in the form in which it has been adopted by Massachusetts.

MANY FEDERALISTS.

JOHN JAY,
ALEXANDER HAMILTON,
ISAAC ROOSEVELT,
ALEXANDER McCOMB,
R. C. LIVINGSTON,

GULIAN VERPLANCK,
DANIEL PHENIX,
WILLIAM NEILSON,
WILLIAM MAXWELL.

NEW-YORK, April 28, 1788.

During the election campaign of 1788, Hamilton and eight other Federalists addressed this broadside to New York's voters.

[New York, May 19, 1788]
Some days since I wrote to you, My Dear Sir. . . .

I then mentioned to you that the question of a majority for or against the constitution would depend upon the County of Albany. By the latter accounts from that quarter I fear much that the issue there has been against us.

As Clinton is truly the leader of his party, and is inflexibly obstinate I count little on overcoming opposition by reason. Our only chances will be the previous ratification by nine states, which may shake the firmness of his followers; and a change in the sentiments of the people which have been for some time travelling towards the constitution, though the first impressions made by every species of influence and artifice were too strong to be eradicated in time to give a decisive turn to the elections. We shall leave nothing undone to cultivate a favourable disposition in the citizens at large.

The language of the Antifoederalists is that if all the other states adopt, New York ought still to hold out. I have the most direct intelligence, but in a manner, which forbids a public use being made of it, that Clinton has in several conversations declared his opinion of the *inutility* of the UNION. Tis an unhappy reflection, that the friends to it should by quarrelling for straws among themselves promote the designs of its adversaries.

We think here that the situation of your state is critical. Let me know what you now think of it. I believe you meet nearly at the time we do. It will be of vast importance that an exact communication should be kept up between us at that period; and the moment *any decisive* question is taken, if favourable, I request you to dispatch an express to me with pointed orders to make all possible diligence, by changing horses &c. All expences shall be thankfully and liberally paid.

The final results of the New York election showed the Federalists defeated by a margin of more than two to one. They won only nineteen contests in four counties, while the Antifederalists won forty-six elections in nine counties. Despite this setback, however, Hamilton could approach the last *Federalist* essays with a degree of optimism. When he wrote the first number, no state convention had met to consider the Constitution; but by the time the last essays were published on May 28, 1788, seven states had ratified the new system, and by the end of May, an eighth had given its assent. Furthermore, few Antifederalists still felt that the Constitution should be rejected out of hand, arguing instead that the new government would be palatable only if it contained some protection for individual rights and civil liberties. Amid this new climate of opinion, Hamilton altered his approach in his last essays. Although a "bill of rights" had been discussed for several months, Hamilton did not mention its absence from the Constitution until the eighty-fourth *Federalist*, the next to last in the series.

[New York, May 28, 1788]

The opposers of the new system in this state, who profess an unlimited admiration for its constitution, are among the most intemperate partizans of a bill of rights. To justify their zeal in this matter, they alledge two things; one is, that ... the constitution of New-York ... contains in the body of it various provisions in favour of particular privileges and rights, which in substance amount to the same thing; the other is, that the constitution adopts in their full extent the common and statute law of Great-Britain, by which many other rights not expressed in it are equally secured.

To the first I answer, that the constitution proposed by the convention contains, as well as the constitution of this state, a number of such provisions. . . .

A copy, by the secretary of the New York senate, of the resolution appointing Hamilton a delegate to Congress for the year 1788

To the second, that is, to the pretended establishment of the common and statute law by the constitution, I answer, that they are expressly made subject "to such alterations and provisions as the legislature shall from time to time make concerning the same." They are therefore at any moment liable to repeal by the ordinary legislative power, and of course have no constitutional sanction. . . .

[Further, Hamilton argued, an explicit bill of rights could endanger the liberties it was designed to protect.]

Why for instance, should it be said, that the liberty of the press shall not be restrained, when no power is given by which restrictions may be imposed? . . . it would furnish, to men disposed to usurp, a plausible pretence for claiming that power. They might urge with a semblance of reason, that the constitution ought not to be charged with the absurdity of providing against the abuse of an authority, which was not given, and that the provision against restraining the liberty of the press afforded a clear implication, that a power to prescribe proper regulations concerning it, was intended to be vested in the national government. . . .

There remains but one other view of this matter to conclude the point. The truth is, after all the declamation we have heard, that the constitution is itself in every rational sense, and to every useful purpose, A BILL OF RIGHTS. The several bills of rights, in Great-Britain, form its constitution, and conversely the constitution of each state is its bill of rights. And the proposed constitution, if adopted, will be the bill of rights of the union. Is it one object of a bill of rights to declare and specify the political privileges of the citizens in the structure and administration of the government? This is done in the most ample and precise manner in the plan of the convention. . . . Is another object of a bill of rights to define certain immunities and modes of proceeding, which are relative to personal and private concerns? This we have seen has also been attended to . . . in the same plan. Adverting therefore to the substantial meaning of a bill of rights, it is absurd to allege that it is not to be found in the work of the convention. . . . It certainly must be immaterial what mode is observed as to the order of declaring the rights of the citizens, if they are to be found in any part of the instrument which establishes the government.

Hamilton's reasons for opposing a bill of rights became clear in the last *Federalist*. Advocates of the measure had seized upon the idea of incorporating these amendments as "previous conditions" to ratification by the states that had not yet acted. Hamilton believed that he could not afford to strengthen the Antifederalist cause by admitting that there was any merit in their arguments.

[New York, May 28, 1788]

Concessions on the part of the friends of the plan, that it has not a claim to absolute perfection, have afforded matter of no small triumph to its enemies. Why, say they, should we adopt an imperfect thing? Why not amend it, and make it perfect before it is irrevocably established? This may be plausible enough, but it is only plausible. In the first place I remark, that the extent of these concessions has been greatly exaggerated.... No advocate of the measure can be found who will not declare his sentiment, that the system, though it may not be perfect in every part, is upon the whole a good one, is the best that the present views and circumstances of the country will permit, and is such an one as promises every species of security which a reasonable people can desire....

[In closing the *Federalist* series, Hamilton quoted the British political scientist David Hume, who had written that "no human genius" could, alone, establish an effective government for "a large state or society."]

New York State's coat of arms

"The judgments of many must unite in the work: EXPERIENCE must guide their labour: Time must bring it to perfection: And the FEELING of inconveniences must correct the mistakes which they *inevitably* fall into, in their first trials and experiments." These judicious reflections contain a lesson of moderation to all the sincere lovers of the union, and ought to put them upon their guard against hazarding anarchy, civil war, a perpetual alienation of the states from each other, and perhaps the military despotism of a victorious demagogue, in the pursuit of what they are not likely to obtain, but from TIME

191

and EXPERIENCE. It may be in me a defect of political fortitude, but I acknowledge, that I cannot entertain an equal tranquillity with those who affect to treat the dangers of a longer continuance in our present situation as imaginary. A NATION without a NATIONAL GOVERNMENT is, in my view, an awful spectacle. The establishment of a constitution, in time of profound peace, by the voluntary consent of a whole people, is a PRODIGY, to the completion of which I look forward with trembling anxiety. I can reconcile it to no rules of prudence to let go the hold we now have, in so arduous an enterprise, upon seven out of the thirteen states; and after having passed over so considerable a part of the ground to recommence the course. I dread the more the consequences of new attempts, because I KNOW that POWERFUL INDIVIDUALS, in this and in other states, are enemies to a general national government, in every possible shape.

Federalist strategy at the New York Convention that was to meet at Poughkeepsie in mid-June depended on the success of the Constitution elsewhere. Hamilton had already made arrangements for obtaining reports from the Virginia Convention. New Hampshire's convention had met in February, adjourned without taking action on the Constitution, and was to reconvene in June. Early in that month Hamilton outlined his plans to John Sullivan, a New Hampshire Federalist.

New York, June 6, 1788.
You will no doubt have understood that the Antifederal party has prevailed in this State by a large majority. It is therefore of the utmost importance that all external circumstances should be made use of to influence their conduct. This will suggest to you the *great advantage* of a speedy decision in your State, if you can be sure of the question, and a prompt communication of the event to us. With this view, permit me to request that the instant you have taken a decisive vote in favor of the Constitution, you send an express to me at Poughkeepsie. Let him take the *shortest route* to that place, change horses on the road, and use all possible diligence. I shall with pleasure defray all expenses, and give a liberal reward to the person. As I suspect an effort will be made to precipitate us, all possible *safe* dispatch on your part, as well to obtain a decision as to communicate the intelligence of it, will be desirable.

State seal of New Hampshire

Two days later, Hamilton, writing to James Madison in Virginia, speculated on the course of events in the New York campaign for ratification.

The Critical Period. FISKE

A view of Poughkeepsie, New York, seen from across the Hudson River

[New York, June 8, 1788]

[The Antifederal party] have a majority of two thirds in the Convention and according to the best estimate I can form of about four sevenths in the community. The views of the leaders in this City are pretty well ascertained to be turned towards a *long* adjournment say till next spring or Summer. Their incautious ones observe that this will give an opportunity to the state to *see how the government works and to act according to circumstances.*

My reasonings on the fact are to this effect. The leaders of the party hostile to the constitution are equally hostile to the Union. They are however afraid to reject the constitution at once because that step would bring matters to a crisis between this state and the states which had adopted the Constitution and between the parties in the state. A separation of the Southern district from the other part of the state it is perceived would become the object of the Foederalists and of the two neighbouring states. They therefore resolve upon a long adjournment as the safest and most artful course to effect their final purpose....

For my own part the more I can penetrate the views of the Antifoederal party in this state, the more I dread the consequences of the non adoption of the Constitution by any of the other states, the more I fear an eventual disunion and civil war. God grant that Virginia may accede. Her example will have a vast influence on our politics. New Hampshire, all accounts give us to expect, will be an assenting state.

The Federalist advantage at Poughkeepsie would be time. If New Hampshire or Virginia became the ninth state to ratify it, the Constitution would be the law of the land. On June 17, the New York Convention met. George Clinton was named chairman and rules were adopted. To insure delay, Hamilton and Robert R. Livingston drafted a resolution providing that no vote would be taken on the Constitution until all its articles had been considered "Clause by Clause." Two days later, Hamilton sent a terse note to Madison, who faced strong Antifederal opposition in his own convention in Virginia.

[Poughkeepsie, New York, June 19, 1788]
Yesterday, My Dear Sir, The Convention made a house.
That day and this have been spent in preliminary arrangements. Tomorrow we go into a Committee of the whole on the Constitution. There is every appearance that a full discussion will take place, which will keep us together at least a fortnight. It is not easy to conjecture what will be the result. Our adversaries greatly outnumber us. The leaders gave indications of a pretty desperate disposition in private conversations previous to the meeting; but I imagine the minor partisans have their scruples and an air of moderation is now assumed. So far the thing is not to be despaired of. A happy issue with you must have considerable influence upon us.

The decision to discuss the Constitution in detail turned the convention into a debating society in which "Antis" and "Feds" delivered long orations to prove their points. Nothing could have suited Hamilton and his friends better: Federalist delegates were skilled public speakers and might be able to overshadow their opposition, but most important, this procedure took time. In his first speech, Hamilton answered Antifederalists who had minimized the national crisis. He opened with a theme that he used during the whole convention—that the Confederation could not and should not be revised, and that only the new Constitution would protect America's liberties and independence.

[Poughkeepsie, New York, June 20, 1788]
What then shall we do? Shall we take the Old Confederation, as the basis of a new system? Can this be the object of the gentlemen? certainly not. Will any man who entertains a wish for the safety of his country, trust the sword and the purse with a single Assembly organized on principles so defective—so rotten? Though we might give to such a government certain powers with safety, yet to give them the full and unlimited powers of taxation and the national forces would be to establish a despotism; the definition of which is, a government, in which all power is concentred in a single body. To take the Old Confederation, and fashion it upon these principles, would be establishing a power which would destroy the liberties of the people. These considerations show clearly, that a government totally different must be instituted. They had weight in the convention who formed the new system. It was seen, that the necessary powers were too

great to be trusted to a single body: They therefore formed two branches; and divided the powers, that each might be a check upon the other. This was the result of their wisdom; and I presume that every reasonable man will agree to it.

The next morning, Hamilton continued his speech and answered the objections of Antifederalists who feared that the House would be too small to represent America's diverse interests. Specifically, critics in the convention proposed that each congressman be elected from a district with twenty thousand inhabitants, not thirty thousand as the Constitution provided.

[Poughkeepsie, New York, June 21, 1788]
I would ask, by what rule or reasoning it is determined, that one man is a better representative for twenty than thirty thousand? . . . I agree with the gentleman, that a very small number might give some colour for suspicion: I acknowledge, that ten would be unsafe; on the other hand, a thousand would be too numerous. But I ask him, why will not ninety-one be an adequate and safe representation? This at present appears to be the proper medium. Besides, the President of the United States will be himself the representative of the people. From the competition that ever subsists between the branches of government, the President will be induced to protect their rights, whenever they are invaded by either branch. On whatever side we view this subject, we discover various and powerful checks to the encroachments of Congress. The true and permanent interests of the members are opposed to corruption: Their number is vastly too large for easy combination: The rivalship between the houses will forever prove an insuperable obstacle: The people have an obvious and powerful protection in their own State governments: Should any thing dangerous be attempted, these bodies of perpetual observation, will be capable of forming and conducting plans of regular opposition. Can we suppose the people's love of liberty will not, under the incitement of their legislative leaders, be roused into resistance, and the madness of tyranny be extinguished at a blow? Sir, the danger is too distant, it is beyond all rational calculations. . . .

[Hamilton hammered away at the basic theme of his

Antifederalist Melancton Smith was known as "Mr. Hamilton's most persevering and formidable opponent" in the New York State ratifying convention.

convention speeches—the delegates must examine real problems and discard old prejudices.]

Sir, we hear constantly a great deal, which is rather calculated to awake our passions, and create prejudices, than to conduct us to truth, and teach us our real interests. I do not suppose this to be the design of the gentlemen. Why then are we told so often of an aristocracy? For my part, I hardly know the meaning of this word as it is applied. If all we hear be true, this government is really a very bad one. But who are the aristocracy among us? Where do we find men elevated to a perpetual rank above their fellow citizens; and possessing powers entirely independent of them? The arguments of the gentlemen only go to prove that there are men who are rich, men who are poor, some who are wise, and others who are not—That indeed every distinguished man is an aristocrat.

The New York State Convention of 1788 met at the Van Kleek house, then a tavern, at Poughkeepsie.

Revolution, LOSSING

Hamilton's speech did not convince George Clinton, who still insisted that the Congress was not "comprehensive" enough and that "there will be more safety in the state than in the federal government." Parrying the Governor's thrust, Hamilton accused Clinton of seeking to destroy the Union.

[Poughkeepsie, New York, June 21, 1788] [This] is a species of reasoning, sometimes used to excite popular jealousies, but . . . I do not suppose that the honorable member who advanced the idea, had any such design: He, undoubtedly, would not wish to extend his argument to the destruction of union or government; but this, Sir, is its real tendency. It has been asserted, that the interests, habits and manners of the Thirteen States are different; and hence it is inferred, that no general free government can suit them. . . . I acknowledge, that the local interests of the states are in some degree various; and that there is some difference in their habits and manners: But this I will presume to affirm; that, from New-Hampshire to Georgia, the people of America are as uniform in their interests and manners, as those of any established in Europe. This diversity, to the eye of a speculatist, may afford some marks of characteristic discrimination, but cannot form an impediment to the regular operation of those general powers, which the

Constitution gives to the united government. . . . Though the difference of interests may create some difficulty and apparent partiality, in the first operations of government, yet the same spirit of accommodation, which produced the plan under discussion, would be exercised in lessening the weight of unequal burthens. Add to this that, under the regular and gentle influence of general laws, these varying interests will be constantly assimilating, till they embrace each other, and assume the same complexion.

When Clinton replied that he was as firm a believer in the Union as any man, Hamilton blandly denied that he had ever said anything to the contrary.

[Poughkeepsie, New York, June 21, 1788]
I only rise to observe that the gentleman has misunderstood me. What I meant to express was this; that if we argued from possibilities only; if we reasoned from chances, or an ungovernable propensity to evil, instead of taking into view the controul, which the nature of things, or the form of the constitution provided, the argument would lead us to withdraw all confidence from our fellow-citizens, and discard the chimerical idea of government.

After the convention adjourned for the day, Hamilton had time to reply to the promising reports that he had been receiving from James Madison in Virginia.

[Poughkeepsie, New York, June 21, 1788]
I thank you for your letter . . . and am glad to learn that you think the chance is in your favour. I hope no disagreeable change may happen. Yet I own I fear something from your indisposition.

Our debate here began on the clause respecting the proportion of representation &c. which has taken up two days. Tomorrow I imagine we shall talk about the power over elections. The only good information I can give you is that we shall be sometime together and take the chance of events.

The object of the party at present is undoubtedly conditional amendments. What effect events may have cannot precisely be foreseen.

I believe the adoption by New Hampshire is certain.

The movement for "conditional" ratification was unmistakable. As delegates debated each article, conditional amendments were proposed. On June 24, for instance, in an examination of the section pertaining to the Senate, an Antifederalist suggested that no man be allowed to serve two consecutive terms in the upper house and that state legislatures be empowered to "recall" their United States Senators. In rebuttal, Hamilton explained the nature and functions of the Senate.

[Poughkeepsie, New York, June 24, 1788]
In the commencement of a revolution, which received its birth from the usurpations of tyranny, nothing was more natural, than that the public mind should be influenced by an extreme spirit of jealousy.... In forming our confederation, this passion alone seemed to actuate us, and we appear to have had no other view than to secure ourselves from despotism.... But, Sir, there is another object, equally important, and which our enthusiasm rendered us little capable of regarding. I mean a principle of strength and stability in the organization of our government, and vigor in its operations. This purpose could never be accomplished but by the establishment of some select body, formed peculiarly upon this principle. There are few positions more demonstrable than that there should be in every republic, some permanent body to correct the prejudices, check the intemperate passions, and regulate the fluctuations of a popular assembly....

Now, Sir, what is the tendency of the proposed amendment? To take away the stability of government by depriving the senate of its permanency: To make this body subject to the same weakness and prejudices, which are incident to popular assemblies, and which it was instituted to correct; and by thus assimilating the complexion of the two branches, destroy the balance between them. The amendment will render the senator a slave to all the capricious humors among the people.... [Thus] he never can possess that firmness which is necessary to the discharge of his great duty to the union.

According to this 1788 newspaper cartoon, Virginia's approval of the Constitution would bring a New York vote for ratification.

On June 25, the Poughkeepsie Convention learned that New Hampshire had ratified the Constitution—the Confederation was dead. Still, New York Antifederalists balked at unconditional approval. That day, Hamilton wrote to Madison in Virginia.

[New York, June 25, 1788]
I am very 'sorry to find by your letter...that your

prospects are so critical. Our chance of success here is infinitely slender, and none at all if you go wrong. The leaders of the Antifederalists finding their part seems somewhat squeamish about rejection, are obliged *at present* to recur to the project of conditional amendments. We are going on very deliberately in the discussion and hitherto not without effect.

Even though the Constitution had been ratified by nine states, the convention at Poughkeepsie continued to consider each clause at a stately pace. When the delegates reached the article on taxation, an amendment was introduced limiting Congress to laying imposts and excise taxes on foreign goods. Hamilton's reply to the proposal revealed his growing impatience.

The notes of John McKesson, the convention secretary, on Hamilton's remarks of June 27, 1788.

[Poughkeepsic, New York, June 27, 1788] It is more easy for the human mind to calculate the evils, than the advantages of a measure; and vastly more natural to apprehend the danger, than to see the necessity, of giving powers to our rulers. Hence I may justly expect, that those who hear me, will place less confidence in those arguments which oppose, than in those which favour, their prepossessions.

After all our doubts, our suspicions and speculations ... we must return at last to this important truth—that when we have formed a constitution upon free principles, when we have given a proper balance to the different branches of administration, and fixed representation upon pure and equal principles, we may with safety furnish it with all the powers, necessary to answer, in the most ample manner, the purposes of government.... Now what do gentlemen mean by coming forward and declaiming against this government? Why do they say we ought to limit its powers, to disable it, and to destroy its capacity of blessing the people? Has philosophy suggested—has experience taught, that such a government ought not to be trusted with every thing necessary for the good of society? Sir, when you have divided and nicely balanced the departments of government; When you have strongly connected the virtue of your rulers with their interest; when, in short, you have rendered your system as perfect as human forms can be; you must place confidence; you must give power.

On the same day, Hamilton wrote to Madison. If Virginia's convention, with a strong Antifederalist faction, voted for ratification, opposition in New York might well collapse.

[Poughkeepsie, New York, June 27, 1788]
A day or two ago General Schuyler at my request sent forward to you an express with an account of the adoption of the Constitution by New Hampshire. We eagerly wait for further intelligence from you, as our only chance of success depends on you. There are some slight symptoms of relaxation in some of the leaders; which authorises a gleam of hope, if you do well; but certainly I think not otherwise.

While waiting for word from Madison, Hamilton carried on his fight against the conditional amendment on taxation. One New York newspaper had already described him as standing "under the federal banner...a political porcupine, armed at all points." But in the middle of the debates on taxation, John Lansing, another New York delegate to the Philadelphia Convention, raised an embarrassing point. He charged that the year before, in Philadelphia, Hamilton had demanded that the states be reduced to "mere corporations," whereas he was now telling the Poughkeepsie Convention that these local governments were necessary parts of the new government. The *Daily Advertiser* carried this account of "the altercation."

[Poughkeepsie, New York, June 28, 1788]
This called up Mr. Hamilton, who entered into a statement of facts; denied what the gentleman had asserted; declared that in the General Convention his ideas had been uniformly the same as on the present occasion: that tho' he at that time declared, as he had constantly and publicly done since, his apprehension that the State governments would finally subvert the general system, unless the arm of the Union was more strengthened than it was even by this Constitution; yet he had through the whole of the business advocated the preservation of the State governments, and affirmed them to be useful and necessary. He accused Mr. Lansing's insinuation as improper, unbecoming and uncandid. Mr. Lansing rose, and with much spirit resented the imputation. He made an appeal to Judge [Robert] Yates, who had taken notes in the Federal Convention for a proof of Mr. Hamilton's expressions. This produced some disorder ...and the Chairman was obliged to call to order.

On June 30, Robert Yates read the notes of Hamilton's speeches in Philadelphia, quoting Hamilton's use of the term "corporate powers" for the states. The *Daily Advertiser* reported the way in which Hamilton and John Jay soothed the Antifederalists.

[Poughkeepsie, New York, June 30, 1788] Mr. Hamilton observed, that corporate was an ambiguous term, and asked Mr. Yates if he understood that he (Mr. Hamilton) used it as descriptive of powers, similar to those of the city of New-York? To which Mr. Yates answered in the negative; adding that he understood the gentleman not to wish such a privation of powers as would reduce the States to mere corporations in the popular acceptation of that term; but only such as would prevent the Members from retarding in any degree, the operations of the united government. Col. Hamilton then asked him if he did not, after the above mentioned debate in the Federal Convention, hear him (Col. Hamilton) say, that his opinion was that the State governments ought to be supported, and that they would be useful and necessary: and further asked him if he did not remember that he (Col. Hamilton) had recommended (as an additional security to the States governments) a Court of Impeachments, to be composed by the Chief Judges of the several States, together with the Chief Justice of the United States. To all which Mr. Yates gave an affirmative answer. On Mr. Jay's proposing to Mr. Yates some questions with a view to set the matter in the most explicit point of light, Mr. Yates answered as before, that Col. Hamilton's design did not appear to him to point at a total extinguishment of the State governments, but only to deprive them of the means of impeding the operation of the Union.

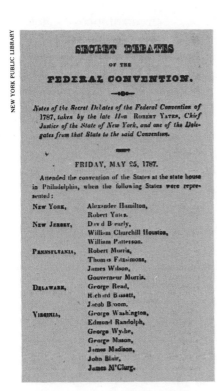

John Lansing, Jr., compiled and published Robert Yates's notes of the secret debates taken at the Philadelphia Convention.

By the beginning of July, Hamilton still had no news from Virginia on that convention's decision. Again, he wrote to Madison.

[Poughkeepsie, New York, July 2, 1788] Your letter of the 20th. came to hand two days since. I regret that your prospects were not yet reduced to greater certainty. There is more and more reason to believe that our conduct will be influenced by yours.

Our discussions have not yet travelled beyond the power of taxation. To day we shall probably quit this ground to pass to another. Our arguments confound, but do not convince. Some of the leaders however appear to me to be convinced *by circumstances* and to be desirous of a retreat. This does not apply to the Chief, who wishes to establish *Clintonism* on the basis of *Antifoederalism*.

As Hamilton had predicted, "circumstances," not "arguments," turned the tide at Poughkeepsie. At noon on July 2, a messenger from New York City interrupted Governor Clinton's speech to announce that Virginia had ratified the Constitution. A few days later, Hamilton reported to Madison that there were signs that the solid Antifederalist front had weakened.

[New York, July 8, 1788]
I felicitate you sincerely on the event in Virginia; but my satisfaction will be allayed, if I discover too much facility in the business of amendment-making. I fear the system will be wounded in some of its vital parts by too general a concurrence in some very injudicious recommendations. . . .

We yesterday *passed* through the constitution. To day some definitive proposition is to be brought forward; but what we are at a loss to judge. We have good reason to believe that our opponents are not agreed, and this affords some ground of hope. Different things are thought of—*Conditions precedent*, or previous amendments; Conditions *subsequent*, or the proposition of amendments upon condition, that if they are not adopted within a limited time, the state shall be at liberty to *withdraw* from the Union, and lastly *recommendatory amendments*. In either case *constructive declarations* will be carried as far as possible. We will go as far as we can in the latter without invalidating the act, and will concur in rational recommendations. The rest for our opponents.

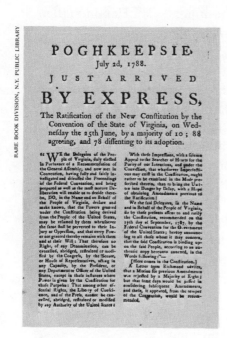

POGHKEEPSIE,
July 2d, 1788.

JUST ARRIVED

BY EXPRESS,

The Ratification of the New Conſtitution by the Convention of the State of Virginia, on Wedneſday the 25th June, by a majority of 10 ; 88 agreeing, and 78 diſſenting to its adoption.

A broadside printed at Poughkeepsie announced Virginia's ratification of the Constitution, June 25, 1788

The next day, the Antifederalists introduced a list of fifty-five amendments to the Constitution arranged under three headings: explanatory, conditional, and recommendatory. Jay introduced a resolution, drafted by Hamilton, that eliminated the "conditional" category, but Antifederalists resisted this move. Hamilton and Jay argued that a ratification with "conditions" would have no force. The *Daily Advertiser* carried this sympathetic account of Hamilton's speech.

[Poughkeepsie, New York, July 12, 1788]
He described in a delicate but most affecting manner the various ungenerous attempts to prejudice the minds of the Convention against him. He had been represented as "an ambitious man, a man unattached to the interests and insensible to the feelings of the people"; and even his supposed talents had been wrested to his dishonor, and produced as a charge against his integrity and virtue. He called on the world to point out an instance in which he had ever deviated from the line of public or private duty. The pathetic appeal fixed the silent sympathetic gaze of the spectators, and made them all his own.

He then proceeded to refute the fallacious reasonings of opposition.... He proved, in the first place, from the series of papers on which the authority of the present Convention was founded, that it had no possible decisive power, but to adopt or reject absolutely: that it had indeed a power to recommend... but it had none to dictate to or embarrass the union by any restrictions or conditions whatever: that the Committee was not a body commissioned to tender stipulations or form a compact, but to dissent from or agree to a plan of government, which could be altered either in its form or exercise only by an authority equal in all respects, to the one which gave it existence. Having made this point clear, he went on to shew that the future Congress would have no authority to receive us into the union on such terms: that this conditional adoption included evidently a disagreement to and rejection of a part of the Constitution: that Congress... must consider such a partial rejection in the light of a total one....

Mr. Hamilton... entreated the Convention in a pathetic strain to make a solemn pause, and weigh well what they were about to do, before they decided on a subject so infinitely important. The orator then closed his address, and received from every unprejudiced spectator the murmur of admiration and applause.

John Jay: a 1781 engraving, after a portrait "drawn from the life"

A week later, trying another tactic, Hamilton and his allies introduced a resolution for adjournment to permit delegates to learn "the Sentiments at present entertained by their Constituents." As both sides knew, these "Sentiments" were now in favor of ratification. On July 17,

Gilbert Livingston, an Antifederalist, made frantic notes of Hamilton's speech before the convention.

[Poughkeepsie, New York, July 17, 1788]
Hamilton: [There are] scarce any new reasons to be offered—they are short & must have their force. It may do good—[it] cannot do evil. While men *hope,* they never become enraged. Both parties hope to succeed, therefore [they] will not heat. Things have changed since we came here. Therefore [it is] decent we should consult our constituents. Good may come, & no evil can come....

[There is a] difference of Opinion respecting the supposed defect. [Some] Gentlemen look at it only to find out the defects and not to discover its securities—& beauties. [It] turns on this, that [the] gentlemen say the state governments will be destroyed. He says they are necessary, & that they will be preserved.

[Hamilton] supposes that if the adoption takes place as proposed we are out of the Union. Some may think we may then enjoy our impost &c., but [Hamilton] lays it down the Union will not permit us to remain so because their interest & safety will not permit it.

Hamilton's speech was interrupted. When he resumed, he made a forceful point by reading a letter from James Madison, written on June 30. Madison reported that Virginia's Antifederalists had decided against appealing to the people over the state convention's decision to ratify the Constitution. If Virginians were content to trust the new government to provide the Constitution with necessary amendments, New York "Antis" had lost vital support. Gilbert Livingston jotted down Hamilton's comments —a series of embarrassing questions for Clinton's supporters.

[Poughkeepsie, New York, July 17, 1788]
Now, what have we to hope for from other states? Assistance? Against what—will they assist us to oppose themselves?

Can we compare our strength against the whole? They will have the power of government and the wealth of the whole country against us; the sea ports [are] all for them. Is there hope of prevailing in so unequal a contest?

Whence are we to derive means of assistance? [From] foreign powers? Whom—France or great Brittain? France is the Ally of the United States. Great Brittain? What object could she have? [She] has totally given up her claim to this country. Will she take the weaker by the hand, to oppose the stronger? Who would wish again to come under her dominion? But she never will because [she has] no interest by it.

This [is] not all. We are divided among our selves: the southern district [is] warmly attached to this government. This [is] a fact and a sentiment which will increase.... Is it in the power of the Northern [district] to compel the southern? [This is] impracticable—they will be aided & protected by the Union. [Hamilton] hopes the election of separation will never be made, [but] it will take place if we reject the Constitution....

... Will Congress overcome the obstacles to receive us? They will not. They are jealous of us and view us as a selfish sister—our neighbours nearest especially.... Their interest in having us with them will be diminished by considering that they can have our [southern] part—the chief source of wealth....

Pause—and suppose the minorities in the other states would go with us to resist. Is this desirable—to have the country divided into martial bands? Who will command? In this case, at any rate, adieu to liberty; a despotism will follow. Can any man wish to run this risk? The cause of republicanism should induce us to avoid this....

[There are] distinguished patriots on both sides, though most [are] for the government: [John] Hancock acquiesces though in a situation that might tempt him to oppose it; [John] Adams—he first conceived the bold idea of independence—he is for it; Governor [William] Livingston, born a republican, he [is] for it; Franklin, this old grey headed patriot looking into the grave, approves it; General Washington came forward. Disinterested, [he] hazarded all without reward. All parties, Whigs and Tories, admired and put confidence in him. At the close of the war, at the head of a discontented army, did he take advantage of the situation of the army or country? No, he proved himself a patriot. This man came forward again and hazarded his harvest of glory. In this case he saw the work he had been engaged in was but half finished. He came forward and approved this Constitution. Is it in human nature to suppose that these good men should lose their virtue and acquiesce in a government that is substantially defective to the liberties of their country?...

Our sister states invite us. They have been as jealous

The Critical Period, FISKE

Portrait of James Madison, based on a painting by Charles Willson Peale

of their liberty as we....All mankind [invites us].
Heaven patronized us—it now invites us.

Is it not wonderful that ten states should adopt it?
Let us take care not to oppose the whole country. If [we
were] on the verge of eternity, [Hamilton] would exhort
us to union.

Antifederalists brought forward another plan—an unconditional ratification under which New York retained the right to secede
from the Union if her conditions were not met. Hamilton wrote to James
Madison, who had recently joined the Congress in New York City, for his
opinion of the new plan.

*The "Federal Ship," named in honor
of Hamilton, is paraded through the
streets of New York to celebrate
ratification of the Constitution.*

[Poughkeepsie, New York, July 19, 1788]
Let me know your idea of the possibility of our being
received on that plan. You will understand that the only
qualification will be *the reservation* of a right to recede
in case our amendments have not been decided upon
in one of the modes pointed out in the Constitution within
a certain number of years, perhaps five or seven.

If this can in the first instance be admitted as a
ratification I do not fear any further consequences.
Congress will I presume recommend certain amendments to render the *structure* of the government more
secure. This will satisfy the more considerate and
honest opposers of the constitution, and with the aid
of time will break up the party.

While Hamilton awaited Madison's reply, he described
deliberations at Poughkeepsie as "debating on amendments without having decided what is to be done with them." At last, on July 23, Melancton
Smith and Samuel Jones broke with other "Antis" to introduce motions for
ratification "in full Confidence" that the conditional amendments would be
added. Their proposals passed by two votes. John Lansing insisted this ratification still included the right of secession if the amendments were not
adopted. Hamilton had just received Madison's opinion that this "reservation" would invalidate the ratification. Gilbert Livingston made notes of
Hamilton's speech.

[Poughkeepsie, New York, July 24, 1788]
Hamilton was in hopes this Morning of Unanimity when
this Motion was first mentioned...[but] since thinks
otherwise. [He] has taken advice with men of character:
they think it will not do. [He] proposed to read a Letter

Hamilton (second column) was among those who signed the New York Convention's act of ratification.

[from James Madison]. [He] reads it. [He] supposes this adoption [is] conditional.... The terms of the constitution import a perpetual compact between the different states; this certainly is not. Treaties and engagements with foreign nations are perpetual; this cannot be under this adoption.... States & men are averse to inequality. They [are] fully bound & we partially.

Should we risk so much on so little? Motives of expediency [are] too much relied on.... Is it not of importance that we join unanimously to procure a convention? The observation of Lansing does not meet the objection as they [the other states] will contemplate wheather this is a ratification. If they have any doubt, they will appoint Congress to meet on certain federal ground. [The] interest of some states [is] against us. If they are driven away by us the people will be dissatisfied &ct.

We have done everything which possibly can insure our wish. This we shall loose by a second state convention. We shall not be represented in Congress & this for no real end. [Hamilton] moves to have the question postponed & that a circular letter be wrote.

Madison's opinion could not be ignored. Hamilton's "circular letter" helped the Antifederalists save face, and on July 25, Lansing's motion on the right of secession was defeated, 31 to 28. By the same margin, the convention agreed to ratify, "in full Confidence" that their list of essential amendments would be enacted. Unanimously they accepted a draft of a circular letter to be sent to the other states concerning the defects of the Constitution. This letter, written by John Jay, with some corrections by Hamilton, was dispatched the next day.

Poughkeepsie, New York, July 26, 1788. "We the members of the Convention of this State, have deliberately & maturely considered the Constitution proposed for the united States. Several articles in it appear so exceptionable to a majority of us, that nothing but the fullest confidence of obtaining a Revision of them by a general convention, and an invincible Reluctance to separating from our Sister States could have prevailed upon a sufficient number to ratify it without stipulating for previous amendments. We all unite in opinion that such a Revision will be necessary to recommend it to the approbation and Support of a numorous Body of our constituents."

It is impossible to point to one isolated incident to prove that Hamilton won the fight for ratification in New York, but it would be equally difficult to imagine how the battle could have been won without him. Colonel Hamilton, that "political porcupine," was always at work. Although *The Federalist* convinced few New Yorkers, its continued publication kept the issues before the public. And although Hamilton's party lost the election in New York, his correspondence with leaders in other states enabled Federalists at Poughkeepsie to plan a strategy by which they prevailed over an Antifederalist majority. A bit arrogant, much too sure of himself, Hamilton could not be ignored. When the time came, he showed enough political sense to withdraw and let his friend Jay conciliate the convention and carry the day for ratification.

Hamilton's role in championing the Constitution was widely recognized in his own day. Three days before the Poughkeepsie Convention adjourned, the city of New York held a belated celebration of the ratification of the Constitution by nine states with a "Grand Fœderal Procession," costing almost ten thousand pounds. The date of the parade had been postponed from July 4 until July 23 so that a "Federal Ship" could be constructed. The ship was pulled along Broadway "with floating sheets, and full sails," and her name was *Hamilton,* to honor the man who had signed the Constitution at Philadelphia for New York and who was still fighting the good fight at Poughkeepsie. In the drizzling rain that Wednesday in July, the painted colors of the *Hamilton*'s flag smeared and ran, but the "Federal Ship" still helped give the parade "a very pompous appearance." Similarly, one Federalist remarked that the Constitution had "undergone an ordeal [by] torture" at Poughkeepsie, but was "preserved, as by fire." Federalism had survived. New York had become the "eleventh pillar" of the new government.

It seemed that there was nothing left for Hamilton to do but insure that the "factions" that had arisen during the Confederacy and rallied under the banner of Antifederalism would be destroyed. The Federalist ship needed a loyal crew and proper officers. For Hamilton, this meant that George Washington must lead the nation and that George Clinton must be replaced as Governor of New York.

Chapter 8

Mr. Secretary

A lexander Hamilton spent only a little more than three decades of his short life as an American. In the first half of this period he had accomplished more than he could have dreamed of when he sailed from St. Croix late in 1772. By the summer of 1788, Hamilton had a devoted wife and a lively family of three sons and a daughter. His personal friends and political allies were among the most powerful men in the country. He had helped win ratification of the Constitution, which established a government that could give America national security and prestige and that would provide him with a stage for his own talents. But Hamilton knew that it was not enough to have established this form of government on paper. In the last sixteen years of his life he fought to see that his own vision of America's "respectability" was insured, by seeking to place the right men in office and by persuading these men to enact legislative and administrative programs that conformed to his ideals. Two weeks after New York had ratified the Constitution, Hamilton undertook the task of insuring that the Presidency would be held by the only man who could unite the nation. In mid-August, he wrote to George Washington.

> [New York, August 13, 1788]
> I take it for granted, Sir, you have concluded to comply with what will no doubt be the general call of your country in relation to the new government. You will permit me to say that it is indispensable you should lend yourself to its first operations—It is to little purpose to have *introduced* a system, if the weightiest influence is not given to its firm *establishment,* in the outset.

In reply, Washington wrote that he could not commit himself on an event that "may never happen." In any case, he confided, it was his "greatest and sole desire to live and die, in peace and retirement" at Mount Vernon. Alarmed, Hamilton wrote again.

New York September 1788

I should be deeply pained my Dear Sir if your scruples in regard to a certain station should be matured into a resolution to decline it; though I am neither surprised at their existence nor can I but agree in opinion that the caution you observe in deferring an ultimate determination is prudent. I have however reflected maturely on the subject and have come to a conclusion . . . that every public and personal consideration will demand from you an acquiescence in what will *certainly* be the unanimous wish of your country. The absolute retreat which you meditated at the close of the late war was natural and proper. Had the government produced by the revolution gone on in a *tolerable* train, it would have been most adviseable to have persisted in that retreat. But I am clearly of opinion that the crisis which brought you again into public view left you no alternative but to comply—and I am equally clear in the opinion that you are by that act *pledged* to take a part in the execution of the government. I am not less convinced that the impression of this necessity of your filling the station in question is so universal that you run no risk of any uncandid imputation, by submitting to it. But even if this were not the case, a regard to your own reputation as well as to the public good, calls upon you in the strongest manner to run that risk.

It cannot be considered as a compliment to say that on your acceptance of the office of President the success of the new government in its commencement may materially depend. Your agency and influence will be not less important in preserving it from the future attacks of its enemies than they have been in recommending it in the first instance to the adoption of the people. Independent of all considerations drawn from this source the point of light in which you stand at home and abroad will make an infinite difference in the respectability with which the government will begin its operations in the alternative of your being or not being at the head of it. . . .

[Hamilton omitted any considerations with "a more personal application," but drew these "inferences" from the factors he had already listed.]

This Gilbert Stuart portrait of George Washington was owned by Hamilton.

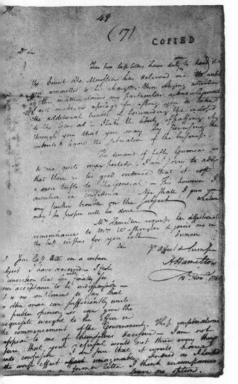

In the postcript of this letter of 1788, Hamilton again tried to persuade Washington to accept the Presidency.

First— In a matter so essential to the well being of society as the prosperity of a newly instituted government a citizen of so much consequence as yourself to its success has no option but to lend his services if called for.... it would be inglorious in such a situation not to hazard the glory however great, which he might have previously acquired.

Secondly. Your signature to the proposed system pledges your judgment for its being such an one as upon the whole was worthy of the public approbation. If it should miscarry... the blame will in all probability be laid on the system itself. And the framers of it will have to encounter the disrepute of having brought about a revolution in government, without substituting any thing that was worthy of the effort. They pulled down one Utopia, it will be said, to build up another. This view of the subject... will suggest to your mind greater hazard to that fame, which must be and ought to be dear to you, in refusing your future aid to the system than in affording it. I will only add that in my estimate of the matter that aid is indispensable.

...I doubt not the considerations mentioned have fully occurred to you, and I trust they will finally produce in your mind the same result, which exists in mine. I flatter myself the frankness with which I have delivered myself will not be displeasing to you. It has been prompted by motives which you would not disapprove.

Although he still did not know whether Washington would serve as President, Hamilton began to weigh the virtues of the candidates for Vice President. Theodore Sedgwick, a political leader in Massachusetts, asked Hamilton for his opinion of John Adams, who was then representing the United States in Great Britain. Hamilton sent his reaction.

[New York, October 9, 1788]

On the subject of Vice President, my ideas have concurred with yours, and I believe Mr. Adams will have the votes of this state....

The only hesitation in my mind with regard to Mr. Adams has arisen within a day or two; from a suggestion by a particular Gentleman that he is unfriendly in his sentiments to General Washington. Richard H Lee who will probably, as rumour now runs, come from Virginia is also in this state. The Lees and Adams' have been in the habit of uniting; and hence may spring up a Cabal very embarrassing to the Executive and of course to the administration of the Government. Consider this. Sound the reality of it and let me hear from you.

What think You of Lincoln or Knox? This is a flying thought.

Sedgwick answered that Adams, "formerly infinitely more democratical than at present," could now be trusted. Massachusetts, he reported, was divided between the supporters of Adams and those of John Hancock for Vice President. Hamilton replied early in November.

[New York, November 9, 1788]
On the question between Mr. H— and Mr. A— Mr. [Rufus] King will probably have informed you that I have upon the whole concluded that the latter ought to be supported. My measures will be taken accordingly. I had but one scruple; but after mature consideration I have relinquished it. Mr. A to a sound understanding has *always* appeared to me to add an ardent love for the public good; and as his further knowlege of the world seems to have corrected those jealousies which he is represented to have once been influenced by I trust nothing of the kind suggested in my former letter will disturb the harmony of the administration.

Two weeks later, Hamilton wrote to James Madison to announce his endorsement of Adams as Vice President.

[New York, November 23, 1788]
My principal reasons are these—First He is a declared partisan of referring to future experience the expediency of amendments in the system... [and this sentiment] is much nearer my own than certain other doctrines. Secondly a character of importance in the Eastern states, if he is not Vice President, one of two worse things will be likely to happen—Either he must be nominated to some important office for which he is less proper, or will become a malcontent and possibly espouse and give additional weight to the opposition to the Government.

As the day approached when the presidential electors would cast their ballots, Hamilton faced another problem: the Constitution made it impossible for electors to indicate which of their votes were for President and which were for Vice President. The situation was further complicated by scattered support in South Carolina for John Rutledge and in Virginia for George Clinton. In January, little more than a week before the Electoral College was to convene, Hamilton advised James Wilson of Pennsylvania of the strategy to be followed if the Rutledge and Clinton electors decided to throw their votes to Adams.

New York, January 25, 1789

As the accounts of the appointments of electors will satisfy the partisans of those Gentlemen in each of those States that they will have no coadjustors elsewhere, it seems not improbable that they will relinquish the attempt in favour of their intended candidates. Here then is a *chance* of unanimity in Adams. Nothing is so apt to beget it as the opinion that the current sets irresistibly towards him. Men are fond of going with the stream. Suppose personal caprice or hostility to the new system should occasion half a dozen votes only to be witheld from Washington—what may not happen? Grant there is little danger. If any, ought it to be run?

...the chance is that there will be Eight votes to spare from Adams leaving him still a majority. Take the probability of unanimity in the North in Adams & of division in the South...and the chances are almost infinite in his favour. Hence I conclude it will be prudent to throw away a few votes say 7 or 8; giving these to persons not otherwise thought of. Under this impression I have proposed to friends in Connecticut to throw away two to others in Jersey to throw away an equal number & I submit it to you whether it will not be well to lose three or four in Pensylvania....for God's sake let not our zeal for a secondary object defeat or endanger a first. I admit that in several important views and particularly to avoid disgust to a man who would be a formidable head to Antifoederalists—it is much to be desired that Adams may have the plurality of suffrages for Vice President; but if risk is to be run on one side or on the other can we hesitate where it ought to be preferred?

John Adams as Vice President, painted by Charles Willson Peale

After the presidential electors met on February 4, 1789, and chose Washington as President and Adams as Vice President, Hamilton turned his attention to the New York campaigns. On February 11, he presided at a meeting in Manhattan, which nominated Antifederalist

Robert Yates for governor. As chairman of "a committee to correspond with the other counties" Hamilton wrote to the supervisors of Albany urging them to support Yates.

[New York, February 18, 1789]

...it is highly necessary that the Chief Magistrate of the State should be free from all temptation wantonly to perplex or embarrass the national Government, whether that temptation should arise from a preference of partial confederacies, from a spirit of competition with the national rulers for personal pre-eminence, from an impatience of the restraints of national authority, from the fear of a diminution of power and emoluments, from resentment or mortification, proceeding from disappointment, or from any other cause whatsoever....

In the consideration of the character most proper to be held up at the ensuing election, some difficulties occurred. Our fellow citizens in some parts of the state had proposed Judge Yates, others had been advocates for the Lieutenant Governor [Pierre Van Cortlandt], and others for Chief Justice [Richard] Morris. It is well known that the inhabitants of this city are...strongly attached to the new constitution, and...that Lieutenant Governor Cortlandt and Chief Justice Morris...were zealous advocates for the same cause. Had it been agreed to support either of them for the office of governor, there would have been reason to fear, that the measure would have been imputed to party, and not to a desire of relieving our country from the evils they experience from the heats of party. It appeared therefore most advisable to select some man of the opposite party, in whose integrity, patriotism and temper, confidence might justly be placed; however little his political opinions on the question lately agitated, might be approved by those who were assembled upon the occasion.

Among the persons of this description, there were circumstances which led to a decision in favor of Judge Yates....It is certain, that as a man and a judge, he is generally esteemed. And though his opposition to the new constitution was such as its friends cannot but disapprove; yet since...its adoption, his conduct has been tempered with a degree of moderation and regard to peace and decorum which entitle him to credit; and seem to point him out as a man likely to compose the differences of the state, and to unite its citizens in the

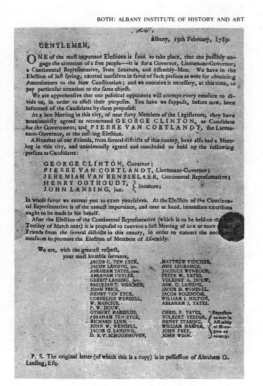

An Antifederalist, pro-Clinton broadside of the heated 1789 elections in New York State

harmonious pursuit of their common and genuine interest.

Of this at least we feel confident, that he has no personal revenge to gratify...nor any promises for personal purposes to be performed at the public expence. On the contrary we trust he will be found to be a man, who looks with an equal eye on his fellow citizens, and who will be more ambitious of leaving a good name, than a good estate, to his posterity.

Hamilton and the Federalists were determined not to repeat their mistakes of 1788, when their opponents had won control of the Poughkeepsie Convention by concentrating on local organization. Hamilton supervised every detail of an all-out statewide campaign against Clinton. Discarding the lofty style of Publius, he used the pen name "H.G." while producing a series of letters that examined Clinton's personal character and public record. In the first of these letters, H.G. reflected on Clinton's early life.

A Federalist broadside published during the 1789 election campaign for the New York governorship

New York, February 20, 1789.

The present Governor was bred to the law, under William Smith, Esquire, formerly of this city. Some time before the late revolution, he resided in Ulster county, and there followed his profession with reputation, though not with distinction. He was not supposed to possess considerable talents; but upon the whole, stood fair on the score of probity. It must however be confessed, that he early got the character with many of being a very *artful* man; and it is not to be wondered at, if that impression, on the minds in which it prevailed, deducted something from the opinion of his integrity. But it would be refining too much to admit such a consequence to be a just one. There certainly are characters (tho' they may be rare) which unite a great degree of address, and even a large portion of what is best expressed by the word CUNNING, with a pretty exact adherence, in the main, to the principles of integrity.

In the dozen years that Clinton had led New York, many of his exploits had been embroidered by popular legend. In his second letter, H.G. sought to puncture the Clinton myth.

New-York, February 21, 1789.

There is...no part of his character, which has been more misrepresented than the military part of it. His

Hamilton's friend John Laurance ran for Congress in the 1789 election.

panegyrists describe him to us as the "war worn veteran"—the complete soldier—the consummate general. One would imagine from their stories of him, that he...was the first of American generals; a Marius in courage, a Caesar in skill, inferior in nothing to a Turenne or a Monteculli, an Eugene or a Marlborough. But trust me, my dear Sir, this is mere rant and romance. That Mr. Clinton is a man of courage, there is no reason to doubt. That he was upon most occasions active and vigorous cannot be justly disputed. In his capacity of governor he was ever ready to promote the common cause—prompt in affording the aid of the militia, when requisite, and scrupling not, when he thought his presence might be of use, to put himself at the head of them. But here his praise as a soldier ends. Beyond this he has no pretension to the wreath of military renown. No man can tell when or where he gave proofs of generalship, either in council or in the field. After diligent enquiry, I have not been able to learn that he was ever more than once in actual combat. This was at Fort Montgomery [in October, 1777], where he commanded in person; and which, after a feeble and unskilful defence, was carried by storm... One particular in this affair deserves to be noticed. It is certain that the governor made a well-timed retreat, (I mean personally, for the greatest part of the garrison were captured), a thing which must have occasioned no small conflict in the breast of a commander nice in military punctilio. But squeamishness on this head, had been ill placed. It was undoubtedly the duty of the BRIGADIER to provide in season for the safety of the GOVERNOR.

The New York polls opened on April 28, and on that day Hamilton issued a last-minute election bulletin to Manhattan voters.
[New York, April 28, 1789]
Hitherto Fellow Citizens you have left no opportunity of manifesting your zeal for the firm establishment of the Constitution of the United States....Your work is now to be completed. We will ask you a few questions, and leave the answers to your own minds. Is there a man in America, who has more early, more decidedly, or more pertenaciously, opposed that constitution than the present governor? Is there a man in America from whose

future opposition to it, so much would be to be feared, as from that of the present governor, if suffered to continue *at the head of this State?* Is it *wise* to continue him in a situation, which will leave it so greatly in his power to counteract what you deem the true interest of your country? Is it *safe,* after all you have seen and known, to put the least confidence in the assurances you receive from those, who advise you to re-elect him...? Are there not appearances which *authorise* you to suppose, that the views of the present governor, in some important respects, have not coincided with the wishes or interests of the city?... These, Fellow Citizens, are serious question. Ponder them well, and act accordingly. Let every man, who believes a change necessary, step forward with the INDEPENDENCE of a FREEMAN and lend his aid!

While Hamilton waited for the verdict of New York's voters (a decision narrowly in favor of George Clinton), Washington was inaugurated on April 30. Five days later, in response to the President's request, Hamilton offered his ideas on the proper etiquette for the Republic's new Chief Executive.

[New York, May 5, 1789]

The public good requires as a primary object that the dignity of the office should be supported. Whatever is essential to this ought to be pursued though at the risk of partial or momentary dissatisfaction. But care will be necessary to avoid extensive disgust or discontent. Men's minds are prepared for a pretty high tone in the demeanour of the Executive; but I doubt whether for so high a tone as in the abstract might be desireable. The notions of equality are yet in my opinion too general and too strong to admit of such a distance being placed between the President and other branches of the government as might even be consistent with a due proportion. The following plan will I think steer clear of extremes and involve no very material inconveniences.

I   The President to have a levee day once a week for receiving visits. An hour to be fixed at which it shall be understood that he will appear and consequently that the visitors are previously to be assembled. The President to remain half an hour, in which time he may converse cursorily on indifferent subjects with such persons as shall strike his attention, and at the end of that half hour

Washington's inauguration

Pages from Hamilton's draft of his suggestions regarding the etiquette to be followed by the President

disappear.... No visits to be returned.

II   The President to accept no invitations: and to give formal entertainments only twice or four times a year on the anniversaries of important events in the revolution.... The members of the two houses of the legislature Principal officers of the Government Foreign ministers and other distinguished strangers only to be invited. The numbers form in my mind an objection— But there may be separate tables in separate rooms. This is practiced in some European Courts....

III   The President on the levée days...to give informal invitations to family dinners on the days of invitation. Not more than six or eight to be invited at a time & the matter to be confined essentially to members of the legislature and other official characters. The President never to remain long at table.

I think it probable that the last article will not correspond with the ideas of most of those with whom Your Excellency may converse but on pretty mature reflection I believe it will be necessary to remove the idea of too immense an inequality....

It is an important point to consider what persons may have access to Your Excellency on business. The heads of departments will of course have this privilege. Foreign Ministers of some descriptions will also be intitled to it. In Europe I am informed ambassadors only have direct access to the Chief Magistrate. Something very *near* what prevails there would in my opinion be right.... I have thought that the members of the Senate should also have a right of *individual* access on matters relative to the *public administration.* In England & France Peers of the realm have this right. We have none such in this Country, but I believe that it will be satisfactory to the people to know that there is some body of men in the state who have a right of continual communication with the President. It will be considered as a safeguard against secret combinations to deceive him.

I have asked myself—will not the representatives expect the same privilege and be offended if they are not allowed to participate with the Senate? There is sufficient danger of this, to merit consideration. But there is a reason for the distinction in the constitution. The Senate are coupled with the President in certain executive functions; treaties and appointments. This makes them in a degree his constitutional counsellors and gives them a *peculiar* claim to the right of access. On the whole, I think the discrimination will be proper. . . .

I have chosen this method of communication, because I understood . . . that it would be most convenient to you. The unstudied and unceremonious manner of it will I hope not render it the less acceptable. And if in the execution of your commands at any time I consult frankness and simplicity more than ceremony or profession, I flatter myself you will not on that account distrust the sincerity of the assurance I now give of my cordial wishes for your personal happiness and the success of your administration.

Hamilton, meantime, was awaiting with special interest the outcome of congressional debate over the functions of Cabinet officers. Special heat was generated in discussions of the office of Secretary of the Treasury, a post for which Hamilton was being considered. The arguments dragged on through the summer of 1789, and not until September 11 was Hamilton's appointment approved. He himself had no doubt as to what must be his first priority. Import duties were the primary source of revenue for the Federal Government, and Hamilton knew that their efficient collection was essential. A practical man, he realized that only reliable statistics would enable him to review the system and make recommendations for reform when Congress reconvened. At the beginning of October he dispatched a circular letter to the collectors of customs.

Treasury Department
New York October 2d. 1789.

As in the first establishment of Revenue systems, imperfections and inconveniencies will naturally present themselves in practice, which could not have been foreseen in their formation; it is of the greatest moment, that the best information should be collected for the use of the Government as to the operation of those, which may have been adopted.

To the obtaining this information, as it respects the plan for the imposition and collection of the duties, the situation of the collectors and naval Officers of the several Ports is in a peculiar manner favourable, and . . . it is equally their duty and their interest to make the best use of their opportunities for that purpose.

Not doubting that their inclination will coincide with both; I am to request that they will carefully note and

Washington's nomination of Hamilton to be Secretary of the Treasury

from time to time communicate to me whatever may serve to discover the merits or defects of that plan, and to point out the means of improving it.

Though the complaints of the Merchants will not always be infallible indications of defects, yet they will always merit attention, and when they occur, I shall be glad to be particularly informed of them.

. . . it was in the contemplation of Congress to employ Boats for the security of the Revenue against contraband. I shall be glad to have your Ideas, as to the expediency of employing them in your quarter, and . . . of the number and kind you deem requisite; their equipments, and the probable expence. . . .

It has been very much apprehended that the number of Ports in several of the States would conduce to great evasions of the duties. It is my wish to be informed how far experience has justified this apprehension, and what can be done to correct the Mischeifs, which may have ensued. . . .

In hinting these particulars it is not my aim to confine your attention to them only; It will give me pleasure to find that your observation has been as diffusive as the object is extensive.

The revenue officers were valuable agents for the new Secretary. When Hamilton decided to allow customs duties to be paid in the notes issued by the Massachusetts Bank in Boston, he offered this suggestion to Benjamin Lincoln, the collector of customs at that port.

Treasury Department November 20th. 1789

It is my wish to have an *eye* on the spot to attend to the operations of the Bank, in order that the measure now adopted may be continued or discontinued, as considerations of safety shall dictate. My own situation with regard to Philadelphia and New York answers this end; but I am too far distant from Boston to have it in my power to pay the same attention there. This hint you will of course perceive to be confidential and designed only for yourself.

Should you therefore at any time perceive it to be unsafe to continue the receipt of the Notes of the Bank of Massachusets or to make that Bank the depository of the public Monies received in your State, I authorize you not only to discontinue the receipt yourself but *as from me* to countermand that receipt at, and . . . the proposed remittance ... from the other ports.

This discretion I confide in you from the intire confidence I have in your prudence and judgement.

Private citizens could serve the Department of the Treasury as well, a fact Hamilton made clear in a letter to William Bingham, a wealthy Philadelphia merchant and director of the Bank of North America. Bingham's knowledge of American and British business made him an excellent source of information.

Private New York October 10th, 1789

There is a species of information highly requisite to the Government in adjusting the policy of its Treaties and Laws respecting Navigation for obtaining which with proper accuracy and detail no regular plan has ever yet been persued in this Country. It relates to the comparative advantages with which the Navigation of the United States and that of other Nations with whom they trade is or can be carried on. The utility of the Knowledge of the facts on which this comparison will depend need not I am sure be explained to you.

Knowing as I do your Zeal for whatever concerns the public good and relying upon your care and intelligence I take the Liberty to request your aid in making the enquiries requisite to the attainment of the Knowledge I have mentioned. ...

May I also take the Liberty to request of you that you will from time to time favor me with communications with regard to the operation of the Revenue and Navigation Laws which have been adopted the defects and inconveniences which have been experienced and the proper remedies. And with any thoughts that may occur to you concerning the Finances and Debts of the United States.

Washington's signature and the presidential seal adorn Hamilton's commission as Treasury Secretary.

Hamilton was aware that the Treasury Department might have problems when Congress reconvened in January, 1790. Indeed, he had already had a taste of James Madison's pronounced anti-British bias in the recent House session, as George Beckwith, Britain's unofficial minister to the United States, reported after a conversation with Hamilton.

[New York, October, 1789]

[Hamilton] ... I confess I was likewise rather surprized at it, as well as that the only opposition to General Washington was from thence. The truth is, that although this gentleman [Madison] is a clever man, he is very little Acquainted with the world. That he is Uncorrupted And incorruptible I have not a doubt; he has the same End in view that I have, And so have those gentlemen, who Act with him, but their mode of attaining it is very different.

If Hamilton considered Madison "little Acquainted with the world," he knew the Virginia congressman was well acquainted with American public opinion. During the congressional recess, while he was preparing for the House a plan for payment of the public debts, Hamilton asked Madison for his thoughts on the subject.

[New York, October 12, 1789]
I dont know how it was but I took it for granted that you had left town much earlier than you did; else I should have found an opportunity after your adjournment to converse with you on the subjects committed to me by the house of Representatives. It is certainly important, that a plan as complete and as unexceptionable as possible should be matured by the next meeting of Congress; and for this purpose it could not but be useful that there should be a comparison and concentration of ideas of those whose duty leads them to a contemplation of the subject.

As I lost the opportunity of a personal communication May I ask of your friendship to put to paper and send me your thoughts on such objects as may have occurred to you for an addition to our revenue; and also as to any modifications of the public debt which could be made consistent with good faith the interest of the Public and of its Creditors?

In my opinion, in considering plans for the increase of our revenues, the difficulty lies, not so much in the want of objects as in the prejudices which may be feared with regard to almost every object. The Question is very much What further taxes will be *least* unpopular?

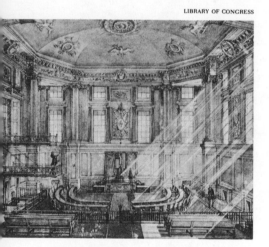

The chambers in New York City's Federal Hall, where the House of Representatives first met in 1789

Provision for the public debt required careful attention to international opinion as well. France, beset by political unrest and economic problems, was an increasingly impatient creditor. With this in mind, Hamilton wrote to his friend the Marquis de Lafayette of his plans for the Treasury Department.

New York October 6th, 1789
The debt due to France will be among the first objects of my attention. Hitherto it has been from necessity neglected. The Session of Congress is now over. It has been exhausted in the organization of the Government, and in a few laws of immediate urgency respecting navigation and commercial Imposts. The subject of the debt foreign and domestic has been referred to the next session which will commence the first Monday in January with an instruction to me to prepare and report a Plan comprehending an adequate Provision for the support of the Public Credit....

From this sketch you will perceive that I am not in a situation to address any thing officially to your administration; but I venture to say to you, as my friend, that if the installments of the Principal of the debt could be suspended for a few years, it would be a valuable accommodation to the United States. In this suggestion I contemplate a speedy payment of the *arrears* of *interest* now due, and effectual Prov[is]ion for the punctual payment of future interest as it arises. Could an arrangement of this sort meet the approbation of your Government, it would be best on every account that the offer should come unsolicited as a fresh mark of good will.

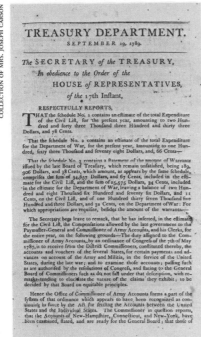

One of Hamilton's first reports to Congress as Treasury Secretary: an account of Government expenditures

During the three months of the congressional recess, while Hamilton was preparing his report on public credit, the Secretary also began publicizing his new administration and its new standards. In mid-December, he issued a circular letter to customs officials concerning the bonds given by shipowners as security for their payment of import duties.

Treasury Department 18 Decr. 1789
As one of the periods for the payment of Bonds taken for Duties is arrived, it is proper that the respective Collectors should be apprised of my expectation with regard to the conduct to be observed by them. It is, that if the Bonds are not paid, *as they fall due* they be immediately put in Suit. On this point, the *most exact punctuality* will be considered as *indispensable....* I am not unaware that the relaxations in this respect, which obtained in many instances under the State Laws, may give an Air of rigor to this Instruction; but I consider its *strict observance* as *essential,* not only to the order of the finances, but even to the propriety of the indulgence, which the Law allows

of procrastinated terms of payment of the Duties, and hence I regard this Strictness, as eventually most convenient to Individuals, as well as necessary to the Public.

The Secretary of the Treasury was equally firm concerning his own standards, as when he replied to Henry Lee of Virginia, who had asked for advance information on the provisions for the payment of the public debt.

[New York, December 1, 1789]
I am sure you are sincere when you say, you would not subject me to an impropriety. Nor do I know that there would be any in my answering your queries. But you remember the saying with regard to Caesar's Wife. I think the spirit of it applicable to every man concerned in the administration of the finances of a Country. With respect to the Conduct of such men — *Suspicion* is ever eagle eyed, And the most innocent things are apt to be misinterpreted.

Public interest in Hamilton's plans for the public credit ran high, but, as he explained to a friend in Philadelphia, he was reluctant to invite discussion in advance.

[New York] November 27, 1789.
With regard to feeling the public pulse about the debt I have several times had an inclination to the measure; but this inclination has given place to the reflection, that bringing on a discussion might be as likely to fix prejudices as to produce good, and that it may be safest to trust to the effect of the Legislative sanction to good measures, and to the reasons that will accompany them at the time.

Early in January, 1790, Hamilton's *Report Relative to a Provision for the Support of Public Credit* was ready for submission to the legislature. In accordance with a rule established by Congress—that officers of the executive departments could not appear personally to present their programs—Hamilton laid his plans before the legislature in a series of massive written reports like this one. The Secretary of the Treasury opened the first of his reports—a major document in the evolution of American government—with a lecture on the benefits of "funding" the national debt: that is, of establishing permanent funds for paying that debt and for converting the various forms of the debt (loan office certificates, certificates issued by the Army, and so forth) into interest-bearing government bonds. Then he dealt with the claims of the various classes of public creditors.

Treasury Department, January 9, 1790.

It is agreed on all hands, that that part of the debt which has been contracted abroad, and is denominated the foreign debt, ought to be provided for, according to the precise terms of the contracts relating to it. The discussions, which can arise, therefore, will have reference essentially to the domestic part of it, or to that which has been contracted at home. It is to be regretted, that there is not the same unanimity of sentiment on this part, as on the other.

The Secretary has too much deference for the opinions of every part of the community, not to have observed one, which has, more than once, made its appearance in the public prints. . . . It involves this question, whether a discrimination ought not to be made between original holders of the public securities, and present possessors, by purchase. Those who advocate a discrimination are for making a full provision for the securities of the former, at their nominal value; but contend, that the latter ought to receive no more than the cost to them, and the interest: And the idea is sometimes suggested of making good the difference to the primitive possessor. . . .

The Secretary, after the most mature reflection on the force of this argument, is induced to reject the doctrine it contains, as equally unjust and impolitic, as highly injurious, even to the original holders of public securities; as ruinous to public credit.

It is inconsistent with justice, because in the first place, it is a breach of contract; in violation of the rights of a fair purchaser. . . .

The difficulties too of regulating the details of a plan for that purpose, which would have even the semblance of equity, would be found immense. It may well be doubted whether they would not be insurmountable, and replete with absurd, as well as inequitable consequences, as to disgust even the proposers of the measure. . . .

[Hamilton knew that his proposal that all public creditors be treated equally would be fiercely debated. His next point, however, was also to raise a great deal of controversy.]

The Critical Period, FISKE

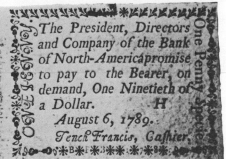

One-penny notes issued by the Bank of North America in August, 1789

The Secretary, after mature reflection on this point, entertains a full conviction, that an assumption of the debts of the particular states by the union, and a like provision for them, as for those of the union, will be a measure of sound policy and substantial justice.

It would, in the opinion of the Secretary, contribute, in an eminent degree, to an orderly, stable and satisfactory arrangement of the national finances.

Admitting, as ought to be the case, that a provision must be made in some way or other, for the entire debt; it will follow, that no greater revenues will be required, whether that provision be made wholly by the United States, or partly by them, and partly by the states separately.

The principal question then must be, whether such a provision cannot be more conveniently and effectually made, by one general plan issuing from one authority, than by different plans originating in different authorities....

If all the public creditors receive their dues from one source, distributed with an equal hand, their interest will be the same. And having the same interests, they will unite in the support of the fiscal arrangements of the government.... These circumstances combined will insure to the revenue laws a more ready and more satisfactory execution.

If on the contrary there are distinct provisions, there will be distinct interests, drawing different ways. That union and concert of views, among the creditors, which in every government is of great importance to their security, and to that of public credit, will not only not exist, but will be likely to give place to mutual jealousy and opposition. And from this cause, the operation of the systems which may be adopted, both by the particular states, and by the union... will be in danger of being counteracted....

[The report next explained how these debts were to be funded into a new issue of government securities. The old domestic debt was to be viewed as a form of annuity. Creditors were entitled to prompt payment of annual interest, but the Government was not required to redeem the principal of the debts at any set time. Hamilton then outlined a complicated system by which public

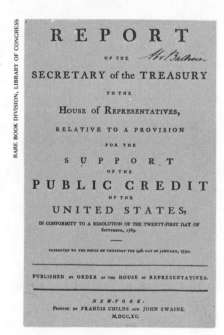

REPORT

OF THE

SECRETARY of the TREASURY

TO THE

House of REPRESENTATIVES,

RELATIVE TO A PROVISION

FOR THE

SUPPORT

OF THE

PUBLIC CREDIT

OF THE

UNITED STATES,

IN CONFORMITY TO A RESOLUTION OF THE TWENTY-FIRST DAY OF
September, 1789.

PRESENTED TO THE HOUSE ON THURSDAY THE 14th DAY OF JANUARY, 1790.

PUBLISHED BY ORDER OF THE HOUSE OF REPRESENTATIVES.

NEW-YORK:
PRINTED BY FRANCIS CHILDS AND JOHN SWAINE.
M,DCC,XC.

The House of Representatives had Hamilton's first report on the public credit printed in 1790.

creditors could accept various forms of bonds, public lands, or annuities for their old certificates. He estimated that government expenses and interest on the debt would require an annual income of $2,839,163.09.]

This sum may, in the opinion of the Secretary, be obtained from the present duties on imports and tonnage, with the additions, which...may be made on wines, spirits, including those distilled within the United States, teas and coffee.

The Secretary conceives, that it will be sound policy, to carry the duties upon articles of this kind, as high as will be consistent with the practicability of a safe collection. This will lessen the necessity, both of having recourse to direct taxation, and of accumulating duties where they would be more inconvenient to trade, and upon objects, which are more to be regarded as necessaries of life.

That the articles which have been enumerated, will, better than most others, bear high duties, can hardly be a question. They are all of them, in reality — luxuries—the greatest part of them foreign luxuries; some of them, in the excess in which they are used, pernicious luxuries. And there is, perhaps, none of them, which is not consumed in so great abundance, as may, justly, denominate it, a source of national extravagance and impoverishment. The consumption of ardent spirits particularly, no doubt very much on account of their cheapness, is carried to an extreme, which is truly to be regretted, as well in regard to the health and the morals, as to the oeconomy of the community....

The Secretary computes the nett product of the duties proposed in this report at about one million seven hundred and three thousand four hundred dollars ...which...will, together with the probable product of the duties on imports and tonnage, complete the sum required....

[Having listed his proposed import duties and taxes, Hamilton promised the House yet another plan.]

...the Secretary...ardently wishes to see it incorporated, as a fundamental maxim, in the system of public credit of the United States, that the creation of debt should always be accompanied with the means of extinguishment. . . .

Under this impression, the Secretary proposes, that the nett product of the post-office, to a sum not exceeding one million of dollars, be vested in commissioners, to consist of the Vice-President of the United States . . . , the Speaker of the House . . . , the Chief Justice, Secretary of the Treasury and Attorney-General of the United States, for the time being, in trust, to be applied, by them, or any three of them, to the discharge of the existing public debt, either by purchases of stock in the market, or by payments on account of the principal, as shall appear to them most adviseable . . . ; to continue so vested, until the whole of the debt shall be discharged. . . .

The Secretary contemplates the application of this money, through the medium of a national bank, for which, with the permission of the House, he will submit a plan in the course of the session.

The violent opposition that greeted Hamilton's report on the public debt made it impolitic for him to present a report on the bank at that time. Worst of all, Hamilton found that chief among the opponents of his program was his old friend James Madison. Two years later, Hamilton recalled his pain and surprise at Madison's behavior in early 1790.

Philadelphia May 26th, 1792

When I accepted the Office, I now hold, it was under a full persuasion, that from similarity of thinking, conspiring with personal goodwill, I should have the firm support of Mr. Madison, in the *general course* of my administration. Aware of the intrinsic difficulties of the situation and of the powers of Mr. Madison, I do not believe I should have accepted under a different supposition.

I have mentioned the similarity of thinking between that Gentleman and myself. This was relative not merely to the general principles of National Policy and Government but to the leading points which were likely to constitute questions in the administration of the finances. I mean 1 the expediency of *funding* the debt 2 the inexpediency of *discrimination* between original and present holders 3 The expediency of *assuming* the state Debts. . . .

Hamilton's military hat and saber and a copy of his report on funding adorn this engraved portrait.

Under these circumstances, you will naturally imagine that it must have been matter of surprize to me, when I was apprised, that it was Mr. Madison's intention to oppose my plan on both the last mentioned points.

Before the debate commenced, I had a conversation with him on my report, in the course of which I alluded to the calculation I had made of his sentiments and the grounds of that calculation. He did not deny them, but alledged in his justification that the very considerable alienation of the debt, subsequent to the periods at which he had opposed a discrimination, had essentially changed the state of the question—and that as to the assumption, he had contemplated it to take place *as matters stood at the peace.*

While the change of opinion avowed on the point of discrimination diminished my respect for the force of Mr. Madison's mind and the soundness of his judgment... Yet my previous impressions of the fairness of Mr. Madison's character and my reliance on his good will towards me disposed me to believe that his suggestions were sincere; and even, on the point of an assumption of the debts of the States as they stood at the peace, to lean towards a cooperation in his view; 'till on feeling the ground I found the thing impracticable, and on further reflection I thought it liable to immense difficulties.

Madison quickly lost his fight to institute a policy of monetary "discrimination" between the Government's original creditors and the men who had later purchased their certificates. The battle over Federal assumption of state debts, however, was longer and more difficult. Alexander White, a Virginian opposed to this provision, argued that debate on the matter was pointless until the House had some information on how the United States might pay the state debts. On March 3, hoping to delay debate, White moved that the Secretary of the Treasury report on funds to be used for the payment of interest on state debts. This delaying action failed and the very next day Hamilton submitted lists of revenues such as those that follow.

[Treasury Department, March 4, 1790]
An increase of the general product of the duties on goods imported, by abolishing the discount of ten per Cent allowed...in respect to goods imported in American bottoms, and adding ten per Cent to the rates specified, in respect to goods imported in foreign bottoms....

229

This change, without impairing the commercial policy of the regulation, or making an inconvenient addition to the general rates of the duties, will occasion an augmentation of the revenue little short of two hundred thousand dollars.

An additional duty on imported Sugars. Sugars are an object of general consumption, and yet constitute a small proportion of the expense of families. A moderate addition to the present rates would not be felt.

House debates on the assumption of state debts raised the old question of state rights and the new question of "constitutionality." Personal attacks were as bitter as they had ever been in the old Continental Congress. When Hamilton learned that Ædanus Burke of South Carolina had denounced him for his supposed insults to southern militiamen, he replied promptly and indignantly.

[New York, April 1, 1790]

I have been informed that in the house of Representatives yesterday, you made use of some very harsh expressions in relation to me.

As I cannot but ascribe so unprovoked an attack to misapprehension or misrepresentation I have concluded to send you an extract from the Eulogium pronounced by me on General Greene, of the part to which alone your animadversions do relate. It is in these words—

"From the heights of Monmouth I might lead you to the *plains of Springfield*, there to behold the Veteran Knyphaussen, at the head of a veteran army, baffled and almost beaten by a General without an army—aided, or rather embarrassed by small fugitive bodies of volunteer militia, *the mimicry of soldiership.*"

From this, you will perceive that the epithets, to which you have taken exception, are neither applicable to the Militia *of South Carolina* in particular, nor to *Militia* in general, but merely to "*small fugitive* bodies of *volunteer* militia."

Having thus Sir stated the matter in its true light it remains for you to judge what conduct, in consequence of the explanation will be proper on your part.

The first sessions of the Senate were held in this chamber in New York City's Federal Hall.

On April 12, the House rejected assumption as part of the funding program. The Senate had yet to act. But, if Congress was slow to adopt Hamilton's financial policies, speculators abroad were eager to invest in the nation's future. Indeed, the Dutch banking house of Willink, Van Staphorst, and Hubbard was too eager, having opened a loan for the United States without any authority from the Federal Government. In May, Hamilton wrote to the bankers in Amsterdam.

The President and his Cabinet, in an engraving by Currier and Ives: from left, Washington, Knox, Hamilton, Jefferson, and Randolph.

Treasury Department May 7th. 1790. The distinguished zeal you have in so many instances shewn for the interests of this country, intitles you upon all occasions to a favourable interpretation of the motives by which you are actuated.... Nor should I be apprehensive, that a sanction to the step you have taken, would form an inconvenient precedent for the future.

But the delays naturally incident to deliberations on a matter of the first consequence, the road to which had not been made easy by the antecedent state of things, having hitherto suspended any definitive resolutions concerning the public debt, I am not now in a situation to speak explicitly in regard to the measure you have undertaken. I can only say that the United States will stand in need of the aid of Loans abroad, and that I expect the requisite provision for making them upon solid, and consequently advantageous terms, will shortly be concluded upon; in which case you will immediately hear from me.

One Virginian, James Madison, had done his best to defeat Hamilton's program in the House; another native of that state soon came to Hamilton's aid. Thomas Jefferson, recently returned from his diplomatic post in Paris, took his oath as Secretary of State on March 22. He and Hamilton discovered several points of mutual interest, such as Jefferson's cherished plan to give America a decimal coinage and standardized system of weights and measures. Hamilton responded enthusiastically.

[New York, June 16, 1790] Mr. Hamilton presents his Compliments to Mr. Jefferson. He has perused with much satisfaction the draft of his report on the subject of weights and measures. There is no view which Mr. H has yet taken of the matter which stands opposed to the alteration of the money-unit as at present contemplated by the regulations of Congress either in the way suggested in the report or in that mentioned in the note of yesterday. And there are certainly strong reasons to render a correspondency desireable. The idea of a general standard among nations ... seems full of convenience & order.

Together, Jefferson and Hamilton solved the problem of Federal assumption of state debts by tying the issue to the debate over the future location of the Federal capital. Many southern Congressmen, opponents of assumption, were anxious to see the capital moved to the Potomac River, whereas many northerners were in favor of assumption but were reluctant to see the capital in the South. The new Secretary of State took credit for persuading Madison to cooperate in a "bargain" by which the South accepted assumption in return for northern votes on the site of the capital city. On July 21, the Senate restored assumption to the House bill on funding; three days later the House agreed to let the amendment stand. Hamilton's program had survived. As he later recalled, he could even forgive James Madison his obstinacy.

> Philadelphia May 26th, 1792
>
> At this time and afterwards repeated intimations were given to me that Mr. Madison, from a spirit of rivalship or some other cause had become personally unfriendly to me; and one Gentleman in particular, whose honor I have no reason to doubt, assured me, that Mr. Madison in a conversation with him had made a pretty direct attempt to insinuate unfavourable impressions of me.
>
> Still I suspended my opinion on the subject. I knew the malevolent officiousness of mankind too well to yield a very ready acquiescience to the suggestions which were made, and resolved to wait 'till time and more experience should afford a solution.

Hamilton could afford to be generous to his critics at the end of July, 1790. His political balance sheet for the last two years had been decidedly in his own favor. Although he had failed to defeat George Clinton in New York, that loss seemed trivial compared to his victory in helping to persuade George Washington to serve as President. With so many of the "right men" in national government, state politics seemed relatively unimportant.

As Congress prepared to adjourn that summer, Hamilton could look forward to working with old friends like John Jay, first Chief Justice of the Supreme Court, and Henry Knox, Secretary of War, and with a new ally, Thomas Jefferson. Hamilton would have agreed with Jefferson's sentiments when the Secretary of State wrote that with debates on funding and assumption "out of the way" there was now room to hope that "nothing else may be able to call up local principles." National principles and "respectable" government seemed assured.

Chapter 9

Public Affairs and a Private One

The spirit of conciliation and nationalism that flowered in the summer of 1790 was short-lived. In fact the compromise of 1790 may have been far less significant than Jefferson believed. There is considerable evidence that many of the senators and representatives who changed their votes on assumption and the location of the capital had made their decisions before the Secretary of State assumed the role of arbitrator. Perhaps the most important aspect of the compromise was that Jefferson believed that it had taken place. In later years, he complained that Hamilton had "duped" him into cooperating in the arrangement, and his sense of betrayal made him an increasingly bitter foe of the Treasury Secretary. Actually, Jefferson had perhaps duped himself by assuming that funding and assumption were the last of Hamilton's innovations. Hamilton had made no secret of the fact that these measures were only the beginning of a new financial system. Indeed, his first *Report on Public Credit* had closed with the promise that he would submit a plan for a national bank—an institution that Jefferson denounced as unconstitutional when it became a reality in 1791.

After the Government moved to Philadelphia in the autumn of 1790 (a temporary move until the new Federal City could be built on the Potomac), Jefferson had ample opportunity to become better acquainted with the Hamiltonian system. The Virginia statesman realized that he had apparently cooperated in a plan completely at odds with his own vision of America's national destiny. At every point the heads of the departments of State and of the Treasury now seemed certain to collide. In foreign policy, Hamilton was working for closer political and commercial ties with Britain, whose profitable trade could benefit the American mercantile community and swell the import duties assigned to funding the domestic debt; Jefferson, who had spent six years as America's minister in Paris, favored France, America's Revolutionary ally and Britain's traditional enemy. In domestic matters, Hamilton's reports on public credit, the bank, and manufactures revealed his conception of a national economy that could take advantage of the Industrial Revolution that was beginning to transform Europe, and that could add commerce and industry to its sources of wealth. Jefferson, however, clung to an almost mystical belief in the virtue of farming as an economic base, and to a Virginia planter's distrust of merchants.

It was a miracle of American political history that Jefferson and Hamilton avoided open conflict as long as they did. In the eighteen months after the passage of assumption, they learned to know each other better and to like each other less, but they managed to confine themselves to private expressions of mutual distrust and growing hostility. For much of this period, Hamilton was too involved in personal problems and with the routine of the Treasury to notice the depth of Jefferson's opposition. Like Jefferson, Hamilton was guilty of some self-delusion concerning the implications of the passage of assumption. His triumph in establishing the funding program made him overconfident. Success did entail a degree of personal inconvenience, for he now had to move his family and office to Philadelphia. But the task was made easier by a friend, to whom Hamilton wrote shortly after his victory in Congress.

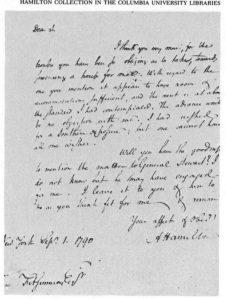

Hamilton's September note thanking Congressman Thomas FitzSimons of Pennsylvania for locating a house for the Hamilton family in Philadelphia

[New York] Augt. 5. 1790

I thank you for the interest you are so obliging as to take in procuring for me a house. My wish has been to have it first ascertained what arrangement would be made, if any, by your Magistracy or other public Men, in regard to *offices* for the accommodation of the department. If any public buildings should be destined to that purpose, my next wish would be to have a house as near my destined office as possible. A cool situation & exposure will of course be a very material point to a New Yorker. The house must have at least six rooms. Good dining and drawing rooms are material articles. I like elbow room in a yard. As to the rent the lower the better consistently with the acquisition of a proper house. But I must leave that to what is practicable.

When Judge [James] Wilson was in Town he obligingly offered to look out for me. Without adverting to your friendly undertaking I requested him to do so. I mention this that you may have the goodness to communicate with him: For *two houses* would be more than I shall *probably* have occasion for.

Congress had authorized the President to open two loans to implement the funding program: one for twelve million dollars, which would pay the foreign debt; and one that would raise two million dollars for the reduction of the domestic debt by purchases of government securities. At last Hamilton could employ the overenthusiastic Dutch bankers who had taken subscriptions for a loan to the United States without his approval. In a letter to Washington, Hamilton outlined his suggestions for using the funds available in Holland.

[New York, August 26, 1790]

The Minister of the Finances of France has...*solicited* that the money arising from the Loan in question, of which he has been apprised, might be applied in part payment of the Debt due to that nation. Its peculiar situation at the present juncture contains an appeal to the sensibility, as well as to the policy and honor of this Country in favor of that requisition.

If these reasons appear to the President sufficient to induce his sanction to the loan in question, it will remain to consider, under what act, it will be most expedient to authorise its being made, whether that of the 4th. or that of the 12th. of the present month, or whether it may not be advisable to authorise it partly under one & partly under the other.

...the business may easily take the latter form...and this is recommended by the consideration that it will contribute in a degree to all the purposes which require to be promoted.

If two thirds of the sum should be borrowed on account of the twelve millions and the remaining third on account of the two millions, the next half years interest in Holland may be discharged, the arrears of Interest on the Debt due to Spain may be paid off, a respectable payment may be made to France as a prelude to more considerable ones, and a sum of consequence to the operation, would remain towards the reduction of our Debt and supporting our funds in conformity to the intention of the last mentioned Act.

Philadelphia's Walnut Street, as it looked about 1790, when Hamilton took up residence there

Shortly thereafter, Elizabeth Hamilton took her children to Albany to visit her parents. Her husband, the only member of the Administration left in New York City, went about his official duties. In mid-September, he wrote to his wife.

[New York] Sep 15. 1790

You do not hope in vain My very Dear love that I am tired of living alone. I was so the very hour after you left me. But I am not sure for all this that it will be possible for

A miniature of Hamilton attributed to Charles Shirreff, circa 1790

me to come to you. . . . I am the only one of the Administration now here, and . . . it might be very awkward for me to be absent also. In this situation, I would press you to come down with your father, who writes me that he must be here by the 27th, if I did not believe that your health may be benefitted by your continuance where you are somewhat longer. . . . But I leave the matter to yourself. If you feel anxious or uneasy you had better come down. If you can prolong your stay with satisfaction it may be of service to you to do it and in that case I would endeavour to return with your father.

If you know My beloved wife how delightful it is to me to have you with me you need not be told how irksome it is to be separated from you & how much I desire to receive you again to my bosom.

Alone in Manhattan, Hamilton pursued one of the plans that would soon put him at odds with Jefferson. In October, 1789, Hamilton had begun a series of conferences with George Beckwith, Britain's unofficial representative in America. Beckwith's report of their first conversation revealed Hamilton's position clearly.

[New York, October, 1789]
[Hamilton:] I have requested to see you on this occasion from a Wish to Explain Certain points, relative to our situation, and from a desire to suggest a measure, which I conceive to be both for the interest of Great Britain, and of this Country to adopt. We have lately Established a Government upon principles, that in my opinion render it safe for any Nation to Enter into Treaties with us, Either Commercial or Political, which has not hitherto been the Case; I have always preferred a Connexion with you, to that of any other Country, *We think in English,* and have a similarity of prejudices, and of predilections. . . . We are a young and a growing Empire, with much Enterprize and vigour, but undoubtedly are, and must be for years, rather an Agricultural, than a manufacturing people. . . .

I am free to say, that Although France has been indulgent to us, in certain points, yet, what she can furnish, is by no means so Essential or so suited to us as Your productions, nor do our raw Materials suit her so well as they do you. . . .

We wish to form a Commercial treaty with you to Every

Extent, to which you may think it for Your interest to go. . . . I am of opinion, that it will be better for Great Britain to grant us admission into her [West Indian] Islands . . . than by a rigid adherence to Your present plan to produce a system of warfare in Commercial matters, which however Encouraged by France in this Country . . . with a view to promote coldness and animosity between the two Countries, I have Ever viewed with much regret, as being directly opposed to that system, which upon Mature reflexion, I have thought it most Eligible for us to pursue.

New problems brought Beckwith back to New York in July, 1790, when the threat of war with Spain made Britain fear that America might seize her posts in the West. Beckwith was anxious to learn if such "hostile designs" existed, and Washington ordered Hamilton to treat the English agent "very civilly" and "to extract as much as he could" from Beckwith. Hamilton's readiness to court Britain's good will and profitable trade became apparent in September after the President left for Virginia. In one conversation with Beckwith, for example, Hamilton "candidly examined" American foreign policy in the event of an Anglo-Spanish war.

[New York, September 26–30, 1790]

You know we have two parties with us; there are gentlemen, who think we ought to be connected with France in the most intimate terms, and that the Bourbon compact [between France and Spain] furnishes an example for us to follow; there are others who are at least as numerous, and influential, who decidedly prefer an English connexion, but the present condition of Great Britain and the States is favorable to the former party, and they are zealous to improve it; the present therefore is the moment to take up the matter seriously and dispassionately, and I wish it done without loss of time.

We consider ourselves perfectly at liberty to act with respect to Spain in any way most conducive to our interests, even to the going to war with that power, if we shall think it advisable to join You.

There would be nothing to criticize in Hamilton's conferences with Beckwith if he had been equally candid with his own Government. It was certainly to the interest of the United States to have at least one Cabinet member at work in the fall of 1790 during this dangerous period in European diplomacy. When the British agent called to investigate reports that America's minister in London, Gouverneur Morris, was on overfriendly terms with the French ambassador, Anne César, Marquis de La Luzerne, and Charles James Fox, the leader of the opposition party in the House of Commons, Hamilton sent this description of his reply to George Washington at Mount Vernon.

MARY EVANS PICTURE LIBRARY, LONDON

Charles James Fox

New York Sepr. 30. 1790

My answer [to Beckwith] was nearly as follows—

I have never heared a syllable Sir, about the matter you mention. It appears to me however very possible [that] an intimacy with both the persons you mention may exist: With the first [La Luzerne], because the situation of the parties had naturally produced such an intimacy, while both were in this Country; and to have dropped and avoided it there would not have been without difficulty, on the score of politeness, and would have worn an extraordinary and mysterious aspect: With the last [Fox], from the patronage of American affairs, which is understood to have been uniformly the part of that Gentleman, and in some degree, from a similarity of dispositions and characters; both brilliant men, men of wit and genius; both fond of the pleasures of society. It is to be hoped that appearances, which admit of so easy a solution will not prove an obstacle to any thing which mutual interest dictates. It is impossible that there can be any thing wrong.

Judging from Beckwith's version of the same conversation, Hamilton had been far more frank with the English agent than his report to Washington indicated, and he had not hesitated to criticize Morris's "prudence" and "fancy."

[New York, September 25–30, 1790]

[Hamilton:] Yes...I believe it in some measure to be true; I am the more inclined to be of this way of thinking from extracts of letters, which I have seen of [Gouverneur Morris], in which he throws out, that such and such were Mr. Fox's opinions on particular subjects, and from the former intimacy, which subsisted here between [Morris] and Monsieur de la Luzerne, as well as from Mr. Fox's line of politics during the war, his general character, and from my knowledge of [Morris] himself.

I do not question this gentleman's sincerity in following up those objects committed to his charge, but to deal frankly with You, I have some doubts of his prudence; this is the point in which he is deficient, for in other respects he is a man of great genius, liable however to be occasionally influenced by his fancy, which sometimes outruns his discretion.

These private conferences in New York were unknown to Jefferson. After the Treasury had moved to Philadelphia in the last week of October, Hamilton began work on a series of reports to Congress—reports that Jefferson could neither endorse nor ignore. These reports, submitted to the House of Representatives on December 13, contained Hamilton's "further provision" for the establishment of public credit, including, first of all, a proposal for paying interest on the state debts assumed by the Union.

Treasury Department December 13th. 1790

The object, which appears to be most immediately essential to the further support of public credit, in pursuance of the plan adopted during the last session of Congress, is, the establishment of proper and sufficient funds, for paying the interest which will begin to accrue, after the year one thousand seven hundred and ninety one, on the amount of the debts of the several States, assumed by the United States; having regard at the same time, to the probable, or estimated deficiency in those already established, as they respect the original debt of the Union....

...the sums requisite for those purposes...Making together Dollars. 826,624.73.

For procuring which sum, the reiterated reflections of the Secretary have suggested nothing so eligible and unexceptionable, in his judgment, as a further duty on foreign distilled spirits, and a duty on spirits distilled within the United States....

The offices of the Secretaries of State and the Treasury were housed in the matching two-story buildings just off the corner of Third and Chestnut streets in Philadelphia.

Hamilton's second report consisted of the plan for a national bank, which he had promised at the conclusion of his first report on the public credit a year earlier. Americans had argued the virtues and evils of banks for decades, and Hamilton knew he would have to meet the criticism of those who disliked the idea of banks and the moneyed power that banks seemed to represent. To him, there was nothing to fear from such institutions if they were properly regulated and made to serve the interests of the society in which they operated. In this famous report he outlined the creation of a national bank that could be as much a "servant" of the people as were the men who held office in the Republic. He opened with this declaration.

Hamilton's original draft (above) and a fair copy (below) of his proposal for a national bank

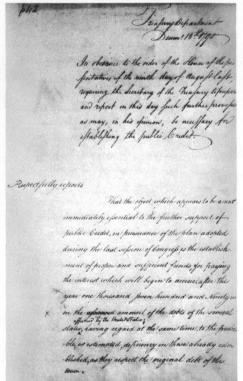

Treasury Department December 13th 1790

That from a conviction...That a National Bank is an Institution of primary importance to the prosperous administration of the Finances, and would be of the greatest utility in the operations connected with the support of the Public Credit, his [the Secretary of the Treasury's] attention has been drawn to devising the plan of such an institution...

There are at present three banks in the United States. That of North America, established in the city of Philadelphia; that of New York, established in the city of New York; that of Massachusetts, established in the city of Boston. Of these three, the first is the only one, which has at any time had a direct relation to the Government of the United States.

The Bank of North America originated in a resolution of Congress of the 26th of May 1781, founded upon a proposition of the Superintendant of finance....

The Directors of this Bank, on behalf of their constituents, have since *accepted* and *acted* under a new charter from the State of Pennsylvania, materially variant from their original one; and which so narrows the foundation of the institution, as to render it an incompetent basis for the extensive purposes of a National Bank....

The order of the subject leads next to an inquiry into the principles, upon which a national Bank, ought to be organised....

[First, however, Hamilton explained what the Bank ought *not* to be: it would have no "plurality of branches" nor would land form part of its capital.]

Considerations of public advantage suggest a further wish, which is, that the Bank could be established upon principles, that would cause the profits of it to redound to the immediate benefit of the State. This is contemplated by many, who speak of a National Bank, but the idea seems liable to insuperable objections. To attach full confidence to an institution of this nature, it appears to be an essential ingredient in its structure, that it shall be under a *private* not a *public* Direction, under the guidance of *individual interest,* not of *public policy;* which would be supposed to be...liable to being too much influenced by *public necessity.* The suspicion of this would most probably be a canker, that would continually corrode the vitals of the credit of the Bank....

The keen, steady, and, as it were, magnetic sense, of their own interest, as proprietors, in the Directors of a Bank, pointing invariably to its true pole, the prosperity of the institution, is the only security, that can always be relied upon, for a careful and prudent administration....

[Now Hamilton described what the bank *ought* to be: an institution whose capital would be limited to ten million dollars, of which two million dollars would be subscribed by the Federal Government. Only one fourth of each share would need to be paid in gold or silver; the rest would be in certificates of the public debt.]

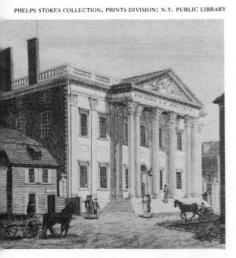

A 1799 engraving by William Birch shows the Bank of the United States on Third Street in Philadelphia.

The combination of a portion of the public Debt in the formation of the Capital, is the principal thing, of which an explanation is requisite. The chief object of this is, to enable the creation of a capital sufficiently large to be the basis of an extensive circulation, and an adequate security for it.... to collect such a sum in this country, in gold and silver, into one depository, may, without hesitation, be pronounced impracticable. Hence the necessity of an auxiliary which the public debt at once presents.

This part of the fund will be always ready to come in aid of the specie. It will more and more command a ready sale; and can therefore expeditiously be turned into coin if an exigency of the Bank should at any time require it....

The debt composing part of the capital... will produce a direct annual revenue of six per centum from the Government, which will enter into the half yearly dividends received by the Stockholders.

In January, 1791, Hamilton wrote his sister-in-law that the success of his financial program meant that the time was "not *very* distant" when he could retire from office. During the following month, however, there were indications that his policies would not be implemented as quickly or as easily as he had hoped. In Congress, James Madison campaigned for commercial restrictions that would favor France at Britain's expense. While Hamilton assured George Beckwith that this was of little consequence, he may have realized that it was a sign of broader, more consistent opposition. Beckwith reported the Secretary's remarks to his superiors in London.

Philadelphia January 19th.[–20] 1791

You know perfectly, that we have different opinions with us, as I have frequently told you; there is a Party which retaining those prejudices that were produced by the civil war, think nothing good can come from Great Britain, and that our obligations to France are never to be forgotten.... There are also worthy individuals with us, who are led to believe that by going into regulations which might cramp your trade to this country, that is, by advocating a system for a discrimination of duties, in favor of nations with whom we have treaties, it would lead to the attainment of a commercial treaty with England which they wish; and there is likewise a party, who ... are convinced, that you are the nation with whom we can trade to the greatest advantage: from these discordant sentiments it is difficult not to do something on this subject, and I think in the course of the present Sessions we shall adopt in a degree the idea furnished by your Navigation Act, the effect of which will be to restrain your shipping from being the carriers to our Markets of other produce or manufacture than that of your own dominions ... or of carrying from hence, excepting to your possessions ... : from the returns in my office, these regulations will not be of any consequence to the shipping of Great Britain.

Hamilton's certificate of election to the American Philosophical Society cited his "distinguished Eminence" and "literary merit."

While Madison was causing problems for Hamilton in the congressional debate on trade policies, Hamilton also found himself increasingly at odds with Jefferson in the Cabinet. When Gouverneur Morris's dispatches from London indicated that it would be impossible to conclude an Anglo-American commercial treaty, Jefferson advised the President to inform Congress of the failure of Morris's mission. Hamilton objected, but Washington made the disclosure to the House and Senate in February, 1791. When George Beckwith demanded the reasons for this decision, Hamilton offered him an explanation.

[Philadelphia, February 16, 1791]

I cannot bring myself to believe that The President's mind is the least influenced by any set of prejudices whatever; he indeed is of opinion from Mr. Morris's letters, *that no commercial treaty is attainable with England,* but I am sure he is not led to make these communications to the Legislature at this time, from any idea of assimilating this with other questions, yet I do not pretend to say that such views may not have struck the minds of certain persons, who have recommended this measure....

In the present state of things, nothing has happened between us and France, to give a tolerable pretence, for breaking off our treaty of Alliance with that Power and immediately forming one with you. A regard for National decorum, puts such a decisive step as this, out of our reach, but I tell you candidly as an individual, that I think the formation of a treaty of commerce, would by degrees have led to this measure, which undoubtedly that Party with us, whose remaining animosities and French partialities influence their whole political conduct, regard with dissatisfaction.

The same day that he commiserated with Beckwith on Anglo-American relations, Hamilton received a letter from Washington enclosing the written opinions of Jefferson and Edmund Randolph, the Attorney General, on the act of Congress establishing a Bank of the United States. Both Virginians had declared the measure to be unconstitutional, and Washington asked for the views of the Secretary of the Treasury. Hamilton replied in a document that must be considered one of the major state papers of the Federal period.

[Philadelphia, February 23, 1791]
It will naturally have been anticipated that, in performing this task he [the Secretary of the Treasury] would feel uncommon solicitude. Personal considerations alone arising from the reflection that the measure originated with him would be sufficient to produce it.... But the chief solicitude arises from a firm persuasion, that principles of construction like those espoused by the Secretary of State and the Attorney General would be fatal to the just & indispensible authority of the United States.

... the objections of the Secretary of State and Attorney General are founded on a general denial of the authority of the United States to erect corporations....

Now it appears to the Secretary of the Treasury, that this *general principle* is *inherent* in the very *definition* of *Government* and *essential* to every step of the progress to be made by that of the United States; namely—that every power vested in a Government is in its nature *sovereign,* and includes by *force* of the *term,* a right to employ all the *means* requisite, and fairly *applicable* to the attainment of the *ends* of such power; and which are not precluded by restrictions & exceptions specified in the constitution; or not immoral, or not contrary to the essential ends of political society....

It is not denied, that there are *implied,* as well as *express* powers, and that the former are as effectually delegated as the latter....

Then it follows, that as a power of erecting a corporation may as well be *implied* as any other thing; it may as well be employed as an *instrument* or *mean* of carrying into execution any of the specified powers, as any other instrument or mean whatever....

[Incorporation, Hamilton argued, was only a means to an end. If that end was "necessary and proper" for an object of the Government described by the Constitution, then incorporation of a bank would be valid. He also quarreled with Jefferson's narrow definition of the word "necessary."]

...the Secretary of State maintains, that no means are to be considered as *necessary,* but those without which the grant of the power would be *nugatory....*

It is certain, that neither the grammatical, nor popular sense of the term requires that construction. According to both, *necessary* often means no more than *needful, requisite, incidental, useful,* or *conducive to.* It is a common mode of expression to say, that it is *necessary* for a government or a person to do this or that thing, when nothing more is intended or understood, than that the interests of the government or person require, or will be promoted, by the doing of this or that thing. The imagination can be at no loss for exemplifications of the use of the word in this sense.

And it is the true one in which it is to be understood as used in the constitution. The whole turn of the clause containing it, indicates, that it was the intent of the convention, by that clause to give a liberal latitude to the exercise of the specified powers.... To understand the word as the Secretary of State does, would be to depart from its obvious & popular sense, and to give it a *restrictive* operation; an idea never before entertained. It would be to give it the same force as if the word *absolutely* or *indispensibly* had been prefixed to it.

A page from Hamilton's memo to Washington that defended the national bank's constitutionality

William Short

Washington accepted Hamilton's opinion of the bank's constitutionality as he had previously taken Jefferson's advice on diplomatic policy. The act incorporating the bank became law on February 25. A few weeks later the President left on a tour of the southern states. The informal, almost makeshift, nature of American government in 1791 was shown by the arrangements made for conducting business in his absence. The Cabinet and the Vice President were to "hold conversations" on "any serious and important cases" that might arise. This procedure was put to the test when Hamilton received a letter from William Short, the American chargé d'affaires in Paris, who had been named the official agent for supervising borrowing in Europe. Short's dispatch announced that a new loan had been obtained in Amsterdam. The Secretary of the Treasury explained his dilemma to the President.

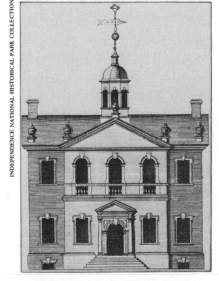

Historic Carpenter's Hall in Philadelphia, first headquarters of the Bank of the United States

Treasury Department April 10 1791. You will recallect that by a particular instruction from you to me, no succeeding *Loan* is to be opened, until *that* preceding has been submitted to you, and received your approbation. As it is very desireable that no delay may attend the progress of the business...to which the loans may be applied, I have concluded to submit Mr. Shorts letter tomorrow to the Vice President, and the heads of Departments, that they may consider, how far the case is within the purview of your letter; and whether it will not be expedient to authorise Mr. Short to proceed upon a further loan to the amount of three millions of guilders....

I request nevertheless to receive your instruction as soon as possible upon the subject. And I submit whether it will not be adviseable to change the restriction above mentioned so as to leave Mr. Short at liberty to open his loans successively for three millions of Dollars each; no new one to commence till after the preceding one has been filled; but without waiting for a ratification from this Country; provided the terms be not in any case less advantageous than those now announced. There is always danger of considerable delay in waiting for approbation from hence, before a new loan can be undertaken; and favourable *moments* may be lost.

Even though the Cabinet approved his plan for a new Dutch loan, Hamilton hesitated to send Short new instructions without Washington's personal authorization. While awaiting the President's instructions, Hamilton explained the gravity of the situation to Jefferson. France's precarious political position had caused her currency to depreciate, while Holland's remained stable in value. Thus a Dutch florin was worth more French livres than had been the case a few years earlier. Hamilton wrote to the Secretary of State, quoting William Short's description of a scheme by which speculators hoped literally to buy the American debt from the hard-pressed French Government.

Treasury Department, 15 April 1791

"The object of this company is, as you will see, to pay livres tournois [French currency] in their present depreciated State & to receive from the United States florins [Dutch currency] at the usual exchange—by this means France would receive from them *as much as she is entitled to receive from us,* but we should be obliged to pay the Company *much more than we are obliged to pay France."*…"I must also add that the house which makes these propositions is *entirely unknown* here & that I never heared even their names at Paris, which proves that *it must be an inconsiderable one."* Consequently the credit of the United States would be in imminent danger of suffering in their hands….

I take it for granted that the Court of France will not attempt any operation with the debt, without the consent of the United States. Any thing of this sort, considering the efforts which are making on our part, to discharge the debt, would certainly be very exceptionable. Indeed I do not see how any valid disposition of the debt of a sovereign power can be made without its consent; but it would be disagreeable to have to use this argument. I trust it will never be rendered necessary.

The bylaws of the Bank of the United States, printed in 1791 by Hamilton's protégé, John Fenno

France's political and financial picture changed quickly, but the United States, hampered by long delays in the exchange of dispatches, could only react slowly. Hamilton did not receive Washington's approval of Short's new instructions until the last week of May—almost six months after Short had written to announce the Dutch loan. With this problem solved, however, Hamilton turned to other business. That summer, Jefferson and Madison found time for a leisurely tour of New York and New England, engaging in conferences along the way with leading northern "republicans" (that is, anti-Hamiltonians). In the meantime, Hamilton remained hard at work at the Treasury Office. Early in June, he undertook the satisfying task of issuing instructions to the captains of the new revenue cutters, who had been given the thankless job of ending a time-honored American occupation —smuggling.

Treasury Department June 4 1791.

While I recommend in the strongest terms to the respective Officers, activity, vigilance & firmness, I feel no less solicitude that their deportment may be marked with prudence, moderation & good temper. Upon these last qualities not less than upon the former must depend the success, usefulness, & consequently *continuance* of the establishment in which they are included. They cannot be insensible that there are some prepossessions against it, that the charge with which they are entrusted is a delicate one, & that it is easy by mismanagement to produce serious & extensive clamour, disgust & odium.

They will always keep in mind that their Countrymen are Freemen & as such are impatient of every thing that bears the least mark of a domineering Spirit.... They will endeavour to overcome difficulties, if any are experienced, by a cool and temperate perseverance in their duty, by address & moderation rather than by vehemence or violence. The former stile of conduct will recommend them to the particular approbation of the president of the United states, while the reverse of it, even a single instance of outrage, or intemperate or improper treatment of any person with whom they have any thing to do in the course of their duty, will meet with his pointed displeasure, & will be attended with correspondent consequences.

SMITHSONIAN INSTITUTION

The key to the first United States Treasury Building in Philadelphia

On learning that Washington had returned to his home at Mount Vernon after his tour of the South, Hamilton sent him this cheerful and confident note.

Philadelphia June 19th. 1791.

I am very happy to learn that the circumstances of your journey have been in all respects so favourable. It has certainly been a particularly fortunate one, and I doubt not it will have been of real utility.

There is nothing which can be said to be new here worth communicating, except generally that all my Accounts from *Europe*, both private & official, concur in proving that the impressions now entertained of our government and its affairs (I may say) *throughout* that quarter of the Globe are of a nature the most flattering & pleasing.

... warmest wishes for your health & happiness...

With these "flattering & pleasing" reports to lighten his labors, the Secretary of the Treasury began work on a plan "for the encouragement and promotion of . . . manufactures" assigned him by the House. In June, he sent this request to the Supervisors of the Revenue in the various states.

> Treasury Department, June 22, 1791.
> I request . . . that you will give me as accurate Information as it shall be in your Power to obtain, *of the Manufactures of every Kind carried on within the Limits of your District, whether incidentally in the domestic Way, or as regular Trades — of the respective Times of their first Establishment — of the Degree of Maturity they have obtained — of the Quantities periodically made — of the Prices at which they are sold — of their respective Qualities — of the impediments, if any, under which they labour — of the Encouragements, if any, which they enjoy under the Laws of the State — whether they are carried on by Societies, Companies, or Individuals.*
>
> It would also be acceptable to me, to have Samples in Cases in which it could be done with Convenience, and without Expence.

One of America's first industrial centers grew up around the Falls of the Passaic in New Jersey.

Hamilton's public interest in manufactures paralleled a private concern. In the spring, he and William Duer, a former Treasury Department official, had discussed the prospect of organizing a "manufacturing Society." Over the summer, Hamilton worked with the organizers of the Society for Establishing Useful Manufactures, a private corporation that was to establish such a "manufactory" in New Jersey. By the end of August, Hamilton had completed this prospectus for the society.

> [Philadelphia, August, 1791]
> What is there to hinder the profitable prosecution of manufactures in this Country, when it is notorious, that . . . provisions and various kinds of raw materials are even cheaper here than in the Country from which our principal supplies come?
>
> The dearness of labour and the want of Capital are the two great objections to the success of manufactures in the United States.
>
> The first objection ceases to be formidable when it is recollected how prodigiously the proportion of manual labour in a variety of manufactures has been decreased by the late improvements in the construction and application of Machines — and when it is also considered to

The journey to the Schuyler summer home at Schuylerville (above) meant a trip across the Hudson at McNeal's Ferry (below).

what an extent women and even children in the populous parts of the Country may be rendered auxiliary to undertakings of this nature. It is also to be taken into calculation that emigrants may be engaged on reasonable terms in countries where labour is cheap, and brought over to the United States.

The last objection disappears in the eye of those who are aware how much may be done by a proper application of the public Debt. Here is the resource which has been hitherto wanted. . . .

To remedy this defect an association of the Capitals of a number of Individuals is an obvious expedient — and the species of Capital which consists of the public Stock is susceptible of dispositions which will render it adequate to the end. . . .

To effect the desired association an incorporation of the adventurers must be contemplated as a mean necessary to their security. This can doubtless be obtained. There is scarcely a state which could be insensible to the advantage of being the scene of such an undertaking. But there are reasons which strongly recommend the state of New Jersey for the purpose. It is thickly populated — provisions are there abundant and cheap. The state having scarcely any external commerce and no waste lands to be peopled can feel the impulse of no supposed interest hostile to the advancement of manufactures.

Despite the demands of the Treasury Department and his work on the *Report on Manufactures,* Hamilton found time to maintain an affectionate correspondence with his wife Elizabeth in the summer of 1791, when she and their children were visiting her parents in Albany. Early in August, Hamilton wrote anxiously on learning that their three-year-old son, James, was ill.

[Philadelphia] Aug. 2, 1791
I thank you my beloved Betsey for your letter announcing your safe arrival; but my satisfaction at learning this has been greatly alloyed by the intelligence you give me of the indisposition of my darling James. Heaven protect and preserve him! I am sure you will lose no time in advising me of any alteration which may happen. I trust he will not be in danger.

Remember the flannel next his skin, and If he should not be better when this reaches, try the bark-waiscoat.

Remember also the benefit he received from Barley
water with a dash of brandy. Be very attentive to his
diet. Indulge him with nothing that will injure him. Not
much fruit of any kind. Be sure that he drinks no water
which has not been first boiled in some iron vessel. I
hope he will have had some rhubarb or antimonial wine.
Paregoric at night in moderation will do him good & a
little bark [quinine] will not do him harm.

Take good care of my Lamb; but I need not recommend....

I am myself in good health & will wait with all the
patience I can the time for your return. But you must
not precipitate it. I am so anxious for a perfect restoration of your health that I am willing to make a great
sacrifice for it.

Alexander Hamilton's "sacrifice" in insisting that his
wife remain in Albany for her health was not as great as it seemed. Years
later, he recounted his experiences during Elizabeth's absence—a personal
adventure so bizarre that some of his later critics have suggested that he
invented the tale to conceal official misconduct.

[August 31, 1797]
Some time in the summer of the year 1791 a woman
called at my house in the city of Philadelphia and asked
to speak with me in private. I attended her into a room
apart from the family. With a seeming air of affliction
she informed that she was a daughter of a Mr. Lewis,
sister to a Mr. G. Livingston of the State of New-York,
and wife to a Mr. Reynolds whose father was in the Commissary Department during the war with Great Britain,
that her husband, who for a long time had treated her
very cruelly, had lately left her, to live with another
woman, and in so destitute a condition, that though desirous of returning to her friends she had not the means—
that knowing I was a citizen of New-York, she had taken
the liberty to apply to my humanity for assistance.

I replied, that her situation was a very interesting one
—that I was disposed to afford her assistance to convey
her to her friends, but this at the moment not being convenient to me (which was the fact) I must request the
place of her residence, to which I should bring or send
a small supply of money. She told me the street and the
number of the house where she lodged. In the evening I

put a bank-bill in my pocket and went to the house. I inquired for Mrs. Reynolds and was shewn up stairs, at the head of which she met me and conducted me into a bed room. I took the bill out of my pocket and gave it to her. Some conversation ensued from which it was quickly apparent that other than pecuniary consolation would be acceptable.

After this, I had frequent meetings with her, most of them at my own house; Mrs. Hamilton with her children being absent on a visit to her father.

In the midst of his liaison with Maria Reynolds, Hamilton was faced with a new crisis for the Treasury. In March, Congress had acted on his suggestion that distilled liquors be taxed. By the end of the summer, opposition to this excise had appeared in Pennsylvania. In a report prepared for President Washington three years later, Hamilton recalled incidents in the four westernmost counties of that state in 1791.

Treasury Department [August 5] 1794

The opposition first manifested itself in the milder shape of the circulation of opinions unfavourable to the law & calculated by the influence of public disesteem to discourage the accepting or holding of Offices under it or the complying with it, by those who might be so disposed; to which was added the show of a discontinuance of the business of distilling. These expedients were shortly after succeeded by private associations to *forbear* compliances with the law. But it was not long before these more negative modes of opposition were perceived to be likely to prove ineffectual. . . .

The officers now began to experience marks of contempt and insult. Threats against them became frequent and loud; and after some time, these threats were ripened into acts of ill-treatment and outrage.

These acts of violence were preceded by certain Meetings of malcontent persons who entered into resolutions calculated at once to confirm inflame and systematize the spirit of opposition.

The first of these Meetings was holden at a place called Red Stone Old Fort, on the 27 of July 1791 where it was concerted that county committe[e]s should be convened in the four Counties at the respective seats of Justice therein. On the 23 of August following one of these committees assembled in the County of Washing-

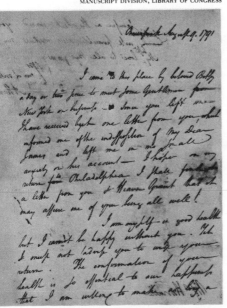

Hamilton wrote this tender letter to his "beloved Betsey" in the midst of his affair with Mrs. Reynolds.

To the Secretary of the Treasury —

A page from Washington's letter authorizing Hamilton to set up a system for collecting a whiskey tax

ton. . . . This Meeting passed some intemperate resolutions . . . containing a strong censure on the law, declaring that any person *who had accepted or might accept an office under Congress in order to carry it into effect should be considered as inimical to the interests of the Country; and recommending to the Citizens of Washington County to treat every person who had accepted or might thereafter accept any such office with contempt, and absolutely to refuse all kind of communication or intercourse with the Officers and to withold from them all aid support or comfort. . . .*

[These meetings, "conducted without moderation or prudence," were not the worst displays of opposition to the excise law in Pennsylvania. Hamilton recounted the experience of one unfortunate revenue collector.]

A party of men armed and disguised way-laid him at a place on Pidgeon Creek in Washington county — seized tarred and feathered him cut off his hair and deprived him of his horse, obliging him to travel on foot a considerable distance in that mortifying and painful situation.

The case was brought before the District Court of Pensylvania out of which Processes issued against John Robertson John Hamilton & Thomas McComb: three of the persons concerned in the outrage.

The serving of These processes was confided by the then Marshall Clement Biddle to his Deputy Joseph Fox, who . . . went into Alleghany County for the purpose of serving them.

The appearances & circumstances which Mr. Fox observed himself in the course of his journey, & learnt afterwards upon his arrival at Pittsburgh, had the effect of deterring him from the service of the processes . . .

Another complication in Hamilton's official life appeared in early August, when France's new minister to the United States, Jean Baptiste de Ternant, presented his credentials to the American Government. After a conversation with Hamilton, Beckwith recorded the Secretary's remarks on the future of Franco-American relations.

Philadelphia August 12th [1791]

Since I saw you, we have got Mr. Ternant, the minister pleniopotentiary from France; I have seen him for a few minutes only. You will find him a man of easy, pleasing manners, and very fit for the objects of his appointment. There has been a sort of alarm in France, and a degree of jealousy of *your* having lately turned your attention more towards this Country than formerly. [Britain had recently named a minister to the United States.]

From the nature of our government foreign affairs are totally in the department of the Secretary of State; we have no Cabinet, and the heads of Departments meet on very particular occasions only, therefore I am a stranger to any special views, that may be in the contemplation of the French government from the appointment of this Minister, but I think it probable, that a revision of their whole commercial condition with *us* may be in agitation, in the Hope of acquiring thereby some share in the trade and consumption of this country; he is a fit man in many respects for such purposes.

Philip Freneau

That same month, Jefferson and Madison completed arrangements for a young New York newspaperman named Philip Freneau, whom they had recruited during their summer tour of the northern states, to move to Philadelphia to serve as a State Department translator and as publisher of a "republican" newspaper. In August, too, Jefferson angrily denounced Vice President Adams for a series of letters signed "Publicola," which he believed Adams had written. In trying to soothe the Secretary of State, Hamilton only damned himself further in the Virginian's eyes. Jefferson made these notes of Hamilton's remarks—remarks that must have made Philip Freneau's venture as a publicist for republicanism seem all the more necessary.

[Philadelphia, August 13, 1791]

A. H. condemning mr Λ's writings...as having a tendency to weaken the present govmt declared in substance as follows. "I own it is my own op[inio]n, tho' I do not publish it in Dan & Bersheba, that the present govmt is not that which will answer the ends of society by giving stability & protection to it's rights, and that it will probably be found expediente to go into the British form. However, since we have undertaken the experiment, I am for giving it a fair course, whatever my expect[atio]ns may be. The success indeed so far is greater than I had expected, & therefore at present success seems more possible than it had done heretofore, & there are still other & other stages of improvemt which, if the present

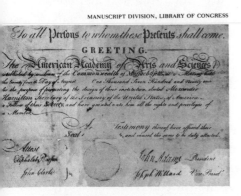

Hamilton's certificate of election to the American Academy of Arts and Sciences, signed and sealed by the Academy's president, John Adams

does not succeed, may be tried & ought to be tried before we give up the republican form altogether for that mind must be really depraved which would not prefer the equality of political rights which is the found[atio]n of pure republicanism, if it can be obtained consistently with order. Therefore whoever by his writings disturbs the present order of things, is really blameable, however pure his intent[io]ns may be, & he was sure mr Adams's were pure."

Increasingly, Jefferson saw Hamilton as the representative of "monarchical" thinking in politics and of the "monied" interest in financial policies. This moneyed interest, which was supposed to have benefited by Federal assumption of state debts and by the establishment of the national bank, was indulging in irresponsible speculation in government securities and bank stock in August, 1791. Activities in the New York stock market were compared to the legendary "South Sea Bubble," which had caused a crash in the British market a half century earlier. Hamilton's natural concern for the New York market was increased by the fact that William Duer, his former assistant in the Treasury Department and co-sponsor of the Society for Establishing Useful Manufactures, was the most notorious of these speculators. In mid-August, the Secretary wrote to Duer.

Philadelphia Aug 17 1791

The conversation here was—"Bank Script is getting so high as to become a bubble" in one breath—in another, "'tis a South Sea dream," in a third, "There is a combination of knowing ones at New York to raise it as high as possible by fictitious purchases in order to take in the credulous and ignorant"—In another "Duer [William] Constable and some others are mounting the balloon as fast as possible—If it dont soon burst, thousands will rue it" &c &c.

As to myself, my friend, I think I know you too well to suppose you capable of such views as were implied in those innuendoes, or to harbour the most distant thought that you could wander from the path either of public good or private integrity. But I will honestly own I had serious fears for you—for your *purse* and for your *reputation,* and with an anxiety for both I wrote to you in earnest terms.... My friendship for you & my concern for the public cause were both alarmed. If the infatuation had continued progressive & any extensive mischiefs had ensued you would certainly have had a large portion

William Duer

of the blame. Conscious of this I wrote to you in all the earnestness of apprehensive friendship.

Hamilton's comment that "the Stocks are all too high" was repeated in New York, and the Secretary found it necessary to defend himself to Senator Rufus King.

Rufus King, by C. W. Peale

[Philadelphia, August 17, 1791]
I observe what you say respecting the quotation of my opinion. I was not unaware of the delicacy of giving any & was sufficiently reserved 'till I perceived the extreme to which Bank Script and with it other stock was tending. But when I saw this I thought it adviseable to speak out, for a bubble connected with my operations is of all the enemies I have to fear, in my judgment, the most formidable—and not only not to promote, but as far as depends on me, to counteract delusions, appears to me to be the only secure foundation on which to stand. I thought it therefore expedient to risk something in contributing to dissolve the charm.

The "charm" of Hamilton's affair with Maria Reynolds was also dissolving in late August. This relationship cannot be described as any classic tale of romantic love. A restless married man had taken advantage of his wife's absence to have an extramarital fling. By the time he wrote this letter to Elizabeth, Alexander Hamilton had begun to regret his venture in adultery.

[Philadelphia, August 21, 1791]
You said that you would not stay longer at Albany than twenty days which would bring it to the first of September. How delighted shall I be to receive you again to my bosom & to embrace with you my precious children. And yet much as I long for this happy moment, my extreme anxiety for the restoration of your health will reconcile me to your staying longer where you are upon condition that you really receive benefit from it, and that your own mind is at ease. But I do not believe that I shall permit you to be so long absent from me another time.

By the first week of September, some of the complications in Hamilton's public and private life had begun to disappear. The New

York market had recovered, and Hamilton had persuaded Maria Reynolds to return to her husband. Elizabeth Hamilton was on her way to Philadelphia, and Hamilton sent this apologetic note when he realized he could not meet her in New Jersey.

A view of the Palisades along the Hudson—a prospect enjoyed by Elizabeth Hamilton en route south.

[Philadelphia, September 4, 1791]

I hoped with the strongest assurance to have met you at Eliz Town; but this change of weather has brought upon me an attack of the complaint in my kindneys, to which you know I have been sometimes subject in the fall. So that I could not with safety commit myself to so rude a vehicle as the stage for so long a journey....

But dont alarm yourself nor hurry so as to injure either yourself or the children. I am not *ill* though I might make myself so by the jolting of the carriage were I to undertake the journey. I am indeed better than I was, this Evening, and if I can get a proper machine I shall make use of a warm bath to which I am advised and from which I am persuaded I shall receive benefit.

A month later, Hamilton received word from William Short that American credit in Europe seemed shaky. Having dealt with a troubled stock market and a demanding mistress, Hamilton showed little alarm in writing to the Government's bankers in Amsterdam.

Treasury Department October 3d. 1791.

I have learnt with some surprise, through Mr. Short, that the price of the effects of the United States had undergone a sudden depression in the market of Amsterdam.

This is so different from the tenor of the hopes I had built upon those expressed by you, and so contrary to all the calculations I can form on the *natural course* of the thing, that I cannot but be curious for a particular devellopment of its cause.

It will therefore be satisfactory to me to receive from you, as early as may be, a full explanation of the circumstances which shall appear to you to have occasioned so unexpected a turn of the thing.

Logo of the National Gazette

As the day approached when he would submit the last of his famous reports to Congress, Hamilton seemed as confident as ever. "Republican" criticism of his programs did not appear serious, and although Philip Freneau's *National Gazette* began publication in Philadelphia in October, its contents seemed harmless enough. There was, however, one sign that Hamilton's "arrangements" for American finances were not progressing as he had wished. Without his knowledge, the directors of the new Bank of the United States had voted to establish branches in the major commercial cities. Nevertheless, after learning of the development, Hamilton wrote reassuringly to William Seton of the Bank of New York.

[Philadelphia] November 25. 1791

A letter from Hamilton to William Seton of the Bank of New York

Strange as it may appear to you, it is not more strange than true, that the whole affair of branches was *begun*, *continued* and *ended*; not only without my participation but *against my judgment*. When I say against my judgment, you will not understand that my opinion was given and overruled, for I never was consulted, but that the steps taken were contrary to my private opinion of the course which ought to have been pursued.

I am sensible of the inconveniences to be apprehended and I regret them; but I do not know that it will be in my power to avert them.

Ultimately it will be incumbent upon me to place the public funds in the keeping of the branch; but *it may be depended upon* that I shall *precipitate nothing*, but shall so conduct the transfer as not to embarrass or distress your institution.

In retrospect, the incident did not appear particularly significant. Meanwhile, Hamilton does not seem to have doubted that his *Report on Manufactures* would be as successful as his earlier recommendations to Congress had been. The report, which is now recognized as one of the most imaginative and innovative aspects of his Treasury program, demonstrates that Hamilton saw his proposals as much more than a means of preserving America's credit or of furnishing badly needed capital in the young nation. Important as these goals were, they were but part of a larger program, under which Hamilton dreamed of giving the American people, through careful government planning, an opportunity to take advantage of all the nation's resources. His report showed flexibility, foresight, and common sense in outlining the methods that could be used to develop a strong, balanced economy that would make the United States as independent of European trade policies as it was now free of foreign rule.

In presenting his report to the House, the Secretary did not ignore the fact that many members felt that it was unwise to encourage manufactures at the expense of agriculture; but he opened his proposals with the assumption that this idea had been "pretty generally" discarded.

[Philadelphia, December 5, 1791]

The embarrassments, which have obstructed the progress

of our external trade, have led to serious reflections on the necessity of enlarging the sphere of our domestic commerce: the restrictive regulations, which in foreign markets abrige the vent of the increasing surplus of our Agricultural produce, serve to beget an earnest desire, that a more extensive demand for that surplus may be created at home: And the complete success, which has rewarded manufacturing enterprise, in some valuable branches, conspiring with the promising symptoms, which attend some less mature essays, in others, justify a hope, that the obstacles to the growth of this species of industry are less formidable than they were apprehended to be. . . .

[Using the arguments employed in the prospectus for the Society for Establishing Useful Manufactures, Hamilton said both land and factories could be productive. Further, he pointed out that America put herself at the mercy of "foreign demand" by concentrating on agriculture.]

The consequence of it is, that the United States are to a certain extent in the situation of a country precluded from foreign Commerce. They can indeed, without difficulty obtain from abroad the manufactured supplies, of which they are in want; but they experience numerous and very injurious impediments to the emission and vent of their own commodities. . . .

In such a position of things, the United States cannot exchange with Europe on equal terms; and the want of reciprocity would render them the victim of a system, which should induce them to confine their views to Agriculture and refrain from Manufactures. A constant and encreasing necessity, on their part, for the commodities of Europe, and only a partial and occasional demand for their own, in return, could not but expose them to a state of impoverishment, compared with the opulence to which their political and natural advantages authorise them to aspire. . . .

[At this time, American factories had a great disadvantage in competing with foreign goods, since European governments subsidized their native industries. America, too, could aid her manufacturers, and the new financial

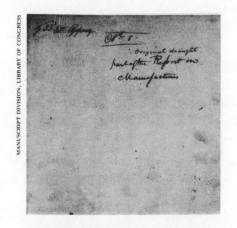

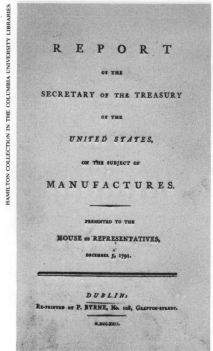

Title pages from Hamilton's draft (top) and from a published edition of his Report on Manufactures

system would end the scarcity of capital for investment.]

In order to a better judgment of the Means proper to be resorted to by the United States, it will be of use to Advert to those which have been employed with success in other Countries. The principal of these are.

I Protecting duties—or duties on those foreign articles which are the rivals of the domestic ones, intended to be encouraged...

II. Prohibitions of rival articles or duties equivalent to prohibitions...

III Prohibitions of the exportation of the materials of manufactures...

IV Pecuniary bounties...

V. Premiums...

VI The Exemption of the Materials of manufactures from duty...

VII Drawbacks of the duties which are imposed on the Materials of Manufactures...

VIII The encouragement of new inventions and discoveries, at home, and of the introduction into the United States of such as may have been made in other countries; particularly those, which relate to machinery...

IX Judicious regulations for the inspection of manufactured commodities...

X The facilitating of pecuniary remittances from place to place is a point of considerable moment to trade in general, and to manufactures in particular....A general circulation of Bank paper...will be a most valuable mean to this end....

XI The facilitating of the transportation of commodities.

...There is perhaps scarcely any thing, which has been better calculated to assist the manufactures of Great Britain, than the ameliorations of the public roads of that Kingdom, and the great progress which has been of late made in opening canals. Of the former, the United States stand much in need; and for the latter they present uncommon facilities.

Shares of stock in the Society for Establishing Useful Manufactures, signed by William Duer

His official duty done, Hamilton found time for more personal business, such as writing to his eldest son, Philip, who had been sent to a boarding school in Trenton, New Jersey.

Philadelphia December 5 1791

Your Mama and myself were very happy to learn that you are pleased with your situation and content to stay as long as shall be thought for your good....

Your Master also informs me that you recited a lesson the first day you began, very much to his satisfaction. I expect every letter from him will give me a fresh proof of your progress. For I know that you can do a great deal, if you please, and I am sure you have too much spirit not to exert yourself, that you may make us every day more and more proud of you....

You remember that I engaged to send for you next Saturday and I will do it, unless you request me to put it off. For a promise must never be broken; and I never will make you one, which I will not fulfil as far as I am able. But it has occurred to me that the Christmas holidays are near at hand, and I suppose your school will then break up for some days and give you an opportunity of coming to stay with us for a longer time than if you should come on Saturday. Will it not be best for you, therefore, to put off your journey till the holidays? But determine as you like best and let me know what will be most pleasing to you.

A good night to my darling son. Adieu

A HAMILTON

As he looked forward to the Christmas holidays in December, 1791, Hamilton must have congratulated himself on having made several narrow escapes in that year. Gouverneur Morris's mission in London had failed, but Britain's new minister to the United States might have better luck in improving Anglo-American ties. He had betrayed his wife with Maria Reynolds, but his mistress had returned to her husband and seemed to be losing interest in her former lover. The New York stock market had shaken public confidence in the "funds," but no disastrous "bubble" had burst over the head of the Secretary of the Treasury.

With the *Report on Manufactures* in the hands of Congress, the last of the major pieces in the Hamiltonian system had been submitted. Its implementation, he hoped, would crown the success of his plan for America's economic development and permit Hamilton to retire. His successes in 1790 and 1791 had required hard work, skill, and foresight. Difficult as his tasks had been, he could consider himself a fortunate and contented man. Before the end of winter, however, Hamilton would meet a series of misfortunes that threatened to offset his earlier triumphs.

Chapter 10

Crisis in the Cabinet

The fate of his *Report on Manufactures* may have warned Hamilton that his policies would no longer win support so easily. Its recommendations were simply ignored by Congress. There were new issues and new divisions in the House in 1791–92 that left little time to consider subsidies for American industry or protective tariff policies. In that session, the "factions" that were supposed to have been banished under constitutional government reappeared. In the *Federalist* essays, James Madison had argued eloquently against the potential dangers of these divisive political groups. With ratification, so the theory went, Antifederalists would disappear and all Americans would unite in support of the new Administration. But new controversies, centering on the Department of the Treasury, created new factions, although Jefferson and Madison would have denied that they had inaugurated a party system. When they began to speak and write of a "republican interest" or "republican party," they saw themselves as defenders of American liberties who had to mount a counterattack against an alleged "monarchical party." There is no evidence that such a party ever existed, but fear of this shadowy force was a powerful motive for Republicans.

In some ways Hamilton's attitude toward this new faction was as unfair and unrealistic as the Republican fear of monarchy. To him it was not a political movement by men who honestly disagreed with his policies, but a plot to destroy "good government." When American Democratic-Republicans allied themselves with the cause of the new French Republic in early 1793, the "plot" seemed all the more threatening. The French Revolution had progressed through a period of constitutional monarchy to a republican regime that guillotined the former monarch and quarreled with all of Europe. Hamilton could not imagine that any man with a due regard for "proper" or "respectable" government could support such a nation.

The joint threat of French and American republicanism developed swiftly in 1792 and early 1793. The eighteen months after the completion of his *Report on Manufactures* must have seemed among the most discouraging in Hamilton's life. Everything that could have gone amiss with his "system" had occurred. Had he been a superstitious man, Hamilton might have taken a warning from the events of December 15, 1791. He later remembered how the day had begun with a note from Maria Reynolds.

[August, 1798]

One day, I received a letter from her...intimating a discovery by her husband. It was matter of doubt with me whether there had been really a discovery by accident, or whether the time for the catastrophe of the plot was arrived.

The same day, being the 15th of December 1791, I received from Mr. Reynolds the letter...by which he informs me of the detection of his wife in the act of writing a letter to me, and that he had obtained from her a discovery of her connection with me, suggesting that it was the consequence of an undue advantage taken of her distress....

[Then, as Hamilton recalled, he sent Reynolds a note asking him to call at the Treasury office. Reynolds complied immediately.]

He in substance repeated the topics contained in his letter, and concluded as he had done there, that he was resolved to have satisfaction.

I replied that he knew best what evidence he had of the alleged connection between me and his wife, that I neither admitted nor denied it—that if he knew of any injury I had done him, intitling him to satisfaction, it lay with him to name it.

He travelled over the same ground as before, and again concluded with the same vague claim of satisfaction, but without specifying the kind, which would content him. It was easy to understand that he wanted money, and to prevent an explosion, I resolved to gratify him. But willing to manage his delicacy, if he had any, I reminded him that I had at our first interview made him a promise of service, that I was disposed to do it as far as might be proper, and in my power, and requested him to consider in what manner I could do it, and to write to me. He withdrew with a promise of compliance.

Two days after, the 17th of December, he wrote me.

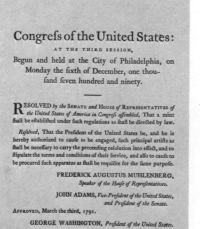

Above, the act of Congress that established the United States Mint; below, the first Mint building

Suspecting a plot against himself, Hamilton alerted a friend to the impending danger prior to his "rendezvous" with James Reynolds.

...The evident drift of this letter is to exaggerate the injury done by me, to make a display of sensibility and to magnify the atonement, which was to be required. It however comes to no conclusion, but proposes a meeting at the *George Tavern,* or at some other place more agreeable to me, which I should name....

I called upon Reynolds, and assuming a decisive tone, told him, that I was tired of his indecision, and insisted upon his declaring to me explicitly what it was he aimed at—He again promised to explain by letter.

On the 19th, I received the promised letter ["Sir I have Considered on the matter Serously. I have This preposial to make to you. give me the Sum Of thousand dollars and I will leve the town and take my daughter with me and go where my Friends Shant here from me and leve her to Yourself to do for as you [think] proper."] the essence of which is that he was willing to take a thousand dollars as the plaister of his wounded honor.

I determined to give it to him, and did so in two payments...dated the 22d of December and 3d of January.

Assured that Reynolds's injured feelings could be "plaistered" with cash, Hamilton returned to work. Britain's new minister, young George Hammond, had come to Philadelphia to conduct formal negotiations with Thomas Jefferson. In private, Hammond found Hamilton as "candid" as had George Beckwith. Reporting to his superiors in London in the first week of 1792, Hammond recorded the Secretary's comments on a list, prepared by Jefferson, of British infractions of the peace treaty of 1783.

[Philadelphia, January 1–8, 1792]

Mr. Hamilton expressed his conviction that the surrender of the posts was the only one which could produce any lengthy or difficult investigation. Upon this head he intimated that although he did not imagine this country could be easily induced to consent to a dereliction of any part of its territory acquired by the Treaty, it might perhaps still be possible to grant to his Majesty's subjects such privileges and immunities in the respective posts as would protect and secure them in the undisturbed prosecution of the Fur Trade....

...Upon the subject of the British Creditors, which he considered as the chief ground of complaint on the part of Great Britain, he assured me that in all cases of this kind, which had been brought before the federal Courts,

Patterns for the first U.S. half dollar; the House found the image of Washington too "monarchical" and substituted the figure "Liberty."

their determinations had been uniformly founded upon the treaty of peace, and had been consequently favorable to the British Creditors. . . .

In treating of the commercial arrangements between the two countries, Mr Hamilton readily admitted the importance of the British Commerce to the United States, and expressed his sanguine hopes that some system might be established mutually satisfactory to both countries. He did not fail to urge with much force and emphasis the anxiety of this country to obtain a small participation in the carrying trade with the West Indies, and the expediency of granting it.

A few days later, Hamilton received the flattering news that a group of New York merchants had commissioned John Trumbull to execute his portrait. The merchants suggested that a part of his "Political Life" would be an appropriate setting for the picture, but Hamilton demurred.

Philadelphia January 15 1792

The mark of esteem on the part of fellow Citizens, to whom I am attached by so many ties, which is announced in your letter . . . is intitled to my affectionate acknowlegements.

I shall chearfully obey their wish as far as respects the taking of my Portrait; but I ask that they will permit it to appear unconnected with any incident of my political life. The simple representation of their fellow Citizen and friend will best accord with my feelings.

Although pleased with the compliment from his friends in the business community, Hamilton well knew that they could damage the Treasury's programs if left to their own devices. Memories of the speculative fever of August, 1791, were still fresh at the end of February, 1792, when the "superstructure of Credit" collapsed completely. Worst of all, from Hamilton's point of view, the crash was triggered by the failure of his friend and former aide, William Duer. Prices of government securities fell sharply, and Hamilton did his best to save the market with purchases for the Sinking Fund. Too impatient to wait for the commissioners of the fund to argue legal technicalities before giving him formal authorization to act, he wrote to William Seton at the end of March asking him to buy securities in the New York stock market—with the following proviso.

Phila. 25th March 1792

You will not however declare on whose account you act,

John Trumbull, by S. L. Waldo

because tho there is, as to a purchase on that principle, no difference of opinion among the Trustees, the thing is not formally aranged and this is Sunday.

It will be very probably conjectured that you appear for the Public; and the conjecture may be left to have its course but without confession. The purchase ought in the present state of things to be at Auction and not till to-morrow evening. But if the purchase at Auction will not tend as well to the purpose of relief as a different mode — it may be departed from. . . . I have just received a Letter from Mr. Short . . . by which he informs me that he has effected a loan for Three Millions of Florins at 4 [Per] Cent Interest on account of the United States. This may be announced; and as in the present moment of suspicion some minds may be disposed to consider the thing as a mere expedient to support the Stocks, I pledge my honor for its exact truth.

The commissioners of the Sinking Fund met the next day and gave Hamilton the powers to make these purchases. But the Secretary now faced new problems. Philip Freneau's *National Gazette* had declared war on the Treasury. Attacks on Hamilton began in mid-March, and on April 2, the paper carried an essay by "Brutus" (James Madison) assailing those who "pampered the spirit of speculation." The next day, at a meeting of the commissioners, Thomas Jefferson objected that the prices being offered for purchases were unrealistically high and would favor the hated speculators. Such criticisms may have prompted Hamilton to make these comments in the instructions he sent to William Seton.

Philadelphia April 4th 1792

I am pained, beyond expression, at the picture you and others give me of the situation of my fellow Citizens — especially as an ignorance of the extent of the disorder renders it impossible to judge whether any adequate remedy can be applied.

You may apply another 50 000 Dollars to purchases at such time as you judge it can be rendered most useful. . . .

I have doubt however whether it will be best to apply this immediately or wait the happening of the crisis which I fear is inevitable. If as is represented a pretty extensive explosion is to take place — the depression of the funds at such a moment will be in the extreme and then it may be more important than now to enter the market in force. I can in such case without difficulty add

William Seton

a hundred thousand Dollars probably a larger Sum....

How vexatious that imprudent speculations of Individuals should lead to an alienation of the National property at such under rates as are now given!

Still another of Hamilton's projects suffered as a result of the market crisis. He had envisioned government securities as a means of furnishing capital for investment at home. The failure of William Duer and other leaders in the Society for Useful Manufactures brought the society's operations to a halt. Hamilton gave the directors firm, sensible advice on salvaging what they could from the situation.

Philadelphia April 14. 1792

The following appears to me to be the course proper to be pursued.

1 To appoint the principal Officers of the Institution and regulate their duties. I mean a Superintendant, an Accountant, and a Cashier, especially the first. Tis impossible that any thing can proceed with vigour or efficiency till this is done....

The Cashier ought...to be of a character and *in a situation* to inspire the most thorough confidence.

No time ought to be lost in determining upon the place and contracting for the land and commencing the buildings. Under present circumstances I would advise that the latter be begun upon a moderate scale yet so as to be capable of extension.

I would also advise that the Society confine themselves at first to the cotton branch.... A complication of objects will tend to weaken still further a confidence already too much impaired.

If a loan should be wanted I would if requisite cooperate to endeavour to procure one on favourable terms.

Means should be taken to procure from Europe a *few essential* workmen; but in this too there ought to be *measure* and circumspection. Nothing should be put in jeopardy....

...I will only add this general observation that nothing scarcely can be so injurious to the affairs of the Society as a much longer suspension of operation.

The validity of Hamilton's views on promoting industry in America would have to be proved by the success of such private under-

NEW-YORK HISTORICAL SOCIETY

William Duer published this notice to his creditors the day after being imprisoned for his debts.

takings as the Society for Useful Manufactures, since Congress had shown less interest in adopting the *Report on Manufactures* than in harassing its author. Nor did Hamilton's trials end when Congress adjourned. His plans for reconciliation with Britain continued to be thwarted by Jefferson, who insisted on giving George Hammond a strongly worded statement of American grievances—despite Hamilton's pleas that he modify his tone. Hammond, after a meeting with Hamilton at the end of May, described the Secretary's attempts to minimize the importance of Jefferson's letter.

[Philadelphia, May 29–June 2, 1792]

This Gentlemen treated me (as he has done upon every occasion) with the strictest confidence and candour. After lamenting the intemperate violence of his colleague Mr Hamilton assured me that this letter was very far from meeting his approbation, or from containing a faithful exposition of the sentiments of this government. He added that at the time of our conversation the President had not had an opportunity of perusing this representation: For having returned from Virginia in the morning only on which it had been delivered to me, he had relied upon Mr Jefferson's assurance, that it was conformable to the opinions of the other members of the executive government.

The conflict between Federalists and Republicans erupted in a brawl on the floor of the House in 1798.

The outraged Hamilton lashed out at his enemies in a letter to his old friend Edward Carrington of Virginia. He concluded with a lengthy indictment of Madison and Jefferson.

Philadelphia May 26th, 1792

It was not 'till the last session that I became unequivocally convinced of the following truth—*"That Mr. Madison cooperating with Mr. Jefferson is at the head of a faction decidedly hostile to me and my administration, and actuated by views in my judgment subversive of the principles of good government and dangerous to the union, peace and happiness of the Country."*...

This conviction in my mind is the result of a long train of circumstances; many of them minute. To attempt to detail them all would fill a volume. I shall therefore confine myself to the mention of a few.

First—As to the point of opposition to me and my administration.

Mr. Jefferson with very little reserve manifests his dislike of the funding system generally; calling in question the expediency of funding a debt at all. Some expressions

A share of stock and a certificate of ownership issued by the U.S. Loan Office and signed by Hamilton

which he has dropped in my own presence...will not permit me to doubt on this point, representations, which I have had from various respectable quarters....

In various conversations with *foreigners* as well as citizens, he has thrown censure on my *principles* of government and on my measures of administration. He has predicted that the people would not long tolerate my proceedings & that I should not long maintain my ground. Some of those, whom he *immediately* and *notoriously* moves, have *even* whispered suspicions of the rectitude of my motives and conduct. In the question concerning the Bank he not only delivered an opinion in writing against its constitutionality & expediency; but he did it *in a stile and manner* which I felt as partaking of asperity and ill humour towards me. As one of the trustees of the sinking fund, I have experienced in almost every leading question opposition from him. When any turn of things in the community has threatened either odium or embarrassment to me, he has not been able to suppress the satisfaction which it gave him....

With regard to Mr. Madison—the matter stands thus. I have not heard, but in...one instance...of his having held language unfriendly to me in private conversation. But in his public conduct there has been a more uniform & persevering opposition than I have been able to resolve into a sincere difference of opinion. I cannot persuade myself that Mr. Madison and I, whose politics had formerly so much the *same point of departure*, should now diverge so widely in our opinions of the measures which are proper to be pursued. The opinion I once entertained of the candour and simplicity and fairness of Mr. Madisons character has, I acknowledge, given way to a decided opinion that *it is one of a peculiarly artificial and complicated kind....*

In respect to our foreign politics the views of these Gentlemen are in my judgment equally unsound & dangerous. *They have a womanish attachment to France and a womanish resentment against Great Britain.* They would draw us into the closest embrace of the former & involve us in all the consequences of her politics, & they would risk the peace of the country in their endeavours to keep us at the greatest possible distance from the latter. This disposition goes to a length particularly in

In a Federalist cartoon of 1790, Washington leads troops against French "cannibals," while Gallatin, Genêt, and Jefferson (right) try to hold back the Federal chariot.

Hamilton's promise to contribute money for a "water engine" to keep down the dust on Walnut Street

Mr. Jefferson of which, till lately, I had no adequate Idea. Various circumstances prove to me that if these Gentlemen were left to pursue their own course there would be in less than six months *an open War between the U States & Great Britain....*

Mr. Jefferson, it is known, did not in the first instance cordially acquiesce in the new constitution for the U States; he had many doubts & reserves. He left this Country before we had experienced the imbicillities of the former....

Mr. Madison had always entertained an exalted opinion of the talents, knowledge and virtues of Mr. Jefferson. The sentiment was probably reciprocal. A close correspondence subsisted between them during the time of Mr. Jefferson's absence from this country. A close intimacy arose upon his return.

Whether any peculiar opinions of Mr. Jefferson concerning the public debt wrought a change in the sentiments of Mr. Madison (for it is certain that the former is more radically wrong than the latter) or whether Mr. Madison seduced by the expectation of popularity and possibly by the calculation of advantage to the state of Virginia was led to change his own opinion—certain it is, that a very material *change* took place, & that the two Gentlemen were united in the new ideas. Mr. Jefferson was indiscreetly open in his approbation of Mr. Madison's principles, upon his first coming to the seat of Government. I say indiscreetly, because a Gentleman in the administration in one department ought not to have taken sides against another, in another department....

Another circumstance has contributed to widening the breach. 'Tis evident beyond a question, from every movement, that Mr Jefferson aims with ardent desire at the Presidential Chair. This too is an important object of the party-politics. It is supposed, from the nature of my former personal & political connexions, that I may favour some other candidate more than Mr. Jefferson when the Question shall occur by the retreat of the present Gentleman. My influence therefore with the Community becomes a thing, on ambitious & personal grounds, to be resisted & destroyed...

In such a state of mind, both these Gentlemen are prepared to hazard a great deal to effect a change. Most of the important measures of every Government are connected with the Treasury. To subvert the present head of it they deem it expedient to risk rendering the Government itself odious; perhaps foolishly thinking that they can easily recover the lost affections & confidence of the people....

[To this end, rumors had been spread in Virginia that Hamilton headed a "Monarchical party meditating the destruction of State & Republican Government." Denying the existence of such a party, Hamilton ended his letter to Carrington with this observation.]

If I were disposed to promote Monarchy & overthrow State Governments, I would mount the hobby horse of popularity—I would cry out usurpation—danger to liberty &c. &c—I would endeavour to prostrate the National Government—raise a ferment—and then "ride in the Whirlwind and direct the Storm." That there are men acting with Jefferson & Madison who have this in view I verily believe. I could lay my finger on some of them. That Madison does *not* mean it I also verily believe, and I rather believe the same of Jefferson; but I read him upon the whole thus—"A man of profound ambition & violent passions."

A broadside reporting on the hurricane that struck Philadelphia and New York on July 1, 1792

Hamilton's battle with his enemies paralleled his campaign to persuade the most important agent of "proper" government to remain in office. George Washington dreaded the prospect of another four years as President. Hamilton, Jefferson, and Madison had all urged him to accept a second term, but retirement was tempting to the sixty-year-old soldier, plagued with bad health and failing hearing. When the President left Philadelphia for Mount Vernon in mid-July, 1792, he was still undecided, and Hamilton pleaded with him in this letter.

Philadelphia July 30th [–August 3] 1792

I received the most sincere pleasure at finding in our last conversation, that there was some relaxation in the disposition you had before discovered to decline a reelection. Since your departure, I have lost no opportunity of sounding the opinions of persons, whose opinions were worth knowing, on these two points—1st the effect of your declining upon the public affairs, and upon your own reputation—2dly. the effect of your continuing, in reference to the declarations you have made of your disinclination to public life—And I can truly say, that I have not found the least difference of sentiment, on either point. The impression is uniform—that your declining would be to be deplored as the greatest evil, that could befall the country at the present juncture, and as critically hazardous to your own reputation—that your continuance will be justified in the mind of every friend to his country by the evident necessity for it. Tis clear, says every one, with whom I have conversed, that the affairs of the national government are not yet firmly established—that its enemies, generally speaking, are as inveterate as ever— ...that if you continue in office nothing materially mischievous is to be apprehended— if you quit much is to be dreaded— ...and, in fine, that on public and personal accounts, on patriotic and prudential considerations, the clear path to be pursued by you will be again to obey the voice of your country; which it is not doubted will be as earnest and as unanimous as ever.

Much of Washington's distaste for office stemmed from the growing spirit of "party" opposition, for Hamilton was now doing his best to counter Republican criticism. The day after he wrote to the President, the *Gazette of the United States* carried the first of Hamilton's letters as "An American" exposing the history of Philip Freneau's appearance in Philadelphia.

[Philadelphia, August 4, 1792]

Mr. Freneau before he came to this City to conduct the National Gazette was employed by Childs & Swaine Printers of the Dayly Advertiser in the City of New York in capacity of editor or superintendant. A paper more devoted to the views of a certain party of which Mr. Jefferson is the head than any to be found in this City was wanted. Mr. Freneau was thought a fit instrument. ...A negotiation was opened with him, which ended in the establishment of the National Gazette under his direction. There is good ground to believe that Mr. Madison while in New York...was the medium of that Negotiation.

Mr. Freneau came here at once Editor of the National Gazette and Clerk for foreign languages in the department of Mr. Jefferson. ...

Mr. Freneau is not then, as he would have supposed,

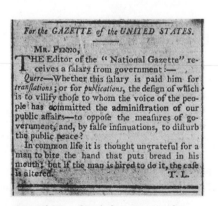

One of Hamilton's letters attacking Philip Freneau, the Antifederalist editor of the National Gazette

the Independent Editor of a News Paper, who, though receiving a salary from Government has firmness enough to expose its maladministration. He is the faithful and devoted servant of the head of a party, from whose hand he receives the boon. The whole complexion of his paper is an exact copy of the politics of his employer foreign and domestic, and exhibits a decisive internal evidence of the influence of that patronage under which he acts.

The need to defend the principles of constitutional government must have seemed even more pressing to Hamilton when he received a letter from Washington concerning public criticism of the Administration. The President sent Hamilton a list of "a variety of matters" for which the Government had been attacked and asked for his "ideas upon the discontents." Many of the "objections" were old arguments against a national bank, funding, and the Federal assumption of state debts. But Hamilton's opponents now claimed that these programs were part of a scheme in which "barren & useless speculation" was being used to corrupt Congress and nourish "vice & Idleness" in the people. Hamilton defended himself in a letter to Washington.

Philadelphia Aug 18. 1792

To uphold public credit and to be friendly to the Bank must be presupposed to be *corrupt things* before the being a proprietor in the funds or of bank Stock can be supposed to have a *corrupting influence*. The being a proprietor in either case is a very different thing from being ... a Stock jobber. On this point of the corruption of the Legislature one more observation of great weight remains. Those who oppose a *funded* debt and mean any provision for it contemplate an *annual* one. Now, it is impossible to conceive a more fruitful source of legislative corruption than this. All the members of it who should incline to speculate would have an annual opportunity of speculating upon their influence in the legislature to promote or retard or put off a provision. Every session the question whether the annual provision should be continued would be an occasion of pernicious caballing and corrupt bargaining. In this very view when the subject was in deliberation, it was impossible not to wish it declared upon once for all & out of the way....

[The intent of the speculators and "corrupt" legislators, so the whispering campaign went, was to overthrow the

Portrait of Alexander Hamilton by John Trumbull painted in 1792

Republic and to establish a monarchy. Hamilton knew that some of his own "theoretical" remarks had been responsible for this charge.]

A letter from the president of Harvard informing Hamilton that he had been awarded an honorary Doctor of Laws degree

This is a palpable misrepresentation. No man, that I know of, contemplated the introducing into this country of a monarchy. A very small number (not more than three or four) manifested theoretical opinions favourable in the abstract to a constitution like that of Great Britain, but every one agreed that such a constitution except as to the general distribution of departments and powers was out of the Question in reference to this Country. The Member [of the Philadelphia Convention] who was most explicit on this point (a Member from New York) declared in strong terms that the republican theory ought to be adhered to in this Country as long as there was any chance of its success—that the idea of a perfect equality of political rights among the citizens, exclusive of all permanent or hereditary distinctions, was of a nature to engage the good wishes of every good man, whatever might be his theoretic doubts—that it merited his best efforts to give success to it in practice—that hitherto from an incompetent structure of the Government it had not had a fair trial, and that the endeavour ought then to be to secure to it a better chance of success by a government more capable of energy and order.

There is not a man at present in either branch of the Legislature who, that I recollect, had held language in the Convention favourable to Monarchy.

The wide range of "discontents" that Washington had pointed out may have caused Hamilton to suspend temporarily his newspaper campaign against the Republicans. For the rest of August, local papers carried no articles that can definitely be attributed to him. By the end of the month, the Treasury had more than enough business to occupy the Secretary. The distillers and farmers of western Pennsylvania were obstructing the excise law more vigorously than ever. Congress had revised the tax in May, 1792, but opposition continued. Two years later, when the crisis came to a head, Hamilton gave the President a history of the affair.

[Philadelphia, August 5, 1794]

The first Law had left the number and positions of the Offices of Inspection, which were to be established in each District...to the discretion of the Supervisor. The

273

(5)

1 Sect. XV. *And be it further enacted and declared,* That the du-
2 ties hereby laid shall continue in force for the same time, and are
3 hereby pledged and appropriated to and for the same purposes,
4 as those in lieu of which they are laid, and pursuant to the act,
5 intitled, " An Act repealing, after the last day of June next, the
6 duties heretofore laid upon distilled spirits imported from abroad,
7 and laying others in their stead, and also upon spirits distilled
8 within the United States, and for appropriating the same."

1 Sect. XVI. *And be it further enacted,* That to make good any
2 deficiency which may happen in consequence of the reduction
3 hereby made in the rates of the duties on spirits distilled within
4 the United States, and on stills, so much of the product of the du-
5 ties laid by the act, intitled, " An Act for raising a farther sum
6 of money for the protection of the frontiers, and for other pur-
7 poses therein mentioned," as may be necessary, shall be, and is
8 hereby pledged and appropriated to the same purposes, to and for
9 which the duties, hereby reduced, were pledged and appro-
10 priated.

1 Sect. XVII. *And be it further enacted,* That the President of
2 the United States be authorized to make such allowances for
3 their respective services, to the supervisors, inspectors and other
4 officers of inspection, as he shall deem reasonable and proper, so
5 as the said allowances, together with the incidental expenses of
6 collecting the duties on spirits distilled within the United States,
7 shall not exceed seven and an half per centum of the total pro-
8 duct of the duties on distilled spirits, for the period to which
9 the said allowances shall relate, computing from the time that
10 the act, intitled " An Act repealing, after the last day of June
11 next, the duties heretofore laid upon distilled spirits imported
12 from abroad, and laying others in their stead, and also upon spi-
13 rits distilled within the United States, and for appropriating the
14 same," took effect :—*And provided also,* That such allowance
15 shall not exceed the annual amount of seventy thousand dollars,
16 until the same shall be further ascertained by law.

1792, *May the 2d—Passed the House of Representatives.*

Printed by John Fenno.

*A copy of the controversial act of
1792 imposing duties on spirits
distilled within the United States*

second [of May, 1792], to secure a due accommodation to Distillers, provides peremptorily that there shall be one in each County.

The idea was immediately embraced, that it was a very important point in the scheme of opposition to the law to prevent the establishment of Offices in the respective Counties. For this purpose, the intimidation of well disposed inhabitants was added to the plan of molesting and obstructing the Officers by force or otherwise, as might be necessary. So effectually was the first point carried, (the certain destruction of property and the peril of life being involved) that it became almost impracticable to obtain suitable places for Offices in some of the Counties—and when obtained, it was found a matter of necessity in almost every instance to abandon them.

After much effort The Inspector of the Revenue succeeded in procuring the house of William Faulkner a captain in the army for an Office of Inspection in the County of Washington. This took place in August 1792. The office was attended by the Inspector of the Revenue in person, till prevented by the following incidents.

Capt Faukner, being in pursuit of some Deserters from the troops, was encountered by a number of people ...who reproached him with letting his house for an Office of Inspection—drew a knife upon him, threatened to scalp him, tar and feather him, and reduce his house and property to Ashes, if he did not solemnly promise to prevent the further use of his House for an Office.

Captain Faulkner made the promise demanded of him. Hamilton, who sent a revenue officer to investigate the situation, at first advised the President to use any means necessary to suppress "the spirit of disobedience." But conferences with the Secretary of War and the Attorney General persuaded him that the Government could afford to show moderation. Meanwhile, Washington had learned of the newspaper war in Philadelphia and had written to Hamilton, Jefferson, and Randolph on the painful subject of dissension in the Cabinet. To his Secretary of the Treasury, the President suggested that the "irritating charges" in "some of our Gazettes" might "tare the Machine asunder" and must give way to "mutual forebearances and temporising yieldings *on all* sides." Hamilton promptly replied.

Philadelphia September 9 1792

The feelings and views which are manifested in that

letter are such as I expected would exist. And I most sincerely regret the causes of the uneasy sensations you experience. It is my most anxious wish, as far as may depend upon me, to smooth the path of your administration, and to render it prosperous and happy. And if any prospect shall open of healing or terminating the differences which exist, I shall most chearfully embrace it; though I consider myself as the deeply injured party. The recommendation of such a spirit is worthy of the moderation and wisdom which dictated it; and if your endeavours should prove unsuccessful, I do not hesitate to say that in my opinion the period is not remote when the public good will require *substitutes* for the *differing members* of your administration. The continuance of a division there must destroy the energy of Government, which will be little enough with the strictest Union. On my part there will be a most chearful acquiescence in such a result.

...I cannot conceal from you that I have had some instrumentality of late in the retaliations which have fallen upon certain public characters and that I find myself placed in a situation not to be able to recede *for the present.*

I considered myself as compelled to this conduct by reasons public as well as personal of the most cogent nature. I *know* that I have been an object of uniform opposition from Mr. Jefferson, from the first moment of his coming to the City of New York to enter upon his present office. I *know,* from the most authentic sources, that I have been the frequent subject of the most unkind whispers and insinuating from the same quarter. I have long seen a formed party in the Legislature, under his auspices, bent upon my subversion. I cannot doubt... that the National Gazette was instituted by him for political purposes and that one leading object of it has been to render me and all the measures connected with my department as odious as possible....

As long as I saw no danger to the Government, from the machinations which were going on, I resolved to be a silent sufferer of the injuries which were done me....

But when I no longer doubted, that there was a formed party deliberately bent upon the subversion of measures, which in its consequences would subvert the Government ...I considered it as a duty, to endeavour to resist the

A page from Washington's letter to Hamilton admonishing against the dissension he found in the Cabinet

torrent, and as an essential mean to this end, to draw aside the veil from the principal Actors. To this strong impulse, to this decided conviction, I have yielded. And I think events will prove that I have judged rightly.

Nevertheless I pledge my honor to you Sir, that if you shall hereafter form a plan to reunite the members of your administration, upon some steady principle of cooperation, I will faithfully concur in executing it during my continuance in office. And I will not directly or indirectly say or do a thing, that shall endanger a feud.

Hamilton's promise to do nothing "that shall endanger a feud" apparently did not include retirement from the public press. Three days after he wrote to Washington, a letter from "Civis" (Hamilton's current pen name) was published in the *National Gazette* in reply to "Mercator."

[Philadelphia, September 11, 1792]

The actual benefits or actual evils of the measures connected with the Treasury Department present and future would be cheerfully submitted to the *Test* of *Experience*. Happy would it be for the country, honorable for human nature, if the experiment were permitted to be fairly made.

But the pains which are taken to misrepresent the tendency of those measures, to inflame the public mind, to disturb the operations of Government are a decided proof, that those to whom they are attributable dare not trust the appeal to such a *Test*. Convinced of this, they have combined all their forces and are making one desperate effort to gain an ascendancy, in the public councils, by means of the ensuing election, in order to precipitate the laudable work of destroying what has been done.

The importance of the "ensuing election" would not permit Hamilton to keep silent. Washington had not yet announced that he would run for reelection, and George Clinton appeared to be making progress in his campaign for John Adams's office. Aaron Burr, the junior Senator from New York, was also making a bid for the Vice Presidency, and although Hamilton at first viewed the Senator as no more than "a diversion in favour of Mr. Clinton," to be safe he began moving against Burr's candidacy. While both Burr and Clinton were Republicans in politics, to Hamilton the Governor was far preferable in his morals and ethics. Adding "Fact" to his list of pen names, Hamilton began attacking the Senator in the public press; in private, he sent letters like this one to friends unacquainted with Burr.

Philadelphia September 21. 1792

Mr. Clinton's success I should think very unfortunate. I am not for trusting the Government too much in the hands of its enemies. But still Mr. C— is a man of property, and, in private life, as far as I know of probity. I fear the other Gentleman is unprincipled both as a public and private man. When the constitution was in deliberation, his conduct was equivocal; but its enemies, who I believe best understood him considered him as with them. In fact, I take it, he is for or against nothing, but as it suits his interest or ambition. He is determined, as I conceive, to make his way to be the head of the popular party and to climb...to the highest honors of the state; and as much higher as circumstances may permit. Embarrassed, as I understand, in his circumstances, with an extravagant family—bold enterprising and intriguing, I am mistaken, if it be not his object to play the game of confusion, and I feel it a religious duty to oppose his career.

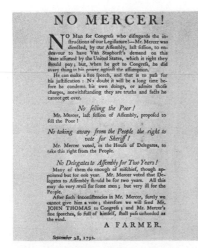

Hamilton published this broadside in 1792 to refute charges that he had engaged in financial speculation while he was Treasury Secretary.

I t was not long before another possibility occurred to Hamilton: the Burr and Clinton candidacies might be part of a plot to elect Jefferson, as he warned Charles Cotesworth Pinckney, a leading South Carolina Federalist.

Philadelphia October 10th 1792

A particular attention to the election for the next Congress is dictated by the vigorous and general effort which is making by factious men to introduce every where and in every department persons unfriendly to the measures, if not the constitution, of the National Government.

Either Governor Clinton or Mr. Burr of New York, both decidedly of the description of persons, I have mentioned, is to be run in this quarter as Vice President in opposition to Mr. Adams....It will be a real misfortune to the Government if either of them should prevail. Tis suspected by some that the plan is only to divide the votes of the N & Middle States to let in Mr. Jefferson by the votes of the South. I will not scruple to say to you in confidence that this also would be a serious misfortune to the Government. That Gentleman whom I once very much esteemed, but who does not permit me to retain

A broadside, found among Hamilton's papers, opposing the reelection of Congressman John Mercer, who had charged Hamilton with malfeasance

that sentiment for him, is certainly a man of sublimated and paradoxical imagination—entertaining & propagating notions inconsistent with dignified and orderly Government. Mr. Adams whatever objections may be against some of his theoretic opinions is a firm honest independent politician.

Hamilton's fears of Jefferson's vice-presidential ambition proved groundless. The Secretary of State wanted nothing so much as to resign and retire to Monticello at the end of Washington's term in office. Still, even though the President had decided to serve for four more years—and was, of course, reelected—and even though John Adams also won a second term, there was not much to cheer the Secretary of the Treasury. A new revolutionary government in France had "suspended" the King, and Republicans had made gains in congressional races. Hamilton scarcely needed more troubles, but more were on the way. On the morning of December 15, 1792, exactly a year after his meeting with James Reynolds, he welcomed three visitors to the Treasury office: Frederick Muhlenberg, former Speaker of the House, Senator James Monroe, and Representative Abraham Venable of Virginia. Later, Hamilton told the story.

Hamilton's letters to congressmen Muhlenberg, Monroe, and Venable, demanding copies of all documents relating to the Reynolds affair

[August, 1798]

Mr. Muhlenberg...introduced the subject by observing to me, that they *had discovered a very improper connection* between me and a Mr. Reynolds: extremely hurt by this mode of introduction, I arrested the progress of the discourse by giving way to very strong expressions of indignation. The gentlemen explained, telling me in substance that I had misapprehended them—that they did not intend to take the fact for established—that their meaning was to apprise me that unsought by them, information had been given them of an improper pecuniary connection between Mr. Reynolds and myself; that they had thought it their duty to pursue it and had become possessed of some documents of a suspicious complexion—that they had contemplated the laying the matter before the President, but before they did this, they thought it right to apprise me of the affair and to afford an opportunity of explanation; declaring at the same time that their agency in the matter was influenced solely by a sense of public duty and by no motive of personal ill will....

I replied, that the affair was now put upon a different footing—that I always stood ready to meet fair inquiry with frank communication—that it happened, in the present instance, to be in my power by written documents to remove all doubt as to the real nature of the business, and fully to convince, that nothing of the kind imputed to me did in fact exist. The same evening at my house was . . . appointed for an explanation.

Some weeks before this meeting, James Reynolds and Jacob Clingman had been arrested for bribing a witness so that they could win a financial claim against the Treasury. In their desperate attempts to escape prosecution, Clingman had hinted to Muhlenberg (a former employer) that Reynolds could prove that Hamilton had advanced him money to be used for speculation. It was this tale that brought Muhlenberg and the two members of Congress to see Hamilton, but at his home that evening Hamilton told them his version of the story—an account that reflected on his private, not his public, morality.

[August, 1798]

I stated in explanation, the circumstances of my affair with Mrs. Reynolds and the consequences of it and in confirmation produced the documents. . . . One or more of the gentlemen . . . was struck with so much conviction, before I had gotten through the communication that they delicately urged me to discontinue it as unnecessary. I insisted upon going through the whole and did so. The result was a full and unequivocal acknowlegement on the part of the three gentlemen of perfect satisfaction with the explanation and expressions of regret at the trouble and embarrassment which had been occasioned to me. Mr. Muhlenberg and Mr. Venable, in particular manifested a degree of sensibility on the occasion. Mr. Monroe was more cold but intirely explicit.

One of the gentlemen, I think, expressed a hope that I also was satisfied with their conduct in conducting the inquiry. I answered, that they knew I had been hurt at the opening of the affair—that this excepted, I was satisfied with their conduct and considered myself as having been treated with candor or with fairness and liberality.

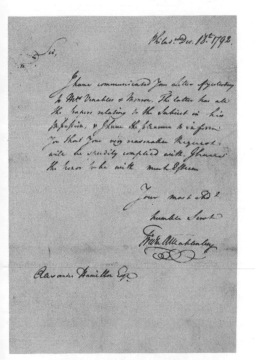

Muhlenberg's reply assuring Hamilton that his request (opposite) would be "speedily complied with"

Three days later, Hamilton belatedly replied to letters from his old friend John Jay. It was clear that his usual self-confidence had been badly shaken.

Frederick A. Muhlenberg

Philadelphia Decembr 18, 1792

Tis not the load of proper official business that alone engrosses me; though this would be enough to occupy any man. Tis not the extra attentions I am obliged to pay to the course of legislative manoevres that alone add to my burthen and perplexity. Tis the malicious intrigues to stab me in the dark, against which I am too often obliged to guard myself, that distract and harrass me to a point, which rendering my situation scarcely tolerable interferes with objects to which friendship & inclination would prompt me.

In the first months of 1793, Hamilton's enemies attacked again—not with "intrigues . . . in the dark," but with public charges to which Hamilton could respond. William Branch Giles of Virginia introduced a series of resolutions in the House calling for extensive investigation of Treasury operations. The resolutions were worded more as accusations than as requests for information, and Giles doubtless believed that Hamilton could never answer the charges before the end of the session. The challenge of hard work seemed to revive the Secretary's morale, and early in February Hamilton submitted his first reply.

William Branch Giles

Treasury Department, February 4th, 1793.

The resolutions, to which I am to answer, were not moved without a pretty copious display of the reasons, on which they were founded. These reasons are before the public through the channel of the press. They are of a nature, to excite attention, to beget alarm, to inspire doubts. Deductions of a very extraordinary complexion may, without forcing the sense, be drawn from them.

I feel it incumbent on me to meet the suggestions, which have been thrown out, with decision and explicitness. And, while I hope, I shall let fall nothing inconsistent with that cordial and unqualified respect, which I feel for the House of Representatives, while I acquiesce in the sufficiency of the motives, that induced, on their part, the giving a prompt and free course to the investigation proposed—I cannot but resolve to treat the subject, with a freedom, which is due to truth, and to the consciousness of a pure zeal for the public interest.

Soon the House was flooded with Hamilton's tables, accounts, and exhibits. There seemed no end to his reports, and one has the sense that he relished the hard work necessary to confound Giles. But during the congressional debate a new issue arose—one that would occupy more and more of Hamilton's time and energy. The Secretary was asked to justify his decision to suspend payments on the French debt in October, 1792, when he learned that Louis XVI had been deposed in favor of a new government. The fate of the French Republic soon became a focal point of party differences and helped persuade Jefferson to remain in the Cabinet. Hamilton, who had long doubted the possibility of orderly, democratic government in the Bourbon kingdom, had grown even more skeptical when the Revolution changed from a movement for a limited monarchy to one for a republic. In November, 1792, the French minister, Ternant, applied for funds to be used in the French colony of Santo Domingo. Hamilton warned Washington that it might be unwise to oblige Ternant because of the situation in France.

The rebellious mob that marched on Versailles on October 5, 1789

> Treasury Department November 19th 1792
> If a restoration of the King should take place, I am of opinion, that no payment which might be made in the Interval would be deemed regular or obligatory. The admission of it to our credit would consequently be considered as a matter of discretion, according to the opinion entertained of its merit and utility. A payment to the newly constituted power, as a reimbursement in course, or in any manner, which would subject it to be used in support of the change, would doubtless be rejected.

Granting aid to France was an especially delicate matter, since the new Republic was on the point of war with all her neighbors. Among members of the Cabinet, Hamilton stood alone in his determination to maintain American neutrality and to do as little as possible for the new French Government. When he finally learned that Louis XVI had been executed and that France had declared war on England, Holland, and Spain, Hamilton immediately set to work devising policies for meeting the crisis. The "continuance of peace" was essential to his program and could not be left to chance; and the imminent arrival of the new French minister, Edmond Genêt, made the American position even more delicate. Seeking the advice of a friend, Hamilton wrote two letters to John Jay in the same day.

> Philadelphia April 9 1793
> When we last conversed together on the subject we were both of opinion that the Minister expected from France should be received.
> Subsequent circumstances have perhaps induced an

One American broadside depicts the fate of France's Louis XVI (above); another (below) laments the death of the King, America's former ally.

additional embarrassment on this point and render it adviseable to reconsider the opinion generally and to raise this further question—Whether he ought to be received *absolutely* or with *qualifications?*

The King has been decapitated. Out of this will arise a Regent, acknowleged and supported by the Powers of Europe almost universally—in capacity to Act and who may himself send an Ambassador to the United States. Should we in such case receive both? If we receive one from the Republic & refuse the other, shall we stand on ground perfectly neutral?

If we receive a Minister from the Republic, shall we be afterwards at liberty to say—"We will not decide whether there is a Government in France competent to demand from us the performance of the existing treaties. What the Government in France shall be is the very point *in dispute.* 'Till that is decided the *applicability* of the Treaties is suspended. When that Government is *established* we shall consider whether such changes have been made as to render their continuance incompatible with the interest of the U States." If we shall not have concluded ourselves by any Act, I am of opinion, that we have at least a right to hold the thing suspended till the point in dispute is decided. I doubt whether we could *bona fide* dispute the ultimate obligation of the Treaties. Will the unqualified reception of a Minister conclude us?

If it will ought we so to conclude ourselves?

Ought we not rather to refuse receiving or to receive with qualification—declaring that we receive the person as the representative of the Government *in fact* of the French Nation reserving to ourselves a right to consider the applicability of the Treaties to the *actual situation* of the parties?

Philad April 9. 1793

I have already written you by this Post. A further Question occurs. Would not a proclamation prohibitting our citizens from taking Com[missio]ns. &c on either side be proper?

Would it be well that it should include a declaration of Neutrality?

If you think the measure prudent could you draft such a thing as you would deem proper? I wish much you could.

With debate heating up over the French crisis, Washington returned hastily to Philadelphia. On April 18, the Cabinet members met to give their opinions on "a general plan of conduct for the Executive," and, the next day, agreed to a Proclamation of Neutrality. This by no means settled American policy toward France, however. Hamilton and Secretary of War Henry Knox, who still differed sharply with Jefferson and Randolph over the reception to be given Genêt on his arrival, presented the President with their joint opinion (drafted by Hamilton) that the French minister should be received "with qualification." After discoursing at length on international law and the obligations of treaties, Hamilton came to the crucial point of his argument.

Philadelphia May 2. 1793

Are the United States bound, by the principles of the laws of nations, to consider the Treaties heretofore made with France, as in present force and operation between them and the actual Governing powers of the French Nation? or may they elect to consider their operation as suspended, reserving also a right to judge finally, whether any such changes have happened in the political affairs of France as may justify a renunciation of those Treaties?...

The conclusion from the whole is, that there is an option in the United States to hold the operation of the Treaties suspended—and that in the event, if the form of Government established in France shall be such as to render a continuance of the Treaties contrary to the interest of the United States, they may be renounced.

If there be such an option, there are strong reasons to shew, that the character and interest of the United States require, that they should pursue the course of holding the operation of the Treaties suspended.

Their character—because it was from Louis the XVI, the then sovereign of the Country, that they received those succours, which were so important in the establishment of their independence and liberty—It was with him his heirs and successors, that they contracted the engagements by which they obtained...succours....

To throw their weight into the scale of the New Government, would it is to be feared be considered by Mankind as not consistent with a decent regard to the relations which subsisted between them and Louis the XVI....

The character of the United States may be also con-

Silhouette of Edmond Charles Genêt

cerned in keeping clear of any connection with the Present Government of France in other views.

A struggle for liberty is in itself respectable and glorious. When conducted with magnanimity, justice and humanity it ought to command the admiration of every friend to human nature. But if sullied by crimes and extravagancies, it loses its respectability. Though success may rescue it from infamy, it cannot in the opinion of the sober part of Mankind attach to it much positive merit or praise. But in the event of a want of success, a general execration must attend it.

It appears thus far but too probable, that the pending revolution of France has sustained some serious blemishes. There is too much ground to anticipate that a sentence uncommonly severe will be passed upon it, if it fails.

The Cabinet had plenty of time to consider Genêt's reception, since the new minister had landed at Charleston, South Carolina, and seemed in no hurry to reach Philadelphia. Washington accepted Jefferson's advice to receive Genêt unconditionally, but even before the French diplomat arrived in the capital, there seemed to be good reason to regret the decision. George Hammond protested Genêt's activities in Charleston, and Hamilton presented this "state of facts" to Washington.

[Philadelphia, May 15, 1793]

Mr. Jenet Minister Plenipotentiary from the Republic of France arrives at charsletown. There he causes two privateers to be fitted out, to which he issues Commissions, to cruise against the enemies of France. There also, the Privateers are manned and partly with citizens of the United States, who are inlisted or engaged for the purpose, without the privity or permission of the Government of this Country; before even Mr Jenet has delivered his credentials and been recognized as a public Minister. One or both these Privateers make captures of British Vessels, in the neighbourhood of our Coasts, and bring or send their prizes into our Ports.

The British Minister Plenipotentiary among other things demands a restitution of these prizes. Ought the demands to be complied with?

I am of opinion that it ought to be complied with, and for the following reasons.

The proceedings in question are highly exceptionable

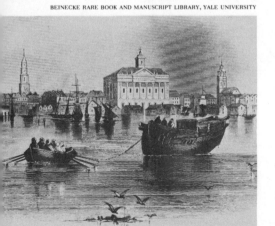

A view of Charleston, South Carolina, as it appeared in 1780

History of Philadelphia BY THOMPSON WESTCOTT

Genêt's house in Philadelphia

both as they respect our rights and as they make us an instrument of hostilities against Great Britain.

The jurisdiction of every *Independent* Nation, within its own territories, naturally excludes all exercise of authority, by any other Government, within those Territories, unless by its own consent, or in consequence of stipulations in Treaties. . . .

The equipping manning and commissioning of Vessels of War, the inlisting, levying or raising of men for military service, whether by land or sea—all which are essentially of the same nature—are among the highest and most important exercises of sovereignty.

It is therefore an injury and affront of a very serious kind, for one Nation to do acts of the above description, within the territories of another, without its consent or permission.

Hamilton's suspicions of a Republican "plot" were multiplied when Genêt reached Philadelphia on May 16. As soon as the French minister presented his credentials, he demanded advances on payments of the debt to France. Washington overruled Hamilton's suggestion that the request be declined abruptly; Genêt was refused, but he was refused as Jefferson wished, with courtesy. Taking heart, Genêt then refused to pay bills drawn by the Santo Domingo authorities under an agreement between his predecessor, Ternant, and the United States. Hamilton was furious and poured out his anger to George Hammond, who afterward wrote an account of the Secretary's remarks.

[Philadelphia, June 10–July 6, 1793]

A very influential member of the American administration . . . informed me . . . that Mr. Genêt's conduct was a direct violation of a formal compact, originally entered into with Mr. Ternant and subsequently confirmed by himself both in conversation and in writing, and on the faith of which the last payment of the installment due had been made: but notwithstanding the precise conditions of the contract, Mr. Genêt had not only refused payment of the bills in question, but had treated all the remonstrances of the government on the subject, with the utmost arrogance, and contempt. My informant farther said that this circumstance was extremely embarassing to the government, as it stood pledged to its own citizens that these bills should be paid. In consequence of which it would be under the necessity of anticipating as much of the installment due next September as would discharge these bills.

The unpaid bills were forgotten temporarily as the privateers commissioned at Charleston sent in more captured British prizes. Washington chose a middle course in dealing with these ships: the privateers were to leave American ports, although their prizes could remain, and Genêt was warned to cease commissioning privateers. The Frenchman simply disregarded the order. His privateers were seized in New York and Philadelphia, but George Hammond protested that two more ships were being armed in Baltimore. The Cabinet responded with limp assurances that it would consider "whether any practicable arrangement can be adopted to prevent the augmentation of the [privateer] force..." The Cabinet's attitude helped Hamilton to make a difficult decision: on June 21, he notified Washington that he would resign as Secretary of the Treasury.

Philadelphia June 21. 1793

Considerations, relative both to the public Interest and to my own delicacy, have brought me, after mature reflection, to a resolution to resign the office, I hold, towards the close of the ensuing session of Congress.

I postpone the final act to that period, because some propositions remain to be submitted by me to Congress, which are necessary to the full developement of my original plan, and, as I suppose, of some consequence to my reputation—and because, in the second place, I am desirous of giving an opportunity, while I shall be still in office, to the revival and more deliberate prosecution of the Inquiry into my conduct, which was instituted during the last session.

I think it proper to communicate my determination, thus early, among other reasons, because it will afford full time to investigate and weigh all the considerations, which ought to guide the appointment of my successor.

In September, 1792, Hamilton had warned Washington that the "public good" would soon "require *substitutes* for the differing members of your administration." He had remarked, as well, that "on my part there will be a most chearful acquiescence in such a result." By June, 1793, he was convinced that he was the member who would have to be replaced. The fortunes of party politics and war had gone against Hamilton for eighteen months, and he had good reason to feel that his presence in the Cabinet would only weaken the precious union he had so long defended.

A Picture Portfolio

Shaping the Young Republic

ODE
FOR THE
FEDERAL PROCESSION,
Upon the Adoption of the NEW GOVERNMENT.

Composed by Mr. L

I.

EMERGING from Old Ocean's bed,
  When fair Columbia rear'd her awful head
To his enraptur'd view, whose dauntless soul
Heav'n had impell'd t' explore the unknown goal;
The Genius of the solitary waste,
With extacy the god-like man embrac'd,
    Prophetic of her future state:
And smil'd serene, and bless'd th' approaching day,
When older Nations, envious, should survey
    Our Wisdom, Virtue, Pow'r how great!
    But still she sigh'd and dropt a tear,
    And still she entertain'd a fear,
Anticipating what she knew too well;
And what, this memorable day, the Muse
With retrospective ken reluctant views,
And this blest Epocha forbids to tell.†

II.

Distress'd she saw—but, with predictive eyes,
Through scenes of horror future bliss descrys;
Sees greater good from partial evil rise,
She knew how Empires rise and fall;
That all the changes on this terrene ball
    Revolve by Heav'n's command,
    Nor can its will withstand—
Submissive she that Pow'r ador'd,
The Sovereign Universal Lord,
    Almighty, wise and good!
Whose eye omniscient saw 'twas right,
We should attain that glorious height,
    Through Seas of kindred blood.

III.

And, lo! the all-important period's nigh,
  And swells the mighty theme—
An Æra, greater than the golden age
  Of which the Poets dream;
And adds a wond'rous, an illustrious page
To this terrestial Globe's vast history.
    Begin oh Muse,
    And far diffuse
    Th' inspiring news
    To Earth's remotest bound:
Throughout the world let joy like ours be found,
And Echo catch the animating sound,
  Now all our highest hopes are crown'd.
    Through time's incessant round,
    Fame shall resound
    This long desir'd event,
And tell what mighty blessings Heav'n has sent;
    Immortal Fame,
    Whose loud acclaim
  Is deathless as the Poet's song,
To countless ages shall the theme prolong.

IV.

Ten Sovereign States, in Friendship's league combin'd,
Blest with a G'vernment, which does embrace
The dearest Interests of the human race,
    This festive day, to joy resign'd,
    This signal day we celebrate—
    Let ev'ry patriot heart dilate,
    Let ev'ry care be banish'd far,
Nor sught the honors of this solemn season mar.
Behold th' admir'd Procession move along,
Our sister States, the happy ten, to greet—
  What animation in the crouded Street!
    What buzzing eclat from each tongue!
    In beautiful arrangement lo!
    Majestically slow,
    Some thousand souls, a federal band,
    Advancing hand in hand——
Heart-cheering sight! not half so much applause
Did Alexander's pompous entries crown;
Nor did he ever gain such true renown,
This grand display can boast a nobler cause.

    * Columbus.   † Alluding to the late war.

V.

Hail Liberty, thou heav'n-born child!
Young, smiling Cherub, virtuous, mild!
We feel, we feel thy Pow'r divine!
These solemnities are thine!
    Our hearts o'erflow,
    Our bosoms glow,
    Sorrow fades,
    Joy pervades
  Th' intoxicated senses!
Floods of Transport fill the soul,
And Melancholy's haggard train controul,
For now our Country's happiness commences!

VI.

Joy to the Union! Fair Columbia hail!——
Distraction in our Councils now shall fail,
And Strength, Respect and Wisdom join'd, prevail:
  Justice shall lift her well-poiz'd Scale.
With placid aspect, Peace her wand extend,
And white rob'd Virtue from the Sky descend;
Genius shall mount a glorious tow'ring height,
By genial Science foster'd and refin'd,
And never-dying wreaths our Offspring's temples bind—
While dwindled Europe sickens at the sight.
Arts, still encreasing, shall our clime adorn,
Success and Wealth crown millions yet unborn,
Glorious and smiling as the op'ning Morn!
And, if fair Industry but prompt the hand,
The cultur'd Earth shall teem at their command,
And Health and Plenty glad Heav'n's fav'rite land;
Pomona's charge shall grow luxuriant here,
And bounteous Ceres crown the blissful year;
Commerce shall raise her languid head—
The Nation's dignity, which with her fled,
Triumphant shall her place resume,
And Navies start from the tall forest's gloom.

VII.

Joy to our far-fam'd *Chief!* whose peerless worth
Makes Monarchs sicken at their royal birth;
And thou, grown dim with honorable age,
Whose Lore shall grace the scientific page,
Franklin, the patriot, venerable Sage,
Of philosophic memory! And thou,*
Our City's boast, to whom so much we owe;
In whom, tho' last and youngest of the three,
No common share of excellence we see:
In ev'ry grateful heart thou hast a place,
Nor Time, nor Circumstance can e'er erase.
All hail, ye Champions in your Country's cause!
Soon shall that Country ring with your applause—
With such, and with ten thousand Patriots more,
To what vast Fame this Western World shall soar!
Discord shall cease, and perfect Union reign,
And all confess that sweetly-pow'rful chain,
The *Fed'ral System,* which, at once, unites
The Thirteen States, and all the people's rights.
Oh, may those rights be sacred to the end,
And to our vast posterity descend;
That beauteous Structure flourish and expand,
And ceaseless Blessings crown our native Land!

    Alexander Hamilton, Esquire.

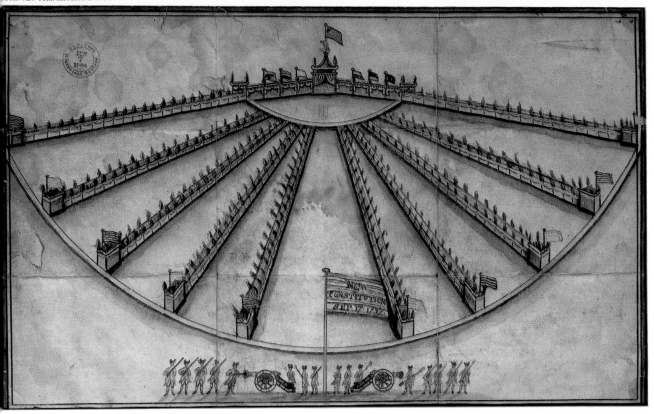

HAMILTONIANA

During the war one of George Washington's other military aides had dubbed Hamilton "the Little Lion," and it proved a sobriquet that suited him well during the difficult political battles he was to fight in the years ahead. When the New York Convention met at Poughkeepsie in June, 1788, to vote on ratification of the Constitution, Hamilton was by then its determined champion. A major voice at the Annapolis Convention of 1786 and the only New York delegate to the Constitutional Convention who had signed what he considered an acceptable compromise, Hamilton was also the author—with John Jay and James Madison—of *The Federalist*. During the tense summer of 1788, he helped sway the heavily Antifederalist New York Convention by his eloquent arguments. When the final vote was taken on July 26, ratification won by a slim vote of 30 to 27. In celebration of ratification by the necessary nine states, New York City had staged a huge federal procession three days earlier. A commemorative ode was written for the occasion (left) calling Hamilton "Our City's boast, to whom so much we owe...." A great float drawn by six white horses carried a ship marked "Hamilton," and L'Enfant designed a banquet pavilion (above) that would seat six thousand people for a celebratory feast. Hamilton at the age of thirty-three was the toast of his adopted town, and someone even suggested calling the city Hamiltoniana.

HAMILTON'S NEW YORK

Following New York's ratification of the Constitution, Hamilton returned to the Continental Congress, to which he had been elected in February, 1788, and successfully campaigned to keep the temporary seat of government in his own New York City. The view below shows the lower tip of Manhattan Island from the Hudson River in Hamilton's day. Just to the right of the ship's mast is the dome of the old City Hall, a block away from Trinity Church on Wall Street. Modernized and renamed Federal Hall, it became the first Capitol of the United States (right); Washington took his oath as first President on the balcony in 1789. Hamilton lived and had his law office at 56 and 57 Wall Street, which became known as Bank Row in 1792 when the first Bank of the United States opened at 52 Wall. At the northeast corner of Wall and William streets (right, below) stood the Bank of New York, founded in 1784 by Hamilton. All these water colors were done in the 1790's by Archibald Robertson of the British Army's Royal Engineers.

At the corner of Wall and Water streets was the Tontine Coffee House (left), which housed the New York

Stock Exchange. At far right is the Merchant's Coffee House, a gathering place for merchants and brokers.

THE

REPORT

OF THE

SECRETARY OF THE TREASURY,

(ALEXANDER HAMILTON,)

ON THE SUBJECT OF A

NATIONAL BANK.

Read in the House of Representatives, Dec. 13th, 1790

NEW-YORK:

PUBLISHED BY S. WHITING & CO.
No. 118, Pearl-street.
J. Seymour, print.
1811.

HIGH FINANCE

Two of Hamilton's mentors in the world of finance were Robert Morris and Gouverneur Morris. Robert Morris commissioned Charles Willson Peale to paint the double portrait at left of himself and Gouverneur (seated), his assistant in the Office of Finance, in 1783—the year after he had appointed Hamilton as his financial agent in New York State. As Secretary of the Treasury in 1790, Hamilton—in order to get approval for his fiscal programs—compromised with southerners who wished to move the capital from New York to a site on the Potomac River. The cartoon at lower left shows Robert Morris moving the Capitol to its interim location in Philadelphia. Hamilton himself moved his whole family, which by this time included four children, to Philadelphia and opened the Treasury office just around the corner from his house at 226 Walnut Street. In December, 1790, he submitted to Congress his report (left) urging that a national bank be established. After considerable debate, Congress enacted it into law; and a handsome building on Third Street (below) was built to house the first Bank of the United States.

FIRST SECRETARY OF THE TREASURY

The handsome portrait of Alexander Hamilton at right was painted for the New York Chamber of Commerce by John Trumbull in 1792 — a reflection of the pride that New York took in its illustrious resident. The indefatigable Secretary of the Treasury, by that time, had already issued four of his famous series of state papers, concerning public credit, a national bank, the mint, and manufactures. On most of these important questions Hamilton was opposed, often bitterly, by Thomas Jefferson. Washington's Secretary of State said of Hamilton that he "was not only a monarchist, but for a monarchy bottomed on corruption.... Hamilton was, indeed, a singular character. Of acute understanding, disinterested, honest, and honorable in all private transactions...yet so bewitched and perverted by the British example, as to be under thorough conviction that corruption was essential to the government of a nation." Indeed, about the only issue he and Hamilton agreed on was the decimal system of currency. Jefferson proposed it and Hamilton acted on it. The coins above show a selection issued between 1793 and 1796, including copper half cents and cents; silver half dimes, dimes, twenty-five cents, fifty cents, and dollars; and two and a half, five, and ten dollar gold pieces.

USEFUL MANUFACTURES

In addition to writing his notable *Report on The Subject of Manufactures*, which urged the Government to encourage manufacturing, as well as "the cultivation of the earth, as the primary and most certain source of national supply," Hamilton helped found the Society for Establishing Useful Manufactures. The venture was located in Paterson, New Jersey, alongside the beautiful Falls of the Passaic (below), which furnished the necessary water power for the mills that were built. At right is a lottery ticket issued to raise funds for the project. Unfortunately, the early experiment in American industrialization failed.

PATERSON
LOTTERY.

No.

J. WOODS, Printer.

THIS *TICKET* will entitle the Bearer to such PRIZE as may be drawn against its Number, in the LOTTERY of the SOCIETY FOR ESTABLISHING USEFUL MANUFACTURES, erected by Virtue of an Act of the Legislature of the State of New-Jersey.—Subject to a Deduction of 15 per Cent.

N

The subtle Seducer.

The American Financier.

London, Publish'd by A. Hamilton Jun.ʳ, Fleet Street, Jan.ʸ 10, 1781.

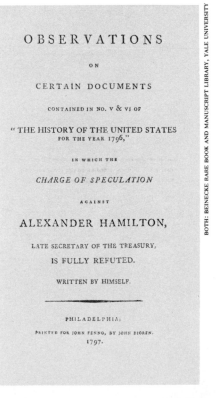

OBSERVATIONS

ON

CERTAIN DOCUMENTS

CONTAINED IN NO. V & VI OF

"THE HISTORY OF THE UNITED STATES
FOR THE YEAR 1796,"

IN WHICH THE

CHARGE OF SPECULATION

AGAINST

ALEXANDER HAMILTON,

LATE SECRETARY OF THE TREASURY,

IS FULLY REFUTED.

WRITTEN BY HIMSELF.

PHILADELPHIA:
PRINTED FOR JOHN FENNO, BY JOHN BIOREN.
1797.

HOME LIFE

Although Hamilton's married life appeared to be a happy one, he asserted under political pressure in 1797 that he had had an affair with Maria Reynolds, which began six years earlier in Philadelphia while Betsey and the children were in Albany. An English publisher inserted stock engravings labeled "The Subtle Seducer" and "The American Financier" as frontispieces to Hamilton's published confession (below, left). He managed to salvage his marriage, however, and built the Grange (left) in the countryside of upper Manhattan as a permanent home for his family. Cerrachi's fine bust (below) was placed in the entrance hall.

A FATAL ENCOUNTER

In 1804, Alexander Hamilton and Aaron Burr, by then bitter political enemies, started down a path from which there would be, for Hamilton, no return. When Burr challenged Hamilton to the fatal duel, Hamilton wrote "some remarks explanatory" of his conduct and motives. "...it is not to be denied that my animadversions on the political principles, character, and views of Col. Burr have been extremely severe.... He may have supposed himself under a necessity of acting as he has done...." The spot chosen for the dueling ground (right foreground) was in Weehawken, New Jersey, just across the Hudson River from New York City.

302

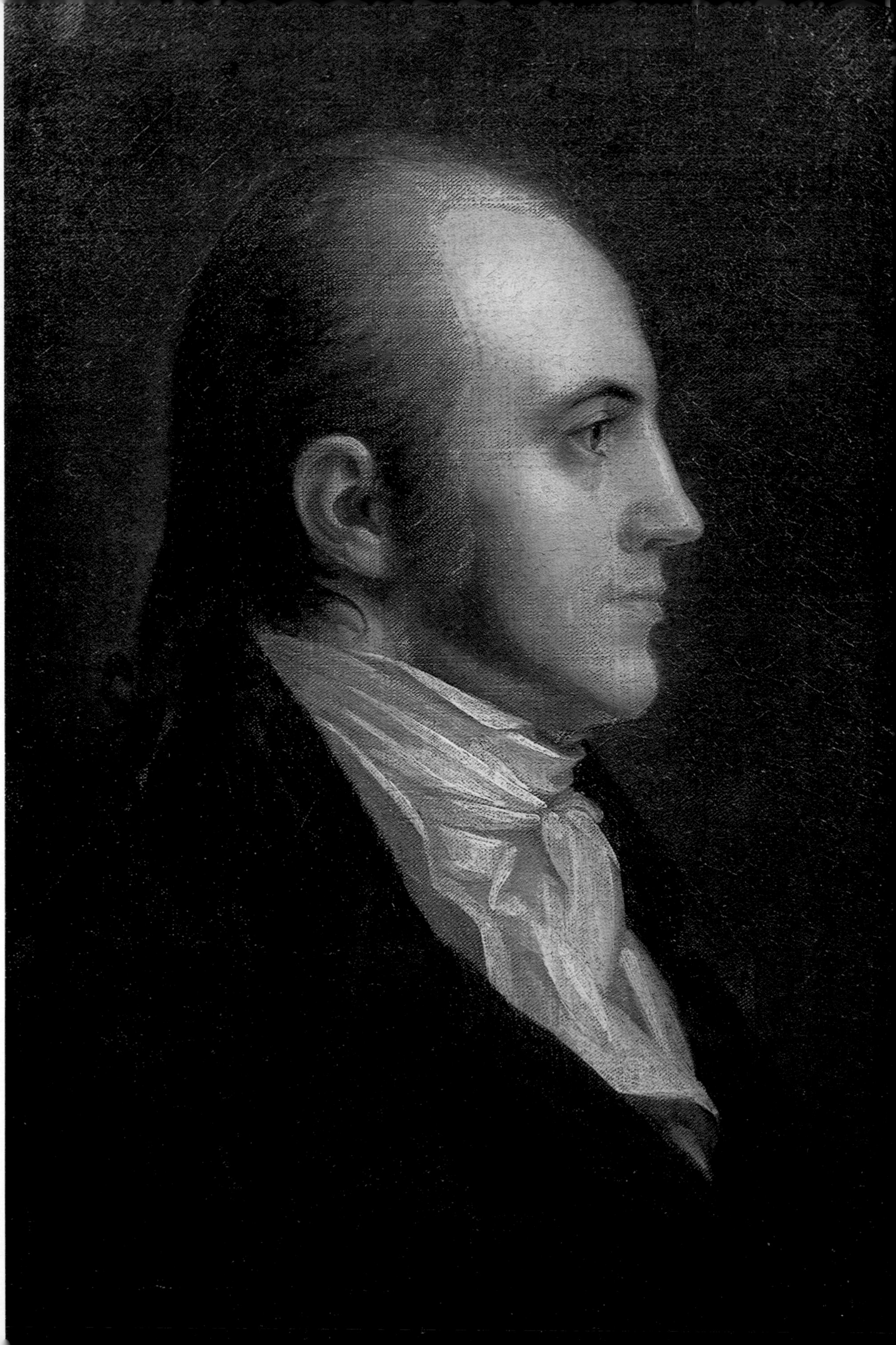

BY JOHN VANDERLYN, 1802; NEW-YORK HISTORICAL SOCIETY

A LIFE CUT TRAGICALLY SHORT

Hamilton had good reason to abhor the practice of dueling. Only a few years earlier his eldest son, Philip, had been killed in a duel, and he never recovered from that terrible shock. But his deep-seated sense of "what men of the world denominate honor, imposed on me . . . a peculiar necessity not to decline the call." He had made up his mind not to shoot to kill Burr (left), but Burr's first bullet found its mark in Hamilton's left side. Dr. David Hosack (bottom left), whom both men had chosen as their attending physician, rushed Hamilton back across the river to the house of William Bayard (bottom right) and informed Betsey, who hastened to the bedside from the Grange. Hamilton's last letter to her, "not to be delivered to you, unless I shall first have terminated my earthly career," reassured her of his "love for you and my precious children." He enjoined her to "Fly to the bosom of your God and be comforted. . . . Adieu best of wives and best of Women." Hamilton died on the afternoon of July 12, 1804. New York and the country mourned him, and among expressions of their grief was the detail below from a memorial handkerchief, "In memory of the lamented Hamilton."

Chapter 11

Creating a Legacy

A t the end of June, 1793, Alexander Hamilton was determined to leave the Cabinet and return to his legal practice in New York. But within a month, the tables were turned: it was Jefferson whose policies were questioned. Shortly thereafter, the Secretary of State announced his own plans for retirement, leaving Hamilton to dominate the Cabinet without serious opposition. His coming months in office would be attended by new hostilities in Europe and by armed resistance to the revenue laws on the Pennsylvania frontier. On the whole, Hamilton was to meet these challenges to America's neutrality and her national honor with considerable success and good sense. But in July, 1793, it was Edmond Genêt and his intrigues that most concerned the Treasury Secretary. In the first week of that month, local authorities learned that Genêt had begun to arm another vessel in the port of Philadelphia. Hamilton sent a detailed account of the incident to Senator Rufus King of New York, as he and Henry Knox had heard it from Governor Thomas Mifflin of Pennsylvania.

> Philadelphia August 13th 1793
> On Saturday the 6th of July last, the warden of this Port reported to Governor Mifflin that the Brig Little Sarah since called The Petit Democrat (an English merchant vessel mounting from two to four Guns taken off our coast by the French Frigate The Ambuscade and brought into this Port) had very materially augmented her Military equipments; having then fourteen Iron Cannon and six swivels mounted; and it being understood that her crew was to consist of one hundred & twenty men.
>
> Governor Mifflin, in consequence of this information sent Mr [Alexander J.] Dallas to Mr Genet to endeavour to prevail upon him to enter into an arrangement for

detaining the vessel in Port without the necessity of employing for that purpose military force.

Mr Dallas reported to Governor Mifflin that Mr Genet had absolutely refused to do what had been requested of him—that he had been very angry and intemperate—that he had complained of ill treatment from the Government and had declared that "he would appeal from the President to the People"—mentioned his expectation of the arrival of three Ships of the line; observing that he would know how to do justice to his country or at least he had a Frigate at his command and could easily withdraw himself from this—said that he would not advise an attempt to take possession of the vessel as it would be resisted.

The refusal was so peremptory that Governor Mifflin in consequence of it ordered out 120 men for the purpose of taking possession of the vessel....

Mr Jefferson on sunday went to Mr Genet to endeavour to prevail upon him to detain the Petit Democrat till the President could return and decide upon the case; but, as Mr Jefferson afterwards communicated, he absolutely refused to give a promise of the kind saying only that she would not probably be ready to depart before the succeeding wednesday, the day of the Presidents expected return. This however Mr Jefferson construed into an intimation that she would remain. Mr Jefferson also informed that Mr Genet had been very unreasonable and intemperate in his conversation....

Mud Island, located in the Delaware River just below Philadelphia, was caricatured as a formidable lady in this British cartoon of 1777.

On Monday, July 8, the Cabinet met to consider the events of the weekend. Hamilton and Knox demanded that Mud Island be fortified to prevent the *Little Sarah* from putting out to sea. Jefferson disagreed strongly, and Hamilton prepared a written list of "reasons" for his and Knox's position. In the fifth section of this document, he presented the basis for all his fears and arguments.

[Philadelphia, July 8, 1793]

It is impossible to interpret such conduct into any thing else than a *regular plan to force the United States into the War*. Its tendency to produce that effect cannot be misunderstood by the Agents of France. The direct advantage of the measure to her is obviously too inconsiderable to induce the persisting in it, contrary to the remonstrances of the Government—if it were not with a

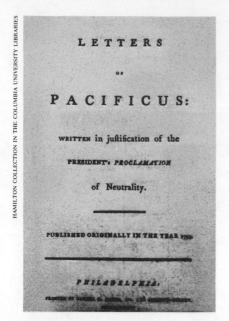

LETTERS

OF

PACIFICUS:

WRITTEN in juſtification of the

PRESIDENT: PROCLAMATION

of Neutrality.

PUBLISHED ORIGINALLY IN THE YEAR 1793

PHILADELPHIA.

*The title page of Hamilton's
collected* Letters of Pacificus

view to the more important end just mentioned: a conduct the more exceptionable because it is accompanied with the fallacious disavowal of an intention to engage us in the War.

...there is satisfactory evidence of a *regular system,* in pursuit of that object, *to endeavour to controul the Government itself, by creating, if possible, a scism between it and the people* and inlisting them on the side of France....

The declaration of the Minister of France to Mr. Dallas, Secretary of the Commonwealth of Pensylvania ...is a further confirmation of the same system. That Declaration, among other exceptionable things, expressed *"That he* (the Minister of France) *would appeal from the President of the United States to the People."* It would be a fatal blindness, not to perceive the spirit, which dictates such language, and an ill-omened passiveness not to resolve to withstand it with energy.

Even before Washington returned to Philadelphia on July 11, Hamilton's carefully drafted "reasons" had lost any practical interest. Genêt, breaking his vague promise to Jefferson, had sent the *Little Sarah* down the Delaware River out of reach of the guns on Mud Island. Since the vessel was still in American waters, her activities were a continued object of concern, and on July 12, the Cabinet referred the problem to the Supreme Court. While he waited for the justices' opinion, Hamilton issued his sixth "Pacificus" letter. Recent proclamations of the French Republic, he wrote, bore an "instructive lesson to the people of this country."

[Philadelphia, July 17, 1793]

It ought to teach us not to over-rate *foreign friendships*— to be upon our guard against *foreign attachments.* The former will generally be found hollow and delusive; the latter will have a natural tendency to lead us aside from our own true interest, and to make us the dupes of foreign influence. They introduce a principle of action, which in its effects, if the expression may be allowed, is *anti-national.* Foreign influence is truly the GRECIAN HORSE to a republic. We cannot be too careful to exclude its entrance. Nor ought we to imagine, that it can only make its approaches in the gross form of direct bribery. It is then most dangerous, when it comes under the patronage of our passions, under the auspices of national prejudice and partiality.

"Foreign friendships" seemed even less reliable when Genêt put the *Little Sarah* out to sea before the Supreme Court could take action. Jefferson, his cause betrayed, informed Washington that he would resign in the fall, and on August 1, the Cabinet voted to demand the French minister's recall. But Genêt's disgrace and the prospect of Jefferson's departure did not end Hamilton's concern that America might be dragged into war. Peace was endangered again at the end of the summer, when Philadelphians learned of a new British directive, issued in London on June 8, ordering English naval commanders to seize all ships carrying provisions to France or to French-occupied ports, and all ships trying to enter a port under British blockade. Hamilton proved more "neutral" than any of his political enemies expected him to be when he reacted to the British infraction of American commercial rights almost as angrily as he had to Genêt's attempts to make the United States a party to France's wars. George Hammond, in a dispatch to his superiors in London, reported Hamilton's reaction to the British maneuver.

AT a MEETING of the Corporation of the city of Burlington, August 30th, 1793, the following recommendations to the citizens was unanimously agreed to.

WHEREAS there is great reason for caution against the malignant Fever or contagious disorder, which prevails in Philadelphia, and it is our duty to use every probable means to prevent the same in the city of Burlington; the Corporation of Burlington after collecting every advice which could be obtained,

RECOMMEND to the Citizens of Burlington,

1. That all unnecessary intercourse be avoided with Philadelphia, that no dry goods, woollen cloths, woollens, cottons or linens, or any packages where straw, hay or shavings are used, be imported within twenty days.

2. That the masters of the boats which ply to and from Burlington to Philadelphia, be very careful that they do not receive on board their vessels, or bring to this city within twenty days, any person or persons but those who appear in good health.

3. That no animal or vegetable substances be thrown or permitted to lay in the streets or alleys, but that all offals, water-melon rinds and substances that putrefy be thrown into the delaware or buried.

4. That no water be permitted to stagnate about the pumps, in the streets or near any houses; but that the wharves, streets, alleys and gutters, ditches, houses, and barnyards, be kept as clean as possible.

5. The Physicians in Burlington are requested to make report to the Mayor or Recorder as soon as possible, after they shall have been called to and visited any person or persons, who shall have the said malignant Fever.

Signed by order of the Corporation,

BOWES REED, *Mayor.*

This broadside was posted in Burlington, New Jersey, to warn the town's citizens of the yellow fever epidemic in Philadelphia.

[Philadelphia, August 21–30, 1793]

Mr. Hamilton... regarded it as a very harsh and unprecedented measure, which not only militated against the principal branch of the present American exports but... appeared to be peculiarly directed against the commerce and navigation of the United States. For these reasons it would be incumbent upon this government, to make a representation on the subject to the Court of London. In the mean time, he earnestly desired me, if I received any exposition of it from your Lordship, to state it to the American administration, as a timely explanation might remove the unfavorable impressions it had made. In my answer I defended it, as well as I was able, on the ground of expediency, and of its not being contrary to the Law of nations.... I however perceived that he was not convinced by *my* reasoning.

Instructions went out to Thomas Pinckney, the American minister to the Court of St. James's, to make appropriate "representations." Toward the end of September, meanwhile, Hamilton and his wife contracted the yellow fever that was then sweeping Philadelphia. During the next two months, more than five thousand Philadelphians would die of the disease, and Hamilton was convinced that he was saved only by the treatment ministered by his boyhood friend from St. Croix, Dr. Edward Stevens. When the Hamiltons recovered, they set off for Albany, where their children had been sent for safekeeping during the epidemic. In October, they returned to their summer home outside Philadelphia. Their children, however, remained in Albany with their grandparents, and there Hamilton sent a bit of fatherly advice to his daughter Angelica.

[Philadelphia, November, 1793]

I was very glad to learn, my dear daughter, that you were going to begin the study of the French language. We hope you will in every respect behave in such a manner as will secure to you the good-will and regard of all those with whom you are. If you happen to displease any of them, be always ready to make a frank apology. But the best way is to act with so much politeness, good manners, and circumspection, as never to have occasion to make any apology. Your mother joins in best love to you. Adieu, my very dear daughter.

Health conditions in Philadelphia were improving, but Hamilton had new worries when he learned that John Fenno, the Philadelphia printer of the Federalist *Gazette of the United States,* faced financial ruin. After an appeal to Rufus King to raise funds in New York, he wrote to John Kean, cashier of the Bank of the United States.

[Philadelphia] Friday Novr. 29 [1793]

Poor *Fenno* is ruined by his Patriotism. His weekly paper is at an end—and he cannot begin again without a loan of at least 1500 Dollars. As I think he deserves assistance from the goodness of his motives and that it is of consequence to the Fœderal cause that he should be enabled to prosecute a paper—I have set on foot a subscription to a loan for his use. The inclosed will shew its progress. Do me the favour to present it to The President [of the Bank of the United States] & such others as you may think adviseable between this & two oClock & then send it to me.

Logo of Philadelphia's Federalist Gazette of the United States

In Cabinet meetings in November, Hamilton and Jefferson continued their quarrel. When Washington and his officers discussed the annual message the President would deliver to Congress on December 3, there were sharp differences on the kind of statement that should be made on foreign policy and American neutrality. Hamilton suggested this paragraph.

[November, 1793]

It is greatly to be lamented, for the sake of humanity, that the flame of War, which had before spread over a considerable part of Europe has within the present year extended itself much further; implicating all those

This Federalist cartoon of 1793 portrays Republicans as a gang of anarchists consorting with Satan.

powers with whom the United States have the most extensive relations. When it was seen here, that almost all the maritime Nations either were, or were likely soon to become parties to the War, it was natural that it should excite serious reflections about the possible consequences to this Country. On the one hand, it appeared desireable, that no impressions in reference to it should exist with any of the powers engaged, of a nature to precipitate arrangements or measures tending to interrupt or endanger our peace. On the other, it was probable, that designing or inconsiderable persons among ourselves might from different motives embark in enterprizes contrary to the duties of a nation at peace with nations at war with each other; and, of course, calculated to invite and to produce reprisals and hostilities. Adverting to these considerations, in a situation both new and delicate, I judged it adviseable to issue a Proclamation.... The effects of this measure have, I trust, neither disappointed the views which dictated it, nor disserved the true interests of our Country.

Washington ignored Hamilton's draft and accepted the advice of the Secretary of State. The annual message was scrupulously "neutral" in the Jeffersonian sense. Hamilton still planned to leave office in the spring of 1794, but he first wished to attend to a piece of unfinished business: replying to the questions raised in Congress about his administration of the Treasury Department. In mid-December, in a letter to the Speaker, he boldly invited the House of Representatives to begin its investigations.

Treasury Department December 16, 1793. It is known that in the last Session certain questions were raised respecting my Conduct in Office, which, though decided in a manner the most satisfactory to me, were nevertheless, unavoidably from the lateness of the period when they were set on foot, so accelerated in their issue, as to have given occasion to a Suggestion that there was not time for due examination. Unwilling to leave the Matter upon such a footing, I have concluded to request of the House of Representatives, as I now do, that a new Inquiry may be without delay instituted, in some mode most effectual for an accurate and thorough investigation—And I will add, that the more comprehensive it is, the more agreeable it will be to me.

More than two months passed before Congress responded to Hamilton's challenge to investigate his department. In the meantime, Jefferson resigned from the Cabinet (he was succeeded by Edmund Randolph), and Genêt was recalled by his Government. Nevertheless, when Congress finally named a special committee to investigate the Treasury in late February, 1794, there was ample evidence that Hamilton had many enemies left in Philadelphia. This committee was more successful than earlier investigators had been in finding an issue with which to embarrass the Secretary of the Treasury. The legislators showed particular interest in the history of the European loans obtained under the statutes of August, 1790, and in the use that had been made of the proceeds. Replying to their request for the "authorities" under which these funds had been allocated, Hamilton insisted that Congress had only a limited right of inquiry into executive affairs.

Treasury department, 24th. March 1794
I ask the Committee . . . to decide, whether they expect from the Secretary of the Treasury, the production of any other authorities from the President to him, in reference to the loans made under the Acts of the 4th. and 12th. of August 1790, except such as regard merely the making of the said loans and the application or disbursement of such part of the proceeds of those loans, as were to be disbursed in foreign countries?

I object to the being required to produce any other authorities, than those excepted, for the following reasons, Viz:

1st Because it results from the constitution of the Treasury department, that all the receipts and expenditures of public money within the United States, must pass through that department, . . . consequently, whenever a loan is made either abroad, or at home, on account of the United States, destined for disbursement within the United States, it becomes, *ex officio,* the province of the Treasury department, to draw the proceeds of such loan into the treasury, and to disburse them thence, according to law.

2nd Because, when it once appears, that the President has constituted the head of a department, his agent, for any general purpose entrusted to him by law, all intermediate authorities from the President to the Agent, being conformable with law, are to be presumed. The proper enquiry for the Legislature must be, "whether the laws have been duly executed or not." If they have been duly executed, the question of sufficiency or deficiency of authority from the President to his Agent, must be, to the Legislature, immaterial and irrelevant.

Hamilton knew that this matter would give his enemies political ammunition. He sent Washington a copy of his letter to the committee, voicing the hope that his opinion on "the proper limits of a Legislative enquiry" would discourage the congressmen. But he asked that the President support his version of the Treasury's transactions should the committee persist in its demands.

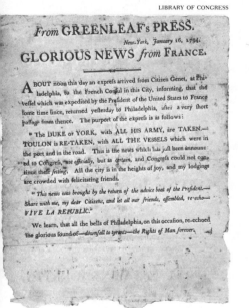

A Republican broadside heralding recent victories of revolutionary France in its war against the First Coalition of European powers

Treasury Dept. Mar. 24. 1794.

In the event of a determination that the enquiry should be general it becomes proper to fix with the President the true view of facts.

The real cause of the transaction has been this. Before I made the disposition of any Loan I regularly communicated to the President my ideas of the proper disposition, designating how much it would be expedient to pay to France—how much to draw to the United States—and always received his sanction for what was adopted & afterwards carried into execution. The communication & the sanction were verbal whenever the President was at the seat of Government. In a case of absence they were in writting. . . .

The sanctions of the President were sometimes expressly and always, as I conceived in their spirit, founded in a material degree on the confidence, that the measures proposed were guided by a just estimate on my part of circumstances, which from situation must have been best known to me—and that they would be always in conformity to the Law.

As Hamilton feared, the select committee was not easily satisfied. Madison gloated to Jefferson that the inquiry "begins to pinch where we most expected"—the occasions when Hamilton had deposited proceeds of the European loans in the Bank of the United States. The committee demanded Hamilton's authority for these decisions. In his reply the Secretary declared that the Treasury had full power to dispose of "all public monies, once obtained." Washington, who had no desire to become involved in the controversy, did furnish Hamilton with a noncommital "certificate" stating that he could not "charge" his "memory with all the particulars" of these transactions. Writing again to the President, Hamilton pointed out the need for a firmer statement.

These nineteenth-century copies of
earlier prints contrast the French and
American versions of liberty

Philadelphia April 8 1794

I . . . find, with regret, that the terms used are such as will
enable those, who are disposed to construe every thing
to my disadvantage, to affirm "That the Declaration of
The President has intirely waved the main point and
does not even manifest an *opinion* that the representation of the Secretary of the Treasury is well founded."

To this it would be added, that the reserve of The
President is a proof that he does not think that representation true—else his justice would have led him to
rescue the officer concerned even from suspicion on
the point. . . .

Under all that has happened Sir, I cannot help entertaining and frankly expressing to you my apprehension,
that false and insidious men, whom you may one day understand, taking advantage of the want of recollection,
which is natural, where the mind is habitually occupied
with a variety of important objects, have found means by
artful suggestions to infuse doubts and distrusts very
injurious to me.

James Madison remarked that Washington's certificate
was "inexpressibly mortifying" to Hamiltonians. Equally annoying was a new
British order in council that permitted the capture of neutral ships carrying
goods to and from the French colonies. The order, which was dated November 6, but which did not reach America until March, gave added support to
Madison's fight for an anti-British commercial policy. Hamilton sent the
President a plan for meeting the British challenge to American trade.

March 8th 1794.

The present situation of the United States is undoubtedly
critical and demands measures vigorous though prudent.
We ought to be in a respectable military posture, because
war may come upon us, whether we choose it or not and
because to be in a condition to defend ourselves and
annoy any who may attack us will be the best method of
securing our peace. If it is known that our principal maritime points are out of the reach of any but formal serious
operations—and that the government has an efficient active force in its disposal for defence or offence on an
emergency—there will be much less temptation to attack
us and much more hesitation to provoke us. . . .

In addition to this, the Legislature ought to vest the
President of the United States with a power to lay an em-

bargo partial or general and to arrest the exportation of commodities partially or generally.

It may also deserve consideration whether the Executive ought not to take measures to form some concert of the Neutral Powers for common Defence.

On March 26, the President approved Congress's thirty-day embargo on vessels bound for foreign ports. With Anglo-American relations now strained more than ever, many Federalists believed that a permanent settlement of differences between the United States and Britain would come only if a special envoy were sent to London. Hamilton realized that Republicans distrusted such a plan for fear that he might be the appointee. He also realized that the plan would not succeed without Republican support. He tempered his remarks accordingly when he sent Washington his suggestions for measures to be taken should the President choose a policy of "preparation for war" and simultaneous negotiations of America's differences with Britain.

Philadelphia April [14] 1794

The mode of doing it which occurs is this—to nominate a person, who will have the confidence of those who think peace still within our reach, and who may be thought qualified for the mission as envoy extraordinary to Great Britain—to announce this to...Congress with an... earnest recommendation that vigorous and effectual measures may be adopted to be prepared for war should it become inevitable....

Knowing as I do Sir that I am among the persons who have been in your contemplation to be employed in the capacity I have mentioned, I should not have taken the present step, had I not been resolved at the same time to advise you with decision to drop me from the consideration and to fix upon another character. I am not unapprised of what has been the byass of your opinion on the subject. I am well aware of all the collateral obstacles which exist and I assure you in the utmost sincerity that I shall be completely and intirely satisfied with the election of another.

I beg leave to add that of the persons whom you would deem free from any constitutional objections—Mr. Jay is the only man in whose qualifications for success there would be a thorough confidence and him whom alone it would be adviseable to send. I think the business would have the best chance possible in his hands.

Even before he had received Hamilton's letter, the President had decided that John Jay would be the most suitable and popular choice for the mission to England. Meanwhile, the British minister, armed with the news that his Government had modified its order against neutral ships caught trading with the French colonies, tried to learn the intentions of the American Administration from the Secretary of the Treasury. George Hammond later described his vain efforts to extract information from Hamilton.

> [Philadelphia, April 15–16, 1794]
> I flattered myself that from communicating to him confidentially and informally the very conciliatory explanations, with which your Lordship [Lord Grenville] furnished me, of the instructions of the 6th of November and of the modifications of them on the 8th of January, I might derive the right of requiring an equal confidential communication on his part with relation to the special commission in question. I was however much surprized at perceiving that he did not receive those explanations with the cordiality I expected, but entered into a pretty copious recital of the injuries which the commerce of this country had suffered from British cruizers, and into a defense of the consequent claim which the American citizens had on their government to vindicate their rights.

Hammond and all of Philadelphia soon learned that Jay had been named to try to "settle all the grounds of dispute" with Britain. Federalist leaders now faced the task of deciding just what Jay's instructions should be. Hamilton urged that Jay should not only negotiate differences arising from Britain's wartime commercial codes and from the treaty of 1783, but should also negotiate a commercial treaty. Washington, however, bowed to Edmund Randolph's opinion that the matter should be left to Jay's "discretion" and was only to be considered if the more important problems were settled first. Hamilton nevertheless sent Jay a copy of his proposals for a trade agreement. In it, he admitted that the American public justly expected substantial reparations for British raids on American shipping; but he suggested that these reparations could be "more laxly dealt with if a truly beneficial treaty of Commerce" was concluded.

> Philadelphia May 6. 1794
> I see not how it can be disputed with you that this Country in a commercial sense is more important to G Britain than any other. The articles she takes from us are certainly precious to her, important perhaps essential to the ordinary subsistence of her Islands.... As a

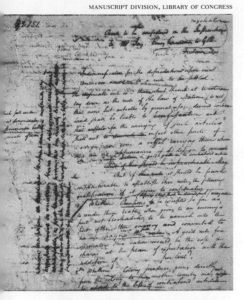

Hamilton's draft of his instructions to John Jay on his peace mission to Great Britain, dated April 23, 1794

Consumer...we stand unrivalled. We now consume of her exports from a milion to [a] milion & a half Sterling more in value than any other foreign country & while the consumption of other countries from obvious causes is likely to be stationary that of this country is increasing and for a long, long, series of years, will increase rapidly....

How unwise then in G Britain to suffer such a state of things to remain exposed to the hazard of constant interruption & derangement by not fixing on the basis of a good Treaty the principles on which it should continue?...

...But you will discover from your instructions that the opinion which has prevailed is that such a Treaty of commerce ought not to be *concluded* without previous reference here for further instruction. It is desireable however to push the British Ministry in this respect to a result that the extent of their views may be ascertained.

Hamilton did his best to see that Jay's mission went as smoothly as possible. One way to insure this was for Hamilton himself to remain in office. Although the select committee of the House had reported favorably on the Secretary's administration of the Treasury, and although Genêt's long-awaited successor, Jean Antoine Joseph Fauchet, seemed a marked improvement over the former French minister, the international situation still seemed too precarious for Hamilton to retire, as he informed Washington late in May.

Philadelphia May 27 1794

I some time since communicated an intention to withdraw from the office I hold, towards the close of the present session.

This I should now put in execution, but for the events, which have lately accumulated, of a nature to render the prospect of the continuance of our peace in a considerable degree precarious. I do not perceive, that I could voluntarily quit my post at such a juncture, consistently with considerations either of duty or character; and therefore I find myself reluctantly obliged to defer the offer of my resignation.

But if any circumstances should have taken place in consequence of the intimation of an intention to resign or should otherwise exist which serve to render my continuance in office in any degree inconvenient or ineligible, I beg leave to assure you Sir that I should yield to

John Jay by Trumbull

them with all the readiness naturally inspired by an impatient desire to relinquish a situation in which even a momentary stay is opposed by the strongest personal & family reasons & could only be produced by a sense of duty or Reputation.

Washington assured Hamilton that there was nothing "inconvenient" or "ineligible" in his decision to remain. Quite the contrary, the President wrote that he was pleased the Secretary would be staying "until the clouds over our affairs, which have come on so fast of late, shall be dispersed." Shortly after Jay sailed for London, the "clouds" broke a bit when the Senate defeated a House motion to extend the embargo. Congress adjourned on June 9, leaving the executive branch to guide America along the path of neutrality during the summer. But in July, family responsibilities began to absorb much of Hamilton's time. His two-year-old son John became seriously ill, and his wife Elizabeth was in the early months of a difficult pregnancy. It was decided to send her and the two youngest boys, James and the ailing John, to Albany. Hamilton took them as far as New York, then returned to Philadelphia on July 30 to look after his older children, Philip, Angelica, and Alexander. The next day he sent a note to Elizabeth.

[Philadelphia] Thursday July 31. 1794

I arrived here, My beloved Eliza, yesterday, too late to write by the Post—but am happy to be able to inform you that the precious little ones we left behind are well. As there is a vacation at this time, I propose sending the two youngest to Mrs. Morris's who has requested it, or to Mrs. Bradford's—I have not intirely determined which.

I shall expect with infinite anxiety a letter from you & heaven Grant that it may bring me good tidings of the health of yourself & the dear Children with you. Alas my beloved Johnny—what shall I hear of you! This question makes my heart sink. Adieu.

With three lively youngsters demanding his attention in Philadelphia, Hamilton must have prayed for an uneventful summer in the Treasury Department. Instead, he was greeted by Francis Mentges, a colonel in the Pennsylvania militia, who had just returned from the disaffected western counties of that state. Mentges reported that a new "insurrection" was brewing on the Pennsylvania frontier, where there was violent opposition to the Federal Government's excise tax on whiskey. The tax, which had been imposed by Congress at Hamilton's urging in order to help pay for the Federal assumption of state debts, was especially hard on western farmers, who converted much of their grain into alcohol to cut down transportation costs. Hamilton carefully recorded Mentges's testimony concerning the rebellion.

[Philadelphia, August, 1794]

... Francis Mentges ... maketh oath That he arrived at Pittsburgh in the County of Alleghanny on the 22 of July last past and continued there until the 25 of the same month. That it was there matter of public notoriety and general conversation that several collections of armed men had on the seventeenth of the same month successively made repeated attacks upon the house of General John Neville Inspector of the Revenue for and on account of his holding and exercising the said Office and to oblige him to relinquish the same ... moreover that David Lenox Marshall of the District had been taken into custody by some of the said armed collections in consequence of his having been there for the service of certain processes in relation to laws of the United States laying duties on distilled spirits and on stills but was afterwards released and that the said Marshall together with the said Inspector of the Revenue had descended the Ohio in a Boat to avoid personal violence or the being compelled by force to enter into engagements or do acts contrary to the duties of their respective Offices.... And the said Deponent further saith that on the twenty fourth of the same month of July he saw & conversed at Pittsburgh aforesaid with Hugh Brackenridge who informed him that he had been the day preceding at a Meeting ... at Mingo Creek Meeting House in the County of Washington consisting generally of the most respectable people of that County ... that it was there proposed that the Meeting should ... pledge themselves to stand by each other until the Excise law was repealed and an Act of Oblivion passed—which proposition was not agreed to but instead of it it was proposed and agreed to that the four Western Counties of Pensylvania and the neighbouring counties of Virginia should be invited to assemble by delegates in a Convention to be holden on the fourteenth of this present Month of August in Mingo Creek ... at Parkinson's [Ferry] ... to take into consideration the situation of the Western Counties and adopt such measures as should appear suited to the

Orders issued by Hamilton as Secretary of the Treasury

exigency. And this Deponent further saith that from the general state of affairs in the said Western Counties of Pensylvania as they came under his observation he doth verily believe that it is intirely impracticable to execute the laws aforesaid by the means of civil process and Judiciary proceeding.

Events in western Pennsylvania were particularly disturbing to Hamilton. As a man concerned with governmental effectiveness and national honor, he found that resistance to Federal law (especially the law that helped finance his funding program) was a challenge that had to be met with prompt, decisive action. Along with other Cabinet members, Hamilton advised Washington to invoke a statute under which the President was empowered to call up the militia if he were "notified" by a member of the Supreme Court that military force was needed to enforce Federal law or suppress disorder. After forwarding the necessary documents to Associate Justice James Wilson, Washington and the Cabinet met with the Governor of Pennsylvania. During the conference, Hamilton responded to an assertion that the state judiciary could deal with the insurgents without the militia. The Secretary's remarks were reported in the minutes of the meeting.

[Philadelphia, August 2, 1794]

[The Secretary of the Treasury] insisted upon the propriety of an immediate resort to Military force. He said that it would not be sufficient to quell the existing riot to restore us to the state in which we were a few weeks back; for, before the present outrages, there was equal opposition to the laws of the U.S., though not expressed in the same manner; but that now the crisis was arrived when it must be determined whether the Government can maintain itself, and that the exertion must be made, not only to quell the rioters, but to protect the officers of the Union in executing their offices, and in compelling obedience to the laws.

Even as Justice Wilson was pondering the wisdom of "notifying" Washington that the militia was needed, Hamilton began planning troop movements. After the conference with Pennsylvania's Governor, he outlined his proposals to Washington.

Treasury Department August 2d. 1794

What force of Militia shall be called out, and from What State or States?

The force ought if attainable to be an imposing one, such if practicable, as will deter from opposition, save the effusion of the blood of Citizens and secure the object to be accomplished.

The quantum must of course be regulated by the resistance to be expected. Tis computed, that the four opposing Counties contain upwards of sixteen thousand males of 16 years and more, that of these about seven thousand may be expected to be armed. Tis possible that the union of the nieghbouring Counties of Virginia may augment this force. Tis not impossible, that it may receive an accession from some adjacent Counties of this state on this side of the Alleghany Mountains.

To be prepared for the worst, I am of opinion, that twelve thousand Militia ought to be ordered to assemble; 9000 foot and 3000 horse....

The Law contemplates that the Militia of a State, in which an insurrection happens, if willing & sufficient shall first be employed, but gives power to employ the Militia of other States in the case either of refusal or insufficiency.

The Governor of Pennsylvania in an Official conference this day, gave it explicitly as his opinion to the President, that the Militia of Pennsylvania alone would be found incompetent to the suppression of the insurrection....

I would submit then, that Pennsylvania be required to furnish 6000 men of whom 1000 to be horse, New-Jersey 2000 of whom 800 to be horse, Maryland 2000 of whom 600 to be horse, Virginia 2000, of whom 600 to be horse.

...The Militia called for to rendezvous at Carlisle in Pensylvania & Cumberland Fort in Virginia on the 10th of September next.

The law requires that previous to the using of force a Proclamation shall issue, commanding the Insurgents to disperse and return peaceably to their respective abodes within a limited time. This step must of course be taken.

James Wilson of Pennsylvania: a signer of the Declaration of Independence; Associate Justice of the Supreme Court, 1789–98

Two days later, Wilson gave the President the necessary "notification." As Washington began work on the proclamation that would precede military operations, Hamilton furnished the President with a history of the "insurrection," ending with an account of what happened when Marshal David Lenox attempted to serve writs on excise violators in July, 1794. Lenox and John Neville, the inspector of revenue in Allegheny County, were first attacked on the road. Then, on July 16, a band of one hundred men besieged Neville's house near Pittsburgh. Neville appealed to local courts, militia officers, and the county sheriff for protection, but was told that no aid could be given him because of the unpopularity of his office.

[Treasury Department, August 5, 1794]

The day following, the Insurgents reassembled with a considerable augmentation of numbers amounting as has been computed to at least 500 and on the 17th of July renewed their attack upon the House of the Inspector; who in the interval had taken the precaution of calling to his aid a small detachment from the garrison of Fort Pit which at the time of this attack consisted of 11 Men, who had been joined by Major Abraham Kirkpatrick a friend & connection of the Inspector.

There being scarcely a prospect of effectual defence against so large a body...and as the Inspector had every thing to apprehend for his person, if taken, it was judged adviseable that he should withdraw from the house to a place of concealment—Major Kirkpatrick generously agreeing to remain with the 11 men, in the intention if practicable to make a capitulation in favour of the property if not to defend it as long as possible.

A parly took place, under cover of a flag, which was sent by the Insurgents to the House to demand, that the Inspector should come forth, renounce his office and stipulate never again to accept an office under the same laws. To this it was replied, that the Inspector had left the house upon their first approach, and that the place to which he had retired was unknown. They then declared that they must have whatever related to his office.... they insisted unconditionally, that the armed men who were in the house for its defence should march out & ground their arms; which Major Kirkpatrick peremptorily refused.... This refusal put an end to the parley.

A brisk firing then ensued between the insurgents and those in the House, which it is said lasted for near an hour; 'till the assailants having set fire to all the neighbouring & adjacent buildings...the intenseness of the heat & the danger of an immediate communication of the fire to the house obliged Maj Kirk: & his small party to come out & surrender themselves.

Henry ("Light Horse Harry") Lee, cavalry officer in the Revolution and later Governor of Virginia

Henry Knox, the Secretary of War, having issued orders to the governors of New Jersey, Pennsylvania, Maryland, and Virginia to call out 12,950 militiamen, then left Philadelphia to look after his business interests in Maine. Hamilton, now Acting Secretary of War as well as head of the Treasury, still found time to write to his wife.

[Philadelphia] August 12. 1794

If my darling child is better when this reaches you persevere in the plan which has made him so. If he is worse —abandon the laudanum & try the cold bath—that is abandon the laudanum by degrees giving it over night but not in the morning—& then leaving it off altogether. Let the water be put in the Kitchen over night & in the morning let the child be dipped in it head foremost wrapping up his head well & taking him again immediately out, put in flannel & rubbed dry with towels. Immediately upon his being taken out let him have two tea spoons full of brandy mixed with just enough water to prevent its taking away his breath.

Observe well his lips. If a glow succeeds continue the bath. If a chill takes place forbear it. If a glow succeeds the quantity of brandy may be lessened after the first experiment.

Household History of the United States, LOSSING

Henry Knox and Hamilton

One burden was lifted from Hamilton's shoulders on August 21, when he learned that his wife and son were well enough to return to Philadelphia. But the news from western Pennsylvania was less encouraging. Three Federal commissioners sent to negotiate with the insurgents reported that they saw little hope for their mission and planned to return to the capital. Washington, Randolph, and Hamilton urged the commissioners to remain as long as possible, but on August 24, agreed to begin mobilizing the militia. To that end, Hamilton wrote to Governor Henry Lee of Virginia.

War Department August 25. 1794

In place of The Secretary at War, who is absent, I am instructed by The President to signify to you his wish and request that you will come forth in the command of the Militia, which is to be detached from Virginia against the Insurgents in the Western parts of Pensylvania; in which case You will have the command of the whole force that may be employed upon that Enterprise.

The President anticipates, that it will be as painful to you to execute, as it is to him to direct, measures of coertion against fellow citizens however misled. Yet he needed not the assurance you have already given him of the sense you entertain of their conduct and its consequences to be convinced that he might count ever on your zealous personal service, towards suppressing an example fatal in its tendency to every thing that is dear and valuable in political society.

In the next two weeks, the Federal commissioners sent encouraging reports of the insurgents' willingness to submit to the excise laws and accept an amnesty for earlier violations. But this did not satisfy the President, and Hamilton issued these orders to the governors involved in the militia call.

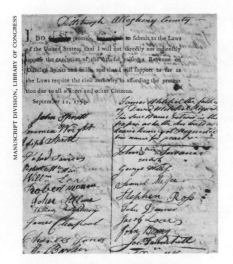

The participants in the Whisky Rebellion were allowed to go free after signing this oath to "submit to the Laws of the United States."

War Department Sepr 10th. 1794
This final resolution has been taken by the President in consequence of a very undecided state of things in the western Counties of this State when the last intelligence from thence came away. It appears that although the restoration of Order had gained powerful advocates & supporters; yet that there is a violent and numerous party which does not permit to count upon a submission to the laws without the intervention of force. Hence the advanced state of the Season considered, it became indispensable to put the force which had been provisionally called for in motion. I advise the appointment of a person in capacity of Quartermaster & Commissary of Military stores to the detachment with a competent Salary, I should think the pay & emoluments of a Major might suffice.

Although occupied with the supervision of troop movements and supply operations, Hamilton, who was still eager for military command, applied to the President for permission to accompany the expedition.

Philadelphia Sept 19 1794.
Upon full reflection I entertain an opinion, that it is adviseable for me, on public ground, considering the connection between the immediate ostensible cause of the insurrection in the Western Country and my department, to go out upon the expedition against the insurgents. In a government like ours, it cannot but have a good effect for the person who is understood to be the adviser or proposer of a measure, which involves danger

to his fellow citizens, to partake in that danger: While, not to do it, might have a bad effect. I therefore request your permission for the purpose.

Pressed by the responsibilities of administering two departments, Hamilton rushed to put his affairs in order in time to join Washington when the President rode west to supervise the assembly of the militia. Finally, by the end of September, having authorized the comptroller, Oliver Wolcott, Jr., to act in his absence, Hamilton was ready to leave. But first he took a moment to write to his two sons at their school in New Jersey.

[Philadelphia, September 29, 1794]

Dear Children

We have been very sorry to hear that our dear Alexander has been unwell but thank God that he was better. We hope he will soon be quite well.

Your Mama will leave this place tomorrow or next day for Trenton to bring you herself to Town.

I expect to set out tomorrow for Carlisle. But you must not be uneasy about it. For by the accounts we have received there will be no fighting and of course no danger. It will only be an agreeable ride which will I hope do me good.

I give you both my best love & blessings as does your Mama. It will give me great pleasure when I come back to know that you have not neglected your studies & have been good boys during the vacation.

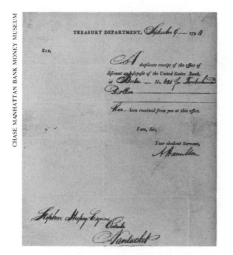

Hamilton signed this Treasury Department receipt for twelve hundred dollars received from a collector of revenue in Nantucket.

On September 30, Hamilton began his "agreeable ride" at Washington's side. When they reached Carlisle, Pennsylvania, on October 4, they found chastened delegates from the insurgents, who begged that the march be halted. Washington promised that there would be no bloodshed if the westerners submitted to Federal authority. The President continued his tour of other units of the militia and then, having set the campaign in motion, he prepared to return to Philadelphia, leaving Hamilton and the citizen-soldiers to continue the march under the command of Governor Lee of Virginia. Before riding east, however, Washington had Hamilton draft instructions for the Governor.

Bedford [Pennsylvania] 20th October 1794.

The objects of the military force are twofold.

1. To overcome any armed opposition which may exist.

325

This painting by Kemmelmeyer shows General Washington reviewing the Western Army at Fort Cumberland at the time of the Whisky Rebellion.

2. To countenance and support the civil officers in the means of executing the laws.

With a view to the first of these two objects, you will proceed as speedily as may be, with the army under your command, into the insurgent counties to attack, and as far as shall be in your power subdue, all persons whom you may find in arms, in opposition to the laws above mentioned. You will march your army in two columns, from the places where they now are assembled...

When arrived within the insurgent Country, if an armed opposition appear, it may be proper to publish a proclamation, inviting all good citizens...to join the standard of the United States....

Of those persons in arms, if any, whom you may make prisoners; leaders, including all persons in command, are to be delivered up to the civil magistrate: the rest to be disarmed, admonished and sent home (except such as may have been particularly violent and also influential)....

The better to effect these purposes, the Judge of the District, Richard Peters Esquire, and the Attorney of the District, William Rawle Esquire, accompany the army.

You are aware that the Judge cannot be controuled in his functions. But I count on his disposition to cooperate in such a general plan as shall appear to you consistent with the policy of the case. But your method of giving a direction to legal proceedings, according to your general plan, will be by instruction to the District Attorney.

He ought particularly to be instructed, (with due regard to time and circumstance)—1st to procure to be arrested, all influential actors in riots and unlawful assemblies...and combinations to resist the laws... who shall not have complied with the terms offered by the Commissioners [the amnesty offered by the Federal commissioners at conferences with the insurgents on August 28 and 29]; or manifested their repentance in some other way, which you may deem satisfactory. 2dly. To cause process to issue for enforcing penalties on delinquent distillers. 3d. To cause *offenders,* who may be arrested, to be conveyed to goals where there will be no danger of rescue....4th. To prosecute indictable offences in the Courts of the United States—those for penalties on delinquents...in the courts of Pennsylvania.

To his wife, Hamilton sent this reassuring note on the eve of Washington's departure for Philadelphia.

> Bedford [Pennsylvania] Oct 20 1794
>
> I am very sorry that some of my sweet angels have been again sick. You do not mention my precious John. I hope he continues well.
>
> The day after tomorrow I march with the army. Be assured that there is not the least appearance of opposition from the Insurgents & that I shall take the greatest care of myself & I hope by the Middle of November to return. Have patience my love & think of me constantly as I do of you with the utmost tenderness.
>
> Kisses & blessings without number to You & my Children

As the militia marched from one tiny farmtown and crossroads village to another, it became obvious that the insurgents had given up any idea of armed resistance. Still, Hamilton was not convinced that the "disaffected country" had been pacified, and he made the following suggestion to Senator Rufus King.

> Jones Mill [Pennsylvania] October 30. 1794
>
> It is of great consequence that a law should if possible be expedited through Congress for raising 500 infantry & 100 horse to be stationed in the disaffected country. Without this the expence incurred will be essentially fruitless.
>
> A law regulating a process of outlawry is also urgent; for the best objects of punishment will fly & they ought to be compelled by their outlawry to abandon their property houses & the UStates. This business must not be skinned over. The political putrefaction of Pensylvania is greater than I had any idea of. Without vigour every where our tranquillity is likely to be of very short duration & the next storm will be infinitely worse than the present one.

Journalist Hugh H. Brackenridge became a justice of the supreme court of Pennsylvania in 1799.

The prospect of seeing the insurgents punished kept Hamilton from returning to Philadelphia. On November 16, he reached Pittsburgh, where he confronted Hugh H. Brackenridge, a local journalist and politician who was suspected of having played a role in the insurrection. By the late summer of 1794, Brackenridge had seen the error of his ways and had assisted the Federal commissioners, but he had neglected to sign the oath of submission to the excise laws before the time limit expired. Later, Brackenridge described his interview with Hamilton.

[Pittsburgh, November 18–19, 1794]
I was received by Hamilton, with that countenance, which a man will have, when he sees a person, with regard to whom his humanity and his sense of justice struggles;—he would have him saved, but is afraid he must be hanged;—was willing to treat me with civility, but was embarrassed with a sense, that, in a short time, I must probably stand in the predicament of a culprit, and be in irons. He began, by asking me some general questions, with regard to any system or plan, within my knowledge, of overthrowing the government. I had known of nothing of the kind. After a number of general questions, to which I had to answer in the negative, I proposed putting an end to that, by giving him a narrative of every thing I did know. It was agreed; and he began to write. I gave him the outlines of the narrative.... the secretary laid down his pen, and addressed himself to me; Mr. Brackenridge, said he, I observe one leading trait in your account, a disposition to excuse the principal actors; and before we go further, I must be candid, and inform you of the delicate situation in which you stand; *you are not within the amnesty; you have not signed upon the day;* a thing we did not know until we came... into the western country; and though the government may not be disposed to proceed rigorously, yet it has you in its power; and it will depend upon the candour of your account, what your fate will be....

[Brackenridge explained his actions to Hamilton all morning and at another conference that afternoon.]

After some time the secretary observed, "My breast begins to ach, we will stop to night; we will resume it tomorrow morning at 9 o'clock." I withdrew, but was struck with his last expression. I was at a loss to know whether his breast ached for my sake, or from the writing; but disposed to construe every thing unfavourable, I supposed it was for my sake, and that he saw I must be arrested....

Waiting on the secretary, at 9 o'clock [the morning of November 19], my examination recommenced. In the course of the narrative, his countenance began to

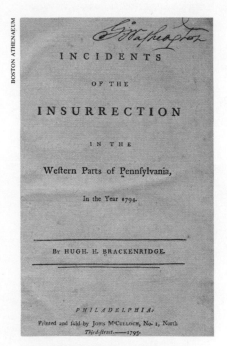

INCIDENTS

OF THE

INSURRECTION

IN THE

Weſtern Parts of Pennſylvania,

In the Year 1794.

By HUGH. H. BRACKENRIDGE.

PHILADELPHIA:
Printed and ſold by JOHN M'CULLOCH, No. 1, North *Third-ſtreet.*——1795.

The title page of Brackenridge's account of the Whisky Rebellion, from George Washington's library

brighten, and having finished the history, there was an end. "Mr. Brackenridge," said he, "in the course of yesterday I had uneasy feelings, I was concerned for you as for a man of talents; my impressions were unfavourable; you may have observed it. I now think it my duty to inform you, that not a single one remains. Had we listened to some people, I do not know what we might have done. There is a side to your account; your conduct has been horribly misrepresented, owing to misconception. I will announce you in this point to governor [Henry] Lee, who represents the executive. You are in no personal danger. You will not be troubled, even by a simple inquisition by the judge; what may be due to yourself with the public, is another question."

Later that day, Hamilton left Pittsburgh for Philadelphia, the insurrection having been suppressed without bloodshed. Feeling free at last to retire, Hamilton conferred with Washington, then informed Congress that he would resign from office at the end of January, 1795. When he wrote to his sister-in-law, Angelica Church, it was in a lighthearted vein.

Philadelphia, December 8, 1794.

You say I am a politician, and good for nothing. What will you say when you learn that after January next, I shall cease to be a politician at all? So is the fact. I have formally and definitely announced my intention to resign at that period, and have ordered a house to be taken for me at New York.

My dear Eliza has been lately very ill. Thank God, she is now quite recovered, except that she continues somewhat weak. My absence on a certain expedition was the cause. . . .

Don't let Mr. Church be alarmed at my retreat—all is well with the public. Our insurrection is most happily terminated. Government has gained by it reputation and strength, and our finances are in a most flourishing condition. *Having contributed to place those of the Nation on a good footing, I go to take a little care of my own; which need my care not a little.*

Hamilton's draft of his last major report to Congress as Secretary of the Treasury, January, 1795

On January 16, Hamilton submitted his last major report to Congress. Although James Madison complained that the Secretary had "got it in" by parliamentary trickery, the document was not the less valuable for the methods used to introduce it to the House. This, like his first great report, dealt with public credit and outlined the means by which the United States could erase the principal as well as the interest of the domestic debt. Perhaps its greatest virtue was not Hamilton's carefully considered recommendations, but the closing paragraphs, which captured the spirit of Hamilton's vision of the Treasury's role. Madison called the address a "valedictory," and indeed, it was a heartfelt, almost poetic, plea to Congress to guard the credit Hamilton had fought to establish for more than five years.

Treasury Department January 16. 1795
Credit public and private is of the greatest consequence to every Country. Of this, it might be emphatically called the invigorating principle. No well informed man, can cast a retrospective eye over the progress of the United States, from their infancy to the present period, without being convinced that they owe in a great degree, to the fostering influence of Credit their present mature growth....

There can be no time, no state of things, in which Credit is not essential to a Nation, especially as long as nations in general continue to use it, as a resource in war. It is impossible for a Country to contend on equal terms, or to be secure against the enterprises of other nations without being able equally with them to avail itself of this important resource. And to a young Country with moderate pecuniary Capital and not a very various industry, it is still more necessary than to Countries, more advanced in both; a truth not the less weighty for being obvious and frequently noticed....

But Credit is not only one of the main pillars of the public safety—it is among the principal engines of useful interprise and internal improvement. As a substitute for Capital it is little less useful than Gold or silver, in Agriculture, in Commerce, in the Manufacturing and mechanic arts....

If the individual Capital of this Country has become more adequate to its exigencies than formerly, 'tis because individuals have found new resources in the public *Credit*, in the funds to which *that* has given value and activity. Let Public Credit be prostrated, and the deficiency will be greater than before. Public and private Credit are closely allied, if not inseparable. There is perhaps no example of the one being in a flourishing, where the other was in a bad, state. A shock to public Credit would therefore not only take away the additional means

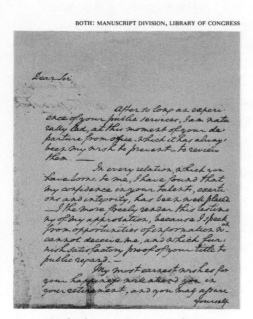

In this letter (above and opposite) Washington assures his retiring Treasury Secretary of his "sincere esteem, regard and friendship."

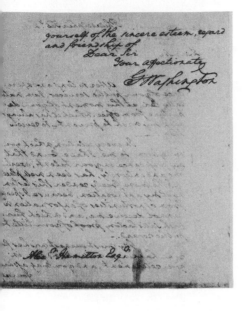

which it has furnished, but by the derangements, disorders distrusts and false principles, which it would engender and disseminate, would diminish the antecedent resources of private Credit. . . .

Credit is an *intire thing*. Every part of it has the nicest sympathy with every other part. Wound one limb, and the whole Tree shrinks and decays. The security of each Creditor is inseperable from the security of all Creditors. . . .

'Tis Wisdom in every case to cherish what is useful and guard against its abuse. 'Twill be the truest policy in the United States to give all possible energy to Public Credit, by a firm adherence to its strictest maxims, and yet to avoid the ills of an excessive employment of it, by true œconomy and system, in the public expenditures, by steadily cultivating peace, and by using sincere, efficient and persevering endeavors to diminish present debts, prevent the accumulation of new, and secure the discharge within a reasonable period of such as it may be matter of necessity to contract.

This, then, was the underlying theme of the seemingly unrelated incidents of Hamilton's years as Secretary of the Treasury. Funding, assumption, foreign relations, the defeat of recalcitrant distillers in the Pennsylvania mountains—all were part of a pattern that would give America firm public credit, which in turn would give the new nation a reputation for financial trustworthiness that would provide public security and an economic base for future expansion.

It was, too, Hamilton's best and most lasting legacy. While he often misunderstood the American people and their political leaders, Hamilton realized from the beginning that the young nation could not prosper without the "invigorating principle" of fiscal respectability. In part, he pursued this goal because of his concern for national honor. More practically, he knew that the United States could not preserve its independence or safety without the ability to borrow money in times of national emergency. Although Hamilton laid this foundation of credit for the "proper" government of his country, that foundation was solid enough to support the administrations of Federalists and Jeffersonian Republicans alike. Long after Hamilton's political theories and political allies had fallen into disrepute, that "pillar" he had described in his report of January 16, 1795, would stand.

Fifteen days after having made that report, Hamilton tendered his resignation and turned his office over to Oliver Wolcott, Jr. With the nation's credit assured, he could, at last, look to his own fortunes.

Chapter 12

A Man of Influence

When Hamilton left his post at the Treasury, he could feel confident that the administration was in good, if not brilliant, hands. Oliver Wolcott, although he might not be very imaginative, could supervise the progress of the programs Hamilton had inaugurated in capable fashion; and Henry Knox's successor in the War Department, Timothy Pickering, was an experienced military administrator. The government of Hamilton's home state, however, must have given him reason for dread. A New York "republican interest" had emerged in the gubernatorial campaign of 1792, just as it had on the national level that same year. While the New York Republicans were largely heirs to the Clintonian and Antifederalist factions, they had also recruited some of Hamilton's old friends and former allies. A variety of personal disappointments and ambitions had caused these defections from Federalist ranks. Chancellor Robert R. Livingston and his youngest brother, Edward, had led their family to the Republican side, and even Commodore James Nicholson, the naval hero who commanded the ship *Hamilton* in the 1788 ratification parade, worked for Clinton's election in 1792. But the fact that George Clinton had kept his office that year only by resorting to legalized election fraud demonstrated that the "republican interest" was not yet an effective Republican party.

Hamilton's policies in the Treasury gave New York's Republicans the incentive and issues they needed to create a meaningful organization after 1792. George Clinton embraced the French cause and even welcomed Edmond Genêt into his family as a son-in-law. British raids on neutral shipping gave Clinton's men a useful rallying point in a city that depended on trade, and in the spring of 1794, local Republicans were "clear for war." Although John Jay's mission to England had quieted them, they had still made large gains in local elections, and the Federal Government's suppression of the Whisky Rebellion that autumn may have helped Republicans win a majority of New York's congressional delegation.

Yet, although Hamilton had unwittingly helped the opposition "interest" become a strong "party," the state picture was not entirely dark when he returned to New York. In January, 1795, after Clinton announced that he would not seek another three-year term, the way was clear to run John Jay for office again despite his absence in London. If Jay returned to the United States with an agreement that settled Anglo-American differences and insured peace and prosperity for New York, the Republicans would lose their most important issue. With Jay in the governor's chair, the "friends of government," as the Federalists called themselves, could regain the congressional seats they had lost in 1794.

In general, then, Hamilton could congratulate himself on having discharged his public duties in such a way that he could at last concentrate on his obligations to his own family. His work in preserving America's credit and peace had forced him to neglect his wife and children too long. His sons would soon require the expensive educations necessary to fit them for their proper places in business and society. His wife had a special claim on his time and attention, since, when her sixth pregnancy ended in miscarriage, he had disregarded her pleas that he leave his militia command in western Pennsylvania to be with her in Philadelphia. Determined now to provide for his family's financial and emotional needs, Hamilton had, by mid-February, 1795, completed arrangements for moving his wife, sons, and daughter to New York. He and his family then traveled north to Albany for an extended visit with the Schuylers. Along the way, unable to forget his commitment to the maintenance of the public credit, Hamilton returned briefly to business matters. Having learned that Congress had rejected some minor proposals on the domestic debt, he wrote to Senator Rufus King.

> Kingston [New Jersey] Feby. 21. 1795
>
> The unnecessary capricious & abominable assassination of the National honor by the rejection of the propositions respecting the unsubscribed debt in the House... haunts me every step I take, and afflicts me more than I can express. To see the character of the Government and the country so sported with, exposed to so indelible a blot puts my heart to the Torture. Am I then more of an American than those who drew their first breath on American Ground? Or What is it that thus torments me at a circumstance so calmly viewed by almost every body else? Am I a fool—a Romantic quixot—Or is there a constitutional defect in the American Mind?

There was little sign of a "Romantic quixot" in Hamilton's letter to his sister-in-law two weeks later, when he outlined very practical plans for his professional future.

[Albany, March 6, 1795]

Eliza & our children are with me here at your fathers house who is himself at New York attending the Legislature. We remain till June, when we become stationary at New York, where I resume the practice of the law. For My Dear Sister, I tell you without regret what I hope you anticipate, that I am poorer than when I went into office. I allot myself full five or six years of more work than will be pleasant though much less than I have had for the last five years.

The Federalist campaign to elect Jay was running smoothly in the spring of 1795, and Hamilton was able to concentrate on his own plans. Robert Troup, a New York attorney, suggested that he and Hamilton accept a retainer from a group of English and Dutch "Capitalists" who planned to buy lands in the Northwest Territory. Troup offered to arrange the transaction so that the former Secretary could invest in the speculation as well as serve as a legal adviser—and do so in complete secrecy. But Hamilton was determined to guard his reputation as carefully in private life as he had done while serving in the Treasury. Hamilton showed little interest in such ventures after his retirement, and profitable as this scheme might have been, he displayed no regrets when he wrote to Troup declining the offer.

Albany April 13. 1795

Tis not my Dear Friend that I think there is any harm or even indelicacy in the thing—I am now in no situation that restrains me—But 'tis because I think there is at present a great crisis in the affairs of [man]kind which may in its consequences involve this country in a sense most affecting to every true friend to it—because concerns of the nature alluded to, though very harmless in the *saints,* who may even fatten themselves on the opportunities or if you please spoils of office, as well as profit by every good thing that is going...[without] hazarding their popularity yet those who are not of the *regenerat[ing]* tribe may not do the most unexceptionable things without its being thundered in their ears—without being denounced as speculators peculators British Agents &c. &c. Because there must be some *public fools* who sacrifice private to public interest at the certainty of ingratitude and obloquy—because my *vanity* whispers I ought to be one of those fools and ought to keep myself in a situation the best calculated to render service....

Bust of John Jay by John Frazer

The game to be played may be a most important one. It may be for nothing less than true liberty, property, order, religion and of course *heads*. I will try Troupe if possible to guard yours and mine.

Hamilton was called upon to "render service" shortly after his family moved to New York City at the end of May. The treaty negotiated in London by John Jay was kept secret even after the Senate began debates on ratification in early June, but gossip about its provisions spread quickly. The twelfth article, limiting American trading privileges in the West Indies, was particularly controversial, and Hamilton made a shrewd suggestion to Rufus King.

New York June 11. 1795

It is to be observed that no time is fixed for the ratification of the Treaty. It may then be ratified with a collateral instruction to make a declaration that the UStates consider the article in question aggregately taken as intended by the King of G B as a privilege; that they conceive it for their interest to forbear the exercise of that privilege...till an explanation in order to a new modification of it shall take place on a more acceptable footing or *till an article to be sent to our minister containing that modification shall be agreed upon between him & the British Court as a part of the Treaty*—the ratification not to [be] exchanged without further instruction from this country unless accepted in this sense and with this qualification.

In 1795 Hamilton was granted the "freedom of the city" by the mayor and aldermen of New York, in testimony of their high esteem.

This was the course the Senate took, voting on June 24 to ratify all of Jay's treaty except the twelfth article. Officially, the treaty remained a "mystery." Unofficially, its provisions were published in the New York press three days after John Jay took office as governor on July 1, 1795. But new British captures of American ships made Washington reluctant to sign the agreement, and he sought Hamilton's opinion. The former Secretary promptly sent the President his "Remarks."

[New York, July 9–11, 1795]

The truly important side of this Treaty is that it closes and upon the whole as reasonably as could have been expected the controverted points between the two Countries—and thereby gives us the prospect of repossessing our Western Posts, an object of primary consequence in our affairs—of escaping finally from

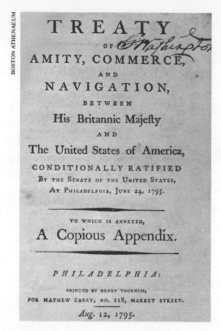

TREATY
OF
AMITY, COMMERCE,
AND
NAVIGATION,
BETWEEN
His Britannic Majefty
AND
The United States of America,
CONDITIONALLY RATIFIED
BY THE SENATE OF THE UNITED STATES,
AT PHILADELPHIA, JUNE 24, 1795.

TO WHICH IS ANNEXED,
A Copious Appendix.

PHILADELPHIA:
PRINTED BY HENRY TUCKNISS,
FOR MATHEW CAREY, NO. 118, MARKET STREET.
Aug. 12, 1795.

*Washington's own signed copy of
Jay's treaty with Great Britain*

being implicated in the dreadful war which is ruining Europe—and of preserving ourselves in a state of peace for a considerable time to come.

Well considered, the greatest interest of this Country in its external relations is that of peace. The more or less of commercial advantages which we may acquire by particular treaties are of far less moment. With peace, the force of circumstances will enable us to make our way sufficiently fast in Trade. War at this time would give a serious wound to our growth and prosperity. Can we escape it for ten or twelve years more, we may then meet it without much inquieture and may advance and support with ener[g]y and effect any just pretensions to greater commercial advantages than we may enjoy.

It follows that the objects contained in the permanent articles are of real and great value to us.... The terms are no way inconsistent with national honor.

Despite Hamilton's arguments, Washington left for Mount Vernon without having signed the treaty. His hesitation only encouraged critics, who called for a meeting at City Hall in New York on July 18 to consider the best "mode of communicating to the President their disapprobation of the English treaty." Hamilton attended as well, and the New York *Journal* described the events of the weekend.

New-York, July 22 [1795].

At the moment the clock struck *twelve*, Mr. *Hamilton*, who was mounted upon a stoop in Broad-street, supported by *Mr. King*...&c. attempted to harrangue the people. He had proceeded no farther than an expression of his ignorance *who called the meeting*, before he was interrupted by the call, "Let us have a chairman;" on which *Col. William S. Smith* was nominated, appointed, and took his stand upon the balcony of the Federal Hall.

Mr. Peter R. Livingston then attempted to address the chair, but was interrupted by Mr. Hamilton; on which a question of order took place, whether Mr. H. or Mr. L. should speak first; this was...carried, by a large majority, in favor of Mr. L. Mr. Livingston then attempted to state the business of the meeting,...but the confusion was so great, that he could not be heard—and, finding that there was an intention, by the oppo-

*This 1797 water color, the only
existing contemporary view of
New York's upper Broad Street,
looks uptown to Federal Hall.*

site party, to defeat the object of the meeting, and prevent the questions being taken on the treaty, he moved, *"That those who disapproved of the treaty, should go to the right, and those who approved of it, to the left;"* which motion was but partly carried into effect; a large body marched up to the church, a large body still remained on the ground, and none, upon the question being reversed, moved to the left....

Finding it impossible to effect a division, those who had drawn off now returned; but finding a great tumult, about 500 of them drew off again, proceeded to the battery, formed a circle, and there BURNT *the treaty*, opposite the government house.

During this interval, Mr. Hamilton introduced a resolution, said to be pened by *Mr.* King, and transmitted it to the Chairman, who attempted to read it, and, behold, a momentary silence took place—but when the citizens found that the resolution *declared it unnecessary to give an opinion on the treaty*, they roared, as with one voice *we'll hear no more of it; tear it up*, &c.

The question was then moved, and carried, for the appointment of a committee of 15, to draft RESOLUTIONS *"expressive of their disapprobation of the treaty."*...

Mr. Hamilton, before the appointment of the Committee, finding the question of his resolutions could not obtain in the *great body*, put the question *(himself)* to those around him, some of whom cried *aye*—after which he called to the *friends of order* to follow him, and they moved off the ground, but the number that followed was small.

New York's customhouse, c. 1796

Not only was Hamilton's circle of friends small that day, but the number of his enemies was increasing. When he tried to play peacemaker between Federalist Josiah Ogden Hoffman and Republican James Nicholson, he found himself the target of Nicholson's anger. Trying to clarify matters, Hamilton later prepared a formal description of his version of the incident.

[New York, July 25–26, 1795]

Mr. Hamilton declares & would repeat that when he interposed in the altercation between Mr. Nicholson & Mr. Hoffman what he said was addressed to both & was purely intended without offence to either to pre-

337

Jay burned in effigy by opponents
of his treaty with Great Britain

vent the continuance of a controversy which might lead to disturbance & riot.

Mr. Nicholson replied very harshly to Mr. Hamilton that he was not the man to prevent his quarrelling called him an Abettor of Tories and used some other harsh expressions which are forgotten.

Mr. Hamilton replied that that was not a place for altercation & Mr. Nicholson & he would discuss it upon a more fit occasion.

Mr. Nicholson replied he & Mr. Hamilton would not pursue the affair for he [Hamilton] had declined an interview upon a former occasion.

Mr. Hamilton replied that no man could affirm that with truth & that he pledged himself to convince Mr. Nicholson of his mistake.

On July 20, Hamilton challenged Commodore Nicholson to a duel. For almost forty-eight hours, Hamilton and Nicholson exchanged notes. Then their seconds tried to work out some form of apology that would settle the affair. Agreement was finally reached, and the Commodore and the Colonel were able to avoid a duel with their reputations intact. This was of considerable value to the Federalists, since Hamilton had begun to publish his monumental defense of Jay's treaty, the essays of "Camillus." This series, titled "The Defence," was signed with the name of the legendary hero who had saved Rome from invasion by the Gauls in the fourth century. The first number, printed in the New York *Argus*, warned Americans of a threat of another kind.

[New York, July 22, 1795]

It is only to know the vanity and vindictiveness of human nature, to be convinced, that while this generation lasts, there will always exist among us, men irreconciliable to our present national constitution....It is a material inference from this, that such men will watch with Lynx's eyes for opportunities of discrediting the proceedings of the government, and will display a hostile and malignant zeal upon every occation, where they think there are any prepossessions of the community to favor their enterprizes. A treaty with Great Britain was too fruitful an occasion not to call forth all their activity.

It is only to consult the history of nations to perceive, that every country, at all times, is cursed by the existence of men, who, actuated by an irregular

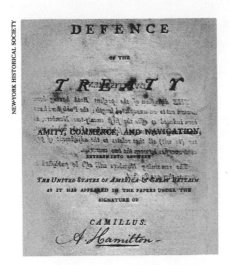

Title page of Hamilton's personal copy of his essays by "Camillus"

ambition, scruple nothing which they imagine will contribute to their own advancement and importance. In monarchies, supple courtiers; in republics, fawning or turbulent demagogues, worshipping still the idol power wherever placed, whether in the hands of a prince, or of the people, and trafficking in the weaknesses, vices, frailties, or prejudices of the one or the other. It was to have been expected, that such men, counting more on the passions than on the reason of their fellow citizens, and anticipating that the treaty would have to struggle with prejudices, would be disposed to make an alliance with popular discontent, to nourish it, and to press it into the service of their particular views.

By the end of August, Washington had signed the treaty, but Hamilton still defended Administration policies in public as "Camillus" and offered advice to the Government in private. More than ever Washington needed the aid of his former Secretary of the Treasury. Edmund Randolph had resigned as Secretary of State after an intercepted dispatch from Fauchet, the former French minister, made it appear that he had solicited a bribe. Randolph's departure and the death of Attorney General William Bradford created two vacancies in the Cabinet. But no one seemed eager to join the Administration, and by the time Washington wrote to Hamilton on October 29 to ask, "What am I to do for a Secretary of State," four men had refused the post. A week later, Hamilton replied, reporting, first of all, that a fifth man, Rufus King, had now rejected the President's offer.

New York November 5th 1795
Circumstances of the moment conspire with the disgust which a virtuous and independent mind feels at placing itself *in but* to the foul and venomous shafts of calumny which are continually shot by an odious confederacy against Virtue—to give Mr. King a decided disinclination to the office.

I wish Sir I could present to you any useful ideas as a substitute. But the embarrassment is extreme as to Secretary of State. An Attorney General I believe may be easily fixed upon by a satisfactory choice....

But for a Secretary of State I know not what to say. [William Loughton] *Smith* [congressman from South Carolina] though not of full size is very respectable for talent & has pretty various information. I think he has

more real talent than the last incumbent of the Office.
But there are strong objections to his appointment. I
fear he is of an uncomfortable temper. He is popular
with no description of men from a certain *hardness* of
character and he more than most other men is considered
as tinctured with prejudices towards the British....

Mr. Innis [James Innes], I fear is too absolutely lazy
for Secy of State. The objection would weigh less as
to Atty General....

Judge [Nathaniel] Pendleton writes well is of respectable abilities and a Gentlemanlike smooth man. If I
were sure of his political views I should be much disposed to advise his appointment under the circumstances. But I fear he has been somewhat tainted with
the prejudices of Mr. Jefferson & Mr. Madison & I
have afflicting suspicions concerning these men....

In fact a first rate character is not attainable. A
second rate must be taken with good dispositions &
barely decent qualifications. I wish I could throw more
light. Tis a sad omen for the Government.

Apparently conceding that a "first rate character"
could not be found, Washington transferred Timothy Pickering to the
State Department. Two months later, Hamilton visited Philadelphia for
the first time since his resignation from the Cabinet. The Government's
case for the constitutionality of the "carriage tax" was being argued before
the Supreme Court, and since this tax had been enacted at his own urging
in June, 1794, Hamilton felt a special responsibility for its vindication.
Opponents contended that it was a "direct" tax, which, under the Constitution, had to be levied in proportion to state population. Hamilton persuaded
the Court to uphold the measure with this common-sense argument on the
definition of "direct" and "indirect" taxes.

February 24, 179[6]

The following are presumed to be the only direct taxes.

Capitation or poll taxes.

Taxes on lands and buildings.

General assessments, whether on the whole property of individuals, or on their whole real or personal
estates....

To apply a rule of apportionment according to numbers to taxes of the above description, has some *rationale*
in it; but to extend an apportionment of that kind to
other cases, would, in many instances, produce...pre-

posterous consequences, and would greatly embarrass the operations of the government....

The Constitution gives power to Congress to lay and collect the taxes, duties, imposts, and excises, requiring that all duties, imposts, and excises shall be uniform throughout the United States.

Here *duties*, *imposts*, and *excises* appear to be contra-distinguished from *taxes*, and while the latter is left to apportionment, the former are enjoined to be uniform.

But, unfortunately, there is equally here a want of criterion to distinguish *duties*, *imposts* and *excises* from taxes.

If the meaning of the word *excise* is to be sought in the British statutes, it will be found to include the duty on carriages... and not liable to apportionment; consequently not a direct tax.

An argument results from this, though not perhaps a conclusive one: yet where so important a distinction in the Constitution is to be realized, it is fair to seek the meaning of terms in the statutory language of that country from which our jurisprudence is derived.

Timothy Pickering

James McHenry's appointment as Secretary of War and Charles Lee's nomination as Attorney General completed the roster of "second rate" men who now made up Washington's official family of advisers. Such men made it more difficult than ever to handle pressing issues, and during Hamilton's stay in Philadelphia the President often turned to him for advice and counsel—particularly concerning Republican opposition to Jay's treaty. Having finally received official notice that ratifications had been exchanged in London, the President had proclaimed the treaty in effect and had submitted it to the House of Representatives on March 1. The House was responsible for voting funds to implement the agreement, and even though congressional Republicans could not undo the treaty, they could still embarrass the Administration. Thus, when Edward Livingston of New York introduced resolutions demanding that House members be allowed to see Jay's official instructions and correspondence, Hamilton wrote to Washington suggesting a plan of action.

New York March 7th. 1796

If the motion succeeds, it ought not to be complied with. Besides that in a matter of such a nature the production of the papers cannot fail to start [a] new and unpleasant Game—it will be fatal to the Negotiating Power of the Government if it is to be a matter of

Hamilton's 1796 certificate to practice law before the United States Circuit Court

course for a call of either House of Congress to bring forth all the communication however confidential.

It seems to me that something like the following answer by the President will be adviseable.

"A right in the House of Representatives, to demand and have as a matter of course, and without specification of any object all communications respecting a negotiation with a foreign power cannot be admitted without danger of much inconvenience. A discretion in the Executive Department how far and where to comply in such cases is essential to the due conduct of foreign negotiations and is essential to preserve the limits between the Legislative and Executive Departments. The present call is altogether indefinite and without any declared purpose. The Executive has no cases on which to judge of the propriety of a compliance with it and cannot therefore without forming a very dangerous precedent comply."

Washington refused the House demand, but the Republicans attacked on another front. On April 15, the House adopted resolutions submitted by Congressman William Blount (and drafted by James Madison) declaring that Congress had a right to pass on portions of treaties involving matters that were the constitutional responsibility of the House, and further, that the President must make available any information that concerned House functions. In effect, these resolutions were intended to justify the House's refusal to vote funds for implementing Jay's treaty. When he heard of these developments, Hamilton wrote to Senator Rufus King.

New York April 15. 1796

To me our true plan appears to be the following....

I The President ought immediately after the House has taken the ground of refusal to send them a solemn Protest....

A copy of this protest to be sent to the Senate for their information. The Senate by resolutions to express strongly their approbation of his principles, to assure him of their firm support & to advise him to proceed in the execution of the Treaty....

Then the Merchants to meet in the Cities & second by their resolutions the measures of the President & Senate further addressing their fellow Citizens to cooperate with them. Petitions afterwards to be handed throughout the U States.

The Senate to hold fast & consent to no adjournment till the expiration of the term of service of the present House unless provision [is] made.

The President to cause a confidential communication to be made to the British stating candidly what has happened; his regrets, his adherence nevertheless to the Treaty....

I prefer that measures should begin with a Protest of the President—as it will be in itself proper & there will be more chance of success if the Contest appears to be with him & the Senate auxiliaries than in the reverse.

But in all this business celerity decision & an imposing attitude are indispensable. The Glory of the President, the safety of the Constitution, the greatest interests, depend upon it. Nothing will be wanting here. I do not write to the President on the subject.

Patrick Henry

Congressional Republicans backed down and voted funds for Jay's treaty, not so much because of merchants' protests as because of Rufus King's threat to make appropriations for this treaty a rider to any and all treaty bills that came to the Senate. Federalists could now concentrate on choosing a candidate to succeed Washington in the fall elections. King had wooed Patrick Henry of Virginia, a former Antifederalist. Thomas Pinckney, America's minister to Britain, was also mentioned prominently. Either of these southerners, it was believed, would have a better chance than would Vice President John Adams. Early in May, Hamilton discussed Federalist strategy with King.

[New York] May 4 1796

I am intircly of opinion that P. H [Patrick Henry] declining Mr. P____ [Pinckney] ought to be our man. It is even an idea of which I am fond in various lights. Indeed on latter reflection, I rather wish to be rid of P.H, that we may be at full liberty to take up Pinckney.

In the event of Pinck[n]ey's return to this Country, I am of opinion all circumstances considered, it is expedient you should replace him. I hope no great question will in a short period agitate our Councils & I am sure you will do much good on the scene in question. I have called on Jay, but happened not to find him disengaged. I shall quickly see him & shall with great pleasure do every thing requisite on my part.

Thomas Pinckney

Senator King admitted that he was "not a little tired" of his legislative burden, and Hamilton passed the information along to Washington. The President reacted promptly by naming King as Thomas Pinckney's successor. Meanwhile, another problem arose that required Hamilton's advice. Rumor had it that members of the French Directory were so displeased with Jay's treaty that they were going to send a special envoy to raise protests and perhaps even demand that the United States aid the French colonies in the West Indies. As yet, no such person had arrived, but Washington was worried about what his response should be, and he asked Hamilton to discuss the matter with Jay. Hamilton replied calmly that it was pointless to be apprehensive before America learned the intentions of the Directory; and he counseled the President about the possibility that France might go so far as to demand a renunciation of Jay's treaty.

New York May 20. 1796

The answer will naturally be that this sacrifice of the positive & recent engagements of the country is pregnant with consequences too humiliating and injurious to us to allow us to believe that the expectation can be persisted in by France since it is to require a thing impossible & to establish as the price of the continuance of Friendship with us the sacrifice of our honor by an act of perfidy which would destroy the value of our friendship to any Nation. That, besides, the Executive . . . is not competent to it—it being of the province of Congress by a declaration of War or otherwise in the proper cases to annul the operation of Treaties. . . .

If the Guarantee of the West Indies should be claimed —The answer may be—

"That the decision of this question belongs to Congress who if it be desired will be convened to deliberate upon it." I presume & hope they will have adjourned. For to [gain] time is every thing.

Hamilton had been conscientiously reporting to Washington every rumor of French attacks on merchant vessels, and the President responded with understandable alarm. Troubled, too, by the conduct of his minister to Paris, James Monroe, who was an enthusiastic supporter of the Directory, Washington asked Hamilton and Governor Jay to discuss, among "other interesting matters," the possibility of sending a new special envoy to France. Hamilton reported the results of these conferences to the President.

New York July 5. 1796

We are both of opinion there is *no* power in the President to appoint an Envoy Extraordinary, without the concurrence of the Senate, & that the information in question is *not* a sufficient ground for extraordinarily convening the senate. If however the President from his *information collectively* be convinced that a dangerous state of things exists between us & France and that an envoy extraordinary to avert the danger is a necessary measure, I believe this would in the sense of the constitution warrant the calling of the Senate for the purpose....

Mr. Jay & Myself though somewhat out of your question talked of the expediency of removing Monroe, and though we perceive there are weighty reasons against it, we think those for it preponderate—if a proper man can be found. But here we feel both immense embarrassment, for he ought to be at the same time a friend to the Government & understood to be *not unfriendly* to the French Revolution. General [Charles Cotesworth] Pinckney is the only man we can think of who fully satisfies the idea, & unfortunately every past experiment forbids the hope that he would accept—though but for a short time. But if a character of tolerable fitness can be thought of, it would seem expedient to send him. At any rate it is to be feared, if...no *actual* & *full* explanation takes place, it will bring serious censure upon the Executive. It will be said that it did not display as much zeal to avoid misunderstanding with France as with G Britain....

As to your resignation, Sir, it is not to be regretted that the declaration of your intention should be suspended as long as possible & suffer me to add that you should *really hold the thing undecided to the last moment.* I do not think it is in the power of party to throw any slur upon the lateness of your decl[a]ration. And you have an obvious justification in the state of things. If a storm gathers, how can you retreat? This is a most serious question.

Washington wears a lace cravat in Adolph Wertmüller's 1795 portrait.

Washington replied that he should have issued a farewell address the day after Congress adjourned and urged Hamilton to finish drafting such a message as quickly as possible. Meanwhile, the President decided to send Charles Pinckney to Paris to replace James Monroe. On July 30, Hamilton completed the manuscript of the President's Farewell Address. He had tried, he told Washington, to make it *"importantly* and *lastingly* useful." With the exception of some of the more partisan passages, Washington found it to be just that. Opening with a declaration that Washington would decline reelection, Hamilton's draft then turned to "some sentiments" on the nation's future course.

[New York, July 30, 1796]

Interwoven as is the love of Liberty with every fibre of your hearts no recommendation is necessary to fortify your attachment to it. Next to this that unity of Government which constitutes you one people claims your vigilant care & guardianship—as a main pillar of your real independence of your peace safety freedom and happiness.

This being the point in your political fortress against which the batteries of internal and external enemies will be most constantly and actively however covertly and insidiously levelled, it is of the utmost importance that you should appreciate in its full force the immense value of your political Union to your national and individual happiness—that you should cherish towards it an affectionate and immoveable attachment and that you should watch for its preservation with jealous solicitude....

The great rule of conduct for us in regard to foreign Nations ought to be to have as little *political* connection with them as possible—so far as we have already formed engagements let them be fulfilled—with circumspection indeed but with perfect good faith. Here let us stop.

Europe has a set of primary interests which have none or a very remote relation to us. Hence she must be involved in frequent contests the causes of which will be essentially foreign to us....

Our detached and distant situation invites us to a different course & enables us to pursue it. If we remain a united people under an efficient Government the period is not distant when we may defy material injury from external annoyance—when we may take such an attitude as will cause the neutrality we shall at any time resolve to observe to be violated with caution...when we may choose peace or war as our interest guided by justice shall dictate.

Why should we forego the advantages of so felicitous a situation? Why quit our own ground to stand upon Foreign ground? Why by interweaving our destiny with any part of Europe should we intangle our prosperity and peace in the nets of European Ambition rivalship interest or Caprice?

Permanent alliance, intimate connection with any part of the foreign world is to be avoided.

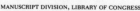

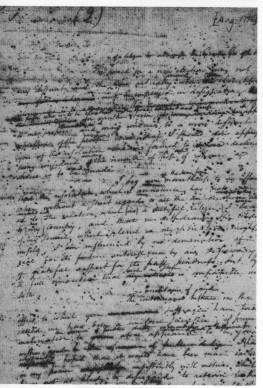

The first page of Hamilton's draft of Washington's Farewell Address

Even when the Farewell Address had been revised and published, Washington was not free of official burdens. Arriving in Philadelphia to serve out the last months of his term, he discovered in an issue of the *Aurora* a letter to Pickering from Pierre Adet, the new French minister, complaining that France's protests had not been answered by the American Government. Because it was not clear whether Adet had taken this step on order from the Directory, Washington—in what was now a familiar pattern—asked Hamilton and Jay to discuss Adet's status. Hamilton sent the President this report.

Pierre Adet

[New York] November 4. 1796

We settled our opinion on one point—(viz) That whether Mr. Adet acted with or without instruction from his Government in publishing his communication, he committed a disrespect towards our government which ought not to pass *unnoticed,* and would most properly be *noticed* to him as the Representative or Agent. That the manner of noticing it, in the first instance at least, ought to be *negative,* that is, by the *personal conduct* of the President towards the Minister. That the true rule on this point would be to receive the Minister...with a *dignified reserve,* holding an *exact medium* between an *offensive coldness* and *cordiality.* The *point* is [a] nice one to be hit, but no one will know better how to do it than the President.

Meanwhile, Washington decided to publish a reply to Adet's appeal, prepared by Secretary Pickering. The exchanges between Adet and the Secretary of State continued until November 15. Then, deliberately timing his announcement to coincide with the American elections, the French minister declared that his Government considered Jay's treaty a violation of the 1778 Franco-American treaties of alliance and commerce and equivalent to an alliance with Great Britain; and that therefore he had been ordered "to suspend...his ministerial functions." Three weeks later, the New York *Minerva* carried Hamilton's essay, "The Answer," which opened with this analysis of French policies.

[December 8, 1796]

The French republic have, at various times, during the present war, complained of certain principles, and decisions of the American government, as being violations of its neutrality, or infractions of the treaty made with France in the year 1778.... They are now not only renewed with great exaggeration, but the French government have directed that it should be done *in the tone of*

James Watson

reproach, instead of the language of friendship. The apparent intention of this menacing tone, at this particular time, is to influence timid minds to vote agreeable to their wishes in the election of president and vice-president, and probably with this view, the memorial was published in the news-papers. This is certainly a practice that must not be permitted. If one foreign minister is permitted to publish what he pleases to the people, in the name of his government, every other foreign minister must be indulged with the same right. What then will be our situation on the election of a president and vice president, when the government is insulted, the persons who administer it, traduced, and the electors menaced by public addresses from these intriguing agents?

Adet's publications came too late to affect the choice of presidential electors in most states, but the New York congressional elections were not held until December. One New York newspaper remarked that Hamilton "patroles the whole city and strains every nerve in favor of the yankey candidate," Federalist James Watson. But when the polls opened on December 13, the incumbent congressman, Republican Edward Livingston, pulled ahead. Within a few days, Hamilton had learned enough about the races for the Electoral College and for the New York delegation to Congress to send this summary of the political picture to Rufus King in London.

New York Decr. 16. 1796

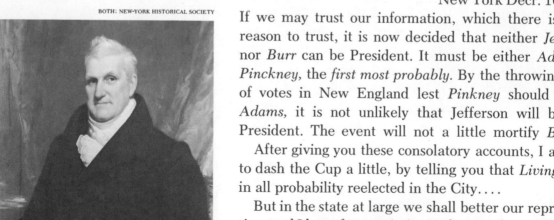

Edward Livingston

If we may trust our information, which there is every reason to trust, it is now decided that neither *Jefferson* nor *Burr* can be President. It must be either *Adams* or *Pinckney,* the *first most probably.* By the throwing away of votes in New England lest *Pinkney* should outrun *Adams,* it is not unlikely that Jefferson will be *Vice* President. The event will not a little mortify *Burr.* . . .

After giving you these consolatory accounts, I am now to dash the Cup a little, by telling you that *Livingston* is in all probability reelected in the City. . . .

But in the state at large we shall better our representation, and I hope for a majority in the next house of Representatives. As an omen of this, there are several *new members* in Congress from different states, who hitherto vote with our friends.

The favourable change in the conduct of Great Britain towards us strengthens the hand of the friends of Order & peace. . . .

As Hamilton had predicted, John Adams won election as the second President of the United States. But Washington, even in the last weeks of his term, still faced major problems. Some advisers suggested that a special envoy be sent to Paris, just as John Jay had been sent to London in a similar crisis in 1794; but Washington hesitated to take this step lest it offend his newly appointed minister to Paris, Charles Cotesworth Pinckney. Once again, the President asked Hamilton's advice, and the former Secretary made this suggestion.

[New York, January 25–31, 1797]

I have reflected as maturely as time has permitted on the idea of an extraordinary mission to France, and notwithstanding the objections, I rather incline to it under some shape or other. As an imitation of what was done in the case of Great Britain, it will argue to the people equal solicitude. To France it will have a similar aspect (for Pinckney will be considered there as a mere substitute in ordinary course to Mr. Monroe) and will in some degree soothe her pride. The influence on party, if a man in whom the opposition has confidence is sent, will be considerable in the event of non success. And it will be to France a bridge over which she may more easily retreat.

The best form of the thing in my view is a commission including three persons who may be called "*Commissioners* Plenipotentiary & extraordinary." Two of the three should be Mr. Madison and Mr. Pinckney. A third may be taken from the Northern states and I know none better than Mr. [George] *Cabot*—who or any *two* of whom may be empowered to act. . . .

Or (which however I think less eligible) Mr. Madison & Mr. Pinkney only may be joint Commissioners—without a third person.

Mr. Cabot . . . will I think certainly go. If not the other two may act without him. . . .

Unless Mr. *Madison* will go there is scarcely another character that will afford advantage.

ADAMS NATIONAL HISTORIC SITE

This portrait of John Adams was painted by William Winstanley in 1798, during Adams's Presidency.

Despite Hamilton's urging, Washington did not appoint a commission. Writing to Rufus King, Hamilton saw little reason for optimism in the conduct of Congress or in the new Administration of John Adams.

[New York] Feby. 15. 1797

The present session of Congress is likely to be very unproductive. That body is in the situation which we foresaw certain *anti* executive maxims would bring them to.

Mr. Adams is President, Mr. Jefferson Vice President. Our Jacobins say they are well pleased and that the *Lion* & the *Lamb* are to lie down together. Mr. Adam's *personal* friends talk a little in the same way. Mr. *Jefferson* is not half so ill a man as we have been accustommed to think him. There is to be a united and a vigorous administration. Sceptics like me quietly look forward to the event—willing to hope but not prepared to believe. If Mr. Adams has *Vanity* to plan a plot has been laid to take hold of it. We trust his real good sense and integrity will be a sufficient shield.

On reflection, Hamilton realized that Adams could appoint the commission and might be in a better position to do so than Washington had been. Toward the end of February, Hamilton began his campaign to influence the new Executive with this letter to Adams's old friend Theodore Sedgwick.

[New York] Feby. 26. 1797

It is a fact, that the resentment of the French Government is very much levelled at the actual President. A change of the person (however undespicable in other respects) may give a change to the passion, and may also furnish a bridge to retreat over. This is a great advantage for a new President & the most ought to be made of it. For it is much our interest to preserve peace, if we can with honor, and if we cannot it will be very important to prove that no endeavour to do it has been omitted.

Were I Mr. Adams, then I believe I should begin my Presidency by naming an extraordinary Commission to the French Republic. And I think it would consist of three persons, Mr. Madison Mr. Pinkney & Mr. Cabot.

As a result of dispatches from Paris, opinion in favor of a special mission to France began growing during March. The Directory, having accepted James Monroe's letter of recall, had refused to receive Charles Pinckney as his successor until French grievances were remedied. Hamilton knew the time was propitious to reintroduce his plan. His task was easier, since John Adams had retained all the members of Washington's Cabinet, and these were men who were used to receiving and following the advice of the former Secretary of the Treasury. In mid-March, Hamilton wrote to Secretary of State Pickering.

[New York] March 22. 1797

It is now ascertained that Mr. Pinckney has been refused and with circumstances of indignity. What is to be done? The share I have had in the public administration added to my interest as a Citizen make me extremely anxious that at this delicate Crisis a course of conduct exactly proper may be adopted. I offer to your consideration without ceremony what appears to me such a course.

First. I would appoint a day of humiliation and prayer.... it will be politically useful to impress our nation that there is a serious state of things — to strengthen religious ideas in a contest which in its progress may require that our people may consider themselves as the defenders of their Country against Atheism conquest & anarchy. It is far from evident to me that the progress of the war may not call on us to defend our fire sides & our altars. And any plan which does not look forward to this as possible will in my opinion be a superficial one.

Second. I would call Congress together at as *short a day* as a majority of both houses can assemble.

3 When assembled I would appoint a Commission extraordinary to consist of Mr. Jefferson, or Mr. Madison, together with Mr Cabot & Mr. Pinckney....

4 The Congress should be urged to take defensive measures.

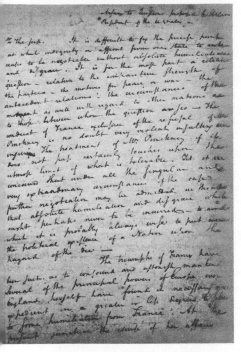

A page from the letter in which Hamilton supplied the answers to the questions John Adams asked of his War Secretary in April, 1797

Pickering replied that Adams had already decided to call Congress into session. From Secretary Wolcott, Hamilton learned that the President had also decided to send a mission to France, although he did not agree with Hamilton's choice of members. Hamilton's first letters to Adams's hand-me-down Cabinet were unsolicited, but the secretaries did not hesitate to seek his opinions, nor were they reluctant to share information with him. Hamilton's most useful channel of influence within the Administration was James McHenry, the Secretary of War. In late April, while occupied in Albany with "court avocations" and his father-in-law's illness, Hamilton received an urgent letter from his friend "Mac," who enclosed a series of questions that Adams had submitted to the Cabinet for written opinions. McHenry asked for Hamilton's "answer at length" and begged him to tell no one of this request. In his reply, Hamilton considered each of Adams's queries on foreign policy, beginning with the question of whether France's rejection of Pinckney was a bar to future negotiations.

[Albany] April 29. 1797

The former relations of the U States to France — the

agency of that power in promoting our revolution—are reasons in the nature of things for not lightly running into a quarrel with—even for bearing and forbearing to a considerable extent. There is perhaps in such a case peculiar dignity in moderation.

France in declining to receive Mr Pinckney has not gone to the *ne plus ultra.* She has declined to receive a minister till grievances, of which she complains, are redressed. She has not absolutely ordered away a minister as the preliminary to war.... It is not even clear that she means to say she will not receive an *extraordinary* minister. This leaves some vacant ground between her act and *rupture.* The U States may occupy it by a further attempt at negotiation. This further attempt seems to be that which must carry us to the point beyond which we cannot go....

But to preserve character abroad—and esteem for the Government at home, it is essential that the idea of further negotiation be accompanied by measures that shall demonstrate a spirit of resistance in case of failure—that shall yield present protection—and promise future security.

With this *adjunct,* it is believed that the Government in pursuing the plan of further negotiation will raise rather than depress the character of the Nation abroad & will preserve the dignity of the American mind & the esteem of the American people.

James McHenry

McHenry found Hamilton's suggestions so useful that he simply recopied the letter, added a few paragraphs, and presented the document to the President as his own work. In May, before a joint session of Congress, Adams outlined his policy toward France. His decisions—to stand firm and to send a commission to Paris—enraged the Republicans and pleased Hamilton. But the "continuance of peace" in Hamilton's private affairs was threatened anew in the first week of July, when James Monroe's return from Paris coincided with the publication of a series of pamphlets entitled "The History of the United States for 1796." The pamphlets charged that Hamilton and other Federalists who had been calling for Monroe's removal from the Paris ministry were seeking revenge for the part Monroe had played in investigating the Reynolds affair in December, 1792. Also printed were the documents concerning that inquiry, along with hints that Hamilton's "volunteer acknowledgement of seduction" concealed grave misconduct in office. As soon as Hamilton read the pamphlets, he wrote indignantly to Monroe and to the other men who had taken part in the investigation, Frederick Muhlenberg and Abraham Venable.

New York July 5. 1797

The peculiar nature of this transaction renders it impossible that you should not recollect it in all its parts and that your own declarations to me at the time contradicts absolutely the construction which the Editor of the Pamphlet puts upon the affair.

I think myself intitled to ask from your Candour and Justice a declaration equivalent to that which was made me at the time in the presence of Mr. Wolcott by yourself and the two other Gentlemen accompanied by a contradiction of the representations in the comments cited above. And I shall rely upon your delicacy that the manner of doing it will be such as one Gentleman has a right to expect from another—especially as you must be sensible that the present appearance of the papers is contrary to the course which was understood between us to be proper and includes a dishonorable infidelity somewhere. . . .

I send you the copy of a Memorandum of the substance of your declaration made by me the morning after our interview. . . .

Memorandum . . . of Messrs. Monroe Mughlenburgh & Venable concerning the affair of J Reynolds.

That they regreted the trouble and uneasiness which they had occasioned to me in consequence of the representations made to them. That they were perfectly satisfied with the explanation I had given and that there was nothing in the transaction which ought to affect my character as a public Officer or lessen the public confidence in my integrity.

A page from Hamilton's memorandum to Monroe, Muhlenberg, and Venable

James Monroe received this letter just as he was about to leave Philadelphia for New York. In Manhattan, his misunderstanding with Hamilton grew more serious. The pamphlets revealed that Monroe had continued to correspond with Jacob Clingman, James Reynolds's partner in crime, after his meetings with Hamilton in December, 1792. This information convinced Hamilton that there was a wide-ranging plot against him. On July 11, he and his wife's brother-in-law John Church went to Monroe's lodgings for a confrontation with the Virginian and his friend David Gelston. Gelston, who left a record of the morning's events, recalled that Hamilton was "very much agitated" when he came to the meeting. Monroe tried to soothe him by explaining that he had received his letter late at night before leaving Philadelphia and had not had time to prepare a joint statement on the subject with Venable and Muhlenberg. Monroe gave assurances that such a statement would be prepared as soon as he returned to Philadelphia, but Hamilton was not satisfied.

> [New York] Tuesday Morning July 11th. 1797
>
> Colo. M then observed if he Colo. H. wished him to give a relation of the facts . . . as they appeared to him, he would do it then. Colo. H. said he should like to hear it, Colo. M. then proceeded upon a history of the business . . . and said that the packet of papers before alluded to he yet believed remained sealed with his friend in Virginia and after getting through Colo. H. said this as your representation is totally false . . . upon which the Gentlemen both instantly rose Colo. M. rising first and saying do you say I represented falsely, you are a Scoundrel. Colo. H said I will meet you like a Gentleman Colo. M said I am ready get your pistols, both said we shall not or it will not be settled any other way. Mr C[hurch] & myself rising at the same moment put our selves between them Mr. C. repeating Gentlemen Gentlemen be moderate . . . we all sat down & the two Gentn, Colo. M & Colo. H. soon got moderate, I observed however very clearly to my mind that Colo. H. appeared extremely agitated & Colo. M. appeared soon to get quite cool and repeated his intire ignorance of the publication & his surprize to find it published, observing to Colo. H. if he would not be so warm & intemperate he would explain everything he knew of the business & how it appeared to him.

John Church

Hamilton was persuaded to let matters rest until Monroe could talk to Muhlenberg and Venable. Although his wife was expecting their sixth child in a few weeks, Hamilton left New York on July 12 to take part in these talks. In Philadelphia, he argued with Monroe and Muhlenberg over the terms of the statement they should issue, and he was determined not to leave until his name was cleared. When his departure was delayed by Monroe's reluctance to produce a satisfactory account of his transactions with Jacob Clingman, Hamilton sent him this bitter complaint.

> [Philadelphia, July 22, 1797]
>
> There appears a design at all events to drive me to the necessity of a formal defence—while you know that the extreme delicacy of its nature might be very disagreeable to me. It is my opinion that as you have been the cause . . .

Engraved portrait of James Monroe

of the business appearing in a shape which gives it an adventitious importance,... it was incumbent upon you as a man of honor and sensibility to have come forward in a manner that would have shielded me completely from the unpleasant effects brought upon me by your agency. This you have not done.

On the contrary by the affected reference of the matter to a defence which I am to make, and by which you profess your opinion is to be decided—you imply that your suspicions are still alive. And as nothing appears to have shaken your original conviction but the wretched tale of Clingman,... it follows that you are pleased to attach a degree of weight to that communication which cannot be accounted for on any fair principle. The result in my mind is that you have been and are actuated by motives towards me malignant and dishonorable; nor can I doubt that this will be the universal opinion when the publication of the whole affair which I am about to make shall be seen.

Shortly after having written this letter, Hamilton rejoined his wife in New York in time for the birth of their fifth son, William. His correspondence with Monroe continued for another two weeks, and at one point it seemed that the affair might end in a duel. Instead, the incident closed with a move by Hamilton that was more puzzling than any of the bizarre events that had occurred earlier. On August 25, a pamphlet appeared in New York with the title *Observations on Certain Documents... in which the Charge of Speculation against Alexander Hamilton... is Fully Refuted. Written by Himself.* The tract was more interesting than its name indicated, for Hamilton included not only the documents involved in the investigation of 1792, but also his correspondence with Maria and James Reynolds and the details of his career as lover and victim of blackmail. Anticipating criticism, Hamilton offered this explanation for his decision to expose his follies.

[August 31, 1797]

I owe perhaps to my friends an apology for condescending to give a public explanation. A just pride with reluctance stoops to a formal vindication against so despicable a contrivance and is inclined rather to oppose to it the uniform evidence of an upright character. This would be my conduct on the present occasion, did not the tale seem to derive a sanction from the names of three men of some weight and consequence in the society:

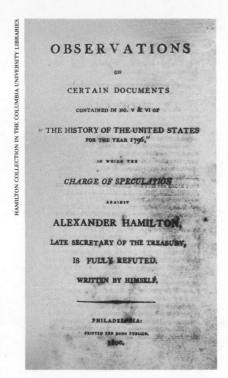

OBSERVATIONS

ON

CERTAIN DOCUMENTS

CONTAINED IN NO. V & VI OF

" THE HISTORY OF THE UNITED STATES
FOR THE YEAR 1796,"

IN WHICH THE

CHARGE OF SPECULATION

AGAINST

ALEXANDER HAMILTON,

LATE SECRETARY OF THE TREASURY,

IS FULLY REFUTED.

WRITTEN BY HIMSELF.

PHILADELPHIA:

PRINTED PRO BONO PUBLICO.

1800.

*Title page of an 1800 edition of
Hamilton's* Observations, *his defense
against charges of speculation*

a circumstance, which I trust will excuse me for paying attention to a slander that without this prop, would defeat itself by intrinsic circumstances of absurdity and malice.

The charge against me is a connection with one James Reynolds for purposes of improper pecuniary speculation. My real crime is an amorous connection with his wife, for a considerable time with his privity and connivance, if not originally brought on by a combination between the husband and wife with the design to extort money from me.

This confession is not made without a blush. I cannot be the apologist of any vice because the ardour of passion may have made it mine. I can never cease to condemn myself for the pang, which it may inflict in a bosom eminently intitled to all my gratitude, fidelity and love. But that bosom will approve, that even at so great an expence, I should effectually wipe away a more serious stain from a name, which it cherishes with no less elevation than tenderness. The public too will I trust excuse the confession. The necessity of it to my defence against a more heinous charge could alone have extorted from me so painful an indecorum.

In the three years of his retirement from the Treasury, Hamilton's life had come full circle. He had left office pinning his hopes for America's peace on a diplomatic mission to England. At the close of 1797, he waited for word of the joint commission to Paris that could save America from "rupture" with the French Republic. He had begun his venture in private life with heavy obligations to his wife and children. There was now another son to be educated, and Elizabeth Hamilton had a stronger claim than ever on her husband's heart and conscience. Hamilton's experiment with withdrawal from public duty had hardly been successful. He felt too strong a commitment to the measures he had begun as Secretary of the Treasury to abandon them. He had challenged James Nicholson to a duel in a dispute over Jay's treaty and shamed his family with the exposure of his affair with Maria Reynolds to uphold his reputation for honesty as a public official. And now, as an unofficial adviser to the Cabinet, he was occupied with the progress of the three-man mission to France. Hamilton would not be a completely private citizen until that mission had succeeded.

Chapter 13

Seeds of Conflict

Hamilton's vows to devote himself to his family and his profession were more seriously threatened by the joint commission to France than they had been by Jay's mission to England. Jay had brought back a controversial treaty for his friend to defend; the reports of the insults that the French Government heaped on the members of the joint commission — Elbridge Gerry, Charles Pinckney, and John Marshall — helped precipitate America into a quasi war with her Revolutionary ally. France's Foreign Minister, Talleyrand, forced the commissioners to bargain through his agents, whom they dubbed "W," "X," "Y," and "Z" in their dispatches. The price of negotiation, they learned, was to be a "loan" to France and a "gift" to Talleyrand himself. When the commissioners' reports of the XYZ affair reached Philadelphia, the United States embarked on a strange undeclared war, which saw no land battles and only a few minor naval engagements.

For Hamilton, the Quasi War offered an opportunity to introduce "respectability" into America's military establishment, as he had done with the nation's finances. Unfortunately, it also gave him a chance for closer contact with President John Adams, who had reacted to Hamilton's part in the 1796 elections by calling him "as great an hypochrite as any in the U.S." It was only a matter of time before the two men would find new reasons for mutual distrust. Hamilton had limited but sincere respect for Adams. He had worked for Adams's election as Vice President in 1789 and 1792 and appreciated the New Englander's support of his program for discharging the public debt via the Sinking Fund Commission. But generally their early relations had not been close. Adams was a proud and suspicious man who resented Hamilton's efforts in 1789 to see that votes in the Electoral College were balanced so that Washington would not accidentally lose the Presidency. To Adams, this was a personal insult that had barred him from an "equal" chance at the office of Chief Executive.

Luckily, Adams was ignorant of Hamilton's work as secret adviser to his

Cabinet in 1798. One reason for this was Adams's habit of leaving Philadelphia as soon as Congress adjourned and remaining at his home in Quincy, Massachusetts, until the legislature reconvened. Had Adams spent more time in the capital, he might have learned sooner of Hamilton's meddling in the Administration. Indeed, if Adams had not been an absentee President, the secretaries might have had less reason to consult Hamilton when prompt decisions were needed. As it happened, the advice Hamilton gave the Cabinet in 1797 and 1798 coincided with the President's own views. But in the progress of the Quasi War their ideas diverged, and Adams learned, as had Thomas Jefferson, that the more he knew of Hamilton, the less he found to admire. When he finally discovered Hamilton's role in the Administration, his anger revealed the depth of his hostility.

At first, however, the President and the former Secretary were united in their determination to assert America's rights and dignity. Even before the Government learned of the extortion attempt by W, X, Y, and Z, James McHenry had asked Hamilton for his suggestions on Administration policy in case the joint mission should fail. The course that Hamilton outlined was remarkably similar to Adams's own conclusions.

[New York, January 27–February 11] 1798

The measures to be taken by the Executive will therefore be—

To communicate to Congress with *manly* but *calm* and *sedate* firmness & without strut, the ill success of the attempt to negotiate & the circumstances attending it—

To deplore the failure of the measure—

To inculcate that the crisis is a very serious one & looking forward to possible events in Europe may involve the safety liberty & prosperity of this Country—

That the situation points out two objects 1 measures of immediate defence to our Commerce and 2 of ulterior security in the event of open Rupture. . . .

The idea to be thrown in that the hope of an accommodation without proceeding to open Rupture ought not to be abandonned or precluded while measures of self preservation ought not to be omitted or delayed & ought to be prosecuted with a vigour commensurate with the present urgency & eventual greatness of the danger. . . .

In addition to these measures Let the President recommend a day to be observed as a day of fasting humiliation & prayer. On religious ground this is very proper—On political, it is very expedient. The Government will be very unwise, if it does not make the most of the religious prepossessions of our people—opposing the honest enthusiasm of Religious Opinion to the phrenzy of Political fanaticism.

February passed with no word from the commissioners. Hamilton rode to Albany to argue the case of Louis Le Guen, a French merchant whose legal problems kept Hamilton profitably employed for several years in a series of trials that became among the most famous in the early history of American business law. Shortly after his return to New York City, Hamilton learned of the humiliating treatment of the American commission by W, X, Y, and Z. Too indignant to keep silent, he protested to Secretary of State Pickering.

American suspicions of French motives were rife when this plan of a supposed French invasion of England and Ireland was published in Philadelphia in April, 1798.

New York March 17. 1798

I look upon the Question before the Public as nothing less than whether we shall maintain our Independence and I am prepared to do it in every event and at every hazard. I am therefore of opinion that our Executive should come forth on this basis.

I wish to see a *temperate*, but *grave solemn* and *firm* communication from the President to the two houses on the result of the advices from our Commissioners. This communication to review summarily the course of our affairs with France from the beginning to the present moment...to consider her refusal to receive our Ministers as a virtual denial of our Independence and as evidence that if circumstances favour the plan we shall be called to defend that Independence our political institutions & our liberty against her enterprizes—to conclude that leaving still the door to accommodation open & not proceeding to final rupture. Our duty our honor & safety require that we shall take vigorous comprehensive measures of defence adequate to the immediate protection of our Commerce to the security of our Ports and to our eventual defence in case of Invas[ion] with a view to these great objects calling forth and organising all the resources of the Country.

In *perfect confidence,*" Pickering responded by giving Hamilton secret details of the XYZ affair, and outlined the Administration's plans to recall the commissioners. As Congress considered the implications of the diplomatic crisis, Hamilton adopted a new pen name, "Titus Manlius," and began treating his readers to a lively exposé of French politics. His basic goal, however, was to persuade Americans and their

Government to arm for their own defense—and to arm "respectably." In his sixth essay, he confronted what was perhaps the greatest barrier to military preparedness: the American people's traditional hostility to a standing army.

A page from Washington's letter assessing the crisis with France and offering Hamilton a position as major general in the event of war

[New York, April 19, 1798]

The resolution to raise an army, it is to be feared, is that one of the measures suggested, which will meet with greatest obstacle; and yet it is the one which ought most to unite opinion. Being merely a precaution for internal security, it can in no sense tend to provoke war, and looking to eventual security in a case, which if it should happen would threaten our very existence as a nation, it is the most important.

The history of our revolution-war is a serious admonition to it. The American cause had nearly been lost for want of creating in the first instance a solid force commensurate in duration with the war....

Suppose an invasion, & that we are left to depend on Militia alone. Can it be doubted that a rapid and formidable progress would in the first instance be made by the invader? Who can answer what dismay this might inspire—how far it might go to create general panic—to rally under the banners of the enemy the false and the timid?...To have a good army on foot will be best of all precautions to prevent as well as to repel invasion.

Hamilton kept himself available for whatever form the "public call" might take in this crisis, although he declined Governor Jay's suggestion that he accept an appointment to an unexpired term in the United States Senate. But Hamilton was not so vain or unrealistic as to think that he would be the first patriot summoned by that "public call." To his mind there was only one man, George Washington, who could lend enough prestige to the new military establishment to make national defense a reality. Accordingly, Hamilton urged the former President to leave his peaceful retirement at Mount Vernon.

New York May 19. 1798

In such a state of public affairs it is impossible not to look up to you; and to wish that your influence could in some proper mode be brought into direct action. Among the ideas which have passed through my mind for this purpose—I have asked myself whether it might not be expedient for you to make a circuit through Virginia and North Carolina under some pretence of health &c. This would call forth addresses public dinners &c. which would give you an opportunity of expressing sentiments in Answers Toasts &c. which would throw the weight of your character into the scale of the Government and revive an enthusiasm for your person that may be turned into the right channel. . . .

You ought also to be aware, My Dear Sir, that in the event of an open rupture with France, the public voice will again call you to command the armies of your Country; and though all who are attached to you will from attachment, as well as public considerations, deplore an occasion which should once more tear you from that repose to which you have so good a right — yet it is the opinion of all those with whom I converse that you will be compelled to make the sacrifice. All your past labour may demand to give it efficacy this further, this very great sacrifice.

Washington replied that he would have no choice but to return to public life if he were called, but would do so with "as much reluctance . . . as I should do to the tombs of my Ancestors." Although the General ruled out a southern tour, Hamilton was encouraged by his response and sent him the following reply.

New York June 2d 1798
It is a great satisfaction to me to ascertain what I had anticipated in hope, that you are not determined in an *adequate emergency* against affording once more your Military services. . . . You intimate a desire to be informed what would be my part in such an event as to entering into military service. I have no scruple about opening myself to you on this point. If I am invited *to a station in which the service I may render may be proportioned to the sacrifice I am to make*, I shall be willing to go into army. If you command, the place in which I should hope to be most useful is that of Inspector General with a command in the line. This I would accept. . . . I have no knowlege of any arrangement contemplated but I take it for granted the services of all the former officers worth having may be commanded & that your choice would regulate the Executive. With decision & care in selection an excellent army may be formed.

A view of Mount Vernon in 1798

By the end of June, Congress had made considerable progress in working out measures for the creation of a larger Navy, an "Additional Army" that would serve during the international crisis, and a "Provisional Army" that would only be called up in an actual state of war. Hamilton, meanwhile, had been spending more and more time sending advice to his friends in the Cabinet. Finding that he could no longer resist giving advice in person, he set off for Philadelphia, arriving in the first week of July. There he learned that Adams had named Washington Commander in Chief of the armed forces, and that the Senate had confirmed the nomination—all without Washington's knowledge. In accepting his appointment, Washington refused to serve in the field unless absolutely necessary and demanded the right to choose his principal staff officers. He submitted a list of these men to Adams, with Hamilton's name first, as Inspector General with the rank of major general. Washington confessed to Hamilton that he expected his former aide to be his "Coadjutor, and assistant," but if the commissions were issued in the order given by the new Commander, Hamilton would have seniority over two other major generals, Henry Knox and Charles Pinckney, who had outranked him at the end of the Revolution. The President postponed sending the commissions lest Knox or Pinckney should take offense. Timothy Pickering loyally reported on this delicate matter, and Hamilton made his position clear in a letter to the Secretary of State.

Hamilton's commission as Inspector General of the Army, signed by President John Adams, July, 1798

[New York] July 17 [1798]

I had contemplated the possibility that *Knox* might come into service & was content to be second to him, if *thought indispensable. Pinckney,* if placed over me, puts me a grade lower. I dont believe it to be necessary. I am far from certain that he will not be content to serve under me—but I am willing that the affair should be so managed as that the relative ranks may remain open to future settlement, to ascertain the effect of the arrangement which has been contemplated. I am not however ready to say that I shall be satisfied with the appointment of Inspector General with the rank & command of Major General on the principle that every officer of higher rank in the late army who may be appointed is to be above me. I am frank to own that this will not accord with my opinion of my own pretensions & I have every reason to believe that it will fall far short of public opinion. Few have made so many sacrifices as myself— to few would a change of situation for a military appointment be so injurious as to myself—if with this sacrifice, I am to be degraded below my just claim in public opinion —ought I to acquiesce?

Even when the Senate approved the list of officers that Washington had prepared, Adams hesitated to take a firm stand on the relative rank of the three generals. The President left for his home in Quincy, Massachusetts, without having dispatched the signed commissions to the major generals. At this point in the growing dispute, Adams was in favor of issuing all the commissions on the same day, with no explicit statement on seniority. The relative rank of the three major generals at the end of the Revolution, he assumed, would determine their standing in the command of the Quasi War. By the end of July, Hamilton had become increasingly annoyed at the delay and a bit more emphatic on what "justice" should be done him—as he showed in a letter to Washington.

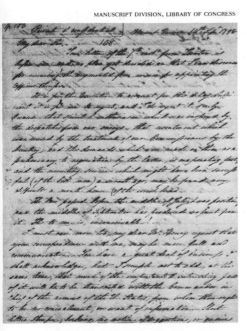

A copy of Washington's letter to James McHenry commenting on John Adams's initial reluctance to appoint Hamilton second-in-command

Philadelphia July 29[–August 1] 1798

With regard to the delicate subject of the relative rank of the Major Generals, it is very natural for me to be a partial judge, and it is not very easy for me to speak upon it. If I know myself however, this at least I may say, that were I convinced of injustice being done to oth[ers] in my favour, I should not hesitate even to volun[teer] a correction of it, as far as my consent could avail. But in a case like this, am I not to take the opinion of others as my guide? If I am, the conclusion is that the Gentlemen concerned ought to acquiesce. It is a fact, of which there is a flood of evidence that a great majority of leading foederal men were of opinion, that in the event of your declining command of the army, it ought to devolve upon me, and that in case of your acceptance, which every body ardently desired, the place of second in command ought to be mine. It is not for me to examine the justness of this opinion....

After saying this much, I [must] add that regard to the public interest is ever predominant with me—that if the Gentlemen concerned are dissatisfied & the service likely to suffer by the preference given to me—I stand ready to submit our relative pretensions to an impartial decision and to wave the preference. It shall never be said, with any color of truth, that my ambition or interest has stood in the way of the public good....

[Next, Hamilton turned to a "matter of far greater moment" than the rank of the general officers.]

It is that my friend, McHenry, is wholly insufficient for his place, with the additional misfortune of not having himself the least suspicion of the fact! This generally

General Henry Knox

will not surprise you, when you take into view the large scale upon which he is now to act. But you perhaps may not be aware of the whole extent of the insufficiency. It is so great as to leave no probability that the business of the War Department can make any tolerable progress in his hands. . . .

My real friendship for McHenry concurring with my zeal for the service predisposed me to aid him in all that he could properly throw upon me. And I thought that he would have been glad in the organisation of the army and in the conduct of the recruiting service, to make me useful to him. With this view I came to this City & I previously opened the way, as far as I could with the least decency. But the idea has been thus far very partially embraced and . . . I shall return to New York without much fruit of my journey. I mention this purely to apprise you of the course of things and the probable results.

Hamilton now concentrated his attention on aiding James McHenry, suggesting that the Secretary of War summon the major generals to begin military planning. Henry Knox, however, refused to accept his appointment unless he were given clear rank over Hamilton and Pinckney. Adams, reluctant to offend Knox for fear of injuring the Government's cause in Massachusetts, finally decided to issue the commissions and to make Knox the senior major general. Learning from McHenry of the President's decision, Hamilton wrote to the Secretary of War.

New York Sepr. 8th. 1798
I postponed a reply 'till to day because I wished first to reflect maturely. My mind is unalterably made up. I shall certainly not hold the commission on the plan proposed, and only wait an official communication to say so.

I return you the inclosures in your letter. You may depend on my fidelity to your friendly confidence. I shall regret whatever of inconvenience may attend you. You doubtless will take care that you retain in your own power all the evidences of this transaction.

But just as Hamilton was about to abandon his "military character," Washington demanded that Adams appoint the general officers in the order that he had indicated when he accepted command of America's provisional and additional forces. Adams acquiesced and sent the signed commissions to the Secretary of War. Summoning all his courage, McHenry issued the commissions and called the new Inspector General to a conference in Philadelphia. Hamilton replied to his timid friend.

N York Oct 19. 1798

It was essential for you to take a decisive course & to leave the blame of further delay at some other door. There can be no doubt of the propriety of combining the aid of General Officers. But *Pinckney* being now arrived, it seems to me very proper & necessary that he also should be called upon. You will learn with pleasure that he sent me a message... purporting his intire satisfaction with the military arrangement & readiness to serve under my command. Communicate this to our friend *Pickering* & *Wolcott,* as I am not well enough to write them by this post.

The matter of "priority" settled, Washington asked Hamilton to "give, without delay, your *full* aid to the Secy of War." Henry Knox having declined his appointment, Hamilton, Pinckney, and Washington were left to bring some order to the War Department and to handle the military arrangements. At Washington's request, Hamilton prepared the staff officers' recommendations on McHenry's requests for information and advice. The reports, which were sent to the Secretary of War over Washington's signature on December 13, revealed Hamilton's own views on the long-range goals of the new armies. His reply to McHenry's questions concerning the wisdom of withdrawing troops from the southern and western frontiers to guard the seaboard, reflected Hamilton's interest in military affairs in the wilderness.

[Philadelphia, December 13, 1798]

It is not adviseable to withdraw any of the troops from the quarters of the Country, which you mention, towards the Atlantic frontier. But the disposition in those quarters probably requires careful revision. It is not impossible that it will be found to admit of alterations favourable both to oeconomy and to the military objects to be attained. The local knowledge of [Brigadier] General [James] Wilkinson [commander of the Western Army] would be so useful in an investigation of this sort, that it is deemed very important to direct him forthwith to repair to Philadelphia. If this be impracticable by land, he may it is presumed come by way of New Orleans. It is observed that in his late communications with the

Spanish Governor he has taken pains to obviate jealousy of the views of the UStates. This was prudent, and he ought to be encouraged to continue the policy. It will also be useful to employ a judicious Engineer to survey our posts on the [Great] Lakes in order that it may be ascertained in the various relations of trade and defence, what beneficial changes, if any, can be made.

Although Hamilton, Washington, and Pinckney had left McHenry with clear guidelines, the Secretary did little to implement their plans. Hamilton, for instance, had been assigned the duty of supervising recruitment of the new troops, but had been issued no official directions. Without these orders, Hamilton received no pay and, as he reminded McHenry, he was reluctant to take more time from his legal practice without some assurance of compensation.

Private New York Decr. 16. 1798
To be frank with you, it is utterly out of my power to apply my time to the public service, without the compensations, scanty enough, which the law annexes to the office. If I were to receive them from the day of the appoint[ment] I should be at least a thousand pounds the worse for my acceptance. From the time it was first known that I had reengaged in military life, the uncertainty of my being able to render services for which I might be retained drove away more than half my professional practice, which I may moderately estimate at four thousand pounds a year. My pecuniary sacrifices already to the public ought to produce the reverse of a disposition every where to compel me to greater than the law imposes. This remark, I am well aware, is not necessary for you personally....

It is always disagreeable to speak of compensations for one's self but a man past 40 with a wife and six Children, and a very *small* property beforehand, is compelled to wave the scruples which his nicety would otherwise dictate.

McHenry's abbreviated version of Washington's recommendations was not submitted to Congress until December 31. Hamilton, unsalaried though he was, took more and more burdens from the Secretary of War in January, drafting legislation for McHenry to present to the House and giving advice on the most minute points. Since Washington refused to take active command until needed in the field, Hamilton and Pinckney were to share responsibility for the additional and provisional forces. McHenry turned to the Inspector General for his "ideas," and Hamilton outlined this division of authority.

A broadside of November 1, 1798, ordering volunteer companies of militia to report for duty

New York January 24th 1799

If I rightly understood the Commander in Chief, his wish was that all the Military points and military force everywhere should be put under the direction of the two Major Generals, who alone should be the Organs of the department of War. The objects of this plan are to disburthen the head of that department of infinite details which must unavoidably clog his general arrangements, and to establish a vigilant military superintendence over all the military points. There is no difficulty in this plan except as to the Western Army. It will be a very natural disposition to give to the Inspector General the command of all the Troops and Posts North of Maryland and to General Pinckney the command of all the Troops and Posts South of the district assigned to the Inspector General. How will this plan as to the Western Army answer? Let all the troops upon the Lakes, including those on the Miami which communicat[es] with Lake Erie, be united under the command of one Officer.... Let all the Troops in Tennessee be united under the command of one Officer.... Let them consider themselves as under the orders of the General who commands the Western Army — and let the whole be placed under the superintendence of the Inspector General....

At the end of January, Hamilton was able to assume his duties and "emoluments" as Inspector General, but his pleasure in his new work was overshadowed by new "attacks" from the "declared enemies" of government in the South. The Kentucky and Virginia legislatures issued angry resolutions against the 1798 Alien and Sedition Acts, and there were even rumors that Virginia was planning armed resistance. Hamilton wrote anxiously to Massachusetts Congressman Theodore Sedgwick.

New York Feby 2. 1799

What, My Dear Sir, are you going to do with Virginia? This is a very serious business, which will call for all the wisdom and firmness of the Government. The following are the ideas which occur to me on the occasion.

The first thing in all great operations of such a Government as ours is to secure the opinion of the people. To this end, the proceedings of Virginia and Kentucke with the two laws complained of should be referred to a special Committee. That Committee should make a report exhibiting with great luminousness and particularity the reasons which support the constitutionality and expediency of those laws—the tendency of the doctrines advanced by Virginia and Kentucke to destroy the Constitution... and, with calm dignity united with pathos, the full evidence which they afford of a regular conspiracy to overturn the government. And the Report should likewise dwell upon the inevitable effect and probably the intention of these proceedings to encourage a hostile foreign power to decline accommodation and proceed in hostility. The Government must [not] merely [de]fend itself [b]ut must attack and arraign its enemies. But in all this, there should be great care to distinguish the people of Virginia from the legislature and even the greater part of those who may have concurred in the legislature from the chiefs; manifesting indeed a strong confidence in the good sense and patriotism of the people, that they will not be the dupes of an insidious plan to disunite the people of America to break down their constitution & expose them to the enterprises of a foreign power.

William Vans Murray, in a portrait painted in London by Mather Brown

With the command of America's forces now divided between himself and Pinckney, Hamilton began working out a plan for securing America's western frontiers. But in mid-February he received word from Sedgwick that John Adams, having consulted neither Congress nor his own Cabinet, had announced that William Vans Murray, the American minister at The Hague, was to represent the nation at Paris. It was the President's intention to ignore French insults to America's pride and to make yet another attempt at peaceful negotiations. Republicans were delighted, but the Federalists balked. As a compromise, Adams was forced to include Murray as part of a new three-man commission. Furthermore, Murray was not to be joined by his colleagues until the American Government had firm reason for believing that the Directory would negotiate. Within a month, Hamilton's hopes for strong American defense policies were threatened again when the citizens of three Pennsylvania counties, led by one John Fries, took up arms to protest a land and house tax enacted to finance military preparedness. Adams proclaimed a state of rebellion, yet even as Hamilton was sending men into the field to suppress Fries' Rebellion, he was writing cautiously to McHenry.

Private   New York March 18. 1799

Beware, my Dear Sir, of magnifying a riot into an insurrection, by employing in the first instance an inadequate force. Tis better far to err on the other side. Whenever the Government appears in arms it ought to appear like a *Hercules,* and inspire respect by the display of strength. The consideration of expence is of no moment compared with the advantages of energy. Tis true this is always a relative question—but tis always important to make no mistake. I only offer a *principle* and a *caution.*

Militia and Regular Army forces prepared to move against the insurgents, but mismanagement plagued the troops more seriously than did Fries and his followers. James McHenry's unwillingness to reform the Army supply system hamstrung Hamilton's efforts to enlist troops, and only after a personal visit to the War Department in Philadelphia could Hamilton send Washington this mildly encouraging report.

Private   New York May 3d. 1799

At length the recruiting for the additional regiments has begun in *Connecticut New York New Jersey Pensylvania* and *Delaware.* The enclosed return of cloathing will sufficiently explain to you that it has commenced at least as soon as the preparations by the Department of War would permit. It might now also proceed in Maryland and Massachusettes, and the next post will I trust enable me to add Virginia—but that I do not think it expedient to outgo our supply of Cloathing. It will have the worst possible effect—if the recruits are to wait a length of time for their cloathing....

The Secretary of War imputes the deficiency in the article of Cloathing to a failure of a contract which he had made and to the difficulty of suddenly finding a substitute by purchases in the market. It is however obvious that the means which have been since pursued have not been the best calculated for dispatch.

Shadow portraits of George and Martha Washington, thought to have been done by Washington's stepgranddaughter, Eleanor Custis

Mount Vernon and its Associations
BY BENSON J. LOSSING, 1883

As Hamilton had predicted, the insurrection was quickly stifled as soon as the Government made a strong show of force. Fries was captured easily, convicted of treason, and sentenced to death, although he was later pardoned. Hamilton's mood improved considerably. The Army, he hoped, would be "at its complement" by autumn. In August, however, worried about the efficient supply of food and clothing during the approaching winter months, Hamilton renewed his campaign to force McHenry to delegate responsibility in the interests of the service.

> New York Aug 19. 1799
>
> It is one thing for business to drag on—another for it to go well. The business of supply in all its branches (except as to provisions) proceeds heavily and without order or punctuality—in a manner equally ill adapted to œconomy on a large scale as to efficiency and the contentment of the army. It is painful to observe how disjointed and peace-meal a business it is. Among other evils is this that the head of the War Department and the Chief of the several divisions of the army exhaust their time in details, which, beyond a general superintendence are foreign to them. And plans for giving perfection to our military system are unavoidably neglected.
>
> Let me repeat, my Dear friend, my earnest advice, that you proceed to organise without delay the several branches of the Department of supply, that is to fix the plan and appoint the agents.... The saving from better management will infinitely overpay the expence of salaries.

Meanwhile, Hamilton was growing increasingly apprehensive about the prospect of peace negotiations. Recent dispatches from William Vans Murray indicated that the Directory might be willing to negotiate, and any sign of peace would shorten the time in which the Adams Administration would allot energy or funds for completing military "arrangements." Hamilton's frayed temper was clear in this letter to James McHenry.

> New York Sepr. 21. 1799
>
> Symptoms bordering on mutiny for the want of pay have been reported to me as having appeared in the twelveth and thirteenth Regiments. And discontents less turbulent have been communicated from several other quarters. An explosion any where would injure and discredit the service, and wherever the blame might really be would be shared by all.
>
> No one can be more deeply impressed than I am with the necessity of a strict adherence to general rules and to established forms. But there will occur circumstances in which these ought to be dispensed with. And it is equally important, to judge rightly when exceptions ought to be admitted as when the general rule ought to be maintained.

The creation of a new army, in which every officer from the highest to the lowest is of new appointment, & in respect to which in and out of the administration there is a deficiency of some essential organs, presents a case which with the utmost diligence and care will require and justify relaxations. . . .

. . . Muster and Pay-Rolls are to be in certain precise forms prescribed by the Treasury. These forms were received by me only four days since, and consequently could not hitherto be in the possession of the commandants of Regiments, It will not be said that I ought to have called for them; because certainly it lies with the department to communicate its own regulations uncalled for. Are the soldiery to suffer a privation of pay for several months, because these forms never prescribed, have not been fulfilled?

A view of Trenton in 1789, when a triumphal arch was erected in honor of Washington, who was on his way to be inaugurated in New York

A few days later, learning that General Charles Pinckney was in Rhode Island, Hamilton urged the General to come to his aid. Pinckney agreed to join Hamilton, McHenry, and Major General James Wilkinson, commander of defenses in the West, for a meeting at Trenton, where the Cabinet had taken refuge from another of Philadelphia's yellow fever epidemics. At the same time that these men were converging on the small New Jersey town, John Adams was on his way south from Quincy to discuss the peace commission with Secretary Pickering, while Chief Justice Oliver Ellsworth and Governor William R. Davie, the two envoys who were to join William Vans Murray in Europe, were journeying to Trenton to learn how a recent "revolution" in the French Directory would affect their appointments. Hamilton later described the results of the coincidental meeting, in mid-October, 1799, of this remarkable assortment of American statesmen—an encounter that ended Hamilton's hopes for the nation's military "respectability."

[September, 1800]

It happened that I arrived at Trenton a short time before the President—Chief Justice Elsworth a short time after him. This was considered as evidence of a combination between the heads of Departments, the Chief-Justice and myself, to endeavour to influence or counteract him [the President] in the affair of the Mission.

The truth, nevertheless, most certainly is, that I went to Trenton with General Wilkinson, pursuant to a preconcert with him of some weeks standing . . . that when I left New-York upon this journey, I had no expectation, whatever, that the President would come to Trenton, and that I did not stay at this place a day longer than was indispensable to the object I have stated. . . .

As to Chief Justice Elsworth, the design of his journey was understood to be to meet his colleague, Governor Davy, at the seat of the Government, where they would be at the fountain head of information, and would obtain any lights or explanations which they might suppose useful. . . .

Yet these simple occurrences were to the jealous mind of Mr. Adams, "confirmations strong," of some mischievous plot against his independence. . . .

[Hamilton's mere presence at Trenton convinced Adams of the existence of a "plot." When the Inspector General tried to dissuade him from sending Ellsworth and Davie to France, the President became implacable. Hamilton later recalled what had taken place.]

When the news of the Revolution in the Directory arrived, Mr. Adams was at his seat in Massachusetts. His Ministers addressed to him a joint letter, communicating the intelligence, and submitting to his consideration, whether that event ought not to suspend the projected mission. In a letter which he afterwards wrote from the same place, he directed the preparation of a draft of instructions for the Envoys, and intimated that their departure would be suspended *for some time*.

Shortly after he came to Trenton, where he adjusted with his Ministers the tenor of the instructions to be given; but he observed a profound silence on the question, whether it was expedient that the Mission should proceed. The morning after the instructions were settled, he signified to the Secretary of State that the Envoys were immediately to depart.

He is reported to have assigned as reason of his silence, that he knew the opinions of his Ministers from their letter; that he had irrevocably adopted an opposite one; and that he deemed it most delicate not to embarrass them by a useless discussion.

Hamilton returned to New York shaken by Adams's abrupt move. The likelihood of the mission's success destroyed his hopes for

Peacefield was John Adams's home in Quincy, Massachusetts.

military reform and restored the reputation of the Jeffersonians, who had been badly hurt by anti-French opinion at the beginning of the Quasi War. Furthermore, peace would put an end to Hamilton's new Army career, returning him inevitably to the hazardous world of partisan politics, where the President was now his avowed enemy. But Hamilton was determined to make some contribution to military reform before leaving his Army post. Realizing there was no longer a chance to create a large, "respectable" army, he concentrated instead on peacetime measures that would give America military security without an unpopular standing army. A central point in his plan was the creation of a "Military Academy," as he reported to James McHenry.

New-York Novr. 23d. 1799

Since it is agreed, that we are not to keep on foot numerous forces instructed and disciplined, military science in its various branches ought to be cultivated, with peculiar care, in proper Nurseries; so that there may always exist a sufficient body of it ready to be imparted and diffused, and a competent number of persons qualified to act as instructors to the additional troops, which events may successively require to be raised. This will be to substitute the elements of an army to the thing itself, and it will greatly tend to enable the Government to dispense with a large body of standing forces, from the facility which it will give of forming Officers and Soldiers promptly upon emergencies.

No sound mind can doubt the essentiality of Military Science in time of war, any more than the moral certainty that the most pacific policy, on the part of a Government, will not preserve it from being engaged in War, more or less frequently. To avoid great evils, it must either have a respectable force prepared for service, or the means of preparing such a force with expedition. The latter, most agreable to the genius of our Government and Nation is the object of a Military Academy.

I propose that this Academy shall consist of five Schools: One to be called "The Fundamental School"—another "The School of Engineers & Artillerists" another "The School of Cavalry"—another "The School of Infantry" and a fifth "The School of the Navy." . . .

These Schools to be provided with proper Apparatus and instruments for philosophical and Chemical experiments, for Astronomical and Nautical observation for surveying and for such other processes as are requisite to the illustration of the several topics of instruction.

The Cadets of the Army and young persons who are destined for military and Naval service ought to study two years in the Fundamental School—and if destined for the Corps of Engineers and Artillerists, or for the Navy two years more in the appropriate School. If for the Cavalry or Infantry one year more in the appropriate School....

In addition to these, Detachments of Officers and non commissioned Officers of the Army ought to attend the Academy in rotation for the purposes of Instruction and Exercise, according to the nature of the corps to which they respectively belong.

To salvage what he could from the wreckage of the Army, Hamilton traveled to Philadelphia in mid-December to confer with McHenry. His stay was marred by the news of Washington's death at Mount Vernon. Deeply grieved, Hamilton wrote to Charles Pinckney.

Philadelphia Decr. [22] 1799

The death of our beloved commander in Chief was known to you before it was to me. I can be at no loss to anticipate what have been your feelings. I need not tell you what are mine. Perhaps no friend of his has more cause to lament, on personal account, than myself. The public misfortune is one which all the friends of our Government will view in the same light. I will not dwell on the subject. My Imagination is gloomy my heart sad.

Writing letters of condolence was no easier for the author of the "Publius" and "Camillus" essays than for other men. It was four weeks after Washington's death before Hamilton could send this message to Martha Washington.

New York Jany. 12. 1800

I did not think it proper, Madam, to intrude amidst the first effusions of your grief. But I can no longer restrain my sensibility from conveying to you an imperfect expression of my affectionate sympathy in the sorrows you experience. No one, better than myself, knows the greatness of your loss, or how much your excellent heart is formed to feel it in all its extent. Satisfied that you cannot receive consolation, I will attempt to offer none. Resignation to the will of Heaven, which the practice of your life ensures, can alone alleviate the sufferings of so heartrending an affliction.

There can be few, who equally with me participate in the loss you deplore.... I cannot say in how many ways the continuance of that confidence and friendship was necessary to me in future relations.

With Washington's death, Hamilton lost his most consistent and influential sponsor in public life. John Adams, more hostile than ever, was left to plague the Inspector General. In the first week of the new year, 1800, Hamilton commented to Rufus King.

Gen. GEORGE WASHINGTON

This memorial portrait of Washington accompanied a funeral oration published the year after his death.

New York January 5 1800

In our Councils there is no fixed plan. Some are for preserving and invigorating the Navy and destroying the army. Some, among the friends of Government, for diminishing both on pecuniary considerations.

My plan is to complete the Navy to the contemplated extent... And finally to preserve the Organs of the existing force; reducing the men to a very moderate number. For this plan there are various Reasons that appear to me solid. I much doubt however that it will finally prevail....

I must hasten to a Conclusion. It was unnecessary for me to have told you that for the loss of our illustrious friend [Washington] every heart is in mourning.

Adieu God bless you

P S   Who is to be the Commander in Chief? Not the next in Command. The appointment will probably be deferred.

As Hamilton predicted, no successor was named for Washington. A new baby daughter, Elizabeth, born in October, gave Hamilton an added motive for looking after his family's welfare, and he now resumed his legal practice. In mid-January, he rode to Albany to argue the case of Louis Le Guen. From there he wrote this fond letter to his wife.

[Albany] Sunday Jany 26 [1800]

I was quite disappointed and pained, My Dear Eliza, when I found, that the Post of Saturday had brought me no letter from you; especially as I was very anxious to hear of the health of my *little* Betsey. But I was consoled in the Evening by your affectionate letter of which *Mr. Leguen* was the bearer. It is absolutely necessary to me when absent to hear frequently of you and my dear Children. While all other passions decline in me, those of love and friendship gain new strength. It will be more and more my endeavour to abstract myself from all pursuits which interfere with those of Affection. Tis here only I can find true pleasure. In this I know your good and kind heart responses to mine.

I hope in about ten days to commence my return-journey. Need I tell that I shall not delay a moment longer than is unavoidable?

But again Hamilton could not forget his public duty. Back in New York in February, his thoughts turned to the presidential election. Congressional Federalists had endorsed Adams as their candidate earlier that winter, and Hamilton wrote to Theodore Sedgwick about the turn of events.

New York, Feb. 27, 1800.

When will Congress probably adjourn? Will any thing be settled as to a certain *Election*? Will my presence be requisite as to this or any other purpose, and when? I observe more and more that by the jealousy and envy of some, the miserlyness of others and the concurring influence of *all foreign powers,* America, if she attains to greatness, must *creep* to it. Well be it so. Slow and sure is no bad maxim. Snails are a wise generation.

P S—Unless for indispensable reasons I had rather not come.

Hamilton's political speculations were momentarily interrupted in March when he received orders to disband all "additional" troops. The Quasi War was dying out. There was now little likelihood that American forces would be called into battle, and a peace settlement was not far off. Meanwhile, New York voters went to the polls in April to choose the state legislators who would select presidential electors in the fall. The Republicans had been demanding that state law be changed to permit direct voting for the Electoral College. The Federalists had ignored their demands. But when the Republicans triumphed at the polls under the skillful leadership of Aaron Burr, the continuance of Federalist rule in America suddenly seemed uncertain. Writing to Governor Jay, Hamilton reconsidered the idea of direct voting.

New York May 7. 1800

The moral certainty therefore is that there will be an Antifœderal Majority in the Ensuing Legislature, and this very high probability is that this will bring *Jefferson* into the Chief Magistracy; unless it be prevented by the measure which I shall now submit to your consideration, namely the immediate calling together of the existing Legislature.

I am aware that there are weighty objections to the measure; but the reasons for it appear to me to outweigh the objections. And in times like these in which we live, it will not do to be overscrupulous. It is easy to sacrifice substantial interests of society by a strict adherence to ordinary rules.

In observing this, I shall not be supposed to mean that any thing ought to be done which integrity will forbid — but merely that the scruples of delicacy and propriety, as relative to a common course of things, ought to yield to the extraordinary nature of the crisis. They ought not to hinder the taking of a *legal* and *constitutional* step, to prevent an *Atheist* in Religion and a *Fanatic* in politics from getting possession of the helm of the State....

The calling of the Legislature will have for object the choosing of Electors by the people in Districts. This... will insure a Majority of votes in the U States for a Fœderal Candidate.

The measure will not fail to be approved by all the Fœderal Party; while it will no doubt be condemned by the opposite. As to its intrinsic nature it is justified by unequivocal reasons of *public safety.*

The reasonable part of the world will I believe approve it. They will see it as a proceeding out of the common course but warranted by the particular nature of the crisis and the great cause of social order.

Theodore Sedgwick

Jay ignored this proposal as "a measure for party purposes wh[ich]. I think it w[oul]d. not become me to adopt." New York's Republican legislature would be allowed to choose the electors. Hamilton, however, had already turned to a new strategy when he suggested to Theodore Sedgwick that Federalists of all states agree to give equal support to Adams and Charles Pinckney. Sedgwick reported that at least one Federalist, Samuel Dexter, hesitated to give such a pledge, since it seemed like an attempt to abandon the President and would "crumble the federal party to atoms." Hamilton would have none of this and sent Sedgwick his opinion of Dexter's arguments.

New York May 10. 1800

He is I am persuaded much mistaken as to the opinion

entertained of Mr Adams by the Fœderal party. Were I to determine from my own observation I should say, *most* of the *most influential men* of that party consider him as a very *unfit* and *incapable* character.

For my individual part my mind is made up. I will never more be responsible for him by my direct support — even though the consequence should be the election of *Jefferson.* If we must have an *enemy* at the head of the Government, let it be one whom we can oppose & for whom we are not responsible, who will not involve our party in the disgrace of his foolish and bad measures. Under *Adams* as under *Jefferson* the government will sink. The party in the hands of whose chief it shall sink will sink with it and the advantage will all be on the side of his adversaries.

Tis a notable expedient for keeping the Fœderal party together to have at the head of it a man who hates and is distrusted by those men of it who in time past have been its most efficient supporters.

If the cause is to be sacrificed to a weak and perverse man, I withdraw from the party & act upon my own ground — never certainly against my principles but in pursuance of them in my own way. I am mistaken if others will not do the same.

The only way to prevent a fatal scism in the Fœderal party is to support G Pinckney in good earnest.

If I can be perfectly satisfied that Adams & Pinckney will be upheld in the East with intire good faith, on the ground of conformity I will wherever my influence may extend pursue the same plan. If not I will pursue Mr. Pinkny as my single object.

Charles Cotesworth Pinckney

The congressional caucus grudgingly agreed to give "equal" support to Adams and Pinckney. Learning that Adams had dismissed Timothy Pickering from the Cabinet and that McHenry had resigned, Hamilton sent this urgent request to the Secretary of State a few days later.

[New York, May 14, 1800]

I perceive that you as well as Mc.Henry are quitting the Administration. I am not informed how all this has been, though I conjecture. Allow me to suggest, that you ought to take with you copies and extracts of all such documents as will enable you to *explain* both *Jefferson* & *Adams.* You are aware of a very curious journal of the latter when he was in Europe, a tissue of weakness and vanity.

The time is coming when men of real integrity & energy must unite against all Empirics.

At the beginning of June, Hamilton received a letter from James McHenry describing the Secretary of War's clash with Adams. The President had called Hamilton "a Bastard" and declared he would rather be Jefferson's Vice President "or even Minister resident at the Hague, than indebted to such a being as Hamilton for the Presidency." Hamilton returned the document with this comment.

> June 6. 1800 New York
> I thank you My *Dear Mac* for the perusal of the Inclosed and wish you had not thought it necessary to forbid my taking a copy. Such a paper to be shewn confidentially would be very important. Charles Carroll of Carrolton ought as soon as possible to be apprized of all the circumstances.
>
> The man is more mad than I ever thought him and I shall soon be led to say as wicked as he is mad.
>
> Pray favour me with as many circumstances as may appear to you...to shew the probability of Coalitions with Mr. Jefferson &c which are spoken of.

In his last month as Inspector General, Hamilton made a tour of New England Army posts to bid farewell to the troops. But he may not have gone north solely out of concern for the undermanned additional army and provisional recruits—loyal soldiers who had never fought a skirmish. Along the way, at meetings with Federalists in New Hampshire, Connecticut, Rhode Island, and Massachusetts, Hamilton found that there was another army in New England: an army of men who were as dissatisfied with Adams as he was. Hamilton returned from his inspection tour with reason to believe that his strategy for electing Charles Pinckney had a good chance for success. The Quasi War had given the nation no fireworks on battlefields, but its aftermath promised an entertaining battle royal between the Federalist President and his Inspector General. For, by the end of that fruitless exercise in military preparedness, Hamilton had learned to dislike John Adams as thoroughly as the Massachusetts statesman had always detested him.

Chapter 14

Last Encounters

The last four years of Hamilton's life were overshadowed by the consequences of his decision to oppose Adams's reelection in 1800. The
electoral system involved any would-be campaign manager in delicate
calculations and complicated bargains that could easily misfire. The flaws
of the Electoral College, where electors could not designate which of their
two ballots was for President and which for Vice President, had become a
major problem with the development of two parties. Each group now had
to guess in advance how many votes could safely be "thrown away" from its
vice presidential candidate to insure that it would elect its own men in the
right order. Had there been effective party discipline, this would have been
easy, but the election of 1796 had shown that there were no guarantees
that Federalists or Republicans would vote as their leaders wished. That
year Adams's supporters had thrown away too many votes, and the Federalist nominee for Vice President had lost to Thomas Jefferson.

In 1800, political observers agreed that the race would be very close.
Hamilton had to convince Federalists in all sections to give "equal" support
to Adams and Charles Cotesworth Pinckney. If New Englanders threw
away a few votes in Adams's favor and southerners threw away a few more
to insure Pinckney's success, Jefferson would win. Beyond this, equal support would result in a tie in the Electoral College, and the final choice would
lie with the House of Representatives. In that quarter, Hamilton might be
able to persuade congressmen to choose Pinckney over Adams as the next
President.

With this plan in mind, Hamilton returned from his tour of New England
at the end of June, 1800. On leaving the office of Inspector General, he had
made the usual resolutions to devote himself to his family. There were also
plans for an impressive country residence on thirty acres of land in upper
Manhattan, which he had purchased in 1799. But both the completion of the
Grange (named after the ancestral home in Scotland) and attention to his

family would have to come after public duty. Back in New York, Hamilton set about convincing Federalists that only an "equal chance" for Charles Pinckney and John Adams would save the party, and that ultimately Adams must be defeated. Hamilton began mobilizing his campaign against the President with letters like this one to Oliver Wolcott.

N Y July 1. 1800

It is essential to inform the most discreet . . . of the facts which denote unfitness in Mr. Adams. I have promised confidential friends a correct statement. To be able to give it, I must derive aid from you. Any thing you may write shall if you please be returned to you. But you must be exact & much in detail. The history of the mission to France from the first steps . . . down to the last proceedings is very important.

I have serious thoughts of writing to the *President* to tell him That I have heared of his having repeatedly mentioned the existence of a British Faction in this Country & alluded to me as one of that faction — requesting that he will inform me of the truth of this information & if true what have been the grounds of the suggestion.

His friends are industrious in propagating the idea to defeat the efforts to unite for Pinckney. The inquiry I propose may furnish an antidote and vindicate character. What think you of the Idea?

For my part I can set Malice at defiance.

Monumental Inscription.

" That life is long which anſwers Life's great end."

YESTERDAY EXPIRED,
Deeply regretted by MILLIONS of grateful Americans,
And by all GOOD MEN.
The FEDERAL ADMINISTRATION
Of the
GOVERNMENT of the *United States :*
Animated by
A WASHINGTON, an ADAMS ;—a
HAMILTON, KNOX, PICKERING, WOL-
COTT, M'HENRY, MARSHALL,
STODDERT and DEXTER.
Æt. 12 years.

Its death was occaſioned by the
Secret Arts. and Open Violence,
Of Foreign and Domeſtic Demagogues:
Notwithſtanding its whole Life
Was devoted to the Performance of every Duty
to promote
The UNION, CREDIT, PEACE, PROSPER-
ITY, HONOR, and
FELICITY of its COUNTRY.

At its birth it found
The Union of the States diſſolving like a Rope of ſnow ;
It hath left it
Stronger than the Threefold cord.

It found the United States
Bankrupts in Eſtate and Reputation ;
It hath left them
Unbounded in Credit ; and reſpected throughout
the World.

In March, 1801, after Jefferson's election to the Presidency, the death of the Federalist party was announced in the Boston Centinel.

Although Wolcott still served in the Cabinet, he was as determined as Hamilton to see that the President did not win a second term. Wolcott replied to Hamilton's letter by hinting that Adams had sent Ellsworth and Davie to France solely to gain political advantage. He encouraged Hamilton to write to Adams concerning the rumors of a "British Faction," and Hamilton sent this message to the President at Quincy.

New York August 1. 1800

It has been repeatedly mentioned to me that you have on different occasions, asserted the existence of a *British Faction* in this Country, embracing a number of leading or influential characters of the *Foederal Party* (as usually denominated) and that you have sometimes named me, at other times plainly alluded to me, as one of this description of persons: And I have likewise been assured that of late some of your warm adherents, for electioneering purposes, have employed a corresponding language.

I must, Sir, take it for granted, that you cannot have

381

made such assertions or insinuations without being willing to avow them, and to assign the reasons to a party who may conceive himself injured by them. I therefore trust that you will not deem it improper that I apply directly to yourself, to ascertain from you, in reference to your own declarations, whether the information, I have received, has been correct or not, and if correct what are the grounds upon which you have founded the suggestion.

By this time, Hamilton had heard accusations that he opposed Adams because of "personal pique" growing out of his failure to be named Washington's successor as Commander in Chief. He began to plan a way to publicize his real motives and wrote to Wolcott.

JOHN ADAMS Prefident of the United States

John Adams, from a 1799 broadside

New York Aug 3. 1800

I have serious thoughts of giving to the public my opinion respecting Mr. Adams with my reasons in a letter to a friend with my signature. This seems to me the most authentic way of conveying the information & best suited to the plain dealing of my character. There are however reasons against it and a very strong one is that some of the principal causes of my disapprobation proceed from yourself & other members of the Administration who would be understood to be the sources of my information whatever cover I might give the thing.

What say you to this measure? I would predicate it on the fact that I am abused by the friends of Mr. Adams who ascribe my opposition to pique & disappointment & would give it the shape of a *defence of myself.*

During the rest of the summer, Hamilton opened "mutual communication of information & opinions" with Federalist leaders in other states and started work on a "letter to a friend" that would expose Adams. Circulation of the draft version was delayed when Hamilton received reactions to the project from New England. George Cabot, for instance, urged restraint, since in the end the party might have to support Adams. Meanwhile, Hamilton had also written to the President, giving Adams a second chance to clarify his remarks about a "British Faction." When Adams ignored this letter from the "Creole bastard," as he had the first, Hamilton delayed no longer. His *Letter... Concerning the Public Conduct of John Adams...* appeared in pamphlet form in early October. Intended for private circulation, the *Letter* traced his differences with Adams's theories and policies since the Revolution, opening with this explanation.

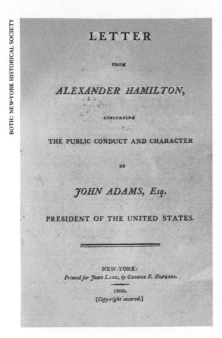

LETTER

FROM

ALEXANDER HAMILTON,

CONCERNING

THE PUBLIC CONDUCT AND CHARACTER

OF

JOHN ADAMS, Esq.

PRESIDENT OF THE UNITED STATES.

NEW-YORK:
Printed for JOHN LANG, by GEORGE F. HOPKINS.
1800.
[Copy-right secured.]

Title pages of Hamilton's pamphlet attacking John Adams (top) and of one published in his defense

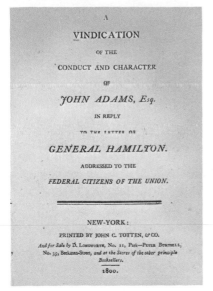

A

VINDICATION

OF THE

CONDUCT AND CHARACTER

OF

JOHN ADAMS, Esq.

IN REPLY

TO THE LETTER OF

GENERAL HAMILTON.

ADDRESSED TO THE

FEDERAL CITIZENS OF THE UNION.

NEW-YORK:

PRINTED BY JOHN C. TOTTEN, & CO.
And for Sale by D. LONGWORTH, No. 11, Park—PETER BURTSELL,
No. 35, Beekman-Street, and at the Stores of the other principle
Booksellers.
1800.

[October 17–21, 1800]

Some of the warm personal friends of Mr. Adams are taking unwearied pains to disparage the motives of those Federalists, who advocate the equal support of Gen. Pinckney, at the approaching election of President and Vice-President. . . .

In addition to a full share of the obloquy vented against this description of persons collectively, peculiar accusations have been devised, to swell the catalogue of my demerits. Among these, the resentment of disappointed ambition, forms a prominent feature. It is pretended, that had the President, upon the demise of General Washington, appointed me Commander in Chief, he would have been, in my estimation, all that is wise, and good and great.

It is necessary, for the public cause, to repel these slanders; by stating the real views of the persons who are calumniated, and the reasons of their conduct.

In executing this task, with particular reference to myself, I ought to premise, that the ground upon which I stand, is different from that of most of those who are confounded with me as in pursuit of the same plan. While our object is common, our motives are variously dissimilar. A part, well affected to Mr. Adams, have no other wish than to take a double chance against Mr. Jefferson. Another part, feeling a diminution of confidence in him, still hope that the general tenor of his conduct will be essentially right. Few go as far in their objections as I do. Not denying to Mr. Adams patriotism and integrity, and even talents of a certain kind, I should be deficient in candor, were I to conceal the conviction, that he does not possess the talents adapted to the *Administration* of Government, and that there are great and intrinsic defects in his character, which unfit him for the office of Chief Magistrate.

It is difficult to understand how Hamilton believed this pamphlet could be kept secret. A confederate of Aaron Burr's, the Republican vice presidential candidate, obtained a copy and extracts were published in the Philadelphia *Aurora* on October 22.

Although Hamilton's friends dissuaded him from further publications, he had already given the Republicans (or Democratic-Republicans, as party members were by then being called) their finest piece of propaganda for the 1800 campaign. Electors met in the states on December 4, and it soon became clear that the vote in the Electoral College would be a tie—not, as Hamilton had planned, between the Federalist nominees, but between the Democratic-Republicans Thomas Jefferson and Aaron Burr. The final outcome would have to be decided in the House of Representatives, and Hamilton wrote to Oliver Wolcott urging that Federalists throw their support to Jefferson as the lesser of two evils.

> New York Decr. 16. 1800
>
> It is now, my Dear Sir, ascertained that Jefferson or Burr will be President and it seems probable that they will come with equal votes to the House of Representatives. It is also circulated here that in this event the Fœderalists in Congress or some of them talk of preferring Burr. I trust New England at least will not so far lose its head as to fall into this snare. There is no doubt but that upon every virtuous and prudent calculation Jefferson is to be preferred. He is by far not so dangerous a man and he has pretensions to character....
>
> But early measures must be taken to fix on this point the opinions of the Fœderalists. Among them, from different motives—Burr will find partisans. If the thing be neglected he may possibly go far.

Having helped to destroy his own party's chances for electing a President, Hamilton now fought to see that Jefferson, not Burr, won the office of Chief Executive. Although his campaign to discredit Burr was the continuation of a long-standing political conflict that would eventually destroy them both, even Hamilton admitted that his personal relationship with Burr was pleasant. The two men had often been joint counsel for the same clients in New York and were cordial to each other outside the courtroom. Had their political views been closer, they might have found enough mutual interests and traits of personality to become friends. Burr came from a distinguished and well-established American family (he was the grandson of Jonathan Edwards), but he, like Hamilton, had grown up without his parents and faced the world with more talents than financial resources. Both were handsome, dapper men who enjoyed the practice of politics and the law. But Hamilton had chosen the road of "respectability" and "propriety" for his public career. In the Revolution, he had been Washington's aide and had won the Commander's support for his later ventures. His marriage to Elizabeth Schuyler placed him in one of New York's leading families. Burr, on the other hand, had aligned himself with Horatio Gates in the military feuds of the war, and his marriage to Theodosia Prevost, a widow ten years his senior with five children, did nothing to advance his ambitions. In public life, Burr chose "democracy," organizing the political clubs of New York and exploiting popular issues with a skill Hamilton both envied and despised. In the election of 1800, Hamilton's campaign against Burr began in earnest. He wrote to his friend Gouverneur Morris, now a United States Senator from New York, who could be counted on to use his influence with Federalists in the lower house of Congress.

New York Decr. 24, 1800

Jefferson or *Burr?*—the former without all doubt. The latter in my judgment has no principle public or private—could be bound by no agreement—will listen to no monitor but his ambition; & for this purpose will use the *worst* part of the community as a ladder to climb to permant power & an instrument to crush the better part. He is bankrupt beyond redemption except by the resources that grow out of war and disorder or by a sale to a foreign power or by great peculation. War with Great Britain would be the immediate instrument. He is sanguine enough to hope every thing—daring enough to attempt every thing—wicked enough to scruple nothing. From the elevation of such a man heaven preserve the Country!

Let our situation be improved to obtain from Jefferson assurances on certain points—the maintenance of the present system especially on the cardinal points of public Credit, a *Navy, Neutrality.*

Make any discreet use you think fit of this letter.

Miniature, by Trumbull, of Oliver Wolcott, Hamilton's successor as Treasury Secretary, and later elected Governor of Connecticut

The votes of the Electoral College would not be officially tallied until February, and Hamilton used the next weeks to persuade wavering Federalists of the perils that would follow Burr's election. Because congressmen were to vote by states, Delaware's single Representative, James Bayard, would cast a vote equal to that of the larger delegations from New York and Virginia. Bayard accordingly became an important object of Hamilton's attention and a frequent recipient of his letters.

New-York Jany. 16th. 180[1]

I was glad to find my dear sir, by your letter, that you had not yet determined to go with the current of the Foederal Party in the support of Mr *Burr* & that you were resolved to hold yourself disengaged till the moment of final decision. Your resolution to separate yourself, in this instance, from the Foederal Party if your conviction shall be strong of the unfitness of Mr Burr, is certainly laudable. So much does it coincide with my ideas, that if the Party shall by supporting Mr Burr as President adopt him for their official Chief—I shall be obliged to consider myself as an *isolated* man. It will be impossible for me to reconcile with my notions of *honor* or policy, the continuing to be of a Party which according to my apprehension will have degraded itself & the country.

On Tuesday, February 17, House Federalists gave Jefferson the Presidency on their thirty-fifth ballot. The deadlock was broken when Federalist members of three delegations cast blank ballots; Bayard of Delaware was one of these. Hamilton's letters had not persuaded him to back Jefferson, but at the last minute he had withdrawn support from Burr. Hamilton made one more stand for Federalist principles in the spring of 1801 when he campaigned against George Clinton, who had emerged from retirement to seek another term as governor. Clinton won, and Hamilton discarded politics for the time to tend to business and plan the finishing touches for the Grange. In May, he sent Elizabeth this note.

Fish Kill Sunday Evening [May 10, 1801]

Wife Children and *hobby* are the only things upon which I have permitted my thoughts to run. As often as I write, you may expect to hear something about the *latter*.

Don't lose any opportunity which may offer of ploughing up the new garden spot and let the waggon make a tour of the ground lately purchased to collect the dung upon it to be scattered over that spot.

When it is too cold to go on with grubbing, our men may be employed in cutting and clearing away the underbrush in the Grove and the other woods; only let the *center* of the principal wood in the line of the different rocks remain rough and wild.

The Country people all agree that to fat fowls, it is essential to keep them well supplied with gravel. One, of whom I inquired, informed me, that sea shore gravel, not too large, is particularly good. They also say the coops must be cleaned out every two or three days. After the Fowls have had a sufficient opportunity of drinking, the remaining water must be removed.

The life of a prosperous attorney and country gentleman seemed to satisfy Hamilton. That summer New York Republicans

Jefferson, by Rembrandt Peale

celebrated Independence Day by gathering at Manhattan's Brick Church to hear a violently anti-Federalist speech by Captain George Eacker, but Hamilton made no comment on the oration. Collecting legal fees and "Setts of Italian Marble" for his new home seemed more worthwhile. Much of Hamilton's contentment as a private citizen came from his pleasure at seeing the progress of his brilliant eldest son, Philip. When the boy graduated from Columbia College in 1800 and began studying for the law, Hamilton had drawn up these strict but affectionate guidelines for the young student.

[New York, 1800]

This 1781 view of upper Manhattan and the Hudson River looks north toward Fort Washington and the site of Hamilton's home, the Grange.

Rules for *Mr Philip Hamilton*

From the first of April to the first of October he is to rise not later than Six Oclock. The rest of the year not later than Seven. If Earlier he will deserve commendation. Ten will be his hour of going to bed throughout the year.

From the time he is dressed in the morning till Nine o clock (the time for breakfast Excepted) he is to read law.

At nine he goes to the office & continues there till dinner time. He will be occupied partly in the writing and partly in reading law.

After Dinner he reads law at home till five O clock. From this hour till seven he disposes of his time as he pleases. From Seven to ten he reads and studies what ever he pleases.

From twelve on Saturday he is at liberty to amuse himself.

On Sunday he will attend the morning Church. The rest of the day may be applied to innocent recreations.

He must not Depart from any of these rules without my permission.

But on the evening of November 20, 1801, Philip visited a New York theater, where he started a quarrel with George Eacker, the Republicans' Fourth of July orator. On November 23, Eacker and young Hamilton crossed the Hudson to New Jersey, where gentlemen could still legally defend their honor by dueling. Philip fell, mortally wounded, and was brought back to Manhattan, where his parents watched his sufferings for almost twenty hours. At the funeral, Alexander Hamilton "was with difficulty supported to the grave of his hopes." He could not bring himself to answer any letters of condolence. Instead he buried himself in a furious attack on Thomas Jefferson's recent message to Congress. The *New-York*

Evening Post (which Hamilton had helped found earlier that year) carried the first of eighteen installments of Hamilton's *Examination* ten days after Jefferson had presented his program at Washington.

[December 17, 1801]

Whoever considers the temper of the day, must be satisfied that this message is likely to add much to the popularity of our chief magistrate. It conforms, as far as would be tolerated at this early stage of our progress in political perfection, to the bewitching tenets of that illuminated doctrine, which promises man, ere long, an emancipation from the burdens and restraints of government; giving a foretaste of that pure felicity which the apostles of this doctrine have predicted. . . . And should the viands, which they offer, prove baneful poisons instead of wholesome aliments, the justification is both plain and easy — *Good patriots must, at all events, please the People.* But those whose patriotism is of the OLD SCHOOL, who differ so widely from the disciples of the new creed, that they would rather risk incurring the displeasure of the people, by speaking unpalatable truths, than betray their interest by fostering their prejudices; will never be deterred by an impure tide of popular opinion, from honestly pointing out the mistakes or the faults of weak or wicked men, who may have been selected as guardians of the public weal.

The Message of the President, by whatever motives it may have been dictated, is a performance which ought to alarm all who are anxious for the safety of our Government, for the respectability and welfare of our nation. It makes, or aims at making, a most prodigal sacrifice of constitutional energy, of sound principle, and of public interest, to the popularity of one man.

Life of Alexander Hamilton BY ALLAN MCLANE HAMILTON, 1910

Hamilton's eldest son, Philip,
as he looked at the age of twenty

Hamilton's *Examination* distracted him from his grief that winter. By February, 1802, he was again making public appearances, speaking against Jefferson's plan to repeal the Judiciary Act, which had been passed by the "lame duck" Federalist Congress a year earlier. By repealing the act, Jefferson could simply do away with the new judicial posts that Adams had filled with Federalists before he left office. Hamilton was enraged at this threat to the independence of the judiciary, but his pleas that Federalists oppose the repeal measure in a temperate and dignified manner only irritated others in his party. In February, he wrote sadly to Gouverneur Morris, who was battling the repeal bill in the Senate.

[New York, February 27, 1802]

Mine is an odd destiny. Perhaps no man in the UStates has sacrificed or done more for the present Constitution than myself—and contrary to all my anticipations of its fate, as you know from the very begginning I am still labouring to prop the frail and worthless fabric. Yet I have the murmurs of its friends no less than the curses of its foes for my reward. What can I do better than withdraw from the Scene? Every day proves to me more and more that this American world was not made for me....

You, friend Morris, are by *birth* a native of this Country but by *genius* an exotic. You mistake if you fancy that you are more a favourite than myself or that you are in any sort upon a theatre s[uited] to you.

Jefferson's repeal bill was passed, but the battle had restored Hamilton's spirits and he was at last able to reply to his friends' notes of sympathy at Philip's death. At the end of March, he wrote to Dr. Benjamin Rush, a Philadelphia physician who had entertained Philip in his home.

New York March 29. 1802

I felt all the weight of the obligation which I owed to you and to your amiable family, for the tender concern they manifested in an event, beyond comparison, the most afflicting of my life. But I was obliged to wait for a moment of greater calm, to express my sense of the kindness.

My loss is indeed great. The highest as well as the eldest hope of my family has been taken from me. You estimated him rightly. He was truly a fine youth. But why should I repine? It was the will of heaven; and he is now out of the reach of the seductions and calamities of a world, full of folly, full of vice, full of danger—of least value in proportion as it is best known. I firmly trust also that he has safely reached the haven of eternal repose and felicity.

You will easily imagine that every memorial of the goodness of his heart must be precious to me. You allude to one recorded in a letter to your son. If no special reasons forbid it, I should be very glad to have a copy of that letter.

Mrs. Hamilton, who has drank deeply of the cup of

Benjamin Rush

sorrow, joins me in affectionate thanks to Mrs. Rush and yourself. Our wishes for your happiness will be unceasing.

Through all the personal difficulties of the past months, Hamilton had not lost his interest in reorganizing the Federalist party. He saw an opportunity to achieve that goal when he learned to his satisfaction that Virginia's Democratic-Republicans were growing increasingly distrustful of Vice President Aaron Burr. Federalists in Congress planned a caucus to "concert an uniform plan" for taking advantage of the situation. At James Bayard's request, Hamilton sent his advice, suggesting that Federalists borrow Democratic-Republican methods to achieve their own ends.

New-York April [16–18] 1802

Men are rather reasoning than reasonable animals for the most part governed by the impulse of passion. This is a truth well understood by our adversaries who have practised upon it with no small benefit to their cause.

It is no less true that the Foederalists seem not to have attended to the fact sufficiently; and that they erred in relying so much on the rectitude & utility of their measures, as to have neglected the cultivation of popular favour by fair & justifiable expedients. . . . Yet unless we can contrive to take hold of & carry along with us some strong feelings of the mind we shall in vain calculate upon any substantial or durable results. Whatever plan we may adopt, to be successful must be founded on the truth of this proposition. And perhaps it is not very easy for us to give it full effect; especially not without some deviations from what on other occasions we have maintained to be right. But in determining upon the propriety of the deviations, we must consider whether it be possible for us to succeed without in some degree employing the weapons which have been employed against us, & whether the actual state & future prospect of things be not such as to justify the reciprocal use of them. I need not tell you that I do not mean to countenance the imitation of things intrinsically unworthy, but only of such as may be denominated irregular, such as in a sound & stable order of things ought not to exist. Neither are you to infer that any revolutionary result is contemplated. In my opinion the present Constitution is the standard to which we are to cling. Under its banners . . . must we combat our political foes, rejecting all changes but through the channel itself provides for amendments. . . . I now offer you the outline of the plan. . . . Let an Association be formed to be denominated, "The Christian Constitutional Society." It's objects to be, 1st The support of the Christian Religion. 2nd The support of the Constitution of the United States. . . .

[This society, Hamilton explained, would have a national "directing council," a "sub-directing council" in each state, and local societies under the "sub-directing" boards. He then outlined "Its Means."]

1st   The diffusion of information. For this purpose not only the Newspapers but pamphlets must be la[r]gely employed & to do this a fund must be created. 5 dollars annually for 8 years, to be contributed by each member who can really afford it. . . . It is essential to be able to disseminate *gratis* useful publications. Whenever it can be done, & there is a press, clubs should be formed to meet once a week, read the newspapers & prepare essays, paragraphs &ct

2nd   The use of all lawful means in *concert* to promote the election of *fit men*. A lively correspondence must be kept up between the different Societies.

3rd   The promoting of institutions of a charitable & useful nature in the management of Fœderalists. The populous cities ought particularly to be attended to. Perhaps it will be well to institute in such places 1st Societies for the relief of Emigrants—2nd. Academies each with one professor instructing the different Classes of Mechanics in the principles of Mechanics & Elements of Chemistry.

James A. Bayard of Delaware

Bayard replied regretfully that such "Clubs" would only "revive a thousand jealousies & suspicions," and concluded that Federalists must let the Democratic-Republicans defeat themselves. But although Hamilton's proposals for Federalist reorganization had failed, his personal fortunes seemed to be on the rise once again. The continuing war in Europe, with its raids on neutral shipping, was providing Hamilton with a lucrative practice in insurance law. In June, Elizabeth gave birth to a baby boy, who was named Philip, after his dead brother, and six months later, the Hamiltons moved into their new country home in upper Man-

391

hattan. It was as one gentleman farmer to another that Hamilton wrote to Charles Pinckney at the end of December.

PRINTS DIVISION, N.Y. PUBLIC LIBRARY

The Grange

Grange (NY) Decr. 29. 1802

A garden, you know, is a very usual refuge of a disappointed politician. Accordingly, I have purchased a few acres about 9 Miles from Town, have built a house and am cultivating a Garden. The melons in your country are very fine. Will you have the goodness to send me some seed both of the Water & Muss Melons?

My daughter adds another request, which is for three or four of your peroquets [parakeets]. She is very fond of birds. If there be any thing in this quarter the sending of which can give you pleasure, you have only to name them. As Farmers a new source of sympathy has arisen between us; and I am pleased with every thing in which our likings and taste can be approximated.

Amidst the triumphant reign of Democracy, do you retain sufficient interest in public affairs to feel any curiosity about what is going on? In my opinion the follies and vices of the Administration have as yet made no material impression to their disadvantage. On the contrary, I think the malady is rather progressive than upon the decline in our Northern Quarter. The last *lullaby* message [Jefferson's message to Congress], instead of inspiring contempt, attracts praise. Mankind are forever destined to be the dupes of bold & cunning imposture.

With no national or statewide elections to tempt him from his "garden," Hamilton's first winter at the Grange was a quiet one. There was more sorrow for the family in March, 1803, when Elizabeth Hamilton's mother died in Albany. While his wife traveled to the funeral, Hamilton stayed in New York and sent her this affectionate report on their household.

Sunday Evening March 20 [1803] Grange

I am here my beloved Betsy with my two little boys *John* & *William* who will be my bed fellows to night. The day I have passed was as agreeable as it could be in your absence; but you need not be told how much difference your presence would have made. Things are now going on here pretty and pretty briskly. I am making some innovations which I am sure you will approve.

The remainder of the Children were well yesterday.

Eliza pouts and plays, and displays more and more her ample stock of Caprice.

I am anxious to hear of your arrival at Albany & shall be glad to be informed that Your Father and all of you are composed. I pray you to exert yourself & I repeat my exhortation that you will bear in mind it is your business to comfort and not to distress.

Although he made a few appearances on behalf of Federalist candidates in 1803, Hamilton was compelled to concentrate mainly on his private interests. Building the Grange had cost more than expected, and other investments had gone wrong. Richard Peters spoke truer, perhaps, than he knew when he advised Hamilton to make the farm his "Plaything—but see that you have other Business, that you may afford to pay for the Rattle." Despite ill health, Hamilton rode to Albany to earn fees to pay for his "plaything" and wrote to his wife to suggest new embellishments for his expensive toy.

> Claverack [New York] Oct 14. 1803
>
> There are some things necessary to be done which I omitted mentioning to you. I wish the Carpenters to make and insert two Chimnies for ventilating the Ice-House, each about two feet square & four feet long half above and half below the ground—to have a cap on the top sloping downwards so that the rain may not easily enter—the aperture for letting in and out the air to be about a foot and a half square in the side immediately below the cap....
>
> Let a separate compost bed be formed near the present one; to consist of 3 barrels full of the *clay* which I bought 6 barrels of *black mould* 2 waggon loads of the best clay on the Hill opposite the *Quakers place*... and one waggon load of pure cow-dung. Let these be well and repeatedly mixed and pounded together to be made use of hereafter for the Vines.
>
> I hope the apple trees will have been planted so as to profit by this moderate and wet weather. If not done— Let *Tough* be reminded that a temporary fence is to be put up...so as to prevent the cattle injuring the young trees....
>
> Remember that the piazzas are also to be caulked & that additional accommodations for the pidgeons are to be Made.
>
> You see I do not forget the Grange. No that I do not;

nor any one that inhabits it. Accept yourself my tenderest affection. Give my Love to your Children.

Hamilton enjoyed the luxury of private life throughout 1803. But in 1804, state voters were to decide on a President, a governor, and congressmen, and when Hamilton traveled again to Albany in February of that year his business was both legal and political. His legal affairs concerned the case of Harry Crosswell, a Federalist printer indicted for libel a year before. Crosswell had asked Hamilton for help in the summer of 1803, but other obligations kept Hamilton from appearing until the following winter, when a complicated series of appeals and counter-appeals brought Crosswell's case to the New York Court of Errors. In his appearance before the court in February, 1804, Hamilton presented some of the most important arguments on the law of libel and the freedom of the press heard in an American courtroom in the early nineteenth century. His plea for Crosswell centered on the contention that the truth of a publication must be accepted as a defense against a charge of libel, and that juries must be allowed to decide on the truth or falsehood of such statements. As one judge remarked, Hamilton's "whole soul, was inlisted in the cause," and he closed his case for Crosswell with this description of the role of a free press in America.

[Albany, February, 1804]

We have been careful that when one party comes in, it shall not be able to break down and bear away the others. If this be not so, in vain have we made Constitutions, for, if it be not so, then we must go into anarchy, and from thence to despotism and to a master. Against this I know there is an almost insurmountable obstacle in the spirit of the people. They would not submit to be thus enslaved. Every tongue, every arm would be uplifted against it; they would resist, and assist, and resist, till they hurled from their seats, those who dared make the attempt. To watch the progress of such endeavours is the office of a free press. To give us early alarm and put us on our guard against the encroachments of power. This, then, is a right of the utmost importance, one for which, instead of yielding it up, we ought rather to spill our blood.... Never can tyranny be introduced into this country by arms; these can never get rid of a popular spirit of enquiry; the only way to crush it down is by a servile tribunal. It is only by the abuse of the forms of justice that we can be enslaved. An army never can do it. For ages it can never be attempted. The spirit of the country with arms in their hands, and disciplined as a militia, would render it impossible. Every pretence that liberty can be thus invaded, is idle declamation. It is not to be endangered by a few thousand of miserable, pitiful military. It is not thus that the liberty of this country is to be destroyed. It is to be subverted only by a pretence of adhering to all the forms of law, and yet by breaking down the substance of our liberties. By devoting a wretched, but honest man as the victim of a nominal trial.

Hamilton's eloquence did not win Harry Crosswell immediate exoneration: the court divided on the question of granting the printer a new trial. But Hamilton's powers of persuasion were not confined to the courtroom that month. Aaron Burr's personal and political differences with Jefferson had driven him back to local politics. George Clinton had declined another term, and the Democratic-Republicans endorsed Chancellor John Lansing, Jr., as his successor, while a splinter group in the party backed Burr. Many New York Federalists favored joining Burr, and Albany party men were to caucus on this point on February 16. Six days before that meeting, Hamilton spoke in support of Lansing.

[Albany, February 10, 1804]

If he [Burr] be truly, as the foederalists have believed, a man of irregular and insatiable ambition, if his plan has been to rise to power on the ladder of Jacobinic principles, it is natural to conclude that he will endeavour to fix himself in power by the same instrument, that he will not lean on a fallen [and] falling party, generally speaking of a character not to favour usurpation and the ascendancy of a despotic chief. Every day shews more and more the much to be regretted tendency of governments intirely popular to dissolution and disorder. Is it rational to expect, that a man who had the sagacity to foresee this tendency, and whose temper would permit him to bottom his aggrandisement on popular prejudices and vices would desert this system at a time, when more than ever the state of things invites him to adhere to it?

...If Lansing is Governor his personal character affords some security against pernicious extremes, and at the same time renders it morally certain, that the democratic party already much divided and weakened will moulder and break asunder more and more....

Hamilton's copy of Don Quixote, *from his library at the Grange*

395

May it not lead to a recasting of parties by which the fœderalists will gain a great accession of force from former opponents. At any rate, is it not wiser in them to promote a course of things by which scism [among the] democrats will be fostered and increased [than one likely, upon a] fair calculation to give them a chief better able than any they have yet had to unite and direct them.

When Lansing refused the nomination, the Clintonians chose Chief Justice Morgan Lewis as their candidate. Meanwhile Hamilton, who was the self-appointed chief of the anti-Burr movement, was receiving his full share of personal abuse. In the last week of February, he heard Judge Ebenezer Purdy's accusations that *"Monarchy"* was the Federalists' objective, and that he, Hamilton, had circulated a letter proposing an English prince on an American throne. When confronted, Purdy asserted that George Clinton had seen such a letter in 1787. Hamilton wrote to the Governor, demanding an explanation.

Albany Febr. 27. 1804

It is now a long time since a very odious slander has been in circulation to the prejudice of my character. It has come to my ears in more than one way, but always 'till lately without the disclosure of any source to which I could resort for explanation or detection. Within a few days, Mr. Kane of this City related to me a story as coming from Judge Purdy, in substance very similar to the calumny to which I have alluded....your name is implicated in the transaction, with what warrant it would be improper for me to prejudge. But the very mention of your name adds importance to the affair and increases the motives to investigation.

The charge...is of a nature too derogatory to permit me to pass it lightly over. It is essential that its origin and progress should be traced as fully as may be practicable, in order to the thorough exposure of its falshood and malignity.

The assertions of Judge Purdy authorise me to appeal to you for a frank and candid explanation of so much of the matter as relates to yourself. This explanation I request as speedily as may be.

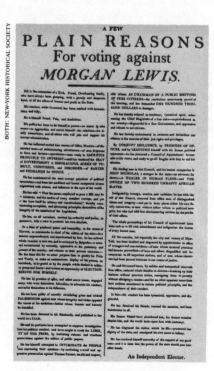

An anti-Lewis broadside of 1804

Clinton replied graciously to Hamilton's questions. While he had seen such a letter, the copy he read had no signature or address, and he declared that he had never believed or said that Hamilton was connected with it. The Governor promised to search for this mysterious letter and send it to Hamilton. He concluded, "I am pleased to find that however much we may differ on other political Subjects we agree in Sentiment as to this." Soon afterward, Hamilton returned to Manhattan to work for the candidacy of Morgan Lewis, thus allying himself with Clinton, his old antagonist. There are no written records of his campaign against Burr, nor any newspaper accounts of speeches he may have made that spring. In the closing days of the gubernatorial race, Hamilton sent this prophetic advice to a friend who had suffered personal reverses.

New York April 13th. 1804

'Tis by patience and perseverance that we can expect to vanquish difficulties, and better our unpleasant condition.

Arraign not the dispensations of Providence—they must be founded in wisdom and goodness; and when they do not suit us, it must be because there is some fault in ourselves, which deserves chastisement, or because there is a kind intent to correct in us some vice or failing, of which, perhaps we may not be conscious; or because the general plan requires that we should suffer partial ill.

In this situation it is our duty to cultivate resignation, and even humility, bearing in mind, in the language of the Poet, that it was *Pride which lost the blest abodes.*

Morgan Lewis, by Charles Curran

Hamilton had no presentiment that his own pride would soon threaten his family. On the contrary, with Burr's defeat, Hamilton probably foresaw for himself nothing but a comfortable life as a Federalist citizen. But, as discreetly as Hamilton had conducted his battle against Burr, the Vice President eventually learned of it. In June, Burr saw printed in a newspaper a letter from Dr. Charles Cooper describing remarks Hamilton had made after a dinner at Albany in February. On June 18, Burr demanded from Hamilton "a prompt and unqualified acknowledgement or denial of the use of any expressions which could warrant the assertions of Dr. Cooper." Hamilton replied two days later, taking refuge in the vagueness of Cooper's language as an excuse for neither admitting nor denying the truth of his charges.

New York June 20, 1804

I have maturely reflected on the subject of your letter... and the more I have reflected the more I have become convinced, that I could not, without manifest impropriety, make the avowal or disavowal which you seem to think necessary.

The clause pointed out...is in these terms, "I could

detail to you a *still more despicable opinion,* which General Hamilton has expressed of Mr. Burr." To endeavour to discover the meaning of this declaration, I was obliged to seek in the antecedent part of the letter for the opinion to which it referred.... I found it in these words "General Hamilton and Judge Kent have declared, *in substance,* that they looked upon Mr. Burr to be a *dangerous man,* and one *who ought not to be trusted with the reins of Government."* The language of Doctor Cooper plainly implies, that he considered this opinion of you, which he attributes to me, as a *despicable* one; but he affirms that I have expressed some other *still more despicable;* without however mentioning to whom, when, or where.... the phrase...admits of infinite shades....

Repeating, that I cannot reconcile it with propriety to make the acknowlegement, or denial, you desire, I will add, that I deem it inadmissible, on principle, to consent to be interrogated as to the justness of the *inferences,* which may be drawn by *others,* from whatever I may have said of a political opponent in the course of a fifteen years competition....

I stand ready to avow or disavow promptly and explicitly any precise or definite opinion, which I may be charged with having declared of any Gentleman. More than this cannot fitly be expected from me; and especially it cannot reasonably be expected, that I shall enter into an explanation upon a basis so vague as that which you have adopted. I trust, on more reflection, you will see the matter in the same light with me. If not, I can only regret the circumstance, and must abide the consequences.

Aaron Burr, as he looked in 1805

With some justice, Burr replied that this note contained "nothing of that sincerity and delicacy which you profess to Value." Hamilton's letter, Burr declared, only "furnished me with new reasons for requiring a definite reply." Burr's friend William Van Ness delivered this message to Hamilton and recorded his reactions.

[New York, June 22, 1804]
General Hamilton perused it, & said it was such a letter as he had hoped not to have received, that it contained several offensive expressions & seemed to close the door to all further reply, that he had hoped the answer he had returned to Col Burr's first letter would have given a

different direction to the controversy, that he thought Mr Burr would have perceived that there was a difficulty in his making a more specific reply, & would have desired him to state what had fallen from him that might have given rise to the inference of Doctor Cooper. He would have done this frankly, & he believed it would not have been found to exceed the limits justifiable among political opponents. If Mr Burr should upon the suggestion of these ideas be disposed to give a different complexion to the discussion, he was willing to consider the last letter not delivered; but if that communication was not withdrawn he could make no reply and Mr Burr must pursue such course as he should deem most proper.

This second evasion did not settle the matter. In the next days, Van Ness tried to work out the problem with Hamilton and Hamilton's friend Nathaniel Pendleton, but Burr was now convinced that Hamilton's remarks in Albany were part of a long-standing plot to blacken his character. On June 25, he demanded a "General disavowal of any intention on the part of Genl Hamilton in his various conversations to convey impressions derogatory to the honor of Mr Burr." Hamilton drafted this reply for Pendleton to present to Van Ness.

> [New York] 26 june 1804
>
> The expectations now disclosed as on the part of Colo. Burr, appear to him [Hamilton] to have greatly changed and extended the original ground of inquiry, and instead of presenting a particular and definite case for explanation, seem to aim at nothing less than an inquisition into his most confidential as well as other conversations through the whole period of his acquaintance with Col Burr. While he was prepared to meet the particular case fully and fairly he thinks it inadmissible that he should be expected to answer at large as to any thing that he may possibly have said in relation to the character of Colo. Burr, at any time or upon any occasion. . . . He does not however mean to authorise any conclusion as to the real nature of his Conduct in relation to Col. Burr, by his declining so loose and vague a basis of explanation; and he disavows an unwillingness to come to a satisfactory, provided it be an honorable accommodation. His objection is to the very indefinite ground which Col. Burr has assumed, in which he is sorry to be able to discover nothing short of predetermined hostility.

This letter sealed Hamilton's fate. The next morning, Van Ness delivered Burr's challenge to a duel that would "vindicate that honor at such hazard as the nature of the case demands." Hamilton received the challenge the evening of July 27 and began preparing for his meeting with the Vice President. Pendleton and Van Ness worked out the details of time and place while the principals put their affairs in order. In the next two weeks, Hamilton finished as much outstanding legal work as possible and prepared a series of documents to be left with Pendleton. While most of these concerned Hamilton's business affairs, one was a summary of his beliefs on dueling in general and his quarrel with Burr in particular.

[New York, June 28–July 11, 1804]

1. My religious and moral principles are strongly opposed to the practice of Duelling and it would ever give me pain to be obliged to shed the blood of a fellow in a private combat forbidden by the laws.

2   My wife and Children are extremely dear to me, and my life is of the utmost importance to them, in various views.

3.   I feel a sense of obligation towards my creditors; who in case of accident to me...may be in some degree sufferers....

4   I am conscious of no *ill-will* to Col Burr, distinct from political opposition....

Lastly, I shall hazard much, and can possibly gain nothing by the issue of the interview.

But it was, as I conceive, impossible for me to avoid it. There are *intrinsick* difficulties in the thing, and *artificial* embarrassments, from the manner of proceeding on the part of Col. Burr.

Intrinsick—because it is not to be denied, that my animadversions on the political principles character and views of Col Burr have been extremely severe, and on different occasions I, in common with many others, have made very unfavourable criticisms on particular instances of the private conduct of this Gentleman.

...The disavowal required of me by Col Burr, in a general and indefinite form, was out of my power.... Yet I wished, as far as might be practicable, to leave a door open to accommodation....

I am not sure, whether under all the circumstances I did not go further in the attempt to accommodate, than a puntilious delicacy will justify. If so, I hope the motives I have stated will excuse me....

To those, who with abhorring the practice of Duelling

A view of Weehawken, New Jersey

may think that I ought on no account to have added to the number of bad examples, I answer that my *relative* situation, as well in public as private appeals, inforcing all the considerations which constitute what men of the world denominate honor, impressed on me (as I thought) a peculiar necessity not to decline the call. The ability to be in future useful, whether in resisting mischief or effecting good, in those crises of our public affairs, which seem likely to happen, would probably be inseparable from a conformity with public prejudice in this particular.

Scrupulously efficient as ever, Hamilton prepared for his duel by arranging for his estate, naming executors, and drawing up his will. Elizabeth was to be his sole beneficiary if anything were left after the payment of his debts. The most difficult part of Hamilton's preparations was providing for his children's "dear Mother." He left two letters for Elizabeth with Pendleton; the first was written a week before he was to meet Burr in New Jersey.

Eastman Johnson made this portrait of Mrs. Alexander Hamilton in 1846. She died in 1854 at the age of ninety-seven, having outlived her husband by fifty years.

[New York] July 4. 1804

This letter, my very dear Eliza, will not be delivered to you, unless I shall first have terminated my earthly career; to begin, as I humbly hope from redeeming grace and divine mercy, a happy immortality.

If it had been possible for me to have avoided the interview, my love for you and my precious children would have been alone a decisive motive. But it was not possible, without sacrifices which would have rendered me unworthy of your esteem. I need not tell you of the pangs I feel, from the idea of quitting you and exposing you to the anguish which I know you would feel. Nor could I dwell on the topic lest it should unman me.

The consolations of Religion, my beloved, can alone support you; and these you have a right to enjoy. Fly to the bosom of your God and be comforted. With my last idea, I shall cherish the sweet hope of meeting you in a better world.

Adieu best of wives and best of Women. Embrace all my darling Children for me. Ever yours

AH

Just before he went to bed on the evening before his duel, Hamilton again wrote to his wife.

[New York, July 10, 1804]
Tuesday Evening 10 O Cl[ock]

The Scruples [of a Christian have deter]mined me to expose my own [life to any] extent rather than subject my[self to the] guilt of taking the life of [another.] This must increase my hazards & redoubles my pangs for you. But you had rather I should die innocent than live guilty. Heaven can [preserve] me [and I humbly] hope will, but in the contrary event, I charge you to remember that you are a Christian. God's will be done! The will of a merciful God must be good.

Once more Adieu My Darling darling Wife

AH

Hamilton had decided to "expose" himself by reserving his first shot in the duel—and perhaps even his second—so that Burr would have "a double opportunity to . . . pause and to reflect." At 5 A.M., July 11, Hamilton crossed the river to Weehawken, New Jersey. By seven o'clock, all parties were present, and the seconds, Van Ness and Pendleton, worked out the details of the duel. Van Ness left this record of the morning's events.

[July 11, 1804]

While his second was explaining these rules [for the duel] Genl Hamilton raised & levelled his pistol, as if to try his position, and lowering it said, I beg pardon for delaying you but the direction of the light, sometimes renders glasses necessary. He then drew from his pocket a pair of spectacles & having put them on, observed that he was ready to proceed. . . .

The parties being . . . asked if they were prepared, being answered in the affirmative he [Pendleton] gave the word *present* as had been agreed on, and both of the parties took aim & fired in succession. . . . The pistols were discharged within a few seconds of each other and the fire of Col: Burr took effect; Genl Hamilton almost instantly fell, Col: Burr then advanced toward Genl H___n with a manner and gesture that appeared to Genl Hamilton's friend to be expressive of regret, but without Speaking turned about & withdrew—Being urged from the field by his friend . . . with a view to prevent his being recognised by the Surgeon and Bargemen who were then approaching. No farther communication took place between the principals and the Barge that carried Col: Burr immediately returned to the City.

This portrait of Hamilton was drawn from memory by Gordon Fairman the year after Hamilton's death.

The account of Dr. David Hosack, the physician whom Burr and Hamilton had chosen to attend the duel, takes up the story after Hamilton fell. The doctor's account appeared in a newspaper two months later.

Dr. Hosack presented this bill for $87.50 to Hamilton's estate for "attendance during his last illness."

[New York] August 17th, 1804. I found him half sitting on the ground, supported in the arms of Mr. Pendleton. His countenance of death I shall never forget—He had at that instant just strength to say, "This is a mortal wound, Doctor;" when he sunk away, and became to all appearances lifeless. I immediately stripped up his clothes, and soon, alas! ascertained that the direction of the ball must have been through some vital part. [On performing an autopsy, Hosack found "the ball struck the second or third false rib, fractured it about in the middle; it then passed through the liver and diaphragm, and...lodged in the first or second lumbar vertebra...."] His pulses were not to be felt; his respiration was entirely suspended; and upon laying my hand on his heart, and perceiving no motion there, I considered him as irrecoverably gone. I however observed to Mr. Pendleton, that the only chance for his reviving was immediately to get him upon the water. We therefore lifted him up, and carried him out of the wood, to the margin of the bank, where the bargemen aided us in conveying him into the boat, which immediately put off. During all this time I could not discover the least symptom of returning life....

[In the boat, Dr. Hosack rubbed Hamilton's face and body with "spirits of hartshorne." Fifty yards from shore, Hamilton regained consciousness. Dr. Hosack's account here is at variance with Van Ness's earlier report that both pistols "were discharged within a few seconds of each other."]

He breathed; his eyes, hardly opened, wandered, without fixing upon any objects; to our great joy he at length spoke: "My vision is indistinct," were his first words. His pulse became more perceptible; his respiration more regular; his sight returned.... Soon after recovering his sight, he happened to cast his eye upon the case of pistols, and observing the one that he had had in his hand lying on the outside, he said, "Take care of that pistol; it is undischarged, and still cocked; it may go off and do harm;

403

—Pendleton knows, (attempting to turn his head towards him) that I did not intend to fire at him." "Yes," said Mr. Pendleton..."I have already made Dr. Hosack acquainted with your determination as to that." He then closed his eyes, and remained calm, without any disposition to speak....He asked me once or twice, how I found his pulse; and he informed me that his lower extremities had lost all feeling; manifesting to me that he entertained no hopes that he should long survive....Perceiving that we approached the shore, he said, "Let Mrs. Hamilton be immediately sent for—let the event be gradually broken to her; but give her hopes." Looking up we saw his friend Mr. [William] Bayard standing on the wharf in great agitation....when I called to him to have a cot prepared, and he at the same moment saw his poor friend lying in the bottom of the boat, he threw up his eyes and burst into a flood of tears and lamentation. Hamilton alone appeared tranquil and composed. We then conveyed him as tenderly as possible up to the house....

Upon our reaching the house he became more languid....I gave him a little weak wine and water. When he recovered his feelings, he complained of pain in his back; we immediately undressed him, laid him in bed, and darkened the room. I then gave him a large anodyne, which I frequently repeated. During the first day he took upwards of an ounce of laudanum [tincture of opium]....Yet were his sufferings, during the whole of the day, almost intolerable.

The Reverend Benjamin Moore

As soon as Hamilton was brought to Bayard's house, a message was sent to Benjamin Moore, Episcopal bishop of New York. Moore went immediately, but delayed giving Hamilton Communion until the General had had "time for serious reflection." A few hours later, Moore wrote, he received another summons.

[New York] Thursday evening, July 12 [1804]. At one o'clock I was again called on to visit him. Upon my entering the room and approaching his bed, with the utmost calmness and composure he said, "My dear Sir, you perceive my unfortunate situation, and no doubt have been made acquainted with the circumstances which led to it. It is my desire to receive the Communion at your hands. I hope you will not conceive there is any impropriety in my request." He added, "It has for some time past been the wish of my heart, and it was my intention to take an early opportunity of uniting myself to the church, by the reception of that holy ordinance." I observed to him, that...however desirous I might be to afford consolation to a fellow mortal in distress; still, it was my duty as a minister of the gospel, to hold up the law of God...and that...I must unequivocally condemn the practice which had brought him to his present unhappy condition. He acknowledged the propriety of these sentiments, and declared that he viewed the late transaction with sorrow and contrition. I then asked him, "Should it please God, to restore you to health, Sir, will you never be again engaged in a similar transaction? and will you employ all your influence in society to discountenance this barbarous custom?" His answer was, "That, Sir, is my deliberate intention."...

[Bishop Moore discussed the meaning of the Communion with Hamilton. At last he questioned the dying man.]

"Do you sincerely repent of your sins past? Have you a lively faith in God's mercy through Christ, with a thankful remembrance of the death of Christ? And are you disposed to live in love and charity with all men?" He lifted up his hands and said, "With the utmost sincerity of heart I can answer those questions in the affirmative—I have no ill will against Col. Burr. I met him with a fixed resolution to do him no harm—I forgive all that happened." I then observed...that I had no reason to doubt his sincerity, and would proceed immediately to gratify his wishes. The Communion was then administered, which he received with great devotion, and his heart afterwards appeared to be perfectly at rest.

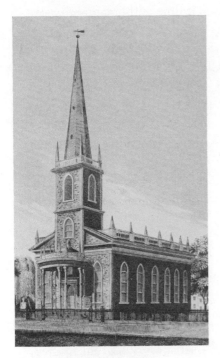

On Saturday, July 14, 1804, Hamilton was buried in Trinity churchyard, at the head of Wall Street in lower Manhattan.

Although Dr. Hosack had "not the shadow of a hope" of Hamilton's recovery, he summoned other medical experts for consultations. These doctors confirmed his gloomy diagnosis, and Hamilton's sufferings continued—as Dr. Hosack later recalled.

[New York] August 17th, 1804. During the night, he had some imperfect sleep; but the succeeding morning his symptoms were aggravated, attended however with a diminution of pain. His mind retained all its usual strength and composure. The great

405

The Hamilton memorial engraving above was published circa 1804.

source of his anxiety seemed to be in his sympathy with his half distracted wife and children. He spoke to me frequently of them—"My beloved wife and children," were always his expressions. But his fortitude triumphed over his situation, dreadful as it was; once, indeed, at the sight of his children brought to the bed-side together, seven in number, his utterance forsook him; he opened his eyes, gave them one look, and closed them again, till they were taken away. As a proof of his extraordinary composure of mind, let me add, that he alone could calm the frantic grief of their mother. *"Remember, my Eliza, you are a Christian,"* were the expressions with which he frequently, with a firm voice, but in a pathetic and impressive manner, addressed her. His words, and the tone in which they were uttered, will never be effaced from my memory.

Bishop Moore returned to Hamilton's bedside the morning of Thursday, July 12, and remained there until 2 P.M., when Hamilton "expired without a struggle, and almost without a groan." Thus the most spirited and vocal warrior of the Federalist cause left his wife and children, his unpaid debts, and his unfulfilled dreams. He left, as well, a great mystery for American historians. His premature death helped make Hamilton a comparatively vague personality among the Founding Fathers. Unlike Jefferson, Madison, and Adams, he had no years of quiet retirement in which to write his memoirs or answer questions about his early career. In his forty-nine years, Hamilton had been too pressed by public duty and family obligations to spare time for reminiscence.

Hamilton's death was perhaps the most puzzling incident in his short life. Biographers return again and again to two questions: Why had he not given Aaron Burr some form of apology and avoided a challenge? And why, once that challenge had been issued, did Hamilton not decline the duel on the grounds of his religious and moral convictions?

Some have speculated that Hamilton was motivated by some sort of "death wish," a subconscious desire for self-destruction. Certainly Hamilton's letters in the last three years of his life reflected a feeling that he was out of place in Jeffersonian America. Politically, both Hamilton and Burr had run the course of their careers by the time they met for their "interview" in Weehawken. In 1802, Hamilton's friends had ignored his suggestions for remodeling the Federalist party, and the party would never fully recover from the bitter division of 1800. Burr in his turn had alienated the southern wing of his party, and his life after the duel was a series of fantastic schemes and pathetic failures. His plans to establish a colony in the West, possibly even to form a new nation, brought him to trial for treason in 1807.

But any attempt to conduct posthumous psychoanalysis on either man is fruitless and quite unnecessary. There is an answer to the riddle of Hamilton's death in the clear patterns of his life. Hamilton could not offer Burr a satisfactory explanation or apology because there was none. In the course of the years, Hamilton had insulted Burr's family, impugned his financial solvency, and accused him of almost everything from accepting bribes to showing cowardice in the Army. If any man deserved "satisfaction" from him, Hamilton knew that it was Aaron Burr. By Hamilton's own standards of "honor," he had given Burr reason for a challenge. Those same standards forced Hamilton to accept Burr's invitation to the meeting at Weehawken. Hamilton would not have criticized any man for refusing to participate in a duel if that man was opposed in principle, as he himself was, to this form of ritual bloodshed; but Hamilton felt a special need to prove his own right to a "reputation," to "honor." A self-made man, Hamilton molded his life after the image of those who had been born to wealth and power in the aristocratic, Colonial tradition. Determined to prove that America, though a new republic, could be "respectable" in the most strict definition of the word, Hamilton demanded as much of himself. If this meant embracing old, outmoded standards of honor, he would do so. And he followed this terrible, relentless logic to its tragic conclusion when he crossed the Hudson to Weehawken.

Other men and other patriots felt concern for national respectability without losing their sense of proportion in this way. But Hamilton had a special reason for guarding the reputation he had earned. As long as there was one man who, like John Adams, could dismiss him as "a bastard brat of a Scotch pedlar," Hamilton's struggle to give his name legitimacy and stature was pointless. If he were to be "useful" to the nation, Hamilton believed that he must preserve that reputation by any means.

At Hamilton's funeral, Gouverneur Morris begged Americans "to remember this solemn testimonial, that he was not ambitious. . . . He was ambitious only of glory." Morris had known Hamilton well and understood his friend's desperate need for recognition. He demanded of his audience at Trinity Church, *I charge you to protect his fame*—it is all he has left—all that these poor orphan children will inherit from their father." And this was all that Hamilton had hoped to leave. It was not power or wealth, but "fame" and "glory" that had driven Hamilton throughout his short life. Thirty years as an American, a career as a soldier and a statesman, a loving family, and warm friends had never erased the fears and frustrations in the heart of Nicholas Cruger's clerk, who longed for a "war" to rescue him from his drudgery. Few men contributed more than Alexander Hamilton to the establishment of the new American nation, which held out the promise of a new life, with new standards of a man's worth. The tragedy of Hamilton's life was that he was so often at odds with the new nation he had helped to create.

Selected Bibliography

Bemis, Samuel Flagg. *Jay's Treaty: A Study in Commerce and Diplomacy.* New York: Macmillan, 1923.

Bowers, Claude G. *Jefferson and Hamilton: The Struggle for Democracy in America.* Boston: Houghton Mifflin, 1925.

Cooke, Jacob E., ed. *The Federalist.* Middletown, Conn.: Wesleyan University Press, 1961.

De Conde, Alexander. *Entangling Alliance: Politics and Diplomacy under George Washington.* Durham: Duke University Press, 1958.

————.*The Quasi-War: The Politics and Diplomacy of the Undeclared War with France, 1797–1801.* New York: Charles Scribner's Sons, 1966.

DePauw, Linda G. *The Eleventh Pillar: New York State and the Federal Constitution.* Ithaca: Cornell University Press, 1966.

Hacker, Louis M. *Alexander Hamilton in the American Tradition.* New York: McGraw-Hill, 1957.

Hamilton, Alexander. *The Law Practice of Alexander Hamilton: Documents and Commentary.* Edited by Julius Goebel, Jr., *et al.* 2 vols. to date. New York: Columbia University Press, 1964 —.

————. *The Papers of Alexander Hamilton.* Edited by Harold C. Syrett *et al.* 19 vols. to date. New York: Columbia University Press, 1961 —.

————. *The Works of Alexander Hamilton.* Edited by John C. Hamilton. 7 vols. New York: J. F. Trow, 1850–51.

————. *The Works of Alexander Hamilton.* Edited by Henry Cabot Lodge. 9 vols. New York: G. P. Putnam's Sons, 1885–86.

Hamilton, Allan McLane. *The Intimate Life of Alexander Hamilton.* New York: Charles Scribner's Sons, 1910.

Hamilton, John C. *A History of the Republic of the United States of America, as Traced in the Writings of Alexander Hamilton and of his Contemporaries.* 7 vols. New York: Appleton, 1857–64.

Lodge, Henry Cabot. *Alexander Hamilton.* Boston: Houghton Mifflin, 1882.

Lycan, Gilbert L. *Alexander Hamilton and American Foreign Policy: A Design for Greatness.* Norman, Okla.: University of Oklahoma Press, 1970.

Miller, John C. *Alexander Hamilton: A Portrait in Paradox.* New York: Harper & Row, 1959.

————. *The Federalist Era, 1789–1801.* New York: Harper & Row, 1960.

Mitchell, Broadus. *Alexander Hamilton.* 2 vols. New York: Macmillan, 1957–62.

Rossiter, Clinton L. *Alexander Hamilton and the Constitution.* New York: Harcourt, Brace & World, 1964.

————. *1787: The Grand Convention.* New York: Macmillan, 1966.

Schachner, Nathan. *Alexander Hamilton.* New York: Yoseloff, 1957.

Stourzh, Gerald. *Alexander Hamilton and the Idea of Republican Government.* Stanford: Stanford University Press, 1970.

Syrett, Harold C., and Cooke, Jean G., eds. *Interview in Weehawken: The Burr-Hamilton Duel, as Told in the Original Documents.* Middletown, Conn.: Wesleyan University Press, 1960.

White, Leonard D. *The Federalists: A Study in Administrative History.* New York: Macmillan, 1948.

Acknowledgments

Unless otherwise specifically credited below, all documents reproduced in this volume are from the Alexander Hamilton Papers, Library of Congress, Washington, D.C., the greatest collection of Hamilton documents in existence, and other collections at the Library of Congress. In addition the Editors would like to thank the following institutions for permission to reprint documents in their possession:

American Philosophical Society, Philadelphia, Penna., page 379(center)

Bank of New York, New York, N.Y., pages 265(bottom)–266(top)

Charleston Library Society, Charleston, S. C., page 392(top)

Columbia University, New York, N.Y., pages 310(center), 337(bottom)–338(top), 370(top), 376(bottom)–377, 393(bottom)–394(top)

Connecticut Historical Society, Hartford, pages 319–320(top), 384

Henry E. Huntington Library, San Marino, Calif., pages 373–74(top)

Historical Society of Pennsylvania, Philadelphia, pages 266(center), 323(bottom)–324(top)

Lehigh University, Bethlehem, Penna., page 353

Library Collection of Philadelphia, pages 389(bottom)–390(top)

Maryland Hall Records, Annapolis, page 324 (center)

Massachusetts Historical Society, Boston, pages 351(top), 359(center), 362, 367(bottom)–368, 378(bottom)–379(top), 381(bottom)–382(top)

National Archives, Washington, D.C., page 247(top)

New-York Historical Society, New York, N.Y., page 146, 327(bottom), 333, 335(center), 336(bottom)–337, 342(bottom)–343(top), 348(bottom)–349(top), 349(bottom)–350(top), 375(center), 400–401(top)

New York Public Library, New York, N.Y., pages 344(bottom)–345, 390–91

New York State Historical Association, Weehawken, pages 397(bottom)–398(top), 398(bottom)–399(top), 399(bottom), 402(bottom)

Pennsylvania Archives, Harrisburg, page 320(center)

Public Records Office, London, pages 285(bottom)–286(top)

Public Records Office—Foreign Office, London, page 316(top)

Rhode Island Historical Society, Providence, page 248(top)

United States Naval Academy, Annapolis, Md., pages 358–59(top)

University of Virginia, Charlottesville, pages 374(bottom)–375

Yale University Library, New Haven, Conn., page 334(bottom)

The Editors also make grateful acknowledgment for the use of documents from the following works:

Hamilton, James A. *Reminiscences of James A. Hamilton; or, Men and Events, at Home & Abroad, During Three Quarters of a Century.* New York, 1869. Page 329(bottom)

Hamilton, John Church. *Life of Alexander Hamilton, a History of the Republic of the United States of America.* Boston, 1879. Page 267(bottom)

The Editors wish to express their appreciation of the many institutions and individuals who made available their pictorial material for use in this volume. In particular the Editors are grateful to:

Mrs. Joseph Carson, Philadelphia, Penna.

Chase Manhattan Bank Money Museum, New York, N.Y.

Columbiana Collection, Columbia University Libraries, New York, N.Y.—Alice Bonnell

Danish Maritime Museum, Kronborg Castle, Helsingor, Denmark

Hamilton Collection, Columbia University Libraries, New York, N.Y.—Kenneth Lohf

Independence National Historical Park Collection, Philadelphia, Penna.

Eva Lawaetz, St. Croix, Virgin Islands

Mr. and Mrs. Walter Lewisohn, Yorktown Heights, N.Y.

Library of Congress, Washington, D.C.—John D. Knowlton

National Archives, Washington, D.C.

New-York Historical Society, New York, N.Y.

New York Public Library, New York, N.Y.

The Royal Library, Copenhagen, Denmark

University of Copenhagen Library, Copenhagen, Denmark

Yale University Art Gallery, New Haven, Conn.

Index

Boldface indicates pages on which illustrations appear.

416

S

be treated of in a

by uniting

^ proceeding ~~measures~~ as may

for that purpose, ...

J. ha...

The President & Directors

of the Bank of the United Sta...